PIMLICO

588

THIRTEEN DAYS

Clive Ponting is a Reader in Politics at the University of
Wales, Swansea. He has written numerous books including
the world-wide bestseller *A Green History of the World*, a
highly controversial revisionist biography of Winston
Churchill and *Armageddon: The Second World War*. His most
recent publications are *The Pimlico History of the Twentieth
Century* and *World History: A New Perspective*, also available in
Pimlico paperback. He is working on a new book about the
Crimean War.

THIRTEEN DAYS

Diplomacy and Disaster:
The Countdown to the Great War

———

CLIVE PONTING

PIMLICO

Published by Pimlico 2003

2 4 6 8 10 9 7 5 3 1

Copyright © Clive Ponting 2003

Clive Ponting has asserted his right
under the Copyright, Designs and Patents Act 1988
to be identified as the author of this work

First published in Great Britain by
Chatto & Windus 2002

Pimlico edition 2003

Pimlico
Random House, 20 Vauxhall Bridge Road,
London SW1V 2SA

Random House Australia (Pty) Limited
20 Alfred Street, Milsons Point, Sydney,
New South Wales 2061, Australia

Random House New Zealand Limited
18 Poland Road, Glenfield,
Auckland 10, New Zealand

Random House South Africa (Pty) Limited
Endulini, 5A Jubilee Road, Parktown 2193, South Africa

The Random House Group Limited Reg. No. 954009
www.randomhouse.co.uk

A CIP catalogue record for this book is available from the British Library

ISBN 0-7126-6826-8

Printed and bound in Great Britain by
Mackays of Chatham Plc, Chatham, Kent

Contents

List of Maps

INTRODUCTION

The reasons for the outbreak of the First World War have been a matter of acute controversy ever since the war began. The debate took a virulent form when, on 28 June 1919 (five years to the day after Archduke Franz Ferdinand and his wife were assassinated at Sarajevo), the German representatives were given no choice but to sign the Treaty of Versailles drafted by the victorious allies. Germany took particular exception to article 231, the so-called *Kriegsschuldfrage*, or 'war guilt' clause. It stated:

> Germany accepts the responsibility of Germany and her allies for causing all the loss and damage to the Allied governments and their nationals imposed on them by aggression of Germany and her allies.

In addition:

> The Allied and Associated Powers publicly arraign William II of Hohenzollern, former German emperor, for a supreme offence against international morality, and the sanctity of treaties.

Over the last eighty years scholars have looked for deep, fundamental causes in the European power structure that made the outbreak of war almost inevitable. A number of different features of Europe before 1914 have been allocated primary responsibility. Apart from internal political and social pressures at least three other factors were thought to be crucial. First, the alliance structure that ensured a limited dispute in the Balkans escalated into a war involving all the major European powers. Second, economic and imperial rivalries stemming from European expansion into Asia and the Pacific and the partition of Africa in the late nineteenth century. Third, a developing arms race between the powers – in particular the building of an ocean-going navy by Germany after 1897 and the British decision that it had to maintain its naval supremacy. The problem with all these interpretations is that they tend to work backwards from the outbreak of war in order to show that it was inevitable and preordained. The common picture is of a Europe reaching boiling point as heat was applied by a number of factors resulting in an inevitable explosion in the summer of 1914. The assassination of Franz Ferdinand was seen as no more than the action that lit the fuse that set off the conflagration.

This book rejects such explanations. It does not deny that the tensions were there, but it does deny that they were inevitably going to cause a European war. Europe had been divided into two alliance structures since the mid-1890s but this had not led to war. Economic and imperial rivalries around the globe were settled by negotiation and Europe was not engaged in a major arms race. On average, defence spending was at the level found in peacetime Europe throughout the twentieth century. Europe did face a large number of diplomatic disputes in the period between 1905 and 1913 – Morocco in 1905–6, Bosnia–Herzegovina in 1908–9, Agadir in 1911 and the vast range of problems stemming from the Balkan Wars of 1912–13 – but the crucial point is that they were all settled through diplomacy. The key question that has to be answered is why the crisis produced by the assassinations at Sarajevo was not resolved by diplomatic means. That can only be answered by studying events in detail. A small number of diplomats, senior officials, army officers and monarchs made all the key decisions. They had to act within the framework established for European relations in the early twentieth century but it was the decisions they made, their mistakes, failures and miscalculations that produced war.

In studying the diplomatic crisis of July 1914, this book rejects the common view of primary German responsibility for the war. That is not to say that Germany can escape all blame for the outbreak of the war. Some of the decisions taken by the German government contributed directly to ensuring that war was the result of the July 1914 crisis. However, other countries cannot escape responsibility. The Russian decision to mobilise was fundamental in tipping an acute diplomatic crisis into war and France did nothing to restrain its ally from pursuing this course. British policy was faltering and unclear and the misunderstandings about its position which this generated contributed significantly to the miscalculations made in Berlin.

This book argues that the First World War only occurred because of the situation in the Balkans. It was the outcome of the two Balkan wars between 1912 and 1913, the changes they precipitated in the strategic balance in the region, together with the struggle for influence between Austria–Hungary and Russia, that led to war. In this respect what began as the 'Third Balkan War' rapidly escalated into a European conflict. The primary responsibility for war therefore lies with three states. First, Serbia, where there was an aggressive, ideologically motivated nationalism, entrenched under the extremists who brought the Karadjordjević dynasty to the throne in the bloody 1903 coup. The extreme nationalists were never reconciled to the Austro-Hungarian annexation of Bosnia-Herzegovina in 1908 which they saw as part of historic Serbia, even though the majority of the population of the provinces were not Serbs. The assassinations at Sarajevo were directed, funded and organised by factions within the Serbian administration. They were carried out by extreme Serb nationalist terrorists. The second state which must bear primary responsibility for the war is Austria-Hungary. It viewed the expansion of Serbia in 1912–13 as a fundamental threat. It was not simply the Serbian desire to gain Bosnia–Herzegovina that made it an enemy of Austria–Hungary. The mere existence of a Serb national state acted as a potential dis-integrating force within the multinational Habsburg empire and tended to encourage other minority populations, not just Serbs, to look outside the empire for support in establishing their own national states. It was the determination of the government in Vienna to use the assas-sinations as an excuse to permanently cripple Serbia through military conquest and dismemberment, and throughout the July crisis to reject any diplomatic settlement, that was a fundamental cause of the out-break of the war. The third state was Russia. It had been expanding westwards for more than two hundred years and saw the Balkans as an important area which should form part of its sphere of influence, even though the attempt to bring this about inevitably brought it into conflict with Austria–Hungary. Russia supported Serbia simply because it was an enemy of Austria–Hungary, although some elements in the Russian government also saw such actions as support for another Slav and Orthodox state. It was the Russian decision not to allow Austria–Hungary to impose a diplomatic humiliation on Serbia, let alone defeat it in a local war, that ensured the outbreak of a European war.

After looking in detail at the assassinations in Sarajevo and examining the most important features of Europe in the first decade of the twentieth century this book concentrates on the diplomatic crisis that followed the killings. It shows how Austria–Hungary and Germany decided to deal with Serbia, and any problems such action might involve. The majority of the book deals with the 'Thirteen Days', from the presentation of the Austro–Hungarian ultimatum to Serbia on 23 July to Britain's entry into the war on 4 August. It examines how the situation escalated out of control, the decisions taken by the various governments that helped ensure this outcome and why diplomatic attempts to resolve the crisis failed. It does so by describing what happened day by day in the various capitals of Europe. The focus of each chapter shifts from capital to capital as the crucial decisions were taken. The book is deliberately structured in this way. Communications between the European capitals were still primitive – telephones and telephone networks were in their infancy and governments had to rely on telegrams that took several hours, often nearly a whole day, to travel from capital to capital. No European politician was able to gain control of the crisis and action was still reliant on ambassadors who might or might not carry out the instructions they were sent. Governments were often unaware of what was happening in the rest of Europe until it was too late. Diplomatic initiatives were frequently started when the problem they were meant to resolve had been overtaken by events. The result was that the crisis rapidly ran out of control. Each chapter tries to gain a dramatic sense of that crisis by showing how each government reacted to the rapidly deteriorating situation.

The thirteen-day crisis led to the outbreak of the First World War, something that no power in Europe wanted. That war ended the old European order for ever. The instability the war produced led to the establishment of Communism in Russia and the rise of Fascism and Nazism. After only a short pause, the second round of what had become a European civil war began in 1939. That in its turn led to the collapse of the European empires across the globe and the eclipse of Europe by the United States and, to some extent, the Soviet Union. It was the assassinations at Sarajevo and the thirteen-day diplomatic crisis in 1914 that were to shape much of European history for the rest of the twentieth century.

PART ONE

Sarajevo, Sunday 28 June 1914

I

THE ASSASSINATION

In late June 1914 Archduke Franz Ferdinand, the heir to the Austro-Hungarian throne, was, as Inspector-General of the armed forces, visiting manoeuvres conducted by the 15th and 16th army corps around Tarčin in the mountains south-west of Sarajevo, the capital of the province of Bosnia–Herzegovina. Franz Ferdinand was the nephew of the eighty-four-year-old Emperor, Franz Josef, but had only become heir through a bizarre series of accidents. Franz Josef's first heir, his younger brother Ferdinand Maximilian Josef, was executed by a Mexican firing squad in June 1867. Franz Josef's son, Crown Prince Rudolf, died in January 1889. Next in line was the second youngest brother of Franz Josef, Archduke Karl Rudolf, the father of Franz Ferdinand. He died in May 1896 after drinking the typhoid infested waters of the River Jordan during a pilgrimage to Jerusalem. In 1898 the thirty-five-year-old Franz Ferdinand was designated as heir to the various Habsburg lands that made up the Austro-Hungarian empire.

Like his father, Archduke Franz Ferdinand was strongly religious and dominated by the priests in his entourage. He had never expected to be heir to the throne and his upbringing had been typical of the Habsburg aristocracy. His career was in the army and his main pastime was hunting – by 1913 he had slaughtered over six thousand deer. He was deeply conservative and disliked the Hungarians who made up a large part of the monarchy and who had, in 1867, been granted a large degree of autonomy and effective equality with the German-speaking part of the Austro-Hungarian empire. He was a supporter of Dr Karl Leuger, the mayor of Vienna and leader of the anti-Semitic Christian Socialist Party, who was a major influence on the young Adolf Hitler. Although Franz Ferdinand also disliked the Serbs, he was generally cautious in foreign policy – he was worried by the growing power of Russia in the Balkans and unwilling to risk a general war. His greatest hatred, however, was reserved for the Italians and he still harboured dreams of regaining Venetia and Lombardy lost fifty years earlier.

Franz Ferdinand's position as heir was deeply affected by his love for Countess Sophie Chotek von Chotkowa und Wogin, who was from an

impoverished Czech aristocratic family. Under the German Con-
federation Act of 1814, the family was not one of those eligible to
marry Habsburg princes. In 1898 Franz Josef banned Franz Ferdinand
from marrying Sophie (his permission was required under the 1839
Familien Statut). Eventually, in 1900, a compromise was reached.
Franz Ferdinand was allowed to marry Sophie but the marriage was to
be morganatic – their children could not inherit the Habsburg throne.
Although Sophie became Princess of Hohenberg on her marriage (and
Duchess in 1907) she was not allowed, on Emperor Franz Josef's
express order, to have the privileges of the wife of an archduke. In court
protocol and on official functions she was ostracised.

The Archduke and his wife travelled by different routes to Sarajevo.
Franz Ferdinand left Trieste by boat and arrived in Sarajevo on 25 June.
He went shopping in the bazaar that evening before spending the next
two days watching the army manoeuvres. The Duchess left Vienna by
train and stayed at the Hotel Bosnia in the spa town of Ilidže. She
visited Sarajevo on both days of the army manoeuvres, before Franz
Ferdinand joined her at the hotel (they had taken over the whole
building) late in the afternoon of 27 June. The programme agreed for
their visit to Sarajevo on 28 June called for them to leave Ilidže by train
at 9.25 a.m. and, on arrival, to inspect a small contingent of troops. At
ten they would drive to the town hall for the official welcome before
leaving at 10.30 to open the new State Museum. This would be
followed by lunch with the governor of Bosnia–Herzegovina, General
Oskar Potiorek, before a drive through the town and a visit to the local
barracks and a carpet factory. The royal couple would leave by train to
Ilidže where, after a brief walk and dinner, they would board the train
at 9 p.m. for their overnight journey to Vienna.

The arrangements for the visit were in the hands of General Potiorek.
Compared with Emperor Franz Josef's visit to the town in 1910, when
a double cordon of soldiers had lined the route, security was very lax.
Dr Edmund Gerde, the chief of the Sarajevo police, had just 120 officers
and six detectives to cover the four-mile route through the town. Gerde
had warned against the visit, considering it far too dangerous because
28 June was *Vidovdan*, the Serb national day commemorating their
catastrophic defeat by the Ottomans at the battle of Kosovo in the late
fourteenth century. It was also the day on which the Serb Miloš Obilić
had assassinated the Ottoman sultan. Gerde asked for a cordon of
soldiers along the route but this was rejected by Potiorek because the
uniforms of the 70,000 troops taking part in the manoeuvres would be

dirty. Gerde also requested that the route of the procession should not be made public until the day before the visit, but the mayor of Sarajevo published the route on 23 June. Potiorek hoped to use the visit to improve his chances of being appointed Army Chief of Staff when Franz Ferdinand became emperor. His contribution to the arrangements was a long correspondence with Franz Ferdinand's office almost entirely confined to protocol – the menu for the dinner, whether the wines should be sweet or dry, whether they should be served at room temperature or chilled and whether a string quartet should play during the lunch. Finally, he ensured that on the manoeuvres the stirrup for Franz Ferdinand's horse was exactly seventy-two centimetres long.

On Sunday 28 June Franz Ferdinand and Sophie attended mass in a specially converted room at the Hotel Bosna and then left for Sarajevo. It was a brilliant, hot, sunny day and Franz Ferdinand was dressed in the uniform of an Austrian cavalry general – blue tunic, black trousers with a red stripe, a hat with pale green feathers and around his waist a gold-braided ribbon with tassels. Sophie wore a white silk dress, a fur of ermine tails over her shoulders and a large white hat. They were met at Sarajevo station by General Potiorek and inspected the guard of honour – the only troops in the town. They then set off in a convoy of cars for the town hall on Appel Quay which ran alongside the Miljačka river. The cars were supplied by the Imperial and Royal Voluntary Automobile Corps, a unit of reserve officers whose function was to provide cars for official visits. In the first car were a few local detectives who acted as the security contingent. The second contained Fehim Effendi Curcic (the mayor of Sarajevo) and Dr Edmund Gerde. The third car was a *Graef und Stift* Viennese sports car with the roof folded back. It was driven by a Czech, Leopold Sojka, and contained Franz Ferdinand and Sophie together with General Potiorek and Lieutenant Colonel Franz Harrach, the transport officer, who owned the car. The remainder of the official entourage travelled in the fourth and fifth cars. Franz Ferdinand asked for the cars to be driven slowly (about 10–12 mph) so that he could see the town.

At about 10.10 the cars were travelling along the Appel Quay through a thin crowd with the buildings decorated with the Habsburg and Bosnian flags. Near the Čumurja Bridge a young man dressed in a long black coat and black hat asked a policeman which was Franz Ferdinand's car and then threw a bomb at it. Sojka, seeing what was happening, accelerated and the bomb hit the folded down roof, bounced off into the street and exploded under the rear wheel of the

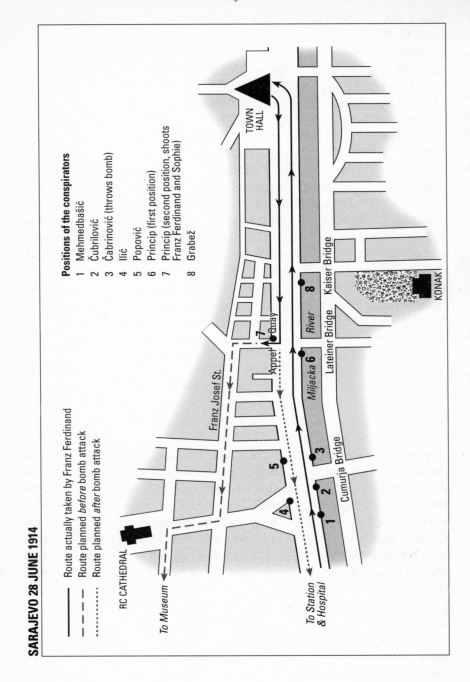

SARAJEVO 28 JUNE 1914

— Route actually taken by Franz Ferdinand
– – Route planned *before* bomb attack
······· Route planned *after* bomb attack

Positions of the conspirators

1 Mehmedbašić
2 Čubrilović
3 Čabrinović (throws bomb)
4 Ilić
5 Popović
6 Princip (first position)
7 Princip (second position, shoots Franz Ferdinand and Sophie)
8 Grabež

RC CATHEDRAL

To Museum

Franz Josef St.

Appel Quay

Cumurja Bridge

Lateiner Bridge

Kaiser Bridge

Miljacka River

KONAK

TOWN HALL

To Station & Hospital

fourth car. The young man then jumped over the wall and fell twenty-six feet into the river below. The first two cars did not know what had happened and continued to the town hall. Franz Ferdinand ordered his car to stop and sent Harrach back to investigate and report. He found that two of the occupants of the fourth car, in particular General Potiorek's aide-de-camp, Colonel Merizzi, were hurt, about twenty spectators were slightly injured and the police were arresting as many bystanders as possible. Franz Ferdinand's car was only slightly damaged and so it continued along Appel Quay to the town hall.

When he arrived, Franz Ferdinand found the official welcoming party arranged on the front steps. In the centre was the mayor. The Muslim councillors, dressed in open waistcoats, baggy trousers and conical hats, were on one side, and the Christian councillors, dressed in tail coats and top hats, were on the other. There was also a representative of the Jewish community present. Not knowing what had occurred, the mayor began his formal speech of welcome. Franz Ferdinand interrupted and, not surprisingly, complained about being welcomed by bombs. After some awkward moments, the mayor continued with his prepared speech and the party moved inside. While Sophie went to meet a group of Muslim women and children on the first floor, there was a discussion in the lobby about plans for the remainder of the visit following the attempted assassination. Franz Ferdinand asked whether it was safe to go on and whether there might be other attempts. Some in his entourage suggested going direct to the governor's residence (the Konak) a short distance away across the Miljačka river. Others argued for an immediate return to Ilidže. General Potiorek accepted full responsibility for the archduke's safety. He suggested continuing with the visit to the museum, although he recommended travelling along the now deserted Appel Quay rather than through the narrow streets of the old town as originally planned. Franz Ferdinand accepted Potiorek's advice although he decided to go first to the military hospital to visit Colonel Merizzi even though he was told that Merizzi's wounds were very minor. Sophie was not due to attend the museum – that was an official function and her status prohibited her taking part. However, she refused to return to Ilidže and decided to accompany her husband to the hospital. Franz Ferdinand dictated a telegram to Franz Josef about the attempted assassination and then left the town hall.

At 10.45 the convoy of cars, in the same order as before, left the town hall for the military hospital. Harrach stood on the left-hand running board of the Archduke's car to protect him from any other assassination attempts. The cars drove at high speed along the quay but at the junction with Franz Josef Street the first two cars turned right in accordance with the original plan for the visit. Potiorek and his staff had forgotten to tell the drivers about the change of route. Sojka followed the first two cars until Potiorek ordered him to stop and go along the quay. As he was putting the car into reverse, a young man stepped forward from the crowd on the corner of Franz Josef Street. He drew a revolver and when a policeman tried to grab his hand another person in the crowd knocked the policeman over. The young man fired shots at close range (about four to five paces). Franz Ferdinand was hit and Sophie was also wounded, almost certainly by a bullet intended for Potiorek. Harrach was standing on the wrong side of the car. Sojka finally managed to reverse the car and then drove rapidly to the governor's residence.

When the car arrived at the Konak at about eleven, it was discovered that Sophie was already dead. She had been killed by a bullet that had penetrated the side of the car and then entered her right side. Franz Ferdinand had been hit on the right side of his neck and the bullet had severed his jugular vein and lodged in his spine. He was pronounced dead at about 11.15. The last rites were administered and the bodies placed in separate rooms at the Konak. At 11.30 all the church bells in Sarajevo began tolling.

2

THE CONSPIRACY

Within minutes of the assassination of Franz Ferdinand and Sophie, the Austro-Hungarian authorities had arrested the two young men who had thrown the bomb and fired the fatal shots. Within hours, the authorities established the outlines of the conspiracy behind the assassination and arrested all but one of the main participants. They knew that those involved were Serbs and that they were linked to elements in the Serbian government in Belgrade. The statements the perpetrators made demonstrated how far their beliefs and actions had been moulded by the most virulent and extreme forms of Serb nationalism that had emerged in the late nineteenth century.

The tiny mountain kingdom of Serbia was effectively autonomous within the Ottoman empire from the mid-nineteenth century but only obtained its formal independence at the Congress of Berlin in 1878. At that Congress Austria–Hungary took over the administration of the Ottoman provinces of Bosnia–Herzegovina although they remained under nominal Ottoman sovereignty. Serbia became a puppet state of Austria-Hungary. In June 1881 a secret agreement bound Serbia not to negotiate or agree a political treaty with another state without Austo-Hungarian approval and not to allow any foreign military forces on to its soil. Serbia also renounced all claims to Bosnia–Herzegovina with its large Serb population. Article 2 of the 1881 treaty stated: 'Serbia will not tolerate political, religious or other intrigues which, taking its territory as a point of departure, might be directed against the Austro–Hungarian monarchy.' In return Austria–Hungary backed the claims of Prince Milan Obrenović to the throne and supported him when he declared himself king in 1882. As a landlocked state Serbia remained dependent on Austria–Hungary for its communications and its richer neighbour was also the main market for its agricultural products. Nine-tenths of the population of Serbia were peasants and eight out of ten people were illiterate. At the beginning of the twentieth century there were just 4,000 industrial workers in the whole country. A national bank to issue currency was only set up in 1884 and the state remained debt-ridden. Only 200,000 people were allowed to vote and political life, which was deeply corrupt, was run by the small educated elite.

Despite the obvious limitations of the Serbian state and economy it was seen by many as the first stage in the rebirth of the Serb nation. Such ideas reflected the growth of an extreme Serb nationalism which, in some respects, was similar to that found in other parts of Europe in the late nineteenth century. Increasingly, nationalism was becoming a deeply conservative force characterised by a rejection of the modern world, a belief in an illusory past and a desire for a Utopian future of unity, stability and order in a nation without internal conflict. The unique attributes of a people were defined by race, language or religion, by special sacred, religious or national sites and by an identity created over time that separated one group of people from another.

Serb nationalism was one of the most extreme of these sets of beliefs. Its origins can be traced back to the late eighteenth and early nineteenth centuries when Vuk Karadižić created the modern Serbian language out of a dialect found in Bosnia. Dositej Obradović (who died in 1811) first asserted the idea that all the inhabitants of Serbia, Bosnia, Herzegovina, Montenegro, Dalmatia and Croatia were racially and linguistically part of a single Serb identity even though they were separated by religion and history. The political claims of Serb nationalism were first set out in the *Načertanije* written by llija Garašanin, a minister in the 'government' of Alexander Karadjordjević (from the family who were the main rivals to the Obrenović dynasty) which ruled Serbia between 1842 and 1860. In the *Načertanije*, which was written in 1844 but not published until 1906, Garašanin laid out the concept of 'Greater Serbia'. It was to include the population of all the areas claimed as Serbian by Obradović, who would be brought under the rule of the Karadjordjević dynasty regardless of their claims to a separate identity as Croats, Muslims, Montenegrins, Hungarians, etc. The Serb task was to continue building the Serbian empire which had been 'interrupted' by the Ottoman conquest at the end of the fourteenth-century. Greater Serbia would include not just the areas listed above but also the historic area of Kosovo together with northern Albania so as to give Serbia access to the sea. The Serbian state would be created on the ruins of the Ottoman empire by absorbing all the 'Serbian people'. This inevitably meant, as Garašanin stated, 'Austria must always be the eternal enemy of a Serbian state'.[1]

One of the defining characteristics of a true Serb was the Orthodox religion. One of the leaders of that Church, Prince-Bishop Petar II

Petrović-Njejos of Montenegro, who ruled that minuscule mountain kingdom between 1830 and 1851 (the title was hereditary in the family and passed from uncle to nephew), set out the more brutal and genocidal aspects of Serb nationalism in his epic poem *Gorski Vijenac* (or 'The Mountain Wreath') published in 1847. One part of the poem set out to glorify Miloš Obilić, the legendary hero of Kosovo. The aim was to rekindle this old spirit so that all Serbs could become free. The main part of the poem was, however, a celebration of the actions of the Montenegin rulers who, on a future Christmas Eve, decide to exterminate all Montenegrins who had converted to Islam. The poem rejoices in the slaughter and bloodshed and implies that it should continue – 'our faiths will swim in blood, the better one will not sink'. *Gorski Vijenac* was published in twenty editions between 1847 and 1913 and became the most widely read work among Serbs. It achieved a mythic status, second only to Kosovo, in the creation of Serbian nationalism.

Serbia continued to be ruled by the Obrenović family, who had set themselves up as the royal dynasty in 1882, until the early twentieth century. However, there was increasing opposition to them from extreme nationalists, particularly in the army, who backed the rival Karadjordjević family and their claim to the throne (they had led the 1806 revolt against the Ottomans and ruled Serbia intermittently in the early nineteenth century). In 1900 the Obrenović ruler, Alexander, married his mistress Draga Mašin, who had been a lady-in-waiting to his mother. This action further discredited the royal family among the extreme Serb nationalists and they staged a military coup. On the night of 11 June 1903, army units broke into the royal palace in Belgrade. It took them two hours to find the King and Queen concealed in a hidden clothes closet. The half-dressed Queen was repeatedly shot as she tried to protect her husband and after their deaths the bodies were hacked to pieces with sabres and thrown out into the courtyard.

Following the coup, the army installed Prince Petar Karadjordjević as the new king. He was married to a Montenegrin princess and was strongly supported by the Russians. The new dynasty (which remained unrecognised by most of Europe for several years) was itself strongly nationalist and also encouraged the much more extreme Serbian nationalists who had put the dynasty on the throne together with their belief in a 'Greater Serbia'. Under its new rulers Serbia was soon in conflict with Austria–Hungary, as it tried to end its subordinate status and achieve some degree of economic and political independence. The decisive turning point came with the Austro-Hungarian decision to annex Bosnia–Herzegovina in 1908 and incorporate it into the Habsburg empire. This was a deliberate and direct challenge to the increasingly extreme Serbian nationalism which saw one of its main avenues of expansion as being northwards into Bosnia–Herzegovina which the nationalists had always seen as being central to any 'Great Serbia'.

The annexation led to the outbreak of an even more extreme Serb nationalism. A new organisation – *Narodna Odbrana* – was created. Its original role was semi-military – to organise volunteers to 'protect' Bosnia–Herzegovina. However, in 1909, when it was deprived of Russian diplomatic support, Serbia was forced to recognise the Austro–Hungarian annexation of Bosnia–Herzegovina. As part of the settlement, the Serbian government was obliged to restrict the activities of *Narodna Odbrana*, which the government in Vienna rightly saw as hostile to its interests. Serbia was to ensure that in future it was devoted solely to promoting Serb culture. To a large extent this did happen, although Narodna Odbrana continued to maintain a network of agents across the newly incorporated Austro-Hungarian province.

The most important outcome of the restrictions on the activities of *Narodna Odbrana*, as well as the humiliation of Serbia in the 1908–9 crisis, was the creation of a highly secret organisation within the Serbian elite. The new organisation – *Ujedinjenje ili Smrt* (Union or Death) – was founded on 22 May 1911 by the group of army officers who had led the 1903 coup. The first president was Colonel Ilija Radivojević who, together with another member of the central committee, Velimir Vemić, had hacked the bodies of the last Obrenović king and queen into pieces. The symbols of *Ujedinjenje ili Smrt* were a skull, crossbones, knife, bomb and poison. Its aims were the 'union' of all Serbs into the 'Greater Serbia' which it defined in Article 7 of its constitution as including Bosnia–Herzegovina, Montenegro, Macedonia, Croatia and Dalmatia. It believed that its aims could best be achieved by 'the racial regeneration of the Serbian people'. However, as an organisation it preferred terrorist action over propaganda (that became the function of *Narodna Odbrana*). It aimed to exercise its influence within the Serbian government, which, it argued, should perform the same role as Piedmont had in the unification of Italy between 1858 and 1870 – it would expand to absorb the Serbs everywhere in the Balkans, including those in Bosnia–Herzegovina. (The newspaper of the organisation, first published in August 1911, was called *Pijemont*.) The members of *Ujedinjenje ili Smrt* took a gruesome oath and were identified only by a number – they were not known to each other, only to the central committee of eleven. As an elite group, membership was restricted to those who had something to offer the organisation and in total it probably did not exceed 2,500.

The main driving force behind *Ujedinjenje ili Smrt*, and its real controller, was the shadowy figure of Colonel Dragutin Dimitrijvić (nicknamed 'Apis' after the Egyptian bull god), who had joined the army in 1893. One of the leaders of the 1903 coup, he remained the accepted head of the group of younger officers who had carried out that coup. In August 1913 he was appointed head of army intelligence, a position from which he was easily able to amalgamate his official duties with those as the effective head of *Ujedinjenje ili Smrt*. He stated that the title of the organisation meant that 'every member must be prepared to give his life for the unification of Serbdom'.[2]

The conspiracy which led to the assassination of Franz Ferdinand and his wife was deeply rooted in extremist Serb nationalism and, in particular, *Ujedinjenje ili Smrt* and its members. The killings, though, were carried out by young Serbs from Bosnia–Herzegovina. After Austria–Hungary took control of the area in 1878, there was a steady programme of public investment, primarily on roads and railways, and schools were set up. However, there were separate schools for each of the communities – Serb, Croat and Muslim. There was no real 'Bosnian' identity, except among a few Muslims, and when, after the annexation, a largely powerless parliament was set up in 1910, it was fundamentally divided. Out of a total population of about two million, 40 per cent were Serbs who were represented by the Serbian National Organisation. It claimed that Bosnia–Herzegovina was Serbian and that the 30 per cent of the population who were Muslims were really Serbs and that the Croats (about 20 per cent of the total) did not count. This last group were represented by the Croatian National Society, a clerical group organised by Archbishop Josef Stadler which stressed Catholicism as the defining element in Croat identity. They believed the Muslims were really Croats. The Muslims were given effective autonomy in 1909, and they, like the Croats, largely supported Austro-Hungarian rule.

The young man who fired the fatal shots on 28 June 1914, Gavrilo Princip, and his accomplice who threw the bomb, Nedeljko Čabrinović, were both Serbs born into this deeply fractured society. Princip was born in 1894 to a peasant family in the Grahovo valley, a remote and poor area of the Krajina in north-west Bosnia. He attended the local primary school between the ages of nine and thirteen. Then, in August 1907, he made the three-day journey to the nearest railway station to travel to Sarajevo where he refused to sleep for even one night at a Muslim inn. His family intended him to join the military school in the town, but through a chance meeting with a shopkeeper friend of the family he went to the merchants' school instead. While in Sarajevo he stayed with Stoja Ilić, a cobbler's widow, and her eighteen-year-old son Danilo (later a central figure in the conspiracy). During the school holidays he returned home to work on the farm. In 1910 he left Sarajevo to attend high school in Tuzla but was expelled in 1912 for participating in pro-Serbian demonstrations during the Balkan War. He went to Belgrade and tried to enlist in the Serbian forces but was turned down by Major Voja Tankosić, who ran the guerrilla training centre at Cuprija in eastern Serbia. Tankosić had been a central figure in the 1903 coup and had personally ordered the murder of Queen Draga's brothers. He was a close associate of 'Apis' and a member of *Ujedinjenje ili Smrt*. He was to play a crucial role in the Sarajevo conspiracy.

Nedeljko Čabrinović was born in Sarajevo in January 1895. His father ran a café and acted as a spy for the police. Čabrinović joined the merchants' school at roughly the same time as Princip but left in 1908 when he failed his exams. He worked as a typesetter, and at numerous other occupations in both Sarajevo and Belgrade where he met Princip again in 1912. Čabrinović left to work in Trieste before returning to Belgrade where he was employed in the state printing office. He hung around many of the cafés where the irregulars who had fought in the Balkan Wars congregated, talked about Serb nationalism and devised numerous plots. Princip, who was attending the First Belgrade High School and had become a fanatical Serb nationalist, could be seen in the same cafés. He knew the *Gorski Vijenac* by heart and had committed himself to a life of action and self-sacrifice in the Serb cause. In 1910 a fellow Serb nationalist, Bogdan Žerajić, had decided to kill the Emperor Franz Josef during the latter's visit to Mostar on 3 June. At the last moment he changed his mind and decided instead to kill the governor of Bosnia–Herzegovina, General Marijan Varešanin. On 15 June he fired five shots at the governor; all of them missed, but Žerajić committed suicide believing he had succeeded in his mission. In 1912 Princip, then aged seventeen, swore an oath on Žerajić's grave in Sarajevo to 'avenge' his death. Later, he brought earth from 'free Serbia' to place on the grave.

The conspiracy to kill Franz Ferdinand was put in motion by the announcement, in March 1914, of his intended visit to Bosnia–Herzegovina. Princip had remained in touch with Danilo Ilić after he left Sarajevo to study in Belgrade. Ilić was a member of *Ujedinjenje ili Smrt* and the main agent for 'Apis' in Sarajevo. He may have told Princip about the visit, but Čabrinović found out when a friend in Sarajevo sent him a newspaper cutting via the only address he knew for Čabrinović – the Café Zlatana Moruna in Belgrade. Princip and Čabrinović, together with a third Serb, Trifko Grabež, who shared lodgings with Princip, decided they should, in the Serb cause, assassinate Franz Ferdinand. There was no specific reason why they chose Franz Ferdinand – he simply represented the main enemy of Serbia and the country that blocked the attainment of a 'Greater Serbia'. It is almost certain that all three conspirators were members of *Ujedinjenje ili Smrt* and it was to that organisation that they turned for help.

The conspirators faced three problems: how to get hold of weapons, how to raise the money to travel to Sarajevo and how to cross the border carrying the weapons without being discovered by the Austro-Hungarian authorities. Princip went to see another member of *Ujedinjenje ili Smrt*, Milan Ciganović. He was a fellow Bosnian Serb who had lived in Belgrade since 1908 and had helped Tankosić run the irregular Serb fighters in the Balkan Wars. He held a sinecure in the Serbian state railway which enabled him to spend his time on various conspiratorial activities. Ciganović realised that he needed the approval of Tankosić for such an operation. Since Princip refused to deal directly with Tankosić because of his rejection in 1912, it was the third conspirator, Grabež, who went with Ciganović to see Major Tankosić. Tankosić agreed to supply the necessary weapons from the various stocks he had left over from the Balkan Wars. He advised the conspirators to practise shooting before leaving Belgrade and told them they would have to take the weapons with them when they crossed the border as he had no means of getting arms into Austria–Hungary. He did, however, promise that he would arrange their journey through his various agents at the frontier and in Bosnia–Herzegovina. He also told them they had to carry cyanide phials so that they could kill themselves after the assassination and not reveal details of the conspiracy. Tankosić provided the conspirators with money – he needed a double signature on the piece of paper authorising the expenditure and this strongly suggests that it was an official *Ujedinjenje ili Smrt* operation, not a piece of private enterprise. All of the evidence implies that 'Apis' knew of and approved the conspiracy in advance.

After the meeting with Tankosić, Grabež left Belgrade to return home to Sarajevo for the Easter school holidays. While there, he must have seen Danilo Ilić and alerted him to the conspiracy. Ilić became the main organiser in Sarajevo. Meanwhile, in Belgrade, Milan Ciganović (the railway employee) acted as the main link to the conspirators, providing them with the money and the weapons. These included four pistols, each loaded with seven bullets, together with a reserve magazine for each. In addition he gave them six nail bombs. He also organised the shooting practice in Košutnjak Park, just outside Belgrade. This was the place where Prince Mihailo Obrenović had been murdered in 1868, probably by Austro-Hungarian agents, when he was about to launch a Serb uprising. The conspirators saw themselves as avenging his death (as well as Žerajić's) and formed themselves into a group of *duhovi* or 'spirits' and 'avengers of Kosovo.'

After a farewell dinner on 28 May 1914, Princip, Čabrinović and Grabež left Belgrade on their journey to Sarajevo. They began their eight-day journey by taking a boat along the River Sava to Sabač. Here, as arranged by Tankosić, they made contact with Captain Rade Popović, an intelligence officer in the frontier guards. (His commanding officer was Major Ljubomir Vulović, a member of the central committee of *Ujedinjenje ili Smrt*.) Popović advised the conspirators that the safest place to cross the border was near Loznica on the River Drina. He bought them cheap rail tickets by signing a warrant saying they were customs officers and wrote a letter to a colleague ordering him to provide assistance. However, after the three left Sabač, Princip and Grabež forced Čabrinović to travel separately and cross the border at Lešnica without any weapons – they thought he was a security risk because he had talked too much, especially on the boat to Sabač. Princip and Grabež travelled by train to Loznica where they met their next contact, Captain Prvanović. He arranged with one of his subordinates, Sergeant Rade Grbić, that they should cross the border in his sector and also arranged for a number of his contacts in Bosnia to escort the conspirators once they were inside Austria–Hungary. Princip and Grabež were taken by these contacts across the border and through Bosnia to Tuzla where they met up with Čabrinović. The three conspirators decided that it was too dangerous to travel to Sarajevo with the weapons and stored them with their *Ujedinjenje ili Smrt* contact in the town, Miško Jovanović. On the train journey to Sarajevo

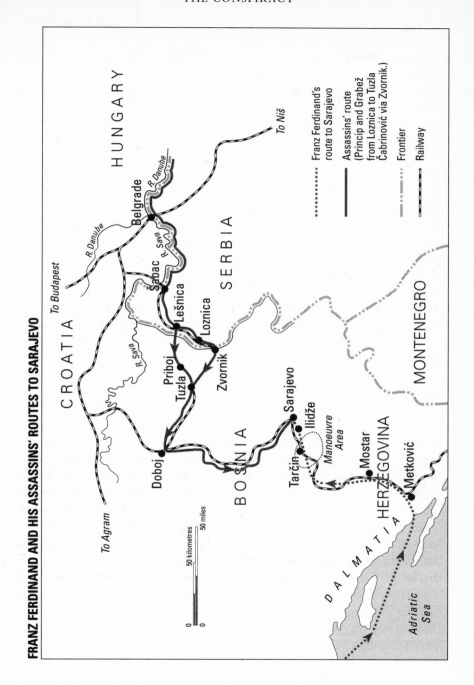

FRANZ FERDINAND AND HIS ASSASSINS' ROUTES TO SARAJEVO

they got into conversation with Ivan Vila – he was a police agent who knew Čabrinović's father, a fellow agent. Vila told them the date of Franz Ferdinand's visit. Princip, Čabrinović and Grabež arrived in Sarajevo late on 4 June – they had over three weeks to wait before they could carry out the assassination attempt.

After they arrived in Sarajevo, the conspirators split up. Čabrinović went to stay with his parents in the town; Grabež went to his parents in Pale. Princip stayed briefly with his brother in Hadžići before moving in with Danilo Ilić. On 15 June Ilić travelled to Tuzla to pick up the stored weapons, took them back to Sarajevo by train and kept them in his house. Ilić had, without the knowledge of the three conspirators from Belgrade, recruited two local Serbs to take part in the assassination, Vaso Čubrilović and Svijetko Popović – both were students at the local teacher training college. The final member of the conspiracy was Muhamed Mehmedbašić, a Muslim carpenter but a fanatical Serb nationalist. Apart from Mehmedbašić, who was twenty-seven, and Ilić, who was twenty-four, all of the conspirators were less than twenty years old.

Princip, Čabrinović and Grabež had left Belgrade a month before the assassination attempt and had been helped at every point on their journey by Serbian government employees. The weapons and money for the operation were supplied by members of the Serbian army. *Ujedinjenje ili Smrt* had penetrated into every area of the Serbian state – in many respects it was the alternative government within Serbia. In view of the consequences of the assassination, one vital question to resolve is whether the Serbian government was aware of the conspiracy. In 1924 Ljuba Jovanović, who was minister of public instruction in 1914, published fragments of his memoirs, entitled *Krv Sloventsva* ('The Blood of Slavism'). In them he claimed that in late May/early June 1914 he told the Serbian prime minister, Nicholas Pašić, that people were crossing into Austria–Hungary with the intention of killing Franz Ferdinand during his visit to Sarajevo. He claimed that Pašić ordered the interior minister, Stojan Protić, to stop the crossings but that his orders were disobeyed because the frontier officials were members of *Ujedinjenje ili Smrt*. Pašić never convincingly denied the story and memoirs by two other senior Serbian officials, Milan Georgević and Colonel Lešanin (the Serbian military attaché in Vienna), confirmed Jovanović's story. There is also circumstantial evidence that Milan Ciganović told Nicholas Pašić about the plot.

Serbian government knowledge of the plot, and their failure to stop the conspirators, seems to be confirmed by the instructions given to the Serbian minister in Vienna, Jovan Jovanović. He was told to give a warning about a likely assassination attempt during the Archduke's visit but he realised that this could only be done in the most general terms without revealing official Serbian knowledge. In addition, Jovanović was disliked in almost every part of the Austro-Hungarian government and rarely saw the foreign minister, Count Berchtold. Jovanović did see his normal contact, Leon Bilinski, the Austro-Hungarian joint finance minister, responsible for the administration of Bosnia–Herzegovina. He appears to have given a warning that was so general that it was ignored. Whether Jovanović could be trusted by the government in Belgrade is doubtful – he was a member of *Ujedinjenje ili Smrt* and supported the groups that were producing a major political crisis in Serbia in the days leading up to the assassination attempt.

Throughout the first half of 1914 there was a dispute in Serbia over the administration of Macedonia, which had been gained during the second Balkan War in 1913. The dispute widened into a struggle for power between the Serbian government under Pašić and the extreme nationalists of *Ujedinjenje ili Smrt* directed by 'Apis' – Colonel Dragutin Dimitrijvić. It also involved the Karadjordjević dynasty and the Russians. The crisis became serious when the Pašić government issued the so-called 'Priority Ordinance', giving precedence to the civilian government rather than the military in the newly conquered territories. The government expected an army coup and was hoping to use the crisis to remove both Apis and Major Tankosić who they felt, with considerable justification, were undermining the government. However, King Petar refused to sign the order dismissing the two army officers and on 2 June, under considerable pressure from the army, Pašić resigned as prime minister. Five day later, Apis issued orders for an army coup in Macedonia but his followers in the area did not support him. At this stage the Russian minister in Belgrade, Nicholas Hartwig, intervened. Hartwig may have known about the Sarajevo assassination plot and even if he did not then his military attaché, General Victor Artamonov, and his deputy, Captain Werchovski, almost certainly did know. Russia was the main supporter of Serbia and Hartwig played a crucial role in Serbian politics. As the British minister in Belgrade reported: 'Serbia is, practically speaking, a Russian province', adding that he had never known the Serbian government to act 'against the directions of the Russian minister'.[3] Hartwig, with the assistance of the heir to the Serbian throne, Alexander (who helped fund the *Pijemont* newspaper), ensured that Pašić was reappointed as prime minister. On 24 June Pašić gained approval for the dissolution of the Skupština (parliament) with elections to be held on 1 August. King Petar resigned as king on 24 June and appointed Alexander as Regent and Commander-in-Chief.

It is almost certain that the assassination conspiracy was supported and promoted by Apis as part of this struggle within the Serbian elite. When the assassination was approved and launched it was intended to be part of a campaign against the Pašić government by the extreme Serb nationalists. If it was successful it was likely to severely embarrass the Pašić government and possibly help lead to its downfall. However, there appear to have been disputes within the leadership of *Ujedinjenje ili Smrt* when, after the Pašić government began asking questions, they discovered, on about 15 June, exactly what Tankosić and Apis had authorised in their name. After this dispute, Apis sent one of his agents – Rade Malobabić, an ex-insurance salesman who ran much of the Serbian army intelligence organisation within Austria–Hungary – to Tuzla. Here he saw Grabež and told him the plot should go ahead. Malobabić also visited Ilić in Sarajevo on the evening before the assassination to give him the same message and Malobabić was probably standing on the town hall steps on the morning of 28 June.

The three conspirators from Belgrade were living, undetected, in Bosnia–Herzegovina from early June. This was not the only lapse in Austro-Hungarian security precautions. The authorities had some information from Serb students at the Pakrac teacher-training college (where the local conspirators Čubrilović and Popović were fellow students) that an attempt might be made on Franz Ferdinand's life but no effective counteraction was taken. Instructions were issued to guards along the border on 27 May (just as the conspirators were setting out from Belgrade) to look out for suspicious people crossing from Serbia but the conspirators were not observed. On 10 June orders were issued for the strict operation of passport rules for all newcomers to Sarajevo after 15 June. Nevertheless, Princip and Čabrinović, who were both known to the police, were registered under their real names and no action was taken against them. Čabrinović, with his usual lack of discretion, even went to Ilidže three times to spy out assassination possibilities but was not detected.

It was only after the programme for Franz Ferdinand's visit was published that the conspirators could start their detailed planning on 24 June. Grabež arrived from Pale the next day and Ilić summoned

Mehmedbašić by telegram on 26 June. On the evening before the assassination, Ilić (apart from seeing Malobabić, his contact with Belgrade) met the local conspirators Čubrilović and Popović in a café and gave them each a pistol and a bomb together with a cyanide phial. Later, he met Mehmedbašić and gave him cyanide and a bomb – there were no pistols left – and explained where he was to stand the next morning. Meanwhile, Princip met Čabrinović, whom he still did not entirely trust, and told him where they would meet in the morning – he would only be given his weapons at the last moment. Ilić, Princip and Čabrinović then went to visit the grave of the Serb 'martyr', Bogdan Žerajić, where they rededicated themselves to the Serb cause.

Sunday 28 June was *Vidovdan* and across Sarajevo church bells were ringing for the special services in memory of Miloš Obilić, the Serb assassin, and the great defeat at Kosovo. In Belgrade the Ujedinjenje ili Smrt newspaper *Pijemont* declared: 'Serbia celebrates Vidovdan today as the victory of Serb national consciousness which has preserved the memory of Kosovo and which in the future must conquer in Bosnia just as it has conquered in Macedonia.' In Sarajevo Čabrinović, Grabež and Ilić met as arranged at the Vlajnić cake shop where Čabrinović ate three cakes. They joined Princip in a rear room and he then gave Čabrinović his weapons. Čabrinović left, and with a friend, Tomo Vučinović, had his photograph taken as a memorial for his parents. The photograph shows that Čabrinović had a copy of the Serb paper *Narod* stuffed into his jacket pocket. The paper contained nothing about the visit by Franz Ferdinand – the front page had a long editorial and a series of poems about Kosovo. After the meeting in the cake shop, Ilić took Grabež back to his house where he was given a bomb. Princip, already armed with a bomb and revolver, went directly to the Appel Quay.

The conspirators were in place shortly before 9 a.m. and stayed there for about seventy-five minutes without any interference from the police. Danilo Ilić walked between the assassins talking to each of them, encouraging them and keeping up their morale. He had only limited success as events showed when the convoy of cars came into view shortly after 10.10. It passed two of the conspirators – Mehmedbašić and Čubrilović – who panicked and took no action (Čubrilović later tried to claim that he did not fire his revolver out of compassion for the Duchess). The one who did act – Čabrinović – threw the bomb at Franz Ferdinand's car. It fell off the roof before it exploded and Čabrinović jumped over the wall of the quay into the river. He was quickly caught, and when he tried to commit suicide he spilled the cyanide and only swallowed enough poison to burn his mouth and throat. He was badly beaten by the crowd and when asked who he was, relied, 'I am a Serbian hero.' He was taken into custody.

After the failure of Čabrinović's bomb, most of the other conspirators – Mehmedbašić, Čubrilović, Popović and Ilić – lost their nerve and fled. They were captured later in the day, apart from Mehmedbašić who managed to cross the border into Montenegro where he was captured but later allowed to escape from jail and reach Serbia. Grabež stayed in his place but twice lost his nerve and took no action when the convoy of cars sped past going to and from the town hall. Princip realised the attempt had failed when he saw Čabrinović captured. He walked away from the quay when the police began clearing the area and stood on the corner of the Appel Quay and Franz Josef Street in front of Moritz Schiller's delicatessen.

Princip expected Franz Ferdinand to drive slowly past him when he returned from the town hall on his way to the museum, as planned in the official programme published a few days earlier. Princip would therefore have failed in his assassination attempt if the drivers of the first two cars in the convoy had been told about the new instructions issued by General Potiorek at the town hall and continued at high speed along the Appel Quay on their way to the hospital. Only when the first two cars turned into Franz Josef Street and Franz Ferdinand's car followed then stopped before trying to reverse, was Princip given his opportunity. He was too hemmed in by the crowd to get the bomb out of his pocket and strike off the detonator. Instead, he drew his revolver. As Princip took aim a policeman tried to knock the revolver out of his hand but a bystander, Mihaljo Pušara, kicked the policeman in the knee and he lost his balance. As the shots were fired, Pušara also assaulted Lieutenant Andreas Freiherr von Morsey, who jumped from one of the cars to attack Princip. After firing the shots, Princip dropped his bomb and put the cyanide phial in his mouth but the dose turned out to be insufficient to kill him. He put his revolver to his head but it was knocked out of his hand by a Croat spectator, Ante Velić. Princip was captured, badly beaten and dragged off to the police station.

In the confusion Mihaljo Pušara managed to escape. He went to a meeting of the local Serb society which had just returned from a memorial service for the dead of Kosovo at the Orthodox church – Pušara was due to sing in the society choir at their celebration of *Vidovdan* later in the day. Pušara was arrested by the police in the evening. He was not an innocent bystander and had stood next to

Princip in order to protect him during the assassination. Pušara had been deeply involved in the conspiracy from the beginning. He had sent the anonymous note to Čabrinović in Belgrade which gave the first information to the conspirators about Franz Ferdinand's visit and set the whole series of events in motion.

In the end the conspiracy hatched among young Serb extremists and backed by elements in the Serbian elite achieved its aim. On 28 June most of the conspirators panicked and the planned assassination was badly bungled, but by chance Princip finally succeeded. However, the consequences of the fatal shots in Sarajevo were to be profound: within little more than a month nearly the whole of Europe was to be at war.

3

THE REACTION

As news of the assassination spread across Sarajevo, anti-Serb demonstrations turned into riots. The Hotel Europa, which was owned by a rich Serb, the Serb school and the premises of two Serb newspapers were wrecked along with numerous Serb shops and houses. The Austro-Hungarian authorities formed bands of Croats and Muslims and left them to attack Serbs across Bosnia–Herzegovina. About five thousand Serbs were arrested (two hundred of them in Sarajevo) and peasants were dragged in from the area around the town. Some of them were hung in the courtyard of the military prison where Princip and Čabrinović were being held. An unknown number of Serbs were murdered across the province. The parliament of Bosnia–Herzegovina met in Sarajevo and all three major parties supported a resolution condemning the assassination. The parliament was then adjourned by the Austro-Hungarian authorities and never met again. The government banned the use of the Cyrillic alphabet and Serb schools were closed. If any Serbs fled to Serbia or joined the Serbian army then their family's property was confiscated.

In Serbia the prime minister, Pašić, was told of the assassination on a train during an electioneering tour to Kosovo. He continued with the tour. He was in a difficult position given the delicate political position in Serbia following his reappointment as prime minister only three days earlier. Alexander had only just taken over as regent, elections were due in a month and the extreme nationalists were waiting to exploit any subservience to Austria–Hungary. All these factors meant that he had little room for manoeuvre. In Belgrade on the evening of 28 June, the festivities for *Vidovdan* were curtailed at 10 p.m. and a period of court mourning was ordered. A flood of condolence telegrams was sent to Vienna and an official government communiqué was issued condemning the killings. The press reaction on the morning of 29 June was predictable. *Pijemont* described Princip as a 'young martyr', *Odjek* blamed Franz Ferdinand for visiting Sarajevo on *Vidovdan* and argued that such a visit 'could not but arouse brutal feelings of resistance, hatred and revenge'. *Balkan* demanded that Austria–Hungary be 'put under international control'.

The ruler of the tiny Serb mountain kingdom of Montenegro, King Nicholas, immediately abandoned his visit to Trieste and returned by steamer to Bar, arriving in his capital, Cetinje, late on 29 June. Montenegro was, as always, in a difficult position, having to strike a balance between its powerful neighbour Austria–Hungary to the north and its emotional ties to Serbia. The French minister Delaroche-Vernet, told Paris that there was 'secret satisfaction' with the assassination and that although King Nicholas did not endorse the killings he 'is delighted with its result'.[1] Nevertheless, the King expressed his personal grief to the Austro-Hungarian minister and when on 1 July demonstrators, organised by groups hostile to the King, tried to congregate in front of the Austro-Hungarian legation, he personally drove his car at them and pushed them away.

News of the assassination reached Vienna in the afternoon of 28 June. Emperor Franz Josef is supposed to have remarked, 'Horrible! The Almighty is not mocked!' or 'It is God's will.' Both quotations are probably apocryphal but do demonstrate the hostility towards Franz Ferdinand and his wife within the Habsburg ruling family and their courtiers. The Austrian public seem to have been remarkably unmoved. Josef Redlich noted in his diary that the Prater Park was not closed on either 28 or 29 June and 'in the town no mood of mourning; in the Prater and with us here in Grienzing music everywhere on both days'.[2] The British ambassador in Vienna, Sir Maurice de Bunsen, heard the news early in the afternoon in a telegram from the British consul in Sarajevo. His wife Bertha kept a diary and she noted that at about 6 p.m. the couple walked to the Belvedere Palace (the official residence of the archduke) 'to see if there was any excitement. None at all.' In the evening the de Bunsens dined at the Volksgarten and Bertha noted that 'except that the band was silent, everyone seemed very gay and not the least upset'. She concluded: 'No one here cares about the Archdukes as they never bow or smile at anyone not even us the Diplomats.'[3] In Bohemia the Social Democrat leader, Gustav Habrman, learned of the assassination from workers leaving an open-air concert in Pilsen, but he too noted that no great sorrow was expressed. Across the Habsburg empire there was no deep mourning and no curtailment of regular activities.

The bodies of Franz Ferdinand and Sophie were taken to the Dalmatian coast. A warship carried them to Trieste from where they were transported by train to Vienna, arriving at 10 p.m. on 2 July.

Earlier that day Franz Josef saw the German ambassador, Tschirschky, and spoke about his hunting plans and the death of General Pollio, the Italian chief of the general staff. He never mentioned the assassination. The arrangements for the official mourning and the funerals reflected the hostility towards the couple. The bodies of the archduke and his wife were escorted by the new heir apparent, Archduke Charles, to the Hofburg Chapel where they were placed side by side but at different levels. Franz Ferdinand's full insignia were placed on his ceremonial coffin. Sophie's coffin had a pair of gloves and a fan on the lid as a reminder of her status as a lady-in-waiting.

Franz Josef was determined to show his continuing disapproval of the couple and personally supervised the arrangements for what was described as 'a third-rate funeral'. No member of the Habsburg royal family was allowed, by Franz Josef's express order, to send any wreaths or flowers for the funeral. Neither were any members of foreign royal families invited to attend and when Kaiser Wilhelm II invited himself (he was a friend of Franz Ferdinand) he was put off with excuses about security problems. The only flowers at the funeral came from the diplomatic corps in Vienna. Franz Josef and a few members of his court did attend the funeral service in the tiny Hofburg Chapel but immediately afterwards the chapel was closed until dark. The coffins were then taken across Vienna to board a train to the tiny country station of Pöchlarn. The train arrived at 1 a.m. and the bodies were left in the waiting room until morning. Then the coffins were taken across the Danube to the memorial chapel at Artstetten. The chapel had been built by Franz Ferdinand to house his body and that of Sophie because his wife was too low-born to be placed in the Habsburg vaults of the Capuchin church in Vienna. The bloodstained clothing of both Franz Ferdinand and Sophie was preserved at the army museum in Vienna.

The reaction to the assassination of Franz Ferdinand was extremely muted in Austria (and in Hungary it was even more so because of his strong anti-Hungarian views). It is, therefore, hardly surprising that across the rest of Europe the news was greeted with indifference and, in some cases, relief. In Germany Kaiser Wilhelm II was told the news during a yacht race at the Kiel regatta where part of the Royal Navy was paying a courtesy visit. Despite his personal attachment to Franz Ferdinand, he continued with the round of entertaining and racing at the regatta. In Berlin on 29 June the executive of the Social Democratic Party was meeting and looking forward to the meeting of the socialist Second International in Vienna during August. The leading German socialist Friedrich Ebert reassured his colleagues and said he did not believe 'that the assassination will have international repercussions and result in greater tension between Austria and Serbia'.[4]

In Italy Franz Ferdinand was seen, rightly, as representative of the deeply conservative, Catholic and military elements in Austria that saw Italy as the real enemy of the Habsburgs and who wanted to regain Venetia and Lombardy. When the news of the assassination was announced in a packed cinema in Rome, the audience applauded and demanded that the Italian national anthem should be played. On 30 June the Russian ambassador, Krupensky, reported to St Petersburg that the Italian foreign minister, San Giuliano, had told him, 'the crime is horrible but world peace will not mourn over it'.[5] At the end of the first week of July, the British ambassador, Sir Rennell Rodd, told the Foreign Office in London that after the formal denunciations of the assassination and expressions of sympathy 'it is obvious that people generally have regarded the elimination of the late Archduke as almost providential'.[6] The British ambassador in St Petersburg, Sir George Buchanan, found the same reaction. He reported to London on 9 July that, once the initial reaction to the killings had passed, the general view was 'one of relief that so dangerous a person was no longer the heir'.[7]

In Britain itself reaction to the assassination was slightly more sympathetic. Franz Ferdinand was moderately popular following his visit in 1913. There was little sympathy for Serbia and after the 1903 coup diplomatic relations had been broken off for four yeas. The new Karadjordjević dynasty was treated with disdain and the British establishment shared Franz Ferdinand's view, expressed when he was in London in 1910 for the funeral of Edward VII, that Alexander, the Crown Prince, was 'a bad copy of a gypsy'.[8] In general the political elite knew little of the complexities of central and south-east European affairs and viewed it as a backward area that was best ignored and, if that could not be done, then patronised. Because the assassination occurred on a Sunday, political leaders and newspaper editors were scattered across the numerous country-house parties that characterised the British weekend. Editorials were hastily put together and, apart from the Tory *Morning Post* and the Labour *Daily Citizen*, they were all sympathetic to Austria–Hungary. The assassination was generally regarded as a Serb plot hatched in Belgrade. On 29 June George V visited the Austro-Hungarian embassy unannounced to express his personal grief and sign the book of condolence. His private secretary,

Lord Knollys, told the ambassador, Count Mensdorff, that the assassins should not be given a long trial as this would only indulge their vanity.

In France the news of the assassination arrived while the whole diplomatic corps and the French political elite, including President Poincaré, were attending the racing at Longchamps. Protocol demanded that the Austro-Hungarian ambassador, Count Miklos Szécsen von Temerin, should withdraw. Everybody else remained to enjoy the racing and watch the Grand Prix being won by Baron de Rothschild's Sardanapale. The assassination was briefly mentioned at the Cabinet meeting on 30 June, but was then ignored as domestic political affairs became the centre of attention just as they did in Britain. On the day of the Cabinet meeting, *L'Humanité* commented that the Sarajevo murders were 'one more rivulet in the stream of blood that has flown in vain in the Balkan peninsula' which was a part of Europe that 'will remain a slaughter-house'.

PART TWO

Prologue

4

EUROPE IN 1914

The assassination of Franz Ferdinand took place at a time when none of the major European powers had fought each other for over forty years. France and Germany had been at peace for forty-three years and Austria–Hungary for almost fifty years. Neither Britain nor Russia had been at war in Europe for sixty years. Indeed, since 1871 the major European powers had only fought wars in Africa and Asia. During that period there had been numerous diplomatic crises, many of them just as serious as that brought about by the Sarajevo killings, but they had all been resolved. In the previous six years the European powers had solved the problems caused by the Austro-Hungarian annexation of Bosnia–Herzegovina in 1908–9, the Agadir crisis of 1911 and the multitude of issues raised by the Balkan Wars of 1912–13. It was certainly not inevitable that the crisis produced by the assassinations would lead to the first war involving all the major European powers for a hundred years.

Historians have, ever since 1914, looked for the 'origins of the First World War' in a variety of factors which were present, or believed to be present, in early twentieth-century Europe. These factors have included the rival alliance systems, an uncontrolled arms race, militarism, imperialism and, a more recent explanation, the nature of domestic politics as the old elites saw themselves losing power to an expanding working class and increasing demands for democracy and greater social justice. However, even if some of these factors did contribute to the outbreak of war in 1914, they do not explain why it was the crisis caused by the assassinations that produced war when other disputes and problems had not. It is equally wrong to view Europe in the early twentieth century as inevitably moving towards war as crisis followed crisis – that is a fault of reading history backwards from 1914. War in 1914 was not inevitable and not preordained by structural factors in the European situation. The reasons for the outbreak of war in late July and early August 1914 can only be understood by examining the actions of the European governments during that crisis. Nevertheless, the underlying preoccupations and concerns of the

European diplomatic and military elites in the summer of 1914 can only be understood in the context of a number of factors.

European Alliances

The most fundamental feature of the European situation was the latent hostility between France and Germany which stemmed from the French defeat in the war of 1870–1. The creation of a unified Germany, in particular its annexation of Alsace and Lorraine, meant that France was always likely to harbour dreams of revanche and revenge. The German chancellor, Bismarck, devoted the main thrust of his foreign policy to ensuring that France remained isolated. This was achieved in 1873 through the *Dreikaiserbund*, a pact between Germany, Austria–Hungary and Russia. French isolation became complete in 1882 when the Dual Alliance of Germany and Austria–Hungary became the Triple Alliance following the accession of Italy. Bismarck was sacked as chancellor in March 1890 and the rapid collapse of the system he had constructed and maintained over the previous twenty years is often blamed on the inadequacies of his successors. In practice it ended because of its inherent contradictions, in particular the growing competition between Austria–Hungary and Russia for influence and control in the Balkans. In May 1891 Germany decided not to renew its agreement with Russia, preferring to side with its main ally, Austria–Hungary. This decision left Russia isolated and it was therefore not surprising that France and Russia drew together. By the summer of 1892, the two states agreed a military convention that was the basis of the alliance which was finally ratified in January 1894. The two sides grew steadily closer, especially as French investment in Russia increased.

The major anomaly in the European alliance structure after the mid-1890s was Italy, the weakest of the 'great powers'. In many respects its alliance with Austria–Hungary was 'unnatural' – Italian unification had partly been achieved through war with the Habsburgs and their expulsion from northern Italy. Italy still harboured ambitions to take over other Austro-Hungarian territories, in particular Trieste and the Ticino, and many in Austria–Hungary (for example, Franz Ferdinand) dreamed about recovering the lost territories of Lombardy and Venezia. Italy and Austria–Hungary were also rivals for influence in the Balkans, especially along the Dalmatian coast and in Albania. Italy was also strategically vulnerable – its long coastline left it open to attack by

Mediterranean sea powers such as France and Britain and it was also heavily dependent on imported coal from Britain for its limited industrialisation. Italy remained a nominal member of the Triple Alliance but effectively undermined the treaty in 1902 with the secret Prinetti-Barrère agreement with France. This provided that Italy would not carry out its obligations under the alliance and would instead remain neutral in any war where French entry had been 'provoked'. After 1902 Italy strove to remain on friendly terms with both France and Britain despite its nominal membership of the Triple Alliance. Although Italy liked to claim great power status in practice, the major European powers treated it with near contempt.

From the mid-1890s, European relations were structured by the divisions between the two alliances. Germany felt the need to support Austria–Hungary on most issues because it was its only significant ally and France saw the alliance with Russia as the only alternative to what might otherwise be a very dangerous isolation. Nevertheless, it is important not to conclude that the outbreak of war in 1914 was the result of the existence of these rival alliance structures. For twenty years the European powers were able to resolve every major problem while maintaining the alliances which they saw as crucial to the maintenance of their security. The rival alliances were central to the 1914 crisis – diplomats and military leaders took decisions based on their alliances and the perceived need to maintain them.

The European power structure was affected as all the major powers industrialised between 1870 and 1914. The main problems for France were that its industrial output was only half that of Germany's (and even less in key areas such as steel and coal production) and its population, at thirty-nine million in 1913, was only two-thirds that of Germany. This made it extremely difficult for France to sustain an army capable of matching Germany, hence the importance of the alliance with Russia. Russia was, in the early twentieth century, still a largely agricultural country although it was industrialising rapidly and was in fact the fourth largest industrial power in the world. However, this reflected its size (a population of about 170 million) – its per capita industrial output was only one-sixth that of Germany's. Until the end of the nineteenth century, the major European industrial power had been Britain, but it had then been overtaken by the phenomenal industrialisation of Germany. By 1913, Germany's share of world manufacturing output was greater than that of Britain and its steel production was over twice as large. In the new chemical and electrical industries it held a significant lead. The other two important European powers – Austria–Hungary and Italy – were only semi-industrial countries. Overall, there was a very rough balance between the two rival alliances – Austria–Hungary and Germany might have smaller armed forces than Russia and France but their combined industrial strength was greater.

The unification of Germany in the period 1866–71 and its subsequent rapid industrialisation has led to the widespread view that it destabilised the European power structure and that its aggressive policies, believed to be encapsulated in rhetoric about 'world power', bore the prime responsibility for the outbreak of war in 1914. These views have been reinforced by the argument, put forward by many historians in the last forty years, that its unique semi-authoritarian political structure meant that the governing elite was prepared to risk a war in the hope that it might unify the nation and ensure that political concessions would not have to be made to the working class and the socialists. In practice Germany was a conservative, cautious power and despite the rhetoric of many groups within it (which was no different from that of similar groups in other European states), not uniquely aggressive. It was broadly content with the European division of Africa and Asia in the late nineteenth century. This was despite the fact that it received only a small and economically poor share of the spoils, while the other states, not just Britain and France but even weak states such as Portugal, Belgium and the Netherlands, had a far greater share. Germany discussed how to increase its share but other powers, in particular Britain, were just as ready to reach agreements such as that between the two powers over how to split up the Portuguese empire to their mutual advantage. German foreign policy was, in practice, characterised by limited arms, limited risks and the willingness to settle for small diplomatic triumphs in the convoluted world of European diplomacy. In 1898 it did begin the construction of a major navy but the rate of expansion was far slower than that of the United States and by 1914 its fleet was still only half the size of the Royal Navy.

Britain

For three-quarters of a century after the final defeat of Napoleon in 1815, Britain took little interest in the affairs of Europe, preferring to concentrate on imperial and commercial expansion across the globe. By the early twentieth century Britain ruled about a quarter of the world but, although it had been the first power to industrialise, its relative economic position was deteriorating as first the United States and then Germany overtook it. Maintenance of a worldwide empire was increasingly difficult as other powers around the globe increased their armed forces. In the first years of the twentieth century Britain decided it could not defend its empire in the western hemisphere against the rising power of the United States. It accepted that it would have to adjust its policies to accept American predominance and withdrew all its forces from Canada. In 1902 it sought an alliance with Japan in the Pacific which left the latter as the effective protector of the empire in the Far East and, consequently, of Australia and New Zealand.

Britain was a status quo power trying to hold on to its empire as the balance of power in the world shifted inexorably to its disadvantage. Its strategic position was well described by Winston Churchill, First Lord of the Admiralty, when at the beginning of 1914 he wrote to his Cabinet colleague David Lloyd George, the chancellor of the Exchequer:

> We have engrossed to ourselves an altogether disproportionate share of the wealth and traffic of the world. We have got all we want in territory, and our claim to be left in unmolested enjoyment of our vast and splendid possession, mainly acquired by violence, largely maintained by force, often seems less reasonable to others than to us.[1]

The key to Britain's strategic dilemma was India, the 'jewel in the crown' of the empire. The main threat to India seemed to come from the Russian advance into central Asia in the second half of the nineteenth century. Although the terrain along the northern border of India made any invasion extremely difficult, the building of Russian railways towards that border made it possible for the Russians to deploy forces far faster than troops could be brought from Britain. As a mainly naval power, Britain did not have an army sufficient to defend India and it could not take the risk of significantly increasing the Indian army given its experience of the 'mutiny' in 1857. Britain also had vast strategic interests in the Gulf – it was vital not only as part of the route to India but also because of the Persian oilfields, now the major provider of fuel for the Royal Navy. The main threat to control of Persia was the increasing Russian penetration into the north of the country and the likelihood that this control would gradually extend southwards into the British zone.

In the early twentieth century the British decided that they could not defend India and would therefore have to reach an agreement with Russia. The best diplomatic route to this objective was through a settlement of colonial disputes with Russia's ally, France. The Anglo-France rivalries were primarily over their respective spheres of interest in Africa and could be resolved through mutual acceptance of British predominance in Egypt and French control of Morocco and much of the Maghreb. The Anglo-French entente of 1904 led to the far more important agreement with Russia in 1907 which provided reassurance about British interests in India and Persia. Britain therefore drifted towards friendship with France and Russia not because of the balance of power in Europe but because these two powers posed the main threat to British imperial interests. As the Foreign Office commented in July 1914, the primary aim of the 1907 agreement with Russia was 'to check Russia's advance to India and the Gulf'.[2]

The maintenance of the friendship with France and, in particular, Russia meant that Britain had to take their side in European disputes. Consequently, it found itself increasingly opposed to Germany, for example during the Moroccan crises of 1905–6 and 1911, where Britain had to support the French interests it had recognised in the 1904 agreement. Hostility towards Germany was made easier by the construction of the German fleet, optimised for action in the North Sea, which Britain had little choice but to see as a threat to its own interests. Keeping the friendship of France and Russia became the paramount objective of British Policy. As the permanent secretary in the Foreign Office, Sir Arthur Nicolson, told the ambassador in Berlin in April 1912, it was 'far more disadvantageous to have an unfriendly France and unfriendly Russia than an unfriendly Germany'.[3] As Russian strength recovered rapidly after its defeat by Japan in 1905, the threat it posed to British interests rose significantly. Nicolson told the ambassador in St Petersburg in April 1914: 'This is such a nightmare that I would at almost any cost keep Russia's friendship.'[4] There was a far greater threat in the background which Nicolson revealed: 'I am also haunted by the same fear as you lest Russia become tired of us and strike a bargain with Germany.'[5] This would leave Britain vulnerable in India, the Gulf and Europe – an impossible strategic situation. Britain's policy during the July crisis of 1914 can only be understood within this wider imperial context and the latent threat posed to the British empire, not by Germany, but by Britain's friends France and Russia.

The Military Balance and Technology

Britain's concerns about the threat posed by Russia reflected its rapidly increasing power in the European balance. Although with the benefit of hindsight we know that under the strain of war Russia collapsed into revolution in early 1917, this was not inevitable. Neither was it how Russia was perceived by the other powers. By 1914, Russian forces had been completely rebuilt from the disaster of 1904–5 and its standing army at 1.3 million men was far bigger than Germany's at 800,000. Russia had also embarked on a further vast expansion of its armed forces in the 'Great Programme' agreed early in 1914. Over 580,000 men would be conscripted every year for a three-year period of service – over twice as many as in Germany. The Russian peacetime army would rise to two million by 1917, two and a half times as big as that of Germany, and as big as the Austro-Hungarian army *after* mobilisation. By 1917, Russian and French forces would outnumber those of Germany and Austria–Hungary by 9.1 million to 6.4 million.

Germany was not uniquely militaristic. It conscripted only a little over a half of its eligible males each year compared with over 80 per cent in France (and the French also made extensive use of North African manpower). Until 1912 the size of the German army was deliberately restricted so as to maintain aristocratic predominance of the officer corps. Its spending on the armed forces was only just over 10 per cent greater than that of Britain. Similarly, although Austria-Hungary had introduced universal military service in 1868, it only conscripted about a fifth of the eligible males every year and they only served for two out of the legal requirement of three years. In 1914 the number of men in the infantry regiments was lower than in 1866 despite the fact that the Austro-Hungarian population had increased by twenty million in the intervening period. Neither was Europe as a whole engaged in an uncontrolled arms race. On average, states were spending between 3 and 5 per cent of their national income on defence every year – the same figure as in other peaceful periods in the first half of the twentieth century and far less than in periods of major tension such as the 1950s.

Military technology changed greatly in the second half of the nineteenth century. Industrial development, in particular the use of primitive machine tools, enabled the mass production of simple weapons such as the rifle and machine gun, together with their bullets. Improvements in communications, especially the construction of railway networks, meant that it was now possible to move large numbers of troops relatively quickly and sustain them over long periods of time with the food and weapons they required. The European powers shifted from having relatively small professional or mercenary armies to the mass conscription of their male population. They also developed the bureaucracies and the mechanisms necessary to enforce this obligation on their citizens. All the European powers (with the exception of Britain) came to rely on the mobilisation of their young male population in the early stages of a war. Plans were developed so that hundreds of thousands of men would go to assembly points where they would form into units, collect their weapons and then be transported to the frontiers. At the beginning of a war, the regular troops would be deployed to secure the frontiers, the railways and the key bridges to enable mobilisation to take place safely. Then over the next two to three weeks the mass units would be formed up for action.

Mobilisation on this scale required elaborate, complex and, inevitably, inflexible plans to be drawn up long in advance by the military staffs. The organisation of the necessary trains, and the provision of the necessary rolling stock, vast arrays of sidings and new signalling arrangements, was a huge task involving very intricate timetables. Once a scheme had been devised it was impossible to alter it at short notice. For example, the German plan involved the movement of three million men and 600,000 horses on 11,000 trains during the first thirteen days of mobilisation. At Cologne the bridge over the Rhine would witness 2,150 trains, each of fifty-four trucks, passing westwards at ten-minute intervals for nearly seventeen days. In total the German railways would be sending 650 trains a day towards the western frontier with France. These mobilisation schemes were on such a huge scale that in 1914 they were still no more than paper plans. No state had either the resources or the time to carry out a trial mobilisation. It was also far too dangerous to do so because mobilisation was seen as leading almost inevitably to war. In 1914 mass mobilisation was tried out for the first time and states discovered whether their military plans were realistic. It is hardly surprising that military staffs in every country were strongly opposed to any modification of their carefully drawn-up schedules. Even the slightest alteration could produce such a degree of chaos that mobilisation might collapse, leaving the state that tried such changes highly vulnerable.

The changes in military technology in the late nineteenth and early twentieth centuries significantly shifted the strategic balance by favouring the defence. Machine guns, barbed wire and railways (which enabled armies to shift troops to threatened sectors of the front rapidly) all aided this strategy, and offensive technologies did not keep pace with these developments. However, all the major powers developed military plans which relied on the offensive. This was not simply a result of military incompetence but reflected a number of other priorities, in particular alliance requirements, and the need to devise plans that, at a minimum, held out some hope of ultimate victory rather than strategic stalemate. In addition, military planners (and politicians and diplomats) assumed that any war, even a major European conflict, would be relatively short. To some extent this was based on the experience of recent European wars, in particular the successful German campaigns against Austria and France in 1866 and 1870–1. The Russo-Japanese war of 1904–5 seemed to reinforce this belief. Military planners assumed that their initial offensives would be successful and that the crucial battles would be fought in the first couple of months of any war. This increased the pressure to begin mobilisation as soon as possible – even a few days gained at this stage might turn out to be significant in a war lasting no more than a few weeks.

Military Plans: Germany

The military plans and mobilisation schedules devised by the European powers had a fundamental impact on the development of the diplomatic crisis in late July 1914. The most difficult military situation was faced by Germany. It had to plan for a two-front war against the numerically superior armies of France and Russia. In the late 1880s German strategy was relatively conservative, reflecting an accurate assessment of the likely balance of forces. It accepted that it could not repeat its unexpected success in 1870 and that a knockout blow against either France or Russia was impossible. This was the German strategy finally adopted in 1915 after the failure of the plan devised by the head of the army, Schlieffen. This plan was an attempt to resolve the problems caused by Germany's position in the centre of Europe. Its aim was to secure a decisive victory by defeating France before the more slowly mobilising Russians could deploy effective forces in the east. It called for a massive flanking movement to bypass the French fortresses along their common frontier. The original 1897 plan envisaged a sweep through the south-eastern corner of Belgium, east of the River Meuse, to outflank the French near Sedan (the site of the comprehensive

German victory in 1870). By 1905, Schlieffen had modified this plan to widen the flanking movement, so as to avoid the Belgian defences at Liège, Namur and along the Meuse valley, by moving through the Netherlands. This required huge forces – three-quarters of the German army would be in the west and seven times as many forces would be on the flanking movement as were left defending the frontier with France. It was a bold strategy but completely unworkable. German troops would have to march long distances whereas the French would be able to demolish bridges to slow up the pace of the attack and move troops by rail to their left flank to stop the offensive. Even if the Germans were successful they would not be able (as they planned) to shift forces eastwards after a few weeks to deal with Russian forces attacking in the east. Their experience in 1870–1 should have shown them that large numbers of troops would be required for months in mopping up French forces, securing control of the interior and maintaining security.

After Schlieffen left office, his successor, Moltke, modified the plan in two ways. First, he removed the planned movement of German forces to the west of Paris to encircle the French capital. There were not enough troops for such a vast manoeuvre, something which Schlieffen had himself come to accept after 1905. However, this meant that, as the German troops passed to the east of Paris, they would expose their right flank to French troops attacking from the capital – exactly what did happen in early September 1914. Second, Moltke removed the need to violate Dutch neutrality by planning to seize the Belgian forts at Liège at the very start of German mobilisation. This action was imperative to secure the bridges over the Meuse for the easy passage of the major German forces a couple of weeks later and their subsequent supply with food and ammunition. German military plans had huge political implications. They meant that for Germany mobilisation was the equivalent of war and that in the opening days of the conflict Belgian neutrality would be violated.

Military Plans: Belgium

The most important political implication of these German plans stemmed from the fact that the major European powers had forced Belgium to be neutral in any European conflict and had themselves guaranteed that neutrality in 1839. During the Franco–Prussian war of 1870–1, both states issued declarations supporting Belgian neutrality. Britain, which had a strategic interest in ensuring a major European power did not control Belgium and the coast opposite Britain, stated in 1870 that it would fight alongside the state which respected that neutrality if it was violated by the other power. By the early twentieth century the question had become less clear-cut as Britain's need for the friendship of France and Russia became more vital. In 1908 the Foreign Office concluded that under the 1839 treaty 'Great Britain is liable for the maintenance of Belgian neutrality whenever Belgium or any of the guaranteeing Powers are in need of, and demand, assistance in opposing its violation'. However, the permanent secretary advised the foreign secretary, Sir Edward Grey, that any British action 'must necessarily depend upon our policy at the time and the circumstances of the moment'. He concluded:

> Supposing France violated the neutrality of Belgium in a war with Germany, it is, under present circumstances, doubtful whether England or Russia would move a finger to maintain Belgian neutrality, while if the neutrality of Belgium were violated by Germany it is probable that the converse would be the case.[6]

The British remained doubtful about the position of Belgium. It seemed clear from German railway construction that they planned to violate Belgian neutrality but this might only affect the far south-east of the country near Luxembourg and in these circumstances the Belgian government might choose not to resist. If the Belgians did not ask for assistance, then Britain would probably not be able to intervene.

The Belgian government was determined to defend its neutrality against all sides, including Britain. Heavily defended forts at Liège and Namur were built with another line of defence around Antwerp. A general staff was created and conscription introduced in 1913. Belgian plans recognised that a German attack in the south-east of the country could be resisted, but that any attempt to do so carried the risk that the army might be cut off from, and unable to defend, the most important parts of the country – Brussels and Antwerp. In these circumstances it might, as the British suspected, be more prudent not to offer substantial resistance. The Belgian government was clear that in this situation the guarantor powers could not intervene without a Belgian request: 'Neutrality persists as long as the Government is standing and possesses the means of making neutrality respected, even if in a restricted sphere.'[7] The Belgian government, which tended to be pro-German and anti-French on political grounds, also distrusted Britain which it felt could not be a disinterested guarantor as it drifted closer to the French camp. The Belgians therefore laid plans to defend themselves against violation of their neutrality whether from Germany or France, or from Britain, who they thought might well land at Antwerp and pull German forces into the centre of the country. The key element of Belgian policy was the principle that the guarantor powers could not decide on their own what to do – at all times it was up to the Belgians to take action to invite the guarantors to help defend their neutrality.

Military Plans: Austria–Hungary

German military planning, based as it was on a massive offensive in the west and a holding operation in the east, had major implications for its ally Austria–Hungary. German strategy depended on the ability of the army in East Prussia to hold any early Russian attack. In doing so, they would be helped if there was an Austro-Hungarian attack in Galicia to divert Russian forces. Like Germany, Austria-Hungary faced a probable two-front war against the small Serbian forces in the south and the larger Russian forces in Galicia and would, like Germany, be outnumbered in this war. (Austria–Hungary even faced the prospect of a four-front war if Italy and Romania became enemies.) Ideally, Austria–Hungary wanted German forces in East Prussia to attack so as to divert Russian forces from Galicia and enable troops to be concentrated against Serbia. In the military discussions between the two allies which began in 1909, Germany simply ignored the Austro-Hungarian demands.

Austro-Hungarian military planners tried to square the circle through a complex mobilisation scheme. The army was divided into three parts. The main part (thirty divisions) would be deployed defensively in Galicia against Russia, with smaller forces (ten divisions) in the south against Serbia. There was a reserve of twelve divisions which would be deployed in whichever area was designated for the offensive. Each of the three parts of the army could be mobilised separately. The fundamental disadvantage of this scheme was that it was necessary to decide at a very early stage where the bulk of the forces were to be deployed and once this had been done it would be very difficult to change course. The worst scenario for Austria–Hungary was the one most likely to occur in any war. A decision to attack Serbia would be made and the bulk of the army would be sent to the south. Only once the Austro-Hungarians were committed to this deployment and Galicia had been left with thin defences would Russia intervene to support Serbia. If this happened Austria–Hungary would need a German attack from East Prussia to divert Russian forces, but such an attack was unlikely because the overwhelming bulk of German forces would be deployed in the west against France. Germany and Austria–Hungary were never able to resolve the inherent contradictions in their military plans.

Military Plans: France

Compared with these problems the strategies of France and Russia were relatively straightforward, although they too had to resolve a number of tensions. The major problem the French faced was that their intelligence about German intentions was poor – until 1911 the war ministry's secret funds for intelligence work were spent on a magnificent Bastille Day lunch. The result was that they expected Germany to deploy twenty divisions in the east – more than double the actual strength. They also expected the Germans to follow their own practice of not using reserve divisions in the initial attack, although there was plenty of information available to indicate that this is exactly what they would do. The result of these two miscalculations was that they assumed Germany could not deploy enough forces for a wide sweep through Belgium and would only move through the south-eastern part of the country. The French army did consider a pre-emptive move into Belgium but the politicians vetoed this violation of neutrality.

The final French war plan (number XVIII) was drawn up by General Joseph Joffre, the chief of the General Staff, in 1913. It was based on extreme optimism about French capabilities and called for an all-out offensive from the start of hostilities, seizing the initiative through a mixture of élan and high morale. The army regulations issued in October 1913 stated: 'The French Army, returning to its traditions, henceforth admits no law but the offensive.' Given the fact that French forces were inferior to those of Germany it is difficult to see the rationale for this strategy. These problems were compounded by the decision to concentrate the bulk of French forces for an offensive into Lorraine even though they expected the weight of the German attack to come through Belgium. The chief consequence of French strategy was that it actually made it easier for the Germans to implement their plans.

Military Plans: Russia

Central to French strategy were Russian capabilities. The French realised they would be facing the bulk of the German army and therefore they needed the earliest and greatest possible Russian offensive to ease this pressure. They were dependent upon their alliance with Russia and had to do everything possible to ensure it continued – without the alliance France would once again be isolated and in a massively inferior position to Germany. These considerations were central to the decision taken in July 1913 to increase the period of peacetime conscription from two years to three (longer than in Germany) as a way of signalling to their ally their determination to resist.

The French needed to do this in order to ensure that Russia did place its main military weight against Germany – if it thought France would be defeated quickly, a more rational Russian strategy would be to attack Austria–Hungary, which it always regarded as its chief enemy. The main Russian problem stemmed from their western frontier in Poland. Although the salient around Warsaw provided a good launching point for an attack towards Berlin, it was extremely vulnerable to a simultaneous attack by Germany from the north and Austria–Hungary from the south. Although an attack southwards into Galicia against Austria–Hungary was the easiest offensive option for the Russians, they realised that the alliance with France depended on their willingness to launch an attack on East Prussia as early as possible – if France was defeated then the Russian position would be untenable.

No Russian plans were credible in the period immediately after the defeat against Japan in 1905. The army needed to be rebuilt and rearmed. In 1909 the minister of war, General Roediger, advised that the army was still incapable of fighting even a defensive war. This situation began to improve and by the summer of 1914 the army leadership was convinced that their forces were now ready to fight and stood a chance of success in a war which they, like most other military chiefs in Europe, expected to last about two to six months. The most important strategic factor, though, was the speed with which Russia could mobilise. The 1906 plans assumed that it would be six to eight weeks before Russia was ready to launch an attack. This was largely because the railway system could only move about 200 trains a day westwards due to the lack of signal boxes, coaling and watering facilities and storage sidings. Improvements to the railway system, especially those funded by the French, reduced mobilisation times steadily. By 1910–12 Russian mobilisation was expected to take about thirty days, although it would be two-thirds complete by the eighteenth day, and the Russians told the French they would launch an attack on Germany even earlier —fifteen days after the start of mobilisation. By 1914 the Russians were able to move 360 trains a day to the west and under the 'Great Programme' of 1914 this would be increased to 560 a day by 1917 when mobilisation would be completed in eighteen days, only three days longer than Germany.

Military Plans: German Apprehensions

This speeding-up of Russian mobilisation posed a major threat to Germany. If by 1917 Russia was able to mobilise almost as fast as Germany (and German military intelligence had very accurate estimates of Russian capabilities), then German strategy was in ruins. Whatever the doubts about the Schlieffen plan (even as modified by Moltke) it would be impossible to send the overwhelming bulk of the German army to the west if Russia was able to launch a major attack just as the German armies sought victory over France. Germany would instead have to divide its forces almost equally and in these circumstances any hope of victory would disappear. The German military planners were right to see their slim hopes of victory in a European war disappearing as Russian capabilities improved rapidly. The temptation was to try and seek victory before the strategic situation deteriorated any further.

Such thoughts do seem to have been prevalent among the German military in the late spring and early summer of 1914. On 18 May General Count von Waldersee, the quartermaster general on the General Staff, wrote a memorandum arguing that 'for the moment we do not have to entertain the possibility that Germany's enemies will begin a war' but he felt they would probably do so in a few years when they were stronger. He went on:

[Germany] has no reason whatever to avoid a conflict, but also, more than that, the chances of achieving a speedy victory in a major European war are today still very favourable for Germany and for the Triple Alliance as well. Soon, however, this will no longer be the case.[8]

Gottlieb von Jagow, the secretary of state for foreign affairs, later recalled that he travelled from Potsdam to Berlin with Moltke sometime in late May/early June 1914. Moltke apparently said:

The prospects for the future oppressed him heavily. In two or three years Russia would have completed her armaments. The military superiority of our enemies would then be so great that he did not know how he could overcome them . . . In his opinion there was no alternative to making preventive war in order to defeat the enemy while we still had a chance of victory . . . [he] proposed that I should conduct a policy with the aim of provoking a war in the near future.[9]

Even though the German military were in a gloomy mood about the impact of Russian power, this does not necessarily mean that the German leadership launched a preventive war in July 1914.

European Diplomacy

Despite these military plans (and the increasing level of militarism found at all levels in every European society), Europe remained at peace. Key decisions in every country were taken by small groups of people – monarchs (except in Britain and republican France), a handful of senior politicians, a few military leaders and, most important of all, diplomats. Policy debates were therefore highly restricted – in Britain, for example, during the crisis in 1914 there was only one parliamentary debate and that was on 3 August after all the crucial decisions had been taken. The discussions within these small policy-making elites show little or no sign of the sort of issues some historians have seen as important in the decisions to go to war, such as imperialism and internal social tensions. Instead, they reflect much vaguer concepts such as 'honour', 'reputation' and 'status'.

These concepts, which seem more suited to a much older style of European diplomacy, and insufficient justifications for war were the language of the European diplomats who dominated the crisis of 1914. In every country these people were drawn from a very narrow social group, with aristocratic, landowning backgrounds and significant private wealth. In Austria–Hungary, of the seventy-two senior diplomats outside Vienna, only two did not have a title and at the foreign ministry (the Ballhausplatz) there was one prince, ten counts, twenty-four barons and thirty-two other titled diplomats. In Russia the foreign ministry at Chorister's Bridge in St Petersburg was staffed by men from a small aristocratic group of diplomatic dynasties. A large private income was required and nearly all the senior members came from a single school – the Imperial Alexander Lycée. In Britain, too, the Foreign Office was staffed by a small, introverted group drawn from the aristocracy and Anglican gentry who were educated at public school and Oxbridge. Few came from commercial, industrial and financial families and there were no Jews. As Sir William Tyrrell (private secretary to the foreign secretary) told the Royal Commission on the civil service in 1914 (in terms that would have been accepted in all the major European capitals):

> All . . . speak the same language; they have the same habits of thought, and more or less the same points of view, and if anybody with a different language came in, I think he would be treated by the whole diplomatic service more or less with suspicion.[10]

Even in republican France the diplomatic service and the Quai d'Orsay were staffed by aristocrats who shared with their counterparts in Britain a contempt for parliament – diplomacy was best left to the experts. Although the diplomatic service suffered badly from factionalism, nearly all its members, as in Russia, came from a single school – the École Libre des Sciences Politiques, which was a deeply conservative private institution. In Italy, too, the foreign office (the Consulta) and the diplomatic service were largely staffed by aristocrats, though they tended to be much poorer than their counterparts elsewhere in Europe.

The European crisis in the summer of the 1914 was the last to be dominated by the 'old diplomacy' before better communications and direct contact between leaders in each country reduced the role of ambassadors. Each country still relied on telegrams as its main means of communication – use of the telephone was limited and mainly restricted to a few messages between Berlin and Vienna. Ambassadors therefore still had considerable leeway over how they acted. It is clear that on some occasions they did not carry out instructions and, in addition, relayed false information back to their capitals. During the July crisis the German ambassador in Vienna, Tschirschky, and the French ambassador in St Petersburg, Paléologue, were particularly prone to this sort of behaviour. The use of telegrams meant that the exchange of information across Europe was slow. Even over the relatively short route from London to Paris, telegrams might take two to three hours to arrive. The time involved between Berlin and Paris varied between one and four hours and sometimes more. Longer distances such as St Petersburg to Paris meant that the quickest telegram took just under three hours but the slowest might not arrive for six. To all these times it was necessary to add that needed for composition, ciphering and then decoding at the other end. When time differences across Europe of up to three hours are included it is clear that rapid action was impossible. Often ambassadors could not carry out instructions and report back in a single day. These problems had a profound impact on the July diplomatic crisis. They meant that it was extremely difficult for any country to gain a grip over the developing crisis as decisions were made across the continent. And the decisions which were taken were often made on the basis of out-of-date information.

There were two groups in Europe particularly opposed to this way of conducting international diplomacy. The Universal Peace Congress was due to meet in Vienna in mid-September 1914 when it was planned that the Emperor Franz Josef would receive the delegates and Count Berchtold the foreign minister would host a reception. Despite its grand name the congress was little more than a talking-shop. Of far greater potential influence was the Second International mainly comprised of the socialist organisations and parties from across Europe. The Tenth International Socialist Congress was due to meet in Vienna about a month before the Universal Peace Congress. Every congress of the International had assumed that socialism was in some way equivalent to, and the main spokesman for, internationalism and peace. The congresses regularly condemned war and militarism and argued about how to resist these two trends, which they rightly foresaw would turn the workers into their main victims. The resolutions of the socialist congresses were generally anodyne, reflecting the very real problems the socialists faced. As national parties, they knew they could not succeed if they appeared to oppose national defence and that in many countries (especially France and Germany) they would face repression and public hostility if they appeared to act against the 'national interest' in a crisis. It was also unclear what action they could actually take. Resolutions and protests were easy but it was far from certain that national parties would even vote against the passage of war credits through their parliaments. More extreme measures such as a general strike had long been regarded as unworkable. In 1912 the Basle congress passed a strong resolution about the responsibility of the ruling classes for any war, but the socialist parties did no more than agree to do 'all they can to prevent war by the use of such means as they find effective'. Any hopes of international working-class solidarity prevailing over national interests were the pipe dream of a few radicals not the socialist leaders of Europe.

The Balkans

The crisis which all of these groups – politicians, diplomats, the military and the socialists – had to face in the summer of 1914 stemmed from the situation in the Balkans. The outbreak of European war cannot be understood outside this context.

The fundamental problem stemmed from the loss of power by the Ottoman empire which had ruled the area since the fifteenth century. Like its major rival, the Habsburg empire, it was a multinational, dynastic empire that incorporated numerous groups in a single political structure and in considerable harmony. The break-up of the empire began in the late eighteenth century as Russia pushed westwards. Greece became independent in 1830 and the other Balkan territories (Serbia, Montenegro and what became Romania) were soon effectively independent too. However, it was not until the Ottomans were defeated by Russia in 1877 that the map of the Balkans was fully redrawn at the Congress of Berlin.

The creation of independent states was inevitable but it resulted in major instability. All the Balkan states made irreconcilable claims to expand further into Ottoman and Habsburg terrorities based on false readings of their ethnic origins and history. The Serbs claimed the territories of 'Greater Serbia' while either ignoring or attacking similar claims to a separate identity by Croats and Muslims. Romania and Bulgaria were almost permanently opposed and the former claimed the Transylvanian territories of Hungary. Serbia, Greece and Bulgaria all asserted their claim to Macedonia. Other groups such as the Albanians made their claims to independence. This potent mixture of competing claims and mutual intolerance was made worse by great power rivalry. As a multinational empire, Austria–Hungary was bound to be threatened by any assertion of national claims, particularly when they involved its own territory, as in Bosnia–Herzegovina. Austria–Hungary also saw itself as fulfilling the traditional Habsburg role (which had been reasserted at the Congress of Vienna in 1815 at the end of the Napoleonic wars) of blocking the westward expansion of Russia. The expansion of a Russian sphere of influence into the Balkans, in particular its support for Bulgaria and Serbia, and its claims to act on a pan-Slav basis (identified partly by Orthodox religion but also through ill-defined racial concepts) was bound to be threatening to Austria–Hungary.

After the Congress of Berlin the region was relatively stable for thirty years as the newly created, politically weak and economically poor

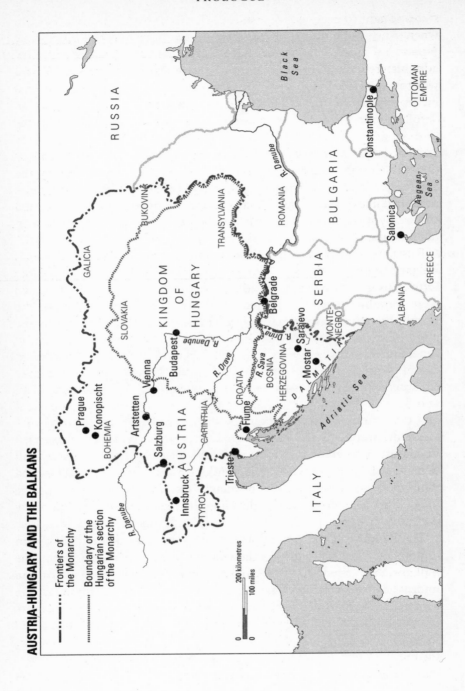

AUSTRIA-HUNGARY AND THE BALKANS

· — · · · Frontiers of
the Monarchy

· · · · · · · Boundary of the
Hungarian section
of the Monarchy

states sought to organise themselves. The situation changed in 1908–9 when Austria–Hungary, taking advantage of the Russian defeat by Japan in 1905, annexed Bosnia–Herzegovina which it had administered, under nominal Ottoman sovereignty, since 1878. Russia was too weak to do other than accept a diplomatic defeat but the legal incorporation of the province greatly alienated the nationalists in Serbia who still dreamed of incorporating it into Greater Serbia. In the Ottoman empire modernisation was producing increasing strain and in 1908 an army coup installed the Committee of Union and Progress as the effective government. Although the process which led to the creation of modern Turkey in 1920–2 had begun, the Ottoman empire remained in existence. Its weakness tempted Italy to expand its colonial empire by trying to conquer Libya in September 1911 and this in turn tempted the Balkan states to take advantage of the situation.

Russia was the main promoter of a Balkan league comprising Serbia, Bulgaria, Greece and later Montenegro which decided to attack the Ottomans in October 1912. The war was successful and the Ottomans were rapidly defeated and expelled from the area west of the Bosphorus. A ceasefire was declared in December 1912, but it took the major European powers, working through a conference of ambassadors in London, until May 1913 to settle the various territorial claims. Within a month of the settlement, the Balkan states fell out over the spoils and a second war resulted between Bulgaria on the one hand and Serbia, Greece and Romania on the other. Bulgaria was defeated and the Ottomans took advantage of the situation to recover Thrace and Adrianople. This time the Balkan powers agreed the Treaty of Bucharest in August 1913 from which Serbia, Romania and Greece all benefited. In parallel with these conflicts a revolt in Albania ensured that it too would become independent – the main problems facing the major European powers were deciding the borders of the new country and who should rule it.

The Balkan Wars not only placed an enormous strain on European diplomacy but they also fundamentally altered the balance in the Balkans. Nevertheless, the European diplomats, working in London under the chairmanship of Sir Edward Grey, were successful in settling the conflicting claims and striking a balance between the interests of the major powers. This was mainly because all the major powers declined to go to extremes in backing their various clients in the region. One of the major reasons why the London conference was relatively successful was the level of cooperation between Britain, which had few interests in the region and did not support Russian aims, and Germany, which on many occasions did not support its ally Austria–Hungary and argued for caution. In particular the German ambassador in London, Lichnowsky, was extremely cooperative – much to the disgust of the government in Vienna who thought he should have supported them more strongly. To both London and Berlin this cooperation seemed a good omen of how they could work together. Just four days before the assassination in Sarajevo, the German chancellor, Bethmann Hollweg, sent a message to Grey though Lichnowsky saying:

> he hoped if new developments or emergencies arose in the Balkans they would be discussed as frankly between Germany and [Britain] as the difficulties that arose during the last Balkan crisis, and that we should be able to keep in close touch.[11]

However, there were a number of disconcerting signs during the Balkan Wars which suggested that a crisis in the area could easily get out of control. In particular Austria–Hungary was becoming more strident and more willing to threaten military action if the small Balkan states did not comply with its demands. In late April 1913, when Montenegro refused to give up the area around Scutari, Austria–Hungary decided to act on its own. The Vienna government consulted its allies in Berlin and Rome before issuing an ultimatum, but the other powers were only told after it was delivered. Forces were mobilised along the frontier and the Montenegrin government rapidly backed down. The Austro-Hungarians had acted on their own, although on this occasion they could claim that they were only trying to enforce a decision already agreed by the London conference. Later, in the autumn of 1913, Serbian troops, trying to put down a revolt by the population of the newly conquered Macedonia (who had been alienated by military occupation and numerous atrocities), moved across the border into Albania in search of 'rebels' and began attacking the local population. On 14 October Austria–Hungary asked Serbia to withdraw its troops but received an evasive reply. Germany supported its ally. France and, more importantly, Russia did not support Serbia. On 18 October Austria–Hungary sent Serbia an ultimatum: they were to evacuate all their troops from Albania within eight days otherwise Vienna would 'have recourse to proper means' to assure the realisation of its demands, Serbia completed its withdrawal within seven days. The lesson the Austro-Hungarian government drew from these episodes was that ultimatums worked and that the small

Balkan states had little choice but to give way to threats.

There were also signs that a diplomatic crisis in the Balkans could easily escalate into a military confrontation between the major powers. The most dangerous sequence of events occurred during the first Balkan War in November 1912. Russia had already retained over 400,000 conscripts due for release and on 19 November Austria–Hungary decided to strengthen its garrisons in Galicia. Three days later Franz Ferdinand and the chief of the General Staff, General Schemua, went to Berlin for talks and received strong support from the German government. On the same day the tsar held a meeting with the minister for war, General Sukhomlinor, and other army leaders. They agreed to start mobilisation in the areas near the border with Austria–Hungary – the Kiev military district and part of the Warsaw district – and to prepare the Odessa district for similar action. It was only at a further meeting on 23 November, when the foreign minister, Sazonov, and the prime minister, Kokovtzov, were present, that the full implications of these decisions were made clear by the civilians. The Tsar was under the illusion that the partial mobilisation agreed on 22 November was feasible (no plans for a partial mobilisation existed) and would only be directed against Austria– Hungary. Kokovtzov pointed out that any mobilisation in the Warsaw area was bound to be seen as aggressive by Germany and would result in counter-mobilisation and war for which Russia was not ready. Sazonov pointed out that under the terms of its alliance Russia was required to consult France before it began any mobilisation. It was decided to postpone any action and the crisis passed. However, this was, in many respects, a dry run for what happened in July 1914 when radically different decisions were taken by the Russian government.

The Vienna government discovered that the cost of the military confrontation with Russia in Galicia was extremely high – it took up the equivalent of the entire military budget for the 1912 financial year. The military also argued that it was demoralising for the troops to be partially mobilised for several months and then asked to stand down. From both perspectives it seemed best to avoid a repeat – the only alternative (apart from discarding the use of military threats) was to mobilise and go to war. The Russian government drew slightly different conclusions from the 1912–13 crisis. They were worried when they discovered that they had not detected the major increase in the Austro-Hungarian forces in Galicia for several weeks. They came to believe that Vienna was able to mobilise secretly placing Russia at a severe disadvantage in any future crisis. The idea of a partial and early mobilisation against Austria–Hungary in the next crisis began to seem an attractive option.

The most fundamental outcome of the Balkan Wars was a major shift in the balance of power in the area and one which the Vienna government felt significantly worsened its position. Serbia, their irreconcilable enemy, expanded considerably through the acquisition of Kosovo and large parts of Macedonia. Bulgaria, which had a German dynasty on the throne but was extremely close to Russia politically, had been severely weakened by Serbia, Romania and Greece at the Treaty of Bucharest in August 1913. However, Bulgaria was seen by Vienna as a vital Balkan state because it had no claims against Austria–Hungary and was bound to be opposed to Serbia because of their competing claims to Macedonia. The problem was that it was incapable of any effective military action after its crushing military defeat in the summer of 1913. In Greece King George had been assassinated in Salonica in 1913 and was succeeded by the strongly pro-German King Constantine (he had been educated in Germany, had served in the German army and was married to one of the Kaiser's sisters). Although Constantine managed to produce some shifts in the traditionally pro-Russian and pro-British orientation of Greek policy, nothing fundamental changed. Under the terms of the 1913 alliance, Greece was obliged to give support to Serbia if it was attacked by either Bulgaria or Austria–Hungary. However, the alliance only papered over the cracks of the fundamental differences between the two states.

Although the tiny, poor, mountainous state of Montenegro had doubled in size since 1878, it still only had a population of 275,000 and its capital Cetinje, with a population of 5,000, was little more than a village. Montenegro was effectively a Russian client state – the Russian military agent in Cetinje had the title 'controller of the subsidy'. King Nicholas had been on the throne since 1860 and he was, after Emperor Franz Josef, the longest serving monarch in Europe. Nicholas had a well-deserved reputation for being one of the shiftiest diplomats in Europe in conducting the careful balancing act required by Montenegro's situation. Nicholas saw himself as the true leader of the Serbs and despite sympathy for Serbia was strongly opposed to the Karadjordjević dynasty. Proposals for union with Serbia, which were supported by Russia, were regarded with suspicion. Nicholas therefore saw Austria–Hungary, which was bound to oppose any union with Serbia (such a union would not only strengthen Serbia but also give it a port on the Adriatic), as a potential protector of Montenegrin independence. He made numerous offers to Vienna between 1912 and

1914 but the Austro-Hungarian government, probably rightly, did not trust him to carry out any agreements he made.

The most pressing problem Austria–Hungary faced in the aftermath of the Balkan Wars was Romania. It had become formally independent in 1881 when a member of the German royal house, Prince Charles of Hohenzollern-Sigmaringen, was crowned as King Carol I. Romania was opposed to Russia (it maintained a claim to parts of Bessarabia lost to Russia in 1877–8) and close to Austria–Hungary and Germany. In 1883 it signed a secret treaty of alliance with these two powers, which was enlarged to include Italy in 1888 and renewed on several occasions up to 1913. The problem was that although this treaty was acceptable to the elite around the King it had to remain secret (even from some members of the government). The reason for the secrecy was that the treaty was fundamentally opposed to Romanian interests, in particular the perceived need to protect the three million Romanians living in Transylvania under Hungarian rule. In these circumstances the alliance was of little real value to either Vienna or Berlin.

During the second Balkan War, Romania had been allied with Serbia against Bulgaria and, following gains made at Bulgaria's expense in the Treaty of Bucharest, had a strong interest in maintaining that alliance. The real worry for Vienna was that Serbia and Romania were the two Balkan states who had claims over Austro-Hungarian territory – Bosnia–Herzegovina and Transylvania respectively. If they began to cooperate against Vienna, the overall political and strategic situation would be very serious. The long Transylvanian border with Romania was undefended and a hostile Romania would make it almost impossible to deploy troops in Galicia against Russia without exposing their right flank to possible attack. In February 1914 negotiations between the Hungarian government and the Romanian national party in Transylvania over the use of the Romanian language broke down and further exacerbated tension between the two countries. The situation was made even worse in early June 1914 when the Tsar and Tsarina visited Romania. Their yacht was in Constanta harbour for twelve hours. During this time Sazonov accompanied the Romanian prime minister, Bratianu, to the royal summer residence of Sinaia and took an unathorised car ride across the border into Transylvania. Although Vienna was perhaps unduly nervous about Russian support for Romania (there were still major disputes between the two states), they did feel that the situation in Bucharest was starting to deteriorate from their point of view.

In the summer of 1914 Austria–Hungary was faced with what they saw as an increasingly unfavourable situation in the Balkans. Their main enemy, Serbia, was greatly strengthened and their most likely supporter, Bulgaria, significantly weakened. Romania seemed about to become a possible threat rather than a friend. Russia, with its pan-Slav ideology and support for Serbia, was Vienna's main competitor and it seemed to be strengthening its position significantly. The question the Austro-Hungarian government faced was how long this deterioration could be allowed to continue before some action was taken to try and remedy the situation.

The crisis that led to the Frist World War can only be understood in this context. It was the Balkan crisis that set the fuse though it was the structure of the European alliance system that ensured that the dispute then developed into a European war. The key to the situation was Serbia (which the British insisted on calling Servia). There was an irreconcilable conflict between an intransigent, extremist, expansionist Serb nationalism making its claim to a Greater Serbia and the multinational Austro-Hungarian empire seeking to preserve its existence. As the British ambassador in Vienna perceptively told the foreign office in London just fifteen months before the July crisis:

> Servia will some day set Europe by the ears, and bring about a universal war on the Continent . . . I cannot tell you how exasperated people are getting here at the continual worry which that little country causes to Austria under encouragement from Russia . . . The next time a Servian crisis arises . . . I feel sure that Austria–Hungary will refuse to admit of any Russian interference in the dispute and that she will proceed to settle her differences with her little neighbour by herself 'coûte que coûte'.[12]

5

THE TWENTY-FOUR DAYS: 29 JUNE–22 JULY

The crisis brought on by the assassinations at Sarajevo occurred in a Europe sweltering in stifling summer heat and where people expected the normal pattern of summer events. Diplomats across Europe were planning their holidays and the usual period of calm and inaction was keenly anticipated. The problems arising from the Balkan Wars appeared to have been satisfactorily resolved apart from the ever-troublesome Albania where there was a widespread revolt against Prince Wilhelm von Wied, the ruler imposed by the European powers (he was to flee into exile in September).

The European diplomatic and military situation seemed unproblematic. In January 1914 Nicolson, the permanent secretary in the foreign office, wrote to Goschen, the ambassador in Berlin, 'I think there is no likelihood of serious friction among the big European Powers.'[1] He reinforced this advice in early May, writing to Goschen: 'Since I have been at the Foreign Office I have not seen such calm waters . . . there is very little of interest taking place at this moment in Europe, and were it not for the troubles in Mexico we should be in comparative calm here.'[2] On 14 May the British Committee of Imperial Defence decided that its planning assumption should be that the current international situation would not change for three to four years. On 15 June Britain and Germany finally concluded their difficult two-year-long negotiations over the construction of a railway through the Ottoman empire to Baghdad. On 23 June a large number of Royal Navy ships arrived in Kiel on a courtesy visit as part of the Kiel regatta. In Belgium the newspaper *Bien Public* noted, as late as 18 July, 'We are entering the period of holidays, a period feared by newsmen who for lack of important events are often obliged to be content with second-rate news.'

Vienna, 29 June–4 July

The crucial decisions which would turn the killings at Sarajevo into a major crisis and lead to a European war were made in Vienna in the immediate aftermath of the assassinations. Central to these discussions were two figures. First, Count Leopold Berchtold, who, at the age of forty-nine, was the youngest foreign minister in Europe. Second, General Franz Conrad von Hötzendorf. He had joined the army in 1863 at the age of eleven and had been sacked as army chief of staff in 1911 but reinstated at Franz Ferdinand's insistence in December 1912. Conrad was an advocate of an aggressive foreign and military policy to compensate for what he saw as the internal weaknesses of Austria–Hungary. He believed that Austria–Hungary had been too cautious in the crisis over the annexation of Bosnia–Herzegovina in 1908–9 and should have eliminated Serbia while Russia was too weak to intervene. After the crises at the end of 1912, he became a proponent of an attack on Serbia followed by its partition in alliance with Bulgaria. He believed in a surprise, preventive war even though his own military plans demonstrated that Austria–Hungary was incapable of such action.

Berchtold was also moving towards a more aggressive policy before the Sarajevo assassinations. He had last seen Franz Ferdinand when he and his wife Nandine, who was a childhood friend of Sophie, visited the Archduke and his wife at their castle of Konopischt on Sunday 14 June. After breakfast and a tour of the gardens, they viewed the archduke's art collection (Berchtold was also a keen collector). During a talk on the terrace of the castle, the two men agreed they needed to take steps to isolate Serbia through an initiative backed by Germany. On his return to Vienna, Berchtold asked the head of the Balkan section in the foreign ministry, Franz von Matscheko, to draft a paper. This was ready on 24 June and recommended an aggressive foreign policy, backed by Germany, to commit Romania publicly to the Triple Alliance so as to break up the alliance formed in the second Balkan War and thereby isolate Serbia. It went on to argue that if this policy failed then Vienna should move to an alliance with Bulgaria and the Ottomans (with whom Germany was extremely close) so as to contain Romania and Serbia and counter any increase in Russian influence. This was an attempt to recreate the more favourable diplomatic balance that existed before the Balkan Wars. No decisions had been made before the assassinations.

As the policy-makers in Vienna gathered on Monday 29 June they faced a difficult dilemma over how to react to the assassination of the heir to the Habsburg throne by Serb terrorists. To do nothing, or simply to protest, under such major provocation, would probably be interpreted as confirming Austro-Hungarian weakness. The likely outcome of this course was that the long-term trends, which seemed to be working against the empire in the Balkans, would intensify. The temptation facing the Vienna government, given its assessment of its strategic position, was to take advantage of the situation to cripple Serbia permanently or at least for a very long period. The problem was whether Russia would allow such action. The general perception in Vienna was that the options for dealing with an increasingly aggressive and difficult Serbia were running out. The 1903 coup, which installed the new nationalistic Karadjordjević dynasty, had ended Serbia's position as a client state. Economic sanctions during the so-called 'pig war' (pigs were Serbia's major export to Austria–Hungary) had failed. In 1909 Serbia had pledged itself to end hostile propaganda but had taken no steps to do so; indeed, open hostility had grown. Austria–Hungary had made concessions in 1912–13 by allowing Montenegro and Serbia to have a common frontier through their partition of the Sanjak area. At the same time partial mobilisation and a series of ultimatums during the Balkan crises had been successful in the short term but they had not resulted in any fundamental change in the situation or Serbian attitudes. The question that had to be answered was whether further diplomatic action, even if it led to a major diplomatic success and the humiliation of Serbia, would be effective in the long term and whether such action was a suitable response given the gravity of the events in Sarajevo. The only other alternative was war.

Shortly before 8 p.m. on 29 June, the day after the assassination, Berchtold and Conrad had their first conversation about what action Austria–Hungary should take. Conrad suggested immediate mobilisation and made it clear that this time mobilisation should lead automatically to war – it would be bad for army morale (and too expensive) to repeat the policy of 1912 – when limited mobilisation had been followed by inaction. Berchtold's initial reaction was that the assassinations did not provide a sufficient excuse to go to war with Serbia and that the public might not support such a course. Instead he suggested 'we send Serbia a demand to dissolve certain societies, relieve the minister of police of his post, etc.'. Conrad still preferred the use of force, arguing that the Muslims and Croats in the monarchy opposed the Serbs and that Russia could be kept out by stressing the need to take action against people who assassinated monarchs (always a sensitive subject in Russia). Berchtold eventually agreed that 'the moment had come to solve the Serbian question' and that he would talk to the Emperor about the possible options.[3]

The following day the German ambassador reported to Berlin that he had spoken to Berchtold who was convinced that the conspiracy had been organised in Belgrade and that the Serbian government had deliberately chosen youths aged under twenty-one who could not be executed under Austro-Hungarian law. Tschirschky said that opinion in Vienna (he clearly meant Berchtold's) was that 'a final and fundamental reckoning should be had with the Serbs'. They would be given a list of demands and if they rejected them then 'energetic' measures would be taken. The ambassador said: 'I take opportunity of every such occasion to advise quietly but very impressively and seriously against too hasty steps.' Vienna, Tschirschky added, needed to think about the attitude of other countries, especially Italy and Romania (he did not mention Russia).[4]

Later that day Berchtold saw the Emperor Franz Josef who agreed that strong action against Serbia was required but that nothing should be done until the investigation underway in Sarajevo produced some evidence and until Count István Tisza, the Hungarian prime minister, who was currently on his way from Budapest to Vienna, could express his view. Under the constitution of Austria–Hungary agreed in 1867 (known as 'dualism'), Hungary had been placed in a strong position within the Habsburg empire. As the leader of the landowning oligarchy that dominated Hungary, Tisza was opposed to any moves towards democracy and devolution of power to the various minorities within the empire (such as the Romanians in Transylvania). Tisza also opposed any moves to eliminate Serbia and incorporate it into the empire – any increase in the number of Serbs would probably end Hungary's privileged position by bringing about a restructuring of the Austro-Hungarian constitution. On 1 July Tisza sent Franz Josef a memorandum advocating a cautious policy. There was, he argued, no evidence available to blame Serbia directly for the assassination and in any case the diplomatic balance did not favour Austria–Hungary – Romania (Tisza's main concern) looked lost to the Triple Alliance and Bulgaria was exhausted by its defeat in the second Balkan War. Tisza thought that there would never be a problem in finding an excuse to attack Serbia when Vienna was ready but first 'a diplomatic constellation must be created which gives us a less unfavourable relative strength'. Germany should be asked to try and get Romania to join the Triple Alliance but if this failed reliance would have to be placed on

Bulgaria. This was no more than the policy the foreign ministry had suggested before the Sarajevo assassinations.[5]

Tisza's cautious views found little support in Vienna – Franz Josef did not respond to his memorandum and did not invite him to policy discussions because he did not agree with him. Conrad was arguing for a hard line and Berchtold was coming round to the same view. In this attitude he was encouraged by the key diplomats in the Ballhausplatz – Count János Forgách, Baron Alexander von Musulin and Count Alexander Hoyos. They were all fervent believers in a strong foreign policy and certainly showed no sign that they believed Austria–Hungary was in long-term decline. Indeed, they argued that Vienna should reassert its position in the Balkans and that if it did so many of the empire's internal problems would be resolved. On 1 July Hoyos saw the German journalist Viktor Naumann who had arrived in Vienna after discussions in the German foreign ministry. Naumann talked about the idea of a preventive war with Russia before its power increased further and said that he thought Germany would support the idea of war against Serbia. Hoyos said in that case 'it would be very valuable to us to be assured that we could in the event count on Germany's covering us in the rear'.[6]

On 2 July Tschirschky saw Franz Josef and Berchtold. He told them that they could rely on Germany standing behind them if Austria–Hungary had to defend its vital interests. However, before taking action they should draw up a clear plan and decide exactly how far they were prepared to go. Then that plan should be put to the German government. During the day, reports from the police in Sarajevo arrived in Vienna. The police had the six major conspirators in custody and they had begun to talk. It was clear that the weapons had come from Ciganović in Belgrade and that Major Tankosić was also involved. Information from Otto Gellinek, the military attaché in Belgrade, explained Tankosić's position in the Serbian military and how 'Apis' was also involved. Vienna now had enough evidence to confirm their original suspicions that this was not simply a Bosnian Serb plot but that elements in the Serbian government were involved. At the same time General Potiorek in Sarajevo was sending messages arguing for military action against Serbia by deliberately exaggerating the level of unrest in Bosnia–Herzegovina.

During the course of 2–3 July, the policy-makers in Vienna (excluding Tisza) decided that they should draw up a firm plan which could be put to their ally for discussion and approval. The first stage was to redraft the relatively cautious memorandum produced in the foreign office military before the assassinations. The passages about forcing Romania to declare itself either for or against the Triple Alliance were taken out – such a move would be too risky if war was planned with Serbia – and the sections on the threats posed by Serbia and a potential Balkan league were expanded. The emphasis on diplomacy was retained but a passage was added stating that even if diplomatic action was successful in changing the balance in the Balkans, Austria–Hungary would:

> still have to reckon with the stubborn, irreconcilable and aggressive enmity of Serbia. All the more important is the need for the Monarchy with a firm hand to sever the threads which its enemies seek to draw close into a net over its head.[7]

In addition, a letter from Franz Josef to the Kaiser was drafted. It blamed Serbia for the assassination and urged an alliance with Bulgaria (which the Kaiser opposed) and diplomatic action with Romania to bring it back into the Triple Alliance. However, it argued that this diplomatic success (which had been the purpose of the original foreign ministry memorandum) would now only be successful if 'Serbia . . . is eliminated as a political power factor in the Balkans'. Reconciliation was no longer possible and the peace 'of all European monarchs' would be menaced 'as long as this focus of criminal agitation in Belgrade lives on unpunished'.[8]

These documents were carefully drafted and did not, because of Tisza's opposition, clearly state that Austria–Hungary wanted approval to go to war with Serbia. (Even so, Tisza objected to the wording, but his comments arrived too late to be taken into account.) Nevertheless, the implications of the two documents were clear. On 4 July Berchtold sent a telegram to the seventy-nine-year-old Austro-Hungarian ambassador in Berlin, Szögyény, telling him that Hoyos would be leaving Vienna by train later that day and that he should seek audiences with the Kaiser and Chancellor Bethmann Hollweg for the next day. Hoyos, himself a hardliner, took with him a clear under-standing that Vienna wanted, subject to German approval, to take radical action and launch an attack on Serbia and eliminate it as a threat for decades to come. Vienna had what it felt were overwhelming reasons for taking strong action against its perpetual enemy. Such an excuse might not occur again. It also felt that it needed to demonstrate to its main ally that it was capable of taking decisive action. Vienna was suspicious that Germany harboured doubts about its ally and may well have thought that if it did not make an effective response after the assassinations, then Germany (and other European states too) might conclude that the Habsburg empire was too weak to be worth supporting. In these circumstances Germany might easily decide to seek an alliance with Russia.

Vienna had rejected a diplomatic victory as insufficient. It wanted a long-term solution to what it saw as the 'Serbian problem'. On 5 July, while Hoyos was in Berlin, Conrad saw Franz Josef. The general suggested that war with Serbia was inevitable. The emperor agreed but said that the position of Germany was vital and explained the background to the Hoyos mission. Conrad asked whether, if Germany supported Austria–Hungary, there would be war with Serbia and Franz Josef replied, 'In that case, yes.'[9]

Berlin, 29 June–5 July

The initial German reaction to the assassinations, particularly in the press, was cautious. On 2 July the Saxon minister in Berlin, Lichtenau, reported to the Saxon minister for foreign affairs, Vitzthum, that he had been to the foreign ministry to discuss the situation. The view there was that the assassinations 'would hardly give cause for any kind of harmful consequences to Europe'.[10] The removal of Franz Ferdinand was seen as beneficial from a policy perspective and it was thought that, although Austria–Hungary would probably take vigorous action, the mood across Europe was so anti-Serbian that even Russia would not intervene. Lichtenau did report (as the Saxon military representative in Berlin confirmed the next day) that the army leaders saw this as an ideal opportunity to have a war with Russia before the situation deteriorated, but he was convinced that the Kaiser strongly favoured peace. Lichtenau was in fact unaware of how the Kaiser was reacting. When, on 2 July, he saw Tschirschky's message of 30 June reporting that he was advising caution in Vienna he strongly disagreed with his ambassador and wrote another of the many emotional marginal notes which he scrawled across his copies of telegrams: 'Now or never . . . The Serbs must be disposed of, and that right soon.'[11] Tschirschky was told of the rebuke and, for the rest of the crisis, altered his line so as to advocate a strong policy on Vienna.

It used to be thought that in the period before Hoyos arrived in Berlin on 5 July the German government was largely inactive. The Kaiser was in Potsdam and the chancellor was, it was believed, isolated on his estate of Hohenfinow. However, since the discovery of Bethmann Hollweg's travel-expense claims in the German archives, it is now known that he was at Potsdam with the Kaiser every day between 29 June and 6 July apart from on 1 July and 3 July. It is inconceivable that during these meetings they did not discuss the options open to Germany following the Sarajevo assassinations. If Austria–Hungary asked its ally for support on an issue which it saw as central to its status and position it would be very difficult for Germany to refuse. Austria–Hungary was Germany's only real ally and if its prestige was not restored then its position in the Balkans, already affected by the gains its enemies had made in the Balkan Wars, might be damaged irreparably. A quick Austro-Hungarian success against Serbia would be highly advantageous and its dismemberment, or even just the loss of the gains it had made in 1912–13, would greatly strengthen Vienna's position and probably lead to further diplomatic gains with Romania and Bulgaria. A Serbian defeat would also be a defeat for Russia and significantly reduce the influence it could wield in the Balkans. The advantages of decisive action were therefore clear. But there were dangers. Russia might not allow any feelings it had about monarchical assassinations to override its interest in not seeing Serbia defeated and dismembered. However, if the military felt that the summer of 1914 was as good an occasion as any to fight Russia, then this might be the time to run risks. If Russia did not intervene and allowed Austria–Hungary to defeat Serbia, huge strategic and diplomatic gains would be made. If they did intervene, then at least the subsequent war would be fought in the most favourable circumstances and with Austria–Hungary strongly tied into the alliance because they had started the quarrel.

This was a significant change in Germany policy. During the Balkan Wars, Germany had acted as a brake on its ally. On 9 November 1912 the Kaiser told his ministers that if the Austro-Hungarian refusal to have Serbia gain a port on the Adriatic provoked a Russian attack, then Germany would not accept it as a cause of war. On 6 July 1913 Bethmann Hollweg warned Vienna that if it took action against Serbia, then a European war would probably be the result and therefore Germany must be consulted first. The clear implication was that Germany would refuse approval for action. However, the situation in July 1914 was different. The quarrel with Serbia was not over territory and influence in the Balkans but over the actions Serbia appeared to have taken in supporting the assassination of the heir to the Habsburg throne. The experience of the crisis produced by the annexation of Bosnia–Herzegovina in 1908–9 seemed to show that if Germany did support its ally (as it had not done consistently through the Balkan crisis of 1912–13), then Russia, after some posturing, would back down. However, Russia had been extremely weak militarily in the 1908–9 crisis and now it felt it had recovered its strength and might be less willing to give way. Even in 1909 Moltke had warned his colleague Conrad: 'I think only an Austrian invasion of Serbia could in the event lead to active intervention by Russia.'[12]

Berlin, 5–6 July

When Hoyos arrived in Berlin on the overnight train from Vienna early on the morning of 5 July, he immediately went to the Austro-Hungarian embassy. Here he showed Szögyény the two documents he had brought with him and briefed him about the strategy that had been agreed but not set out on paper. It is clear that Hoyos told the ambassador that war was Vienna's preferred option. The two men then split up. Hoyos went to see Alfred Zimmerman, the deputy minister at the foreign ministry. (The secretary of state, Jagow, was away on his honeymoon.) During their discussions Hoyos was frank about his government's objectives. Serbia might be allowed to survive but it would be dismembered. Austria–Hungary would take some strategic areas along the border (including the capital Belgrade) but most of the rest of the country would be divided up among its neighbours – Bulgaria, Romania, Albania and, possibly, Montenegro. What remained of Serbia (with the Karadjordjević dynasty removed) would revert to being a client state of Vienna.

The most important discussion that day took place at the Neues Palace at Potsdam where Szögyény had lunch with the Kaiser. Before the meal the Kaiser read the documents brought from Vienna. He commented, as the ambassador reported to Vienna early that evening, that 'he had expected some serious step on our part towards Serbia' but he felt that 'a serious European complication' was possible and that therefore he would have to consult Bethmann Hollweg. The Kaiser was being disingenuous – he must have known the chancellor's views already, as became clear after lunch. It was then that Szögyény pressed the Kaiser for a fuller response. Vienna was told that the Kaiser had replied:

If we really recognised the necessity of military measures against Serbia he would deplore our not taking advantage of the present moment which is so favourable to us . . . we might in this case, as in all others, rely upon Germany's full support.[13]

Later in the afternoon, the ambassador and Hoyos met at the embassy to discuss the German reaction and draft the telegram to go to Vienna.

Meanwhile, in Potsdam, the Kaiser met a number of his advisers at 5 p.m. Present were Bethmann Hollweg, General Baron von Lyncker (head of the Kaiser's military cabinet), General Erich von Falkenhayn (the Prussian minister for war), General Hans von Plessen (the Kaiser's aide-de-camp) and Captain Zencker representing the navy. The Kaiser read out the texts of the Austrian documents. He concluded, as Falkenhayn wrote to Moltke (he had been at the spa of Karlsbad since 28 June), that Vienna had not decided exactly what action to take but that 'energetic' political action was the most likely outcome. Falkenhayn felt that the Austro-Hungarian government was more determined than it had been in the past but 'in no circumstances will the coming weeks bring any decision' and therefore Moltke need not change his holiday plans.[14] The meeting decided that Austria–Hungary should be supported in whatever action it decided to take. Plessen wrote in his diary:

The opinion prevailed among us that the sooner the Austrians make their move against Serbia the better, and that the Russians – though friends of Serbia – will not join in.[15]

It was agreed that Bethmann Hollweg and Zimmerman would meet the Austrians the next day to convey these decisions.

Early on the morning of 6 July the Kaiser saw the only army officer who could be found in Berlin – General Betrab, a map specialist who was head of the cartography section of the general staff. The Kaiser said that he did not expect any further military developments – Russia was not ready to fight and anyway would not take the side of regicides. At 9.15 the Kaiser left for his usual summer cruise off the coast of Norway on board his yacht *Hohenzollern*. Betrab reported on the meeting in a letter to Moltke. He provided a much clearer account of German and Austro-Hungarian policy than Falkenhayn. He said that those at the meeting with the Kaiser on the previous day had approved the decision by Vienna to 'march into Serbia' and that Germany would 'cover Austria in the event of Russia's intervening'. However, the Kaiser 'does not think that Russia will intervene' because the Tsar would not support assassins. The Kaiser therefore 'regards the affair as in the first instance a purely Balkan concern'.[16] The German army, reflecting this relaxed attitude, instituted no measures to prepare for mobilisation, did not interrupt the usual summer routines of the army and took no action to improve its intelligence on what France and Russia were doing.

In Berlin that morning Bethmann Hollweg and Zimmerman saw Szögyény and Hoyos. The telegram, which the two men sent to Vienna later in the day, provides the fullest account of what was agreed between the two allies. Most of the discussion was about possible diplomatic action. Germany agreed that Bulgaria should be persuaded to join the Triple Alliance but this had to be done in such a way as not to violate the existing agreements with Romania (the two Balkan countries were in dispute over numerous territories after the Treaty of Bucharest in 1913). On Serbia, Austria–Hungary 'must judge what is to be done to clear the course' but, whatever was decided in Vienna, Germany would be a faithful ally and friend. However, the German government 'considers immediate action on our part as the best and most thorough-going solution to our difficulties in the Balkans'. The telegram continued: 'Hitherto Bethmann has always advised us to get along with Serbia, but after the recent events, he realises that this is well-nigh impossible.'[17] Hoyos then left to catch the overnight train to Vienna. The telegram which Bethmann Hollweg sent to his ambassador in Vienna was much more general. It merely stated that the Kaiser had not committed himself to any course of action but that Germany would stand by its ally.

The events in Berlin on 5–6 July shaped the subsequent crisis. The German government decided that it had little alternative but to support its ally on such a vital issue, especially when Vienna saw the assassinations as a golden opportunity to improve its position in the Balkans. Austria–Hungary was determined to take decisive action and military action against Serbia was the most likely outcome. Germany, however, left the final decision in the hands of the government in Vienna. Why did Germany give Austria–Hungary the so-called 'blank cheque' by not demanding, in return for its support, the right to be consulted in advance over Vienna's actions? The German government seems, without any evidence, to have convinced itself that Russia would not intervene to protect Serbia. In these circumstances a significant diplomatic or military victory could easily be achieved in a localised conflict between Austria–Hungary and Serbia with Germany giving diplomatic support to its ally. Perhaps in the background of German thinking was the assumption that, even if the Russians did intervene to support Serbia, and a more general war resulted, then this was a good opportunity to fight such a war given that the military situation would only worsen over time. This was a very high-risk strategy. The German and Austro-Hungarian governments were effectively leaving it to the Russians to decide whether it was to be war or not. Once Berlin and Vienna had embarked on such a course it would be very difficult to draw back. On one point the German government was clear. What was needed in Vienna was quick action (in a matter of days) while the other European powers were still disgusted over the assassinations and therefore likely to be sympathetic to any action Austria–Hungary took.

Vienna, 6–7 July

Even as the discussions in Berlin were finishing it was becoming clear in Vienna that there was no hope of the quick action Germany wanted. Conrad discovered that, as usual, harvest leave had been granted. All the army units at Agram (Zagreb), Graz, Pressburg (Bratislava), Cracow and Temesvár (Timi-soara) were on leave until 25 July when they would return to their units for manoeuvres. Altogether, almost half of the army was not available for nearly three weeks. Conrad cancelled further leaves but decided against recalling those soldiers already on leave. Any recall would overload the railways, damage the harvest and alert the other powers that Austria–Hungary was planning military action.

Hoyos arrived back in Vienna early in the morning of 7 July. He immediately went to a meeting with Berchtold, Tisza, Tschirschky and Count Karl Stürgkh, the Austrian prime minister. They discussed the meetings in Berlin and Hoyos gave a frank account of his talk with Zimmerman. This was the first time Tisza had heard the details of how his colleagues intended to dismember Serbia and he was furious. Before the matter could be resolved, Tschirschky withdrew so that the others could attend the council of ministers meeting. The council did not act as a cabinet – it was merely a discussion group for the main figures in the highly fragmented Austro-Hungarian government. Indeed, before 7 July it had only met three times since early October 1913 and on each occasion had only discussed the building of railways in Bosnia–Herzegovina. Nevertheless, its meeting on the morning of 7 July was crucial in setting Austro-Hungarian policy for the rest of the crisis. In addition to Berchtold, Tisza and Stürgkh, two others attended – General Alexander von Krobatin (minister for war) and Leon von Bilinski (joint finance minister). Hoyos was present to take the minutes.[18]

Berchtold opened the meeting by asking his colleagues 'whether the moment had not arrived to render Serbia innocuous once and for all by a display of force?' He said that Germany had given assurances of its 'unconditional support'. Unlike the optimistic assumptions prevailing in Berlin, Berchtold was clear about the wider implications: 'War with Russia would very likely be a consequence of our invading Serbia.' But he argued that Russia was building up a Balkan alliance against Austria–Hungary and therefore 'we should realise that our position in the face of such a policy would grow steadily worse'. In particular, the minorities within the empire would be attracted to these new, strong Balkan states. He concluded that the only logical policy for Austria–Hungary was to 'forestall our adversaries and by a timely settlement of accounts with Serbia check the development which is already in full swing. Later on it will no longer be possible to do so.'

Immediately Berchtold had finished, Tisza put forward the opposite and more cautious position saying that he personally took the view that there was no imperative reason to go to war for the time being. He wanted a series of stiff demands to be put to Serbia but they were not to be so strong that they could not be met. He was convinced that war would not solve any problems because Russia would not allow Serbia to be eliminated. The logical policy was therefore to go for a major diplomatic victory that would humiliate Serbia and at the same time bring Bulgaria into the Triple Alliance so that the power balance in the Balkans was changed in Austria–Hungary's favour. Tisza also made it clear that under no circumstances would he accept any annexation of Serbian territory (increasing the Serb population within Austria–Hungary would tip the balance against Hungary and undermine its privileged position). Berchtold responded by saying: 'A radical solution of the problem raised by the Pan-Serbian propaganda . . . was not possible save by war, by which the Pan-Serb movement would be decapitated once and for all.' When he approved the draft minutes Berchtold changed 'war' to 'energetic intervention'.

Stürgkh spoke next and agreed with Berchtold that it was time 'for a settlement with Serbia by war'. Given the support of Germany if Vienna adopted 'a policy of hesitancy and weakness we run the risk at a later time of being no longer so sure of this unreserved support'. He too felt that the position could not be improved in any way by a diplomatic success. He concluded: 'If on international grounds preliminary diplomatic action was the course taken, it must be taken with the firm resolve that it shall only end in war.' He was supported by Bilinski and Krobatin. The latter argued for a partial mobilisation against Serbia. Once this was complete an unacceptable ultimatum would be sent and its rejection would be followed immediately by war.

After a further discussion the meeting reached some conclusions. All agreed that the matter had to be resolved speedily. Because of Tisza's strong position within the Austro-Hungarian system, a compromise of sorts had to be reached. Demands would be made on Serbia and only if they were rejected would mobilisation begin. The problem with this policy was that it would not produce a speedy resolution – Austro-Hungarian mobilisation was a slow and complex process and weeks would therefore elapse before any war could begin. Apart from Tisza, all the members of the council thought that a purely diplomatic triumph, even if it resulted in a 'resounding humiliation' for Serbia, would not be sufficient. The majority felt that 'such far-reaching demands must be made on Serbia that it will make a refusal almost certain' and therefore lead to war and a 'radical solution'. Tisza said he only agreed that the note could be 'stiff' but not obviously unacceptable. He would resign if he was not consulted over its content.

This 'compromise' could not disguise the fact that Vienna was determined on war with Serbia (even though there would be preliminary diplomatic action). The war was intended to dismember Serbia and render it innocuous for decades. Vienna recognised that its policy would, almost inevitably, mean war with Russia. By implication they therefore accepted the likelihood of a European war which would involve Germany and France as well. Fully aware of these risks, they decided to press ahead.

After lunch, Conrad and the head of the navy, Admiral Kailer, joined the council to assess the military options. Conrad was less than frank in his advice. Even though he knew that the army could not start mobilisation for another fortnight, he, together with Krobatin, called for a surprise attack on Serbia. He also failed to tell the civilian ministers about his knowledge of German plans which he had obtained from Moltke. If Russia did intervene to support Serbia, then Germany would insist on the majority of Austro-Hungarian forces moving to Galicia to help deter a threat to East Prussia, thereby making a successful attack on Serbia very unlikely. Conrad did, however, set out the dilemmas facing the Habsburg military planners very well. Should forces be kept in Transylvania to deal with a potentially hostile Romania? When would a conflict with Russia, which Berchtold thought inevitable, start? Conrad told his colleagues that he would need to know by the fifth day of mobilisation at the latest whether his reserve forces were to go south to the Serbian front or to Galicia to face the Russians – after that date it would be too late to change course. Exactly what was said in the rest of the discussion is unknown except that there was 'a longish debate on the relative strength of the Powers involved and the possible course of a European war'. Hoyos judged that this discussion was too sensitive to record in the minutes. It was, however, agreed that Berchtold would report the conclusions of the meeting to the Emperor on the next day. After the meeting Berchtold saw Wladimir Freiherr von Giesl who was waiting to travel to Belgrade to resume his duties as the Austro-Hungarian minister. Berchtold told him: 'However the Serbs react – you must break off relations and leave; this must lead to war.'[19]

The outcome of the council meeting was that Austria–Hungary had effectively decided (despite Tisza's reservations) that only war would solve the 'Serbian problem' by leading to the dismemberment of Serbia. A diplomatic victory, however great, was judged not to be sufficient. This conclusion was reached despite the clear understanding that Russia would almost certainly intervene and that the consequence of Vienna's actions would therefore be a European war. Once these decisions were taken on 7 July, Vienna did not depart from them in any fundamental respect for the rest of the crisis. Although the primary responsibility for the crisis that led to war lay with Serbia for its active support of the terrorists that carried out the assassinations, Austria–Hungary was just as culpable in its decision to seek a solution through war rather than diplomacy.

Vienna, 8 July

Tisza did not agree with the conclusions his colleagues on the council of ministers had reached on 7 July. He drafted a memorandum which he asked Berchtold to give to Franz Josef when he saw him later in the day (the Emperor still did not want to see Tisza because he disagreed with his views). Tisza correctly stated the conclusions of the meeting on the previous day as being to provoke 'war with Serbia in order to settle accounts once and for all with this arch enemy of the Monarchy'. Tisza said he did not fully agree with this policy because 'any such attack on Serbia would, as far as can humanly be foreseen, bring upon the scene the intervention of Russia and with it a world war'. Romania (always a worry for the Hungarians) might intervene too. In these circumstances, Tisza argued, 'Serbia should be given the opportunity to avoid war by means of a severe diplomatic defeat'. In order to avoid Russian intervention, Italian claims for compensation if Austria–Hungary acquired territory in the Balkans and keep British goodwill, it was essential Vienna made it clear it had 'no intention of annihilating, let alone annexing Serbia'. Austria–Hungary itself would only gain 'frontier rectifications', although annexations by Bulgaria, Romania and Albania and a large indemnity to cripple Serbia for years would be acceptable. Tisza concluded that he could not agree to a 'sole solution by an aggressive war'.[20] The problem with Tisza's position was that, although his reservations over the policy adopted proved to be correct in a matter of weeks, he was reduced to arguing over tactics. He objected to war with Serbia as too dangerous and major annexations as too detrimental to Hungary, but he did agree to a 'stiff' note being sent to Serbia and the dismembering and crippling of the country. The contents of the note were therefore a matter of judgement: what was Serbia likely to accept and what would it reject? The hardliners in Vienna could easily construct an unacceptable note.

After giving his memorandum to Berchtold, Tisza left to return to Budapest. At 3.30 p.m. Berchtold saw Tschirschky so that the latter could tell Berlin what had been decided at the council of ministers on the previous day. Berchtold made it clear that even if the Emperor accepted Tisza's position he would ensure that the terms of the note to Serbia were unacceptable. The ambassador also passed on a message from Berlin which Berchtold then passed on to Tisza, though he may well have strengthened the message. Berchtold told Tisza that in Berlin 'an action of the Monarchy against Serbia is fully expected and that Germany would not understand why we should neglect this opportunity of dealing a blow'. He concluded that 'Germany would interpret any compromise on our part as a confession of weakness' and that this might cause them to re-evaluate the whole alliance.[21]

Berchtold decided to put off his planned audience with Franz Josef while further meetings were held in Vienna. At 6 p.m. he saw Conrad to discuss the integration of diplomatic and military measures. They agreed that an ultimatum with unacceptable demands and a twenty-four- or forty-eight-hour time limit would be sent to Serbia. If Serbia did not accept without qualifications, Austria–Hungary would mobilise, and if subsequently Serbia did accept, there would still be an invasion. Serbia would then be occupied until all Vienna's mobilisation costs were met. Because of army leave, no ultimatum could be sent before 22 July at the earliest and in the meantime all the senior figures in Vienna would keep to their holiday plans in order not to arouse suspicion. The two men were then joined by three members of the foreign ministry – Hoyos, Forgách and Karl von Macchio. Also present was Baron István von Burián, who had been the joint finance minister until 1912 and was now the Hungarian government representative in Vienna. Burián was close to Tisza and was a strong believer in maintaining Hungary's position in the empire. He had been sceptical about strong action against Serbia but now swung round to agree with the majority. He volunteered to go to Budapest to try and persuade Tisza to go along with his colleagues.

Vienna, 9–13 July

On 9 July Berchtold finally went to Bad Ischl to see Franz Josef and get his agreement to the action agreed at the council of ministers. The only source for what took place is the telegram Tschirschky sent to Berlin on the evening of 10 July after he had seen Berchtold on the latter's return to Vienna. According to the ambassador, Berchtold reported that the Emperor thought 'it was necessary now to come to some determination, in order to put an end to the intolerable conditions in connection with Serbia'. The Emperor argued that Berchtold's and Tisza's positions could be reconciled but thought that 'concrete demands should be levelled at Serbia'. Berchtold said that from a wider diplomatic perspective it would be best to make demands on Serbia first rather than just declaring war. He then gave his preliminary thoughts on the contents of the ultimatum. He suggested three demands: 'an Austro-Hungarian agency in Belgrade to monitor propaganda for a Greater Serbia; dissolution of some societies promoting the Greater Serbia idea; and the dismissal of some of the government officials involved in the conspiracy. There would a forty-eight-hour deadline even though that would give Serbia time to consult Russia. Tschirschky reported Berchtold's conclusions:

> If the Serbs should accept all the demands made on them, it would prove a solution which would be 'very disagreeable' to him, and he was still considering what demands should be put that would be wholly impossible for the Serbs to accept.[22]

79

Jagow in Berlin stuck with the 'blank cheque' formula and advised Tschirschky the next day 'we are unable to commit ourselves with respect to the formulation of the demands on Serbia, since this is Austria's concern'.[23]

Indeed, Germany was increasingly anxious that its ally was procrastinating. It was becoming clear that policy would not be settled until Tisza was back in Vienna on 14 July. Tschirschky saw Berchtold again on 11 July to, as he reported to Berlin, 'impress upon the Minister once more, emphatically, that quick action was called for'. He was told that a new demand on Serbia would be made. The King would now have to issue a proclamation and an order to the army that Serbia 'discarded her Greater Serbia policy'. The ambassador was less reassured to hear the ultimatum could not be presented before 23 July, after harvest leave and after the French president had left St Petersburg following his state visit. (Austria–Hungary and Germany did not want the Russians and French co-ordinating their response to the ultimatum at a high level.) A forty-eight-hour time limit would mean that mobilisation could not start until 26 July and it would then take sixteen days to complete. There would, therefore, be no declaration of war on Serbia before 11 August.[24] Any idea of swift action in response to the assassination had disappeared.

On 13 July the Austro-Hungarian foreign office received a telegram from the ambassador in Berlin. Szögyény reported that the Kaiser and the whole government 'are encouraging us emphatically not to neglect the present moment, but to treat Serbia with full energy, so as to clear out the conspirators' nest once for all, and are leaving the choice of means for doing so to our judgement'. He added that Berlin felt Russia was planning a war but was not yet ready. Therefore the German government was 'anything but certain that if Serbia is engaged in a war with us, Russia would lend an armed hand'. They thought Russia would prefer to wait until its rearmament programme was completed in 1917.[25] Later in the day Berchtold saw Tschirschky and told him that he too was 'convinced that speediest action is imperative' and that he hoped to agree the outlines of the ultimatum with Tisza the next day.[26]

Just after lunch on 13 July, Berchtold received a report from Friedrich von Wiesener, the legal counsellor at the foreign ministry, who had been sent to Sarajevo three days earlier to investigate the conspiracy. After his rapid investigation, he concluded that there were 'no proofs that the Serbian Government promoted propaganda . . . but sufficient material to prove that the movement originates in Serbia and is tolerated by the Government'. On the conspiracy itself he argued that there was 'nothing to prove or even to suppose that the Serbian Government is accessory to the inducement for the crime'. Although that might be correct in a strict legal sense, he then went on to set out the evidence, suggesting that elements in the Serbian government were responsible. The crime had been organised in Belgrade by Ciganović and Tankosić who provided the weapons and ordered frontier officials to smuggle the conspirators across the borders. He therefore suggested three demands should be added to the ultimatum: the Serbian government was to stop official involvement in smuggling across the frontier; the officials involved were to be dismissed; and the Serbian government was to prosecute Ciganović and Tankosić. General Potiorek added his comments. He took a more general view than Wiesener's legal opinion, arguing, correctly, that what he called the 'alternative government' in Serbia, especially elements in the army, were responsible for the assassinations.[27]

Vienna, 14 July

In the morning Berchtold, Tisza and Stürgkh met to discuss and agree on the action to be taken against Serbia. Over the last week, under pressure from Burián, Tisza had changed his mind. He did not do so, as is often alleged, because of the German support for Austria–Hungary – he knew that had been promised at the council of ministers meeting on 7 July. For Tisza the decisive factor was his fear that Romania might take advantage of a strong Serbia to foment discontent among the Romanians in Transylvania. He was also reassured by the preliminary diplomatic indications that Bulgaria was moving closer to the Triple Alliance and that Romania might be neutral in any war. Finally, he realised that he was in a minority of one in the Austro-Hungarian government and did not wish to lose all influence over policy-making. He now dropped his objections to sending an ultimatum to Serbia that would be so severe as to ensure rejection and therefore lead to war, even though that war would probably involve Russia. In return for dropping his objections, Tisza was able to insist on two conditions. First, defensive measures would be taken along the Romanian border and, second, a formal undertaking would be given that Austria–Hungary would not annex Serbian territory beyond some changes along the frontier. (This left plenty of scope to dismember Serbia by allowing the other Balkan states to make territorial gains at its expense.)

Following this meeting and final agreement on Austro-Hungarian policy, Berchtold went to see Tschirschky. He told him that Vienna was now absolutely convinced of the necessity of war and that the ultimatum 'is being composed so that the possibility of its acceptance is practically excluded'.[28] Clearly the German ambassador expressed his anxiety about the slow pace of action. Later in the day, Berchtold summoned Tschirschky to explain that the ultimatum could not be sent on 16 July because it was still not drafted. It would not be agreed until a further ministerial meeting on 19 July and Franz Josef's approval would then have to be obtained. Nevertheless, he reassured the ambassador there was no weakening in Vienna. Later, Berchtold wrote to the Emperor to tell him of the agreement with Tisza. He explained, 'the text of the note to be sent to Belgrade . . . is such that we must reckon with the probability of war'. If Serbia did, unexpectedly, agree it 'would signify a downright humiliation for the kingdom' and therefore a blow to Russian prestige in the Balkans. He told Franz Josef that 'even after mobilisation a peaceful arrangement might be possible if Serbia gives way in good time', i.e. during the sixteen-day mobilisation period. If it did so, Serbia would still have to pay the cost of the mobilisation and it would be occupied until the indemnity was paid.[29]

The fundamental decisions had now been made in Vienna (with general approval from Germany). For the next few days the government in Vienna was engaged in settling the details of the ultimatum and the exact diplomatic procedures it would use when it precipitated the crisis. Meanwhile, across Europe other governments, often mainly concerned with domestic politics, were beginning to suspect that Austria–Hungary was about to take some drastic action.

St Petersburg, 14–21 July

On 14 July officials in the Russian foreign ministry decoded a telegram from Berchtold to his ambassador in the Russian capital asking when President Poincaré of France would leave the city at the end of his state visit. Suspicions were immediately aroused. They were reinforced two days later when Baron von Schilling, the head of chancery and most senior official in the foreign ministry, was told by the Italian ambassador, the Marquis Carlotti di Riparbella, that Vienna was going to take 'irrevocable' steps against Serbia on the assumption that Russia would do no more than make a verbal protest. This information was confirmed in a telegram from Shebeko, the Russian ambassador in Vienna, who had heard the news from the British ambassador, de Bunsen, who had been told it by a contact in the foreign ministry.

The foreign minister, Sazonov, returned to St Petersburg from his country estate in Grodno on 18 July. He was met at the station by Schilling who told him about the information received in the ministry. Sazonov was alarmed and saw the Austro-Hungarian ambassador, Count Szápáry, who had only returned to St Petersburg from Vienna on 17 July. Szápáry reassured him that there was 'an entire absence in Austria of any intention of rendering relations with Serbia more acute'.[30] Sazonov seems to have accepted this lie and did not issue any threats about how Russia would react.

On 21 July Sazonov saw the German ambassador, Count Friedrich von Pourtalès. During the discussion, Pourtalès mentioned the strong possibility that the Serbian government was involved not just in propaganda but in the Sarajevo conspiracy itself. Sazonov, who was liable to wild mood swings, sprang to the defence of Serbia. Princip was an Austro-Hungarian subject; if there was propaganda it was because of bad government in Bosnia–Herzegovina, Serbia 'was behaving itself with entire propriety' and, he added, 'a whole country could not be held responsible for the acts of individuals'. Becoming even more emotional, Sazonov said that Vienna just wanted 'the annihilation of Serbia' in which case the whole of Europe would be involved. Sazonov ended the discussion with a clear warning: 'Russia could not look indifferently on at a move at Belgrade which aimed at the humiliation of Serbia . . . in no case should there be any talk of an ultimatum.'[31] This message should have caused real doubts in Berlin about whether the Austro-Hungarian strategy of provoking a war with Serbia on the assumption that Russia would stand aside was realistic. Even if Germany and Austria–Hungary had been willing to change course at such a late stage, the telegram from Pourtalès did not arrive in Berlin until the morning of 23 July, the day the ultimatum was to be delivered.

Paris

The assassinations at Sarajevo had only a transient impact in France where attention was focused on two major political events: the early days of a new government and the sensational Caillaux trial. The Doumergue government collapsed in early June and it took ten days before the ex-socialist René Viviani was able to form a new administration in which he was both prime minister and foreign minister. The government was weak and not expected to last long after the completion of the trial of Madame Caillaux, the wife of the former finance minister, Joseph Caillaux. On 16 March Madame Caillaux had gone to the office of Gaston Calmette, the editor of *Le Figaro*, and shot him six times. She had killed Calmette because, as part of a long-running campaign against her husband, he had published her love letters to Caillaux written while he was still married to his first wife. There were also rumours that Calmette had obtained copies of inter-cepted German telegrams which the French had decoded showing that Caillaux had negotiated with Germany behind the back of his own government during the Agadir crisis in 1911. Caillaux had lied when he specifically denied doing so in a statement to parliament.

After the shooting, Caillaux had resigned from the government, but by early July he was making it clear privately to the government that if they allowed publication of the German telegrams he had material that would embarrass others. He had intercepted telegrams that showed Calmette had been in the pay of the Spanish government. Far more important, he also had information about President Poincaré. Before becoming president he had married a divorcee but then taken part in a secret church wedding specifically authorised by the Vatican. Caillaux had copies of intercepted telegrams detailing Poincaré's dealings with the Holy See which would cause a scandal among anti-clerical political groups in France. During early July, a deal was reached. The govern-ment issued a statement saying that the intercepts of the German telegrams did not exist, even though they did. In return, Caillaux kept his information private. (Foreign governments, not surprisingly, suspected that the French were decoding their telegrams and therefore changed their codes, leaving the French bereft of intelligence during the July crisis.)

Paris, and the rest of France, was eagerly awaiting the opening of Madame Caillaux's trial, which was due to commence on 20 July. Until the trial started most public interest was focused on the last stages of the Tour de France. In Paris the school holidays began as usual after 14 July and most middle-class families left the city, leaving it semi-deserted. All the ambassadors, with the exception of the German representative, Wilhelm Schoen, also left the city. On 13 July Senator Humbert participated in a debate on defence policy and listed a catalogue of French military weaknesses and spoke of the 'flagrant inferiority of our military equipment compared to that of Germany'.

This only served to increase the feeling in Berlin that France would not fight and would therefore restrain Russia. On 14 July the Socialist Party held its annual conference in Paris and agreed a resolution that they would use 'all means' to avoid war but it was left deliberately ambiguous as to what this meant. Even the revoluntionary syndicalist Gustave Hervé insisted that patriotic workers would not respond to any call for a general strike. As the Socialist leader Jean Jaurès insisted in an editorial in *L'Humanité* on 18 July:

> The general strike will never be unilateral . . . No matter what our enemies say, there is no contradiction between the maximum effort for peace and, if we should be invaded, the maximum effort for national independence.

During July, President Poincaré attended the cycling Grand Prix at Vincennes and then, after sorting out the potential scandals surrounding the Caillaux trial, concentrated on the preparations for the state visit to Russia, Sweden, Norway and Denmark which had been arranged at the beginning of the year. He was to be accompanied by René Viviani and the director of the Quai d'Orsay, Pierre de Margerie. The party left Paris on 15 July at 11.30 p.m. by train from the Gare du Nord. At 5.30 a.m. the next morning they embarked at Dunkirk for the voyage to St Petersburg and a trip that was planned to last until 31 July. That they did so shows that they did not expect any major diplomatic developments in their absence. Throughout the trip Viviani was mainly worried about his mistress from the Comédie Française whom he suspected of having an affair. Both politicians were, not surprisingly, also worried about what might happen during the Caillaux trial which would begin just as they arrived in St Petersburg.

St Petersburg, 20–22 July

The French president and his party arrived at Kronstadt harbour at about 2 p.m. on 20 July – on entering the harbour, the battleship on which they were travelling, *France*, hit a tug and nearly collided with her sister ship *Jean Bart*. Later that day, Poincaré had discussions with Tsar Nicholas II and Viviani saw Sazonov. Exactly what was discussed during the visit is unknown – no records seem (somewhat suspiciously) to have survived. It is highly unlikely that, given the information available in St Petersburg, the two allies did not discuss how to react to any Austro-Hungarian action against Serbia. It is almost certain that the French, especially Poincaré who was born in Lorraine and was a strong nationalist, made it clear that they would support Russia in taking a tough line. They may also have agreed that a Russian military response would be appropriate.

There were some indications during the visit that the two powers would react strongly. On the afternoon of 21 July there was a reception for the St Petersburg diplomatic corps at the Winter Palace. The British ambassador, Sir George Buchanan, spoke to Poincaré and said that he feared Austria–Hungary would send a very stiff note to Serbia and suggested direct talks between Russia and Austria–Hungary in Vienna. Poincaré rejected this idea as 'very dangerous' (though it would be only if the French and Russians did not want a settlement). Instead, trying to embroil the British, the president suggested a joint Anglo-French demand for moderation in Vienna.[32] Poincaré then saw the Austro-Hungarian ambassador, Szápáry, and warned him that Russia was a friend of Serbia and France was a friend of Russia. The threat of a wider war stemming from any crisis between Vienna and Belgrade was obvious. That evening the French gave a dinner at the embassy for their Russian hosts. During the meal, a telegram from the French ambassador in Berlin, Jules Cambon, which had been forwarded to St Petersburg, was brought in. Cambon warned, correctly, that Germany would support Austria–Hungary against Serbia and refuse to act as a mediator. All present, especially Sazonov, were worried at this news.

The next day Viviani and Sazonov agreed on joint intervention in Vienna to try to moderate any Austro-Hungarian demands on Serbia. The telegram was sent to Paris for onward transmission but did not arrive there until early on the morning of 24 July (over thirty-six hours after its despatch from St Petersburg) and by then the ultimatum had already been delivered.

London

As in Paris, once the initial shock of the Sarajevo assassinations passed, politicians in London were obsessed with their domestic problems. The death in early July of Joseph Chamberlain, the man who had broken with the Liberals over Home Rule for Ireland and then divided the Conservatives over demands for protectionist tariffs, only seemed to emphasise the growing crisis in Ireland which threatened to plunge Britain into civil war. The Home Rule bill was due to become law about the end of July and discussions were now centred on the terms under which Ulster would be excluded from its operation – what areas were to form part of Ulster and how long that exclusion should last. The heavily armed Protestants in Ulster were on the verge of open revolt and they were supported by elements in the army and by most of the Conservative Party which seemed unworried by the prospect of civil war. During July, negotiations between the parties continued but with little sign that an agreement could be reached.

The diplomats in the Foreign Office were excluded from these debates. The foreign secretary, Sir Edward Grey, was suffering from deteriorating eyesight (partly caused by cataracts) and planned to spend as little time as possible in London (about one visit a fortnight) before going to consult an occulist in Germany in early August. At the beginning of July the diplomats seemed relaxed about the situation. On 5 July the permanent secretary, Nicolson, wrote that he doubted 'whether Austria will take any action of a serious character, and I expect the storm will blow over'.[33] Grey was pleased by the conciliatory attitude of the German ambassador, Lichnowsky, when he saw him on 6 July. Lichnowsky had just returned from a visit to his estates in Silesia. He had stopped in Berlin on both the outward and return journeys on 29 June and 5 July and met Bethmann Hollweg and Zimmerman. However, the chancellor and the acting foreign minister had been less than frank with their ambassador (who they suspected of being too pro-British) and Lichnowsky's reassurances to London that Germany would act as a mediator and restrain Austria–Hungary were wrong. The Foreign Office had doubts about his message, but as Nicolson told de Bunsen in Vienna on 7 July, 'we heard yesterday *privately* that Berlin is most anxious lest Vienna should take measures against Servia of a rather strong character'.[34] When Grey saw Lichnowsky again on 9 July he explained Britain's position – there were no agreements that entailed any 'obligations' to Russia and France although military conversations had taken place. Grey then said he had been trying to 'persuade the Russian Government to adopt a more peaceful view and to assume a more conciliatory attitude toward Austria'. He added that he saw 'no reason for taking a pessimistic view of the situation'.[35] The ambassador in Berlin, Goschen, was on holiday in Britain. On 11 July he wrote to his chargé in Berlin, Sir Horace Rumbold, that he had seen Grey who 'seemed rather nervous as regards Austria and Servia. But I don't think he need be – do you?'[36]

The main worry in the Foreign Office in the first three weeks of July was not Austria–Hungary and Serbia but Britain's relations with Russia. The problem was in Persia, where Britain and Russia had their zones of influence in the south and north of the country respectively with a neutral zone in the middle. Russia seemed to be moving towards the abolition of the neutral zone and its partition – if this happened Russia would secure a port in the Persian Gulf which Britain wanted to avoid. However, they were far from sure that they could stand up to Russia if it meant endangering the security of India and facing threats to British interests elsewhere. As Grey told Buchanan in St Petersburg on 8 June:

> Unless the situation is remedied, and that soon, the whole policy of Anglo-Russian friendship, on which H. M. Government had built, and which was the cornerstone of their foreign relations, would come to a disastrous end.[37]

On 25 June, just three days before the Sarajevo assassinations, Sazonov told Buchanan that he wanted all outstanding Anglo-Russian questions, including Persia, resolved by the end of August.

This demand produced near panic in the Foreign Office and a senior official, Sir George Clerk, was told to draft a position paper which he completed on 21 July. He noted that the primary aim of the 1907 agreement with Russia was 'to check Russia's advance to India and the Gulf' and that therefore 'our Imperial policy requires us to maintain a good understanding with the growing might of Russia'. This growing power meant that the aim of the 1907 agreement could not be sustained in Persia but wider imperial considerations (especially in India) meant that a series of concessions would have to be made to Russia. Clerk set out a series of measures and concluded that these were needed immediately or:

> we shall both endanger our friendship with Russia and find in a comparatively near future that we have sacrificed our whole position in the Persian Gulf and are faced in consequence with a situation where our very existence as an Empire will be at stake.[38]

Sir Edward Grey had not had time to consider the paper before Austria–Hungary precipitated the major diplomatic crisis two days later. But the attitudes behind the paper, and the worries over the British relationship with Russia, illustrate why Britain felt that it had no option but to retain the friendship of France and Russia.

During the third week of July, the British received a number of indications that Austria–Hungary would take drastic action against Serbia and that Germany would support its ally. Nevertheless, Grey remained generally optimistic, relying on the misleading assurances given by Lichnowsky on 6 July. On 16 July de Bunsen in Vienna reported very accurately on what was about to happen:

> The Austro-Hungarian government are in no mood to parley with Servia, but will insist on immediate unconditional compliance, failing which force will be used. Germany is said to be in complete agreement with this procedure.[39]

The next day he sent another telegram revealing his source for this assessment (Count Lützow, who had been Austro-Hungarian ambassador in Rome) and added that Vienna was sure of German support and was 'determined to have her way this time and would refuse to be headed off by anybody'.[40] (De Bunsen was paying one of his rare visits to Vienna – he had been at his estate at Stixenstein since the Archduke's funeral and returned there again on 19 July.)

De Bunsen's information was corroborated on 20 July when the Cabinet minister Lord Haldane, who was generally seen as pro-German, received a letter from Count Hoyos in Vienna trying to justify the action Austria–Hungary was about to take. Haldane forwarded the letter to Grey with his own acute comment:

> This is very serious. Berchtold is apparently ready to plunge Europe into war to settle the Serbian question. He would not take this attitude unless he was assured of German support.[41]

The information from Rumbold, the chargé in Berlin, was that this assessment of the German position was correct. One of the senior officials in the Foreign Office, Sir Edward Crowe (who tended to be anti-German), wrote that the German attitude 'does not bear the stamp of straightforwardness':

> They know what the Austrian Government is going to demand, they are aware that those demands will raise a grave issue, and I think we may say with some assurance that they have expressed approval of these demands and promised support, should dangerous complications ensue.[42]

Just what those complications could be were set out in a telegram from Buchanan on 18 July reporting that 'anything in the shape of an Austrian ultimatum at Belgrade could not leave Russia indifferent, and she might be forced to take some precautionary military measures'.[43]

Rome

By early July diplomatic activity in Rome was declining as the summer heat rose. Most diplomats had left the city. The Italian foreign minister, Marchese Antonio di San Giuliano, was crippled by gout and arthritis and had already departed for the spa of Fiuggi Fonte some fifty miles south-east of the capital. There he shared a hotel with the German ambassador, Hans von Flotow. The British ambassador, Sir James Rennell Rodd, had also left Rome and was on a tour of Tuscany looking for art treasures before he settled for the rest of the summer at the British embassy's villa at Posillipo on the Bay of Naples.

Vienna and Berlin agreed that they would not consult their minor ally over the action to be taken against Serbia. They took this decision for a number of reasons. They thought Italy was too friendly towards Serbia and the other Balkan states and that it would probably leak the details of what was going on to either Serbia or Russia (which is just what the Italians did do). They also thought Italy would want 'compensation' for any territory that Austria–Hungary gained (to which the Italians were entitled under Article VII of the Triple Alliance). Italian actions supported all these doubts. On 14 July San Giuliano told Flotow that 'Italy would not be able to support Austrian claims' and on the next day added that Italy 'could not tolerate' any territorial acquisition by Austria–Hungary.[44] Flotow became convinced that Italy would not support its allies and might even attack Austria–Hungary if it did not get compensation. This assessment caused Berlin to urge Vienna to open discussions with Rome. The initial Austro-Hungarian position was that their actions would not entitle Italy to compensation and therefore they were not even prepared to discuss the matter. However, San Giuliano was determined to see what Vienna might be willing to offer and told the Austro-Hungarian ambassador, Merey (who hated the Italians), that Italy would support Austria-Hungary's demands if they were 'reasonable' (whatever that meant).

Bucharest
Franz Ferdinand had been popular in Bucharest because he was anti-Hungarian and therefore seen (probably wrongly) as a possible supporter of the Romanians in Transylvania. However, the alliance with Germany and Austria–Hungary was not worth the paper it was written on, given the potential disputes between the two countries and the unwillingness of most Romanian politicians to act on the obligations the King had undertaken. The Romanian government's main worry in mid-July was not that they would have to fight alongside

Austria–Hungary but that if the Vienna government did launch an attack on Serbia then the war would spill over to involve the rest of the Balkans. Romania was an ally of Serbia against Bulgaria after the second Balkan War and wanted to keep the gains it had made then. If Bulgaria joined the attack on Serbia then Romania would probably be dragged into the war. Romania might even become a battlefield if Russia joined the war. Neutrality was by far the best option.

During the discussions in Berlin on 5 July between Szögyény and Hoyos and the German government, it was agreed that efforts should be made to bring Bulgaria into the Triple Alliance despite its fundamental differences with Romania. This required careful diplomatic preparation in Bucharest and on 10 July the German chargé, Waldberg, saw King Carol. The King was unenthusiastic, refusing to weaken ties with Serbia and demanding improvements in the conditions of the Romanians in Transylvania before taking any moves that would support Austria–Hungary by seeking agreement with Bulgaria.

Sofia

Vienna and Berlin had more luck with their initiative in Sofia. Despite the agreement in Berlin, Berchtold decided on 8 July not to approach Bulgaria immediately. Instead, the minister in Sofia, Tarnowski, was recalled to Vienna for consultations. When he returned on 16 July, he took with him a draft treaty of alliance based on Bulgarian acceptance of the border with Romania agreed at the Treaty of Bucharest in 1913. (Vienna was still trying to square the circle with these two rival Balkan states.) Tarnowski was told not to approach the Bulgarian government at this time and so when the Bulgarian prime minister suggested renewing discussions on a possible alliance he suggested Bulgaria should put forward its own draft.

The position of the Austro-Hungarian government was set out in a telegram sent to Tarnowski on 23 July for him to use as soon as the crisis broke. He was told that it was essential that Bulgaria remained neutral in any Austro-Hungarian war with Serbia – if Bulgaria attacked Serbia then Romania would help its ally and any chance of localising the war would be lost. To assist in achieving this aim, Tarnowski 'might mention in conversation . . . that at the appropriate moment the Monarchy would bear in mind Bulgaria's historic claim to Macedonia'. (This would be during the planned partition of Serbia.) Meanwhile, the situation for Serbia in the part of Macedonia it had occupied in 1913 could be made worse if the Macedonian terrorists being sheltered by Bulgaria began 'intensive activities', though these should be 'officially disavowed by the Government'. If Romania became actively hostile, then the situation would change radically and Vienna and Berlin would want Bulgaria to attack its neighbours, and in return for this they would 'employ all their resources to obtain the fulfilment of Bulgarian territorial claims'.[45]

Cetinje

On 7 July the Montenegrin government was told by Vienna that one of the Sarajevo conspirators, Mehmedbašić, had fled across the border into the country. He was arrested five days later and taken to the jail in Niksic. On 14 July he escaped and crossed the border into Serbia. The government blamed the escape on the officials in Niksic, but it is more likely that there was government connivance. The escape meant the government no longer had to decide whether to extradite Mehmedbašić to Austria–Hungary.

King Nicholas of Montenegro, as wily as ever, sought to take advantage of what he saw as the inevitable conflict between his two neighbours. Vienna wanted to keep Montenegro neutral in any war with Serbia and on 21 July the Austro-Hungarian minister, Otto, saw both the foreign minister, Plamenac, and King Nicholas. He reassured them that Vienna did not think Montenegro was involved in the Sarajevo plot and would not take any military action against it. As a sweetener he said that Vienna intended to arrange an advance payment of the international loan to the perennially bankrupt country and that it would be made on favourable terms. In response Nicholas set out his terms for neutrality. He said Montenegro had only taken part in the Balkan Wars because they were directed at the Ottomans and he wanted to be friends with Vienna. He suggested territorial gains (Otto thought he envisaged Scutari and northern Albania, exactly the areas Montenegro had lost under Austro-Hungarian pressure in 1913). If this happened 'the danger of union with Serbia would be ended' and Austria–Hungary would gain a friend on whom 'it could uncon- ditionally rely'. (Knowing Nicholas as they did, the Austro-Hungarians were hardly likely to believe that claim.) To make clear the conse- quences of not accepting this blackmail, Nicholas added that the alternative was union with Serbia which would then gain access to the Adriatic and probably take northern Albania too.

Belgrade

The Serbian government was in a difficult position after Sarajevo. Its strong nationalism and the confidence gained from expansion in the Balkan Wars (its population rose by just over a half) was balanced by the weakness of the army which was described by one outside observer as 'a peasant mob'. The government was also weak internally. The crisis of late June, which produced an attempted military coup and a change of monarch, had only just been resolved and Pašić, the prime minister, was fighting an election campaign. Now more than ever he could not afford to be outflanked by the nationalists and groups like *Ujedinjenje ili Smrt* and men like 'Apis'. Neither was he prepared for Serbia to return to its position before 1903 of being an Austro-Hungarian satellite state. In the weeks after Sarajevo, Pašić was passive on the diplomatic front. He hoped that Austria–Hungary would treat the killings as an internal criminal matter and do no more than ask for Serbian help in finding the perpetrators. He was reassured by Vienna's statements that nothing would be done until after the criminal investigation was complete. However, if Austria–Hungary did take action and war was the outcome, then Serbia had no interest in keeping the conflict localised – on their own they would inevitably be defeated. The only chance of Serbian success would be in a wider European war when Austria–Hungary might be defeated and Serbia might then be able to create the 'Greater Serbia' it had long dreamed about.

On one subject the Serbian government was absolutely determined: there could be no investigation of the Sarajevo crime in Serbia. The reasons were obvious. Any investigation would reveal Serbian involvement and the role of 'Apis' and his group. The conspirators were in the Serbian army, some of them at a high level, and Austria–Hungary would never accept that they were acting on their own without formal government approval. Pašić continually rejected suggestions from other powers (Germany, Britain and Italy) that he should hold an inquiry so as to deflect demands from Vienna that they should be involved. The Serbian government could not agree to Austria–Hungary conducting its own investigations in Serbia, not just because it would infringe Serbian sovereignty, but because such investigations might well discover the truth about Sarajevo. Pašić told the Italian chargé (Cora) on 7 July that any such demand from Vienna would be a *'casus belli'*.[46] The chief of the Belgrade police, Vasil Lazarević, did conduct his own inquiry which lasted a week and concluded that there were no Serbian connections with the Sarajevo conspiracy. His conclusions are somewhat surprising because on 25 June he had personally arranged for Ciganović (the man who had supplied the conspirators with weapons) to leave Belgrade and then on the day of the assassinations had removed his name from the official list of railway employees.

The Serbian government also seemed to be doing little to placate Austria–Hungary. On 10 July the Russian minister in Belgrade, Nicholas Hartwig, who had a history of heart problems, collapsed and died while visiting Giesl, the Austro-Hungarian minister. Hartwig was given a state funeral on 14 July, which was attended by most of the Serbian elite. Pašić gave an oration praising Hartwig's services to pan-Slavism and praising Russia as the protector of all Slavs. Three days later the *Leipziger Neueste Nachrichten* published an interview Pašić had given the newspaper just after Hartwig's death. He denied the Serbian government and people had been involved in the assassinations at Sarajevo, spoke of the Austro-Hungarian oppression of the Serbs and said that if Serbia were attacked by a great power then other states would come to its aid. The only action Serbia did take, after strong advice from Russia, was to suspend talks with Montenegro on a possible union, as they would be too provocative to Austria-Hungary.

There were increasing signs that Vienna was going to take a hard line. On 17 July the Serbian minister in London, Bosković, reported that a 'well-informed source' (almost certainly the foreign office after they received de Bunsen's advice from Vienna) advised that Austria–Hungary's peaceful statements should not be believed and that it was planning 'momentous pressure' on Serbia and probably a military attack.[47] Troop movements along the Austro-Hungarian border were also detected. The only substantive action Pašić did take was to send a telegram to all Serbian representatives abroad (with the exception of Vienna) which stated that Serbia could never accept demands that infringed its 'independence and dignity' and asked for help.[48] Pašić was still engrossed in the election campaign. On 20 July he left for a tour of north-east Serbia, returning to Belgrade two days later. He pushed through the appointment of Lazar Paču, the finance minister, as acting prime minister and left by boat for Radujevać and a campaigning visit to southern Serbia.

Vienna and Berlin, 15–22 July

After Tisza had agreed on 14 July that an unacceptable ultimatum could be sent to Serbia, the government in Vienna deliberately set out to lull the rest of Europe into a false sense of security. Conrad and Krobatin went on leave and the newspapers were told not to comment on Serbia. The drafting of the ultimatum was undertaken by Baron Musulin, the head of chancery in the foreign ministry. The main debate was over Article 6. Musulin's original draft only required Serbia to open a judicial inquiry into those Serbians involved in the plot and to prosecute Ciganović and Tankosić. This might have been acceptable to Belgrade. It was Forgach and Berchtold who were determined to make the ultimatum unacceptable and introduced the peremptory wording found in the final ultimatum. The council of ministers, with Conrad, Kailer and Burián also present, met secretly at Berchtold's house on the evening of 19 July, arriving in unmarked cars to avoid detection. The wording of the ultimatum was agreed as was the decision to begin mobilisation as soon as Serbia failed to accept every demand without qualification.

The meeting also accepted Tisza's suggestion that Vienna would issue a declaration that it had no intention of annexing Serbian territory beyond a few frontier 'rectifications' in the hope that this might appease the Russians. But this declaration was riddled with holes and Austria–Hungary could never have been held to it after a successful war against Serbia. The declaration was intended to conceal the aim of ruining Serbia and ending any threat it might pose to Austria–Hungary by putting it into a far worse position than before 1903. The 'rectifications' Berchtold had in mind included pushing Serbia back from the Danube, involving the loss of the capital, Belgrade. The Sabac salient, which jutted out in Bosnia–Herzegovina, would be removed and Austria–Hungary would also take the Negotin area in north-east Serbia to provide a common frontier with Bulgaria. The Sanjak of Novibazar would be reannexed to separate Montenegro and Serbia, and Montenegro would also lose its coastal strip on the Adriatic so that Austria–Hungary had a common frontier with Albania. Bulgaria, Albania and possibly Greece and Romania would be allowed large territorial gains at Serbia's expense. The rump of Serbia would be turned into a tiny mountain kingdom surrounded by enemies. The Karadjordjević dynasty would probably be deposed and Serbia would be forced into a customs union with Austria–Hungary and its railways would be run by Hungary.

The Emperor Franz Josef approved the ultimatum on 21 July but Germany was still trying to find out the exact text. It knew it was intended to be unacceptable and knew some of the demands. Berlin could hardly complain it was being kept in the dark since it had told its ally that it was for them to decide exactly how they dealt with Serbia. The position in Berlin was well set out in a telegram the Bavarian chargé, Schoen, sent to the government in Munich on 18 July. He reported that the foreign office knew of the main demands that would be in the ultimatum but not its complete text. Nevertheless, 'it is perfectly plain that Serbia can not accept any such demands, which are incompatible with her dignity as a sovereign state'. Jagow and Zimmerman were happy for Austria–Hungary to take action 'even at the risk of further complications' because it was 'the sick man of Europe' and only action could cure its weaknesses – 'they are of the opinion here that Austria is face to face with an hour of fate'. Jagow and Zimmerman told Schoen that Germany had to give unconditional support to its only ally because otherwise the long-term trends working to undermine Austria–Hungary would become unstoppable. If Austria–Hungary collapsed then Germany would be left isolated. After the ultimatum was sent, Germany would take diplomatic action to try and ensure localisation of the conflict. As Schoen reported: 'It will claim that the Austrian action has been just as much of a surprise to it as to the other Powers.'[49]

Even before they knew the contents of the ultimatum Germany started taking action. On 19 July an article appeared in the semi-official *North German Gazette* (it had been written by Jagow, the foreign secretary). It spoke of the 'settlement of differences which arise between Austria–Hungary and Serbia' and expressed the hope that they 'should remain localised'. Two days later Bethmann Hollweg sent instructions to the ambassadors in St Petersburg, Paris and London setting out the action they were to take after the ultimatum was delivered. Vienna's position was described as 'fair and moderate' (even though Berlin still did not know the exact text of the memorandum). The ambassadors were to support strongly the Austro-Hungarian position and point out that it might have to take military action 'unless it wishes to dispense for ever with its standing as a Great Power'. After a long-winded justification of Vienna's position they were to stress: 'we urgently desire the localisation of the conflict, as the intervention of any other Power would, as a result of the various alliance obligations, bring about inestimable consequences'. In particular, Pourtalès in St Petersburg was to 'emphasise particularly the view that the problem under discussion is one which it is solely for Austria–Hungary and Serbia to solve'. He should also emphasise the idea of monarchical solidarity and the need to deal 'the death blow to a political radicalism'.[50] The high-risk strategy which Germany was embarking on was well set out in a private letter Jagow sent to Lichnowsky in London. He told him localisation would depend on France and Britain restraining Russia but 'the more boldness Austria displays, the more strongly we support her, the more likely is Russia to keep quiet'.[51]

Germany was also prepared to deceive its allies. On 20 July the Italian ambassador, Bollati, left Berlin for three weeks to take a spa cure after receiving assurances from Jagow that nothing important was likely to happen. It was on the same day that Berlin discovered that Vienna proposed to deliver the ultimatum to Serbia at 5 p.m. on 23 July. The foreign ministry realised that this would be just before Poincaré and his party left St Petersburg and, wishing to leave nothing to chance, advised Vienna to put off the action in Belgrade for another hour. The German ambassador in Vienna was given a copy of the ultimatum on 21 July. However, Tschirschky felt that he had to send it by courier to Berlin. If he sent a telegram containing the text, Vienna would be able to intercept it and, knowing the wording of their own ultimatum, would then be able to break the German diplomatic code. Tschirschky's message arrived in Berlin at 8 p.m. on 22 July, an hour after Szögyény gave a copy of the ultimatum to Jagow. In their memoirs written after the war both Jagow and Bethmann Hollweg claimed that they thought the ultimatum was too strong. In fact, Jagow expressed his agreement.

In Vienna the final preparations that would unleash the diplomatic crisis were being made. The text of the ultimatum was sent to Giesl in Belgrade on 20 July and telegrams went to other ambassadors on how to present the Austro-Hungarian case. In order to minimise the risk that concerted diplomatic action might take place during the forty-eight-hour time limit, the ambassadors were told not to release the text of the ultimatum until the morning of 24 July. Italy, Austria–Hungary's ally, was not to be given the text until then – they would merely be told on 23 July that an ultimatum was being presented. On 20 July Lieutenant Colonel Straub, the head of the railway section in the general staff, began to prepare the railways for war against Serbia. On the next day preparations were made to begin mobilisation immediately Serbia failed to accept the ultimatum.

The government in Vienna was quite clear about the risks it was running. As early as 15 July, Hoyos said privately: 'War has been as good as decided upon . . . if the world war breaks out, it needn't matter to us . . . Germany is in full agreement with us.'[52] On 21 July Berchtold wrote a letter to his old friend Merey, the ambassador in Rome, setting out his thinking. He argued that Austria–Hungary was in an 'exposed position' – Italy was unreliable and jealous, Romania was probably hostile and the Tsar was surrounded by pro-Slav advisers. He admitted that the action about to be taken against Serbia was 'no light one' but 'the responsibility for doing nothing, for letting things take their course till the waves engulf us, seems to me still more grave – if momentarily less arduous'. He was not convinced that the diplomatic triumph that Tisza had argued for would achieve anything – Vienna had gained such successes in 1908–9 and again in 1912–13 but they had had no long-term effect. The aim behind the ultimatum was to show that Austria–Hungary was fully entitled to make demands on Serbia and if the ultimatum was accepted there would be 'a thorough-going purge in Serbia with our co-operation'. If it were rejected there would be 'a settlement by force of arms, followed by the greatest possible weakening of Serbia'.[53]

Austria–Hungary was now ready to take the action that would ignite the European crisis. It felt it was faced by the danger of decline, threatened by Serbia and the long-term changes in the Balkan balance that were working against its position and strengthening that of its rival Russia. If it did not take action after the assassination of the heir to the throne by Serb terrorists (almost certainly aided by Serbia), then its prestige and status might suffer irreparable damage. When it asked its ally for help, Germany was in an almost impossible position. If it argued for moderation in Vienna then its only ally might become so weak as to leave Germany effectively isolated in the European power balance. Berlin decided it had little option but to support its ally in taking action against Serbia. Both Germany and Austria–Hungary realised that it was far from certain that a limited war with Serbia could be fought and that Russia might well intervene. If St Petersburg did decide to take up the challenge and refuse to accept a major diplomatic defeat through a permanent weakening of Serbia, then many in Berlin and Vienna thought it was better to have the war now rather than in a few years when Russian rearmament and railway construction would make them far stronger. It was a high-risk strategy that was reckless in its willingness to risk a European war for the purpose of destroying Serbia. It placed much of the onus for escalating any crisis into a European war on the government in St Petersburg and its attitude to the likely humiliation and dismemberment of its client.

PART THREE

The Thirteen Days

6

THURSDAY 23 JULY

Vienna – Morning/Afternoon
There was only desultory activity in the Austro-Hungarian capital. The ultimatum had been sent to Giesl in Belgrade and advice sent to the ambassadors in the other European capitals. Nothing could be done now but wait until the early evening when the diplomatic crisis would be initiated. Berchtold and Conrad had an inconclusive discussion about the situation. The foreign minister said he was worried about the attitude of Italy and Conrad then said that mobilisation should not start if Italy might intervene – Austria–Hungary could not fight a three-front war. Yet ministers in Vienna had already agreed that mobilisation would start as soon as Serbia failed to accept the Austro-Hungarian terms and before they knew how Italy, let alone Russia, would react. The two men consoled themselves with the thought that Serbia might yield shortly after mobilisation began, thus resolving Vienna's dilemmas.

Rome
Austria–Hungary had decided that Italy could not be given a copy of the ultimatum before it was delivered. The ambassador, Merey, was ill and so it was his deputy, Count Ambrozy, who drove over to Fiuggi to see San Giuliano at 4 p.m. Ambrozy merely said that an ultimatum would shortly be delivered in Belgrade and that it would have a forty-eight-hour time limit. San Giuliano refused to make any comments before he saw the contents of the ultimatum, which Ambrozy promised he would see the next day. The Italian foreign minister did, however, ask whether Vienna proposed to make any annexation of Serbian territory (which would, under Article VII of the Triple Alliance, allow Italy to claim 'compensation'). Ambrozy said Austria–Hungary could not make any commitments and San Giuliano replied that if it did forgo annexation then it would help Italy 'keep in step' with its allies.[1]

San Giuliano was more forthright when he saw Flotow, the German ambassador. He said Italian public opinion, which supported Serbia and its national claims because of the resonance this had for Italian history, would make it difficult for Italy to support Austria–Hungary. He also said, correctly, that it was 'contrary to the spirit of the Triple Alliance to have undertaken such action without first taking counsel with allies'.[2] Vienna and Berlin had done nothing to placate their nominal ally and the initial reaction in Rome must have deepened their suspicion that nothing but trouble with Italy lay ahead. San Giuliano decided to stay at Fiuggi.

Bucharest

Romania received better treatment than Italy. The ambassador, Czernin, had obtained Berchtold's agreement to see King Carol at the same time as the ultimatum was delivered in Belgrade and to read him the text. (The King had already been warned by the Italian minister, Fasciotti, that morning about what was going to happen and was told that he ought to try and moderate Vienna's demands.) King Carol's immediate reaction to Czernin was that there would be a European war within a week. As Czernin reported to Vienna, the King's sympathies 'are on our side but he knows that his country will not make it easy for him to carry out the treaty of alliance'. The King was worried that if Serbia was defeated then Bulgaria would make large gains, so Czernin tried some delicate bribery by suggesting 'Romania can perhaps get something too' (presumably at Serbia's expense).[3] Vienna had tried to be slightly more accommodating towards Romania than to Italy but its efforts had little impact.

London

Political attention was still focused on the Ulster crisis where last-ditch talks were underway at Buckingham Palace under King George V's nominal chairmanship. The chancellor of the exchequer, David Lloyd George, spoke in a debate in the House of Commons about foreign affairs and reported that relations with Germany were 'very much better' than they had been 'a few years ago'. He concluded that 'the two great Empires begin to realise that the points of cooperation are greater and more numerous than the points of possible controversy'.[4]

At the Foreign Office, Sir Edward Grey saw the Austrian ambassador, Count Albert Mensdorff-Pouilly-Dietrichstein, a cousin of the late Edward VII. Grey distrusted the ambassador, but

Mensdorff, with Berchtold's permission, gave him an outline of the terms of the ultimatum, though not its actual text. Berchtold had agreed to this because he wanted to pre-empt Grey giving advice about what Vienna should do. Grey demonstrated for the first time a central feature of his actions over the next few days. He was very slow to appreciate the dimensions of the problem and hence made a number of mistakes that only worsened the situation. He told Mensdorff that it would be terrible if the four great powers – Austria–Hungary, Germany, Russia and France – were involved in war. Vienna, not surprisingly, read this as an indication that Britain would remain neutral in any European war. This was bound to increase their willingness to run risks. The ambassador in Berlin, Goschen, was still on holiday in Britain and he dined with Mensdorff that evening. He noted in his diary that 'Austria means business – and personally I doubt whether anything will stop her'. He added that Mensdorff told him that this time Austria–Hungary 'would certainly move'.[5]

Across London an even more momentous dinner was taking place. A few days earlier Berlin had sent Albert Ballin, the head of the Hamburg-Amerika shipping line, to London. Ballin, who had the confidence of the Kaiser and the political elite in London, had been used on numerous occasions in the past for informal discussions about Anglo-German naval matters. He was sent to discuss the state of the negotiations for an Anglo-Russian naval convention to which Berlin was strongly opposed. His other task was to sound out the British about their attitude to the European situation. That evening he dined with Lord Haldane (the Cabinet minister who was most sympathetic to Germany), Sir Edward Grey and the ageing Lord Morley, who had once been Gladstone's private secretary and was now Lord Privy Seal. Haldane's account of the meeting, written some years after the end of the war, is unreliable when it states that Ballin was warned that Germany should not attack France. A letter Ballin wrote to Haldane a few days after the dinner explains that Haldane told him 'in your very clear manner' that Britain would only intervene militarily in a continental war 'if the balance of power were to be greatly altered by German annexation of French territory'.[6] This was compatible with Grey's statement to Mensdorff earlier in the day but in a more extreme form. Grey was present and does not seem to have intervened to correct any misapprehension Ballin may have gained. The views expressed at this dinner, and other indications given later, convinced Berlin to continue with its highly risky diplomatic policy, on the reasonable assumption that Britain would remain neutral in any major European war.

St Petersburg

The state visit by President Poincaré was now drawing to a close. The last event was a dinner on board *France* for the Tsar, Tsarina and members of the imperial court. Poincaré thought the meal was mediocre. After the final farewells (the Tsar promised to pay a return visit in the summer of 1915) the French warships left Kronstadt harbour for Stockholm and the next part of the tour. The French party had, as Vienna and Berlin intended, left Russian waters before any news of the ultimatum reached St Petersburg. That news arrived very late in the evening when the counsellor at the Italian embassy, Count Montereale, told Butzov, a foreign ministry official, that Austria–Hungary was presenting an unacceptable note to Serbia. He did not, however, know the contents and no action was taken in the Russian capital that evening.

Belgrade

The capital of Serbia was a town with a population of about 100,000 (a third of the size of its fellow Balkan capital Bucharest) and its streets and town square, which had been laid out by two French architects in 1911, were usually jammed with ox carts. Facilities were still primitive – the Hotel Imperial had no baths, though the Grant Hotel did have electricity. Over a quarter of the population were employed by the government. With the forthcoming elections due to be held in 1 August, Pašić was away campaigning and the most senior Cabinet minister left in the capital, Stojan Protić, was at home with a bad foot.

The carefully planned Austro-Hungarian action caught the Serbian government unawares when, at 4.30 p.m. Giesl telephoned the foreign ministry to say that he had an important message to deliver to Prime Minister Pašić at exactly 6 p.m. The only senior minister available, the fat, chain-smoking Lazar Paču (the finance minister), tried to locate Pašić. The prime minister was making election speeches in Zaječar, Knjaževac and Niš accompanied by Sajinović, the head of the political section of the foreign ministry. He was waiting to leave Niš station when the stationmaster summoned him to his office to take a telephone call from Paču shortly after 4.30 p.m. Pašić guessed that Giesl would be delivering a series of demands about Sarajevo. Not knowing of the forty-eight-hour time limit, he thought it would be best to play for time while the Serbian government consulted its friends and diplomacy had some time to work. He refused to return to Belgrade and decided to set off for Salonika in Greece. His coach was attached to the regular train and, together with Sajinović, he set off southwards, away from the capital.

Meanwhile, in Belgrade, Lazar Paču was left with unenviable task of seeing the Austro-Hungarian minister. At the meeting Paču was accompanied by Slavko Gruić, the secretary-general of the foreign ministry. He was needed because Paču did not speak French – the language of European diplomacy (the Austro-Hungarian ultimatum was delivered to Serbia in a French text). At exactly 6 p.m. Giesl handed over the ultimatum and told Paču that the terms had to be answered and accepted within forty-eight hours and that if this was not done he had orders to leave Belgrade immediately and break off diplomatic relations. He also specified that the Serbian reply was to be in both a French and Serbian text so that the two could be compared – Vienna suspected that Belgrade might try to wriggle out of its commitments through deliberate mistranslation. Knowing that Pašić was not returning to Belgrade, Paču tried to play for time by saying that it would be difficult to assemble the Serbian cabinet because of the forthcoming elections. Giesl refused to accept these excuses, saying Serbia was a small country with railways and that anyway it was not his problem. Giesl left to return to his legation.

Gruić translated the ultimatum for Paču who then showed it to two other ministers who were waiting in an adjoining room. What they read shocked and alarmed them. (The full text of the ultimatum is in Appendix A.) The Serbian government was told that in March 1909 they had formally stated that none of their rights had been touched by Vienna's annexation of Bosnia–Herzegovina and that they would therefore change their policy towards Austria–Hungary and 'live in future on terms of friendly and neighbourly relations'. The ultimatum stated that Serbia had not followed this policy and had not suppressed the Greater Serbia movement nor its propaganda. It went on to say that the confessions of the conspirators 'prove that the murder of Sarajevo was prepared in Belgrade'. (An annex to the note gave detailed evidence of this.) As a result Austria–Hungary now required the Serbian government to take certain actions. The first, to take place on 26 July, would be for the King to issue a declaration to the army, and the second, for the government to publish on the first page of the official gazette a statement drafted by Vienna and set out in the ultimatum. Both Serbian statements would condemn propaganda directed against Austria–Hungary, express regret at the horrible consequences of the ambition to annex Bosnia–Herzegovina and that officials had taken part in the conspiracy. Finally, they would warn of harsh action to be taken against any repetition of these actions.

The Serbian government was to give nine specific undertakings. First, to suppress all publications hostile to Austria–Hungary. Second, to dissolve *Narodna Odbrana* and seize its assets together with those of similar organisations. (Austria–Hungary knew about *Ujedinjenje ili Smrt* but felt it could not ask for the dissolution of a secret society whose existence could be denied.) Third, to eliminate all teachers and school books hostile to Austria–Hungary. Fourth, to remove from the army and civil service all those involved in propaganda against Austria–Hungary – the names of those involved would be supplied by the Vienna government. Fifth, to allow Austro-Hungarian officials to assist Serbia in suppressing the subversive movement against Austria–Hungary. Sixth, to establish a judicial inquiry against those involved in the Sarajevo conspiracy and accept that Austro-Hungarian officials 'will take an active part in these inquiries'. Seventh, to arrest Tankosić and Ciganović. Eighth, to stop officials engaging in arms smuggling across the border and to dismiss and severely punish those who helped the conspirators. Finally, to give an explanation of the anti-Austro-Hungarian remarks made by Serbian officials after Sarajevo.

Although no formal meeting of the Serbian cabinet took place that evening, a group of six ministers met to consider the ultimatum. There was general agreement that it could not accepted. According to Gruić, Ljuba Jovanović, the minister for public instruction, summed up the general mood when he said 'we have no other choice than to fight it out'.[7] The first action of the Serbian government was to turn to its protector, Russia. Pač2, as the senior minister, immediately left for the Russian legation where he saw the chargé, Strandtmann, and asked for Russian help. Stradtmannn agreed to send a telegram to St Petersburg – it did not arrive until the next morning. Pač2 then went to see the Regent, Alexander, who said that the note meant European war. He consulted other members of the royal family and it was agreed to send a telegram to all Serbian representatives abroad explaining that the 'demands are such that no Serbian government could accept them in full'.[8] It was also agreed that Pašić should be summoned back to

Belgrade. His train was stopped at Lescovac where the stationmaster handed him a telegram from Alexander recalling him to the capital. Pašić's train was turned round and he headed back to Belgrade. Gruić tried to send telegrams to three of the stops en route with the main points of the ultimatum but could not get the messages to the stations. That night Pašić had only the most general idea about the contents of the ultimatum.

Meanwhile, in Belgrade, ministers decided to start military preparations – they expected Austria–Hungary to attack as soon as the ultimatum expired. The first problem was to assemble the army high command. The chief of staff, Putnik, was actually in Austria, taking the waters at the spa of Gleighenberg in Styria. He was recalled as was his deputy who was also abroad. (Austria–Hungary made no attempt to impede Putnik's return.) The minister of war, Dušan Stefanović, consulted the acting head of the army, Colonel Pavlović, and they agreed to initiate the preliminary measures for mobilisation. All divisional commanders were called up and the five regiments in the north of the country were told to prepare assembly points for mobilisation. The major problem the army commanders faced was that most of the Serbian forces, which were in a very poor condition, were engaged in 'pacifying' the new province of Macedonia and because of the poor transport network it would take a long time to move these units to the north. Nevertheless, the first military moves of the crisis had been made.

Vienna – evening

News of the ultimatum broke in the Habsburg capital in the early evening. There was little immediate action and no signs of public jubilation. The socialist leader, Friedrich Adler contacted Camille Huysmans, the secretary of the International Socialist Bureau, in Brussels to say that it was unlikely that the forthcoming congress could be held in Vienna. Huysmans got in touch with the Swiss socialists about moving the congress to Berne. Elsewhere in the city, the founder of psychoanalysis, Siegmund Freud (who had just suffered the defection of two of his disciples – Adler and Jung), wrote: 'For the first time in thirty years I feel myself to be an Austrian and feel like giving this not very hopeful Empire another chance.' He thought the ultimatum was 'deliverance through a bold-spirited deed' and added in his own inimitable fashion: 'All my libido is given to Austria–Hungary'.[9]

Berlin – Evening

News of the ultimatum produced little reaction in the German capital. The socialist Karl Kautsky wrote to his colleague in Vienna, Victor Adler:

> The ultimatum was a great surprise to me. It came quite unexpectedly. I thought that old Franz Josef and the young one [Archduke Charles] wanted to be 'left in peace'. Now we suddenly have a declaration of war because that is precisely what the ultimatum is. It is war, local war between Austria and Serbia.[10]

Kautsky was shrewd about the purpose of the ultimatum but optimistic about the likely consequences. Bethmann Hollweg was also optimistic, writing to the Kaiser that even if there was a European war 'it is improbable that England will *immediately* enter the fray'.[11]

Across the city the young Czech writer Franz Kafka had been to his fiancée's house to break off their engagement just a month before the wedding. He then sat alone on a bench on the Unter den Linden before joining his fiancée's sister for dinner at the Restaurant Belvedere on the Strahlau Brücke.

At the war ministry General Waldersee, the deputy chief of the general staff, returned to his desk from holiday and ordered the start of more intensive intelligence gathering on Russia. Instructions to keep a close eye on all Russian activities were sent to intelligence units along the eastern border.

7

FRIDAY 24 JULY

Across Europe that morning the various foreign ministries only knew that Austria–Hungary had sent an ultimatum to Serbia. Not until later in the day did they find out about its contents in detail. As Vienna had intended, the time available for any concerted diplomatic action was therefore very limited. The most frantic activity took place in Belgrade as the Serbian government decided how to respond. However, the most fundamental decisions were taken in St Petersburg. It was the response of the Russian government at the very start of the crisis that demolished the highly risky strategy agreed in Vienna and Berlin and helped ensure that the diplomatic crisis resulted in a European war.

Belgrade

Pašić arrived back at Belgrade station shortly after 5 a.m. He read the full text of the ultimatum and realised immediately the difficult position in which it placed Serbia. His first action was to go to the Russian legation where he saw Strandtmann. The chargé reported to St Petersburg that Pašić thought it was 'not possible either to accept or reject the Austrian note' and that more time was needed for diplomatic action. However, he said, 'if war is unavoidable we shall fight', though he added that Belgrade would not be defended.[1] The Serbian cabinet met for an hour at 10 a.m. and although no records were kept of any of its meetings it seems clear that it agreed to reject most of the Austrian demands, especially that requiring the dissolution of the societies promoting the Greater Serbia idea. The cabinet agreed that the Regent should make a direct appeal to the Tsar. The attitude of Russia was bound to be crucial for Serbia. Russia was its protector against Austria–Hungary but that did not mean that support would automatically be forthcoming – in the crises of 1909 and 1912 Russia had advised Belgrade to back down. Alexander appealed to Nicholas II as the protector of the Slavs and of a defenceless Serbia which was about to be attacked. Alexander's appeal said that the Austro-Hungarian note was humiliating but Serbia might agree to any terms that were consistent with its sovereignty or any which Russia advised them to accept and 'those advised by Your Majesty after taking cognizance of them'.[2] Although this was an obvious attempt to pass the responsibility on to Russia, it is clear that if Russia had advised Serbia to accept all the conditions without qualification then Belgrade would have little alternative but to do so.

While the Serbian government was waiting for the Russian reply it tried to assess the diplomatic situation – the outlook was certainly not optimistic. At 11 a.m. Pašić saw Lazar Mijusković, the Montenegrin minister, who promised solidarity. Pašić, who had long experience of Montenegrin duplicity, did not believe him. The minister in Vienna, Jovanović, was asked to sound out Austro-Hungarian intentions which Giesl had refused to discuss the previous evening. Jovanović was able to report nothing more than that Berchtold expected a 'satisfactory reply' before the deadline. If this were not forthcoming, Jovanović advised that war seemed very likely.[3] Pašić assumed, correctly, that Serbia's allies from the Balkan Wars (Greece and Romania) would not provide any help unless Bulgaria intervened and tried to alter the settlement agreed in the Treaty of Bucharest from which all three countries benefited. (Telegrams were sent that evening to the Serbian representatives in Bucharest, Athens and Cetinje instructing them to report on how these governments might react.) The British minister in Belgrade, Des Graz, was away on holiday and so Pašić saw the chargé, Crackanthorpe, to ask if Britain might be able to moderate Vienna's demands. Pašić was unable to speak to a French representative because on 1 July he had asked the French government to recall their minister, Descos. He had done so because of his too honest reporting, especially about the activities of 'Apis' and his group of conspirators. Descos had left Belgrade on 14 July and his replacement, Boppe (who had been specifically requested by the Serbian government), did not arrive in Belgrade until the morning of 25 July.

The Serbian cabinet met again in the afternoon when it agreed that Alexander should send another personal telegram, this time to his uncle the King of Italy. He was asked to urge Austria–Hungary to extend the time limit.[4] The cabinet also agreed further military measures. The bridges over the Sava river were mined, the military took over control of the railways, the first levy of reserve troops was called up and arrangements were also put in hand for the evacuation of the government from Belgrade to Niš. During the evening the cabinet was in almost continual session as Pašić and Stojan Protić (the interior minister) prepared drafts of the reply to Austria–Hungary. Already there were some signs of movement away from outright rejection. It was agreed that *Narodna Odbrana* would be dissolved (point two) and that officials guilty of anti-Austro-Hungarian propaganda would be dismissed (point four) but subject to the Sarajevo inquiry proving their guilt. The strategy which Pašić was to follow in the reply agreed the next day was already clear: Serbia would agree to most of the demands in the ultimatum but put in caveats that would render them almost useless.

Vienna

There was surprisingly little activity in the Austro-Hungarian capital on the day after the delivery of the ultimatum. In the morning Berchtold saw the Russian chargé, Prince Kudaschev, to explain the ultimatum. Berchtold had the effrontery to claim that 'there was nothing further from our mind than to humiliate Serbia' and that he had personally eliminated from the note everything of that kind. The note, he explained, was merely designed to stop Serbia supporting the Greater Serbia movement and to enable Austria–Hungary to check that it was doing so. Kudaschev had no instructions from St Petersburg and so merely expressed his personal opinion that it would be a violation of international law to have the Austro-Hungarian government acting within Serbia.[5] In his report to St Petersburg Kudaschev was frank in his assessment. He said that Vienna 'plainly considers that her demands can be met and is prepared to risk armed conflict in the event of rejection'. He reported that Berchtold had said 'Austria–Hungary had to give proof of her stature as a Great Power, essential to the balance of power in Europe, by an outright *coup de force*'. Berchtold argued that Russia could not want the collapse of Austria–Hungary even though this was what Serbia wanted.[6]

In parallel with this discussion Berchtold despatched a courier by train to St Petersburg with a coded message for the ambassador Szápáry (the courier arrived on the afternoon of 27 July). The ambassador was instructed to give Sazonov a series of misleading undertakings. He was to say that Austria–Hungary was 'territorially saturated and does not covet Serbian possessions' and neither did it intend any 'infringement of the sovereignty of Serbia'. It was hoped that these assurances might induce Russia to give Austria–Hungary a free hand in dealing with Serbia. If this was not the case, Szápáry was to make the explicit threat that Vienna would go to 'extreme lengths' to obtain fulfilment of its demands and that it would not 'recoil from the possibility of European complications.'[7]

Berchtold, probably suspecting that Serbia might try to give a qualified acceptance of the ultimatum to buy more time and ultimately wriggle out of Vienna's demands, sent a message to Giesl to reinforce what he had told him earlier. The minister in Belgrade was instructed that 'any conditional acceptance or one accompanied by reservations is to be regarded as a refusal' and must therefore be followed by the breaking-off of diplomatic relations and his departure.[8]

Berlin

In Berlin, as in Vienna, there was little activity. The intelligence staff instructed its units along the French border to be on the alert and to gather as much intelligence as possible. The main diplomatic event was the meeting which the French ambassador, Jules Cambon, requested with Jagow. Jagow lied and told Cambon that Germany had been unaware of the terms of the ultimatum, though he did add that it supported them. Jagow expected 'a little excitement' ('*un peu d'émotion*' in the original) from Serbia's friends but argued they should give 'wise advice'. Responding to this opening, Cambon said that Germany should give similar 'wise advice' in Vienna. Jagow replied that the problem had to be localised between Austria–Hungary and Serbia. In his report to Paris, Cambon wondered about the high-risk policy Vienna and Berlin had adopted: 'If what is happening is the result of due reflection, I do not understand why all means of retreat have been cut off.'[9]

The British chargé, Rumbold, saw Cambon after this meeting and reported that Cambon thought, correctly, that Vienna and Berlin 'are playing a dangerous game of bluff, and they think they can carry matters through with a high hand.'[10]

Paris

The French government was in disarray with its two senior figures sailing across the Baltic on the *France* bound for Stockholm. It was difficult to communicate with the battleship and as Poincaré wrote in his diary 'little by little we receive fragmentary wireless messages, disquieting in their confusion and obscurity'.[11] Nevertheless, Poincaré,

Viviani and de Margerie discussed the situation and devised a telegram to be sent to St Petersburg for onward transmission to Paris and London. Serbia was advised to accept as much as possible of the ultimatum that was compatible with its honour and to seek a twenty-four-hour extension of the time limit. France was to support this request in Vienna and Russia, France and Britain should suggest an international inquiry into the assassinations. Given the time delays involved, there was little chance that this telegram would have any effect.

In Paris the foreign ministry had been placed in the hands of Bienvenu-Martin, the minister of justice, while Poincaré and Viviani were on their state visit. He had no experience of diplomacy and usually only visited the Quai d'Orsay for about three-quarters of an hour each day. His main adviser was Philippe Berthelot, the deputy head of the foreign ministry. (It was not until the evening that Paul Cambon, the ambassador in London and the brother of the ambassador in Berlin, was instructed to go to Paris and assist Bienvenu-Martin until Poincaré and Viviani returned.) The Austro-Hungarian ambassador, Szécsen, called an Bienvenu-Martin to carry out Vienna's instructions on elucidating the ultimatum. Szécsen reported that Bienvenu-Martin thought 'energetic action' by Austria–Hungary 'could be understood', although he was 'most surprised' at the content of point five about Austro-Hungarian officials acting within Serbia. Nevertheless, he thought 'it was Serbia's duty to take energetic steps against possible accomplices of the murderer of Sarajevo' and he 'expressed the hope that the dispute will be peacefully settled in a manner agreeable to our wishes'. Szécsen added that Bienvenu-Martin 'avoided any attempt to defend or extenuate in any way the attitude of Serbia'.

Szécsen concluded his report to Vienna: 'Monsieur Bienvenu-Martin has of course no influence whatever on the course of foreign policy in France'.[12] This assessment was correct but Bienvenu-Martin's conciliatory words and pro-Austro-Hungarian sentiments were not simply those of a man inexperienced in diplomacy and not representing French policy correctly (even though his approach did differ from that of the hardline nationalist President Poincaré). Szécsen sent a second telegram to Berchtold later in the evening. He explained that Berthelot had also been present at the discussion with Bienvenu-Martin and had said 'the Serbian Government ought at once to declare its acceptance of the note in principle, but ask for explanations and further details on certain points'.[13]

The German ambassador, Schoen, was also reassured when he saw Bienvenu-Martin later in the day. He reported the French minister was 'visibly relieved at our idea that Austro-Serbian conflict was one to be settled exclusively by the two participants. French Government sincerely shares the wishes that conflict remain localised.' However, Bienvenu-Martin did say that Russia would find it difficult to stand aside and also suggested that if the Serbian reply was broadly satisfactory then Vienna should negotiate over the details. Berlin and Vienna could easily interpret these indications from Paris as suggesting that their strategy was working – France seemed to be sympathetic, advising Serbia to be conciliatory and therefore perhaps it might act to restrain Russia.

When the Serbian minister, Vesnic, called on Berthelot (he did not have enough status to see Bienvenu-Martin) and asked for advice, he can hardly have been reassured by the response. Berthelot merely gave his personal opinion that 'Serbia should try to gain time'. It should also offer 'immediate satisfaction' on most points, ask for proof of the Austro-Hungarian allegations and offer to submit the dispute to great power mediation.

London

The morning newspaper reaction was strongly favourable to Austro-Hungary. All condemned the Serbian government and some, such as the liberal *Manchester Guardian* and *Daily Chronicle*, thought Vienna's action was justifiable. The British government took much the same line with Serbia as did the French. The instructions sent to Crackanthorpe in Belgrade were that it was unclear whether Austro-Hungarian military action could be avoided but the 'only chance was to give a favourable reply on as many points as possible' and that Serbia should give the 'fullest satisfaction'.[14]

Around midday Mensdorff called on Grey to give him the full text of the ultimatum. Grey commented that point five surely compromised Serbian sovereignty and, according to Mensdorff, called the note 'the most formidable document that was ever addressed from one state to another'. But he admitted that 'what it said on the guilt of Serbia in the crime of Sarajevo and some of our demands were fully justified'. He also told Mensdorff that he was worried by the situation the ultimatum had created and by the danger that it could lead to a European war.[15] However, despite these fears, Grey did not ask for any extension of the time limit in the ultimatum.

Now that the expected crisis had begun Grey needed to decide what position Britain should adopt. Some Foreign Office officials already saw the issue as a struggle between the alliances and thought Britain should side with France and Russia. The permanent secretary, Nicolson, inclined to this view but saw the problem in the wider imperial context of security of India and the Persian Gulf: 'Our attitude . . . will be regarded by Russia as a test and we must be most careful not to alienate her.'[16] The danger of openly siding with France and Russia was that it would simply make them more intransigent because of the knowledge that they could rely on Britain even in the event of war. The opposite course of declaring neutrality from the beginning would merely make Germany and Austria–Hungary more intransigent. Perhaps the best course was that suggested by Buchanan, the ambassador in St Petersburg, when Sazonov asked for strong British support for Russia and France. Buchanan said he did not think that was possible but, as he reported to Grey:

> I thought you might be prepared to represent strongly at Vienna and Berlin danger to European peace of an Austrian attack on Servia. You might perhaps point out that it would in all probability force Russia to intervene, that this would bring Germany and France into the field, and that if war became general, it would be difficult for England to remain neutral.[17]

This telegram did not arrive in London until 8 p.m. and by then Grey had already embarked on a course which significantly increased the likelihood of German and Austro-Hungarian intransigence by hinting that Britain would stay neutral.

Early in the afternoon Grey saw Paul Cambon. Their meetings were usually difficult. Although Cambon had been the ambassador in London since 1898, he did not like Britain, returned to Paris every fortnight and refused to speak English. Grey could not speak French. In their conversations the two men spoke in their own language and tried as best they could to understand what the other was saying. Grey told Cambon that he would be seeing the German ambassador, Lichnowsky, later in the day. At that meeting he would suggest mediation of the dispute between Vienna and Belgrade by the four major powers not directly involved – Germany, France, Britain and Italy. This was a revival of the process which had been used during the Balkan Wars. It suffered, however, from a fatal defect – it assumed that Germany was prepared to act as a moderating influence over its ally.

All the indications that Grey had received in the days leading up to the ultimatum were that Germany had changed tack and was on this occasion supporting its ally. Grey was therefore wasting his time in trying to revive the tacit cooperation between London and Berlin which had worked reasonably well some eighteen months earlier.

After his talk with Cambon, Grey walked through the archway connecting the Foreign Office and Downing Street for a short meeting of the cabinet which lasted from 3.15 until 4.10. It had been called to discuss the collapse of the talks on Ulster at Buckingham Palace and the total impasse which the government now faced. Civil war was much closer. It was only at the very end of the meeting that Grey mentioned the European situation. According to the prime minister, Asquith, Grey told his colleagues it was 'the gravest event for many years past in Europe'.[18] As usual Asquith spent most of the meeting writing a letter to Venetia Stanley who was his regular correspondent and probably also his lover. He told her the situation was 'about as bad as it can possibly be', that Serbia would reject the ultimatum and then the great powers would be involved. Therefore 'we are within measurable, or imaginable distance of a real Armageddon'. Surprisingly, Asquith was sanguine about Britain's position and concluded 'happily there seems to be no reason why we should be anything more than spectators'.[19] Asquith then made a brief statement in the House of Commons about the situation in Ulster, went to have a haircut and spent the evening playing bridge.

After the meeting Grey saw Lichnowsky. He told him that 'if the Austrian ultimatum to Servia did not lead to trouble between Austria and Russia I had no concern with it'. This was, of course, very close to the German position that the conflict should remain localised between Vienna and Belgrade. Grey said he was worried by how Russia might react but that Britain could exercise almost no influence in St Petersburg, adding that he did not think Russia would advise Serbia to accept the ultimatum. He then made his suggestion for four-power mediation 'in the event of the relations between Austria and Russia becoming threatening'.[20] He hoped Berlin would try to stop Vienna embarking on military action. He then, according to Lichnowsky's account of the meeting, said:

> The danger of a European war, should Austria invade Serbian territory, would become immediate. The results of such a war between four nations – he expressly emphasised the number four, and meant by it Russia, Austria-Hungary, Germany and France – would be absolutely incalculable.

Grey's words were bound to reinforce still further the German impression that Britain would remain neutral in a European conflict and this is exactly how they were interpreted in Berlin. The Kaiser wrote on his copy of the telegram: 'He forgets Italy.'[21] The two hints that Grey gave in this conversation – that Britain would be happy with a localised war and that it would remain neutral – were bound to increase the optimism in Berlin that its high-risk strategy might be working. Even if Germany and Austria–Hungary did face war with France and Russia, their chances of winning would be greatly strengthened if Britain kept out of the conflict.

After Grey had left the Foreign Office to have dinner at his club, a message arrived from Mensdorff asking to see Grey urgently. The foreign secretary was not recalled but instead the chief clerk, Montgomery, called at the embassy on his way home. Mensdorff told him he had had a telegram from Vienna to say that the note to Serbia was not an 'ultimatum' but a démarche with a time limit. If it was rejected, Austria–Hungary would break off relations and begin military preparations, though not military operations. This was an accurate statement of the Austro-Hungarian position and it seemed to give plenty of time for diplomacy to work. In Grey's absence the officials at the Foreign Office sent telegrams to the ambassadors in the major capitals saying 'the immediate situation seems less acute'. Only now was de Bunsen in Vienna finally asked to seek an extension of the time limit in the ultimatum.

Rome

Austria–Hungary did not give the text of the ultimatum to its ally until just before noon when Count Ambrozy handed a copy to the secretary-general of the foreign ministry, Giacomo de Martino. He telephoned the text to San Giuliano who was still at Fiuggi, crippled with gout. The situation following the delivery of the ultimatum was discussed at a meeting lasting several hours between San Giuliano, the prime minister Antonio Salandra and Flotow. Italy faced a number of possible options: it could openly support its allies and argue it should be rewarded for this support with some 'compensation', or it could openly declare that the Austro-Hungarian action was designed to provoke a war which would, under the terms of the Triple Alliance, be a war of aggression which Italy was not bound to support. (Under the terms of the 1902 agreement with

France, Italy had already secretly pledged its neutrality in such a war.)

During the discussion at Fiuggi that afternoon the Italians decided against such a policy in favour of a more mendacious approach. Telegrams were drafted for the ambassadors in Berlin and Vienna telling them that Austria–Hungary had no right to deliver the ultimatum without consulting its allies and that its content showed Vienna 'means to provoke a war'. The German ambassador had therefore been told that Italy 'is under no obligation to go to the help of Austria' even if it was at war with Russia 'since any European war in this case is the consequence of an act of provocation and aggression by Austria'. However, Italy might still take part in such a war if it was in its interest to do so. Public opinion made it difficult to support Vienna and therefore Italy could not join a war unless the government could 'give the country beforehand the certitude of an advantage commensurate with the risks'. This would involve Vienna accepting Italy's interpretation of Article VII of the Triple Alliance and giving it 'compensation'.[22] Italy's position (which it retained for the rest of the crisis) was that Austria–Hungary was provoking an unjust aggressive war which it was under no obligation to support unless it was given enough 'compensation' in which case Italy would regard it as a legitimate defensive war.

In his report to Berlin Flotow described the meeting as 'a rather excited conversation of several hours'. His only achievement was to stop the Italians from issuing any statement about the ultimatum. He argued for unity within the Triple Alliance but concluded 'the only way of holding Italy is to promise her compensations in good time'. The Kaiser's comment was that 'the little thief must always get his bit to gobble up as well'.[23] The next day Flotow sent an even franker letter to Bethmann Hollweg which arrived in Berlin on 27 July. The ambassador thought three factors were determining Italian policy: 'fear of Italian public opinion'; 'the consciousness of military weakness'; and 'the desire to turn the occasion to good account and win something for Italy, if possible the Trentino'. The problem with the latter aim was that the Trentino was Austrian and it was difficult to see that Vienna would be prepared to give up its own territory in the aftermath of a successful war against Serbia. The alternative was for Italy to take sides against Austria–Hungary in the hope of gaining territory that way. Flotow gained the clear impression, although it was not 'directly expressed' by San Giuliano, that Italy might indeed turn against its ally. The ambassador advised Berlin that 'active help from Italy in any European conflict that may arise is scarcely to be counted on' and that its active hostility could only be averted by a 'wise policy' in Vienna.[24]

After the meeting San Giuliano wrote to the King telling him Italy's main aim was 'to assure ourselves of eventual compensations for any increase of territory whatsoever on the part of Austria'.[25] At 9.15 p.m. that evening the Italian ambassador in Berlin, Riccardo Bollati, called at the Wilhelmstrasse where he saw Jagow. This was the opening shot in the Italian campaign to get Germany to use its influence in Vienna on Italy's behalf. Bollati carried some weight in Berlin because of his strongly pro-Triple Alliance views. Following up the instructions he had received from Fiuggi, he told Jagow that 'Italy is prepared to adopt a very benevolent and friendly attitude towards Austria and create no difficulties for her'. However, he emphasised that this would 'only be possible if she received assurances about the interpretation of Article VII' otherwise Italy 'would be obliged to aim at preventing any territorial aggrandizement of Austria–Hungary'. Bollati told Jagow 'in confidence' that Italy would ask for the Trentino and if Vienna took any Albanian territory then Valona on the Albanian coast as well. Jagow told Tschirschky in Vienna that Berlin agreed with Rome's inter-pretation of Article VII because 'compensation' was involved under the terms of the treaty if Austria–Hungary made any gains in the *région des Balkans* and not simply in Ottoman territory as Vienna was trying to claim. He added, 'Moreover, theoretical polemics over interpretation of treaty seem to me now out of place. Decisions are necessary which are consonant with the political situation.'[26] Vienna was about to find out that it faced a difficult position with its minor ally and that Germany was supporting Italy.

Meanwhile, in Rome, the Vatican was making it clear it strongly supported Austria–Hungary as a Catholic power standing up to countries which professed the Orthodox faith. Ritter, the Bavarian chargé to the Holy See, reported to Munich that 'the Pope approves armed measures by Austria against Serbia'. In addition, the cardinal state secretary, Carindal Merry del Val, 'hopes that Austria will this time take a firm stand' against 'a threat to the very existence of Austria'. As Ritter reported: 'Herein is expressed the Curia's intense fear of Pan-Slavism'.[27]

Brussels

The Belgian government immediately foresaw that the Austrian ultimatum could produce a European war that might well involve Belgium. The foreign minister, Davignon, sent a telegram to his diplomats in the countries which were signatories of the 1839 treaty saying that the Belgian army was taking up defensive positions and that neutrality would be maintained. They were told not to deliver the message until they received further instructions. The minister in Berlin, Baron Napoléon Beyens, thought war was unlikely:

> One does not very well see how France, the France of radicalism, the Caillaux trial and of the disturbing revelations of M. Charles Humbert about the state of the army, could accept a European war where its existence would be at stake, in order to save Serbia from an unprecedented humiliation.

He also spoke of 'the indelible strain impressed on the Serbian nation by the assassinations of Sarajevo'.[28] Within a fortnight, Belgium found itself at war as an ally of France and Serbia. This telegram was suppressed when the government in Brussels published its diplomatic correspondence during the crisis.

The Balkans

The governments of the various small Balkan states had to decide how to react to the possibilities opened up by a probable war between Austria–Hungary and Serbia. In Sofia the Austro-Hungarian ambassador, Tarnowski, saw the prime minister, Radoslavov, to give him the text of the ultimatum. Radoslavov immediately saw the opportunity to improve Bulgaria's position and told Tarnowski that the ultimatum was 'perhaps a great and unexpected piece of good fortune for Bulgaria'. However, he realised that Bulgaria would have to be neutral (to avoid Romanian and Greek intervention in maintaining the Treaty of Bucharest) and said that Sofia would do nothing without seeking Vienna's advice first. Tarnowski told Berchtold that Bulgaria clearly hoped to gain Macedonia if Serbia was defeated but because he had received no instructions from Vienna he made no promises.[29]

Bulgaria's rivals took a different view. In Bucharest Czernin, having seen the King to give him a copy of the ultimatum the previous day, now saw the prime minister, Bratianu. The latter thought the note showed that Vienna just wanted war and asked what Austria–Hungary proposed to do with Serbia. Czernin said that they would not annex Serbian territory. Bratianu said Romania would remain neutral in such a war.

Greece, Serbia's other ally from the second Balkan War, and who had signed a treaty pledging support in any war with Austria–Hungary, was being more devious. The prime minister, Eleftherios Venizelos, was in Trieste en route to Brussels where he was due to meet the Ottoman Grand Vizier to conclude an agreement on the Aegean Islands and sign an alliance. He sent a telegram to the foreign minister, Streit, saying that his absence would provide 'plausible reasons' for not replying to any Serbian request for help under the terms of the alliance. He thought Serbia was responsible for the Sarajevo assassinations and should therefore be advised to be very conciliatory.[30]

In Constantinople the Austro-Hungarian ambassador, Margrave Janos von Pallavicini, read out the text of the ultimatum to the Grand Vizier. The latter was very enthusiastic and said it 'exceeded his expectations'. The Ottomans clearly wanted to clamber on to the bandwagon and the Grand Vizier said they hoped to join the Triple Alliance in company with Bulgaria. (Venizelos's trip would be in vain as the Grand Vizier would drop the agreement with Greece.) The Grand Vizier said he had long wanted an alliance with Bulgaria (which was untrue) and that the Ottomans would help them against Romania.[31]

In Cetinje the Austro-Hungarian minister Otto read the ultimatum to King Nicholas and Plamenac, the Montenegrin foreign minister. The King said he hoped Serbia would yield but thought some points, especially about the role of Austro-Hungarian officials in Serbia, would be difficult to accept. He was worried that Montenegro would be dragged into the conflict. The King expressed the same worries to Giers, the Russian minister. Montenegro told other governments what they thought they wanted to hear. In his discussions later in the day, Plamenac told the Italian minister that Montenegro could remain neutral but went further with the French minister, Delaroche-Vernet, saying that Montenegro would break off relations with Vienna when they invaded Serbia because 'the ties of blood are stronger than anything . . . no power could prevent Serbs and Montenegrins from fighting side by side'.[32] However, the government was still weighing up its options. The Austro-Hungarian military attaché reported to Vienna that 'King and Cabinet willing to remain neutral if Austria–Hungary promises concessions to Montenegro. Positive decisions in the matter not yet taken.'[33] In Vienna Conrad suggested simply bribing Montenegro to keep out of the war.

St Petersburg – Morning

Across Europe on the day after the Austro-Hungarian ultimatum, governments had little time to react and devise any effective diplomatic action. However, in St Petersburg the Russian government took a series of decisions which demonstrated that the German and Austro-Hungarian assumption that it might allow Serbia to be humiliated was wildly optimistic. They were also the first steps that ensured the outbreak of a European war. These decisions were taken despite the fact that Russia had no treaty of alliance with Serbia and was under no obligation to support it diplomatically, let alone go to its defence. Russia was guided solely by consideration of its own immediate interests and a determination not to allow Austria–Hungary a diplomatic or military triumph.

The Russian foreign ministry knew the detailed text of the ultimatum early that morning when the telegram sent overnight by Strandtmann in Belgrade reached St Petersburg. When Sazonov arrived at the office shortly before 10 a.m. and read the document he remarked, 'C'est le guerre européenne.'[34] He immediately telephoned Tsar Nicholas II and gave him his own shrewd assessment of the situation. He thought the ultimatum was designed to be rejected, that Vienna intended to attack, and that therefore they must have been given prior German approval. Shortly after 10 a.m. Sazonov began a one-and-a-half-hour discussion with Szápáry. The ambassador began by reading out the ultimatum as instructed by Vienna. Sazonov, in one of his frequent emotional states, kept interrupting, saying: 'I know what it is. You want to go to war with Serbia'; 'You are setting fire to Europe'; 'It will be considered as an unjustified aggression.' Later he described the ultimatum as a 'pretext' for war and objected strongly to the dissolution of Narodna Odbrana and to Austro-Hungarian officials operating in Serbia. He also demolished one of Berlin's favourite arguments by saying: 'The Monarchical idea has nothing to do with this affair at all.' Finally, he told Szápáry: 'What you want is war, and you have burnt your bridges behind you.' Remarkably, Szápáry, in his telegram to Vienna, described Sazonov as 'serene' but 'non-compliant' and 'hostile'.[35]

On leaving this meeting Sazonov saw General Yanushkevich (the army chief of staff) who then summoned General Dobrorolski (the head of the mobilisation section) and asked him to devise, within the hour, a plan for a partial mobilisation against Austria–Hungary. (Yanushkevich needed the information to brief the minister of war.) Sazonov then left the foreign ministry to have lunch at the French embassy with the ambassador, Maurice Paléologue, and the British ambassador, Buchanan. Paléologue took a very tough line which almost certainly reflected the views Poincaré had expressed over the previous few days during the state visit. He said France would give full diplomatic support to Russia and would fulfil all its alliance obligations. Such a strong expression of support was bound to increase Russian intransigence. Buchanan reported that Sazonov thought the Austro-Hungarian action was 'immoral and provocative'. Sazonov then put the case for Britain siding with Russia and France:

> The Serbian question was but a part of general European question and that we could not efface ourselves . . . [Sazonov] expressed the hope that H. M. Govt. would proclaim their solidarity with France and Russia . . . If war did break out we would sooner or later be dragged into it, but if we did not make common cause with France and Russia from the outset we should have rendered war more likely, and should not have played a *beau rôle*.[36]

Given Sazonov's demand a month earlier for a resolution of Anglo-Russian differences (especially on Persia), the threat that lay behind these sentiments was pretty clear.

St Petersburg – Afternoon

Reassured by the strong French support, Sazonov left the embassy to attend the council of ministers that met at 3 p.m. The council was not a cabinet which exercised collective responsibility but merely a meeting of ministers individually responsible to the Tsar. Its composition had changed significantly in recent months. In February 1914 the chairman and finance minister, V. N. Kokovtsov, had been dismissed. He had been a strong opponent of an adventurous foreign policy and a supporter of Sazonov's generally conciliatory policies in the Balkans. In particular his arguments had been decisive in deciding against mobilisation during the November 1912 crisis with Austria–Hungary. Kokovtsov had been replaced as chairman of the council by I. L. Goremykin, a non-entity, and as finance minister by P. L. Bark. The council meeting lasted for a little over two hours and the main source for its discussion is Bark's memoir written while he had access to the minutes.

Sazonov opened the discussion by taking a very different line than in the last Balkan crisis with Austria–Hungary eighteen months earlier. Now he argued that Russia had made concessions in the past but these had only encouraged Germany and Austria–Hungary. Now was the time to make a stand. The ultimatum was designed to turn Serbia into an Austro-Hungarian protectorate and Russia could not abandon its historic mission to secure Slav independence. If it backed down now and lost influence in the Balkans it would be seen as a second-rate state and this would only encourage Vienna to make more demands. But taking a stand did involve the risk of war and he had no idea how Britain would react. A. V. Krivoshein, the minister of agriculture but the dominant figure in the council, spoke next. He felt Russia had recovered from the disasters of 1904–6 and that although the military situation was far from satisfactory (Russia could probably never match Germany and Austria–Hungary) now was the time to make a stand. Conciliation would not reduce the risks of war and the hope now was to make it clear Russia could not make concessions as in 1908–9 and 1912–13:

> All factors tended to prove that the most judicious policy Russia could follow in present circumstances was a return to a firmer and more energetic attitude towards the unreasonable claims of the Central Powers.

General Sukhomlinov, the minister for war, expressed the view that although there had been major improvements in the military situation since 1905 Russia did not have superiority over its potential opponents. Nevertheless, 'hesitation was no longer appropriate' and he saw 'no objection to a display of greater firmness in our diplomatic negotiations'. Bark said that war would endanger Russia's financial and economic stability but further concessions could not be made because 'the honour, dignity and authority of Russia were at stake.'[37]

The council then went on to discuss what action to take. On the diplomatic front Sazonov would contact the other major powers and seek an extension of the deadline so that each country could take a view on the Austro-Hungarian case and the documents it had proving Serbian involvement. (This was exactly the widening of the dispute Vienna and Berlin were determined to avoid.) Serbia was not to be advised to accept the ultimatum and implicitly it was accepted that Belgrade would reject it. Instead, they were to be advised that if they were not able to resist the expected attack they should offer no resistance and instead appeal to the great powers for help. It was also agreed that Russian money should be withdrawn from banks in Germany and Austria–Hungary. The most important discussions, though, were over Russian military measures.

Sazonov had, during his meeting with Yanushkevich in the morning, suggested the possibility of partial mobilisation against Austria–Hungary. Now, on the advice of Sukhomlinov (who was basing his information on what he heard from Yanushkevich before the meeting), the council decided to recommend doing what Russia had refrained from doing in the November 1912 crisis – instituting partial mobilisation. The Tsar would be asked to approve the measure the next day. It involved the mobilisation of the Kiev, Odessa, Moscow and Kazan military districts opposite Austria–Hungary, together with the Baltic and Black Sea fleets. (Mobilisation in the Warsaw district, which also faced Galicia, was rejected because Berlin might interpret the measure as being aimed at them.) Mobilisation was intended to deter Austria–Hungary – by posing a threat in Galicia it would make it more difficult for them to concentrate their forces against Serbia. It would also demonstrate Russian determination. The drawback was that it was a major escalation of the crisis which might lead to countermeasures on the other side. (Austria–Hungary had still made no military moves at this stage, although it was planning to do so.) Russian mobilisation was also bound to have an effect on Germany. The essence of German strategy was to use the time allowed by the relatively slowly mobilising Russians in order to defeat the French. Germany could not allow Russia to gain a significant head start in military preparations without wrecking its whole strategy for a quick victory.

Russian partial mobilisation also had implications for the Franco-Russian alliance because the act of mobilisation was inevitably linked to the first stages of a war. Under Article II of the military convention between the two countries signed in September 1913, either could mobilise immediately and without consulting the other if their primary enemy, Germany, began mobilisation. However, this was not the case if either Austria–Hungary or Italy mobilised. In these circumstances prior consultation was 'indispensable'. In the autumn 1912 crisis, when he was opposed to action, Sazonov argued that prior consultation with France was required. He did not do so now. Russia made no effort to consult its ally or obtain approval for the decision to begin partial mobilisation. Yet the implications for France were profound because of the structure of the alliance systems – a Russian war with Austria–Hungary would almost inevitably drag in Germany and then France.

Why did Sazonov ignore French concerns? The most likely explanation is that Poincaré discussed the issue during the state visit and gave either tacit or explicit approval to how Russia would react to the expected Austro-Hungarian ultimatum to Serbia.

The most fundamental objection to Russian partial mobilisation against Austria–Hungary, about which Sukhomlinov seems to have been blissfully unaware, was that Russia had no plan for such a mobilisation. Ever since the mid-1890s Russian plans had assumed, correctly given the Triple Alliance, that they would fight Germany and Austria–Hungary simultaneously. Russian plans had also, because of French pressure, shifted to placing the focus of mobilisation against Germany in East Prussia, not on Austro-Hungarian forces in Galicia.

The military advice to the council of ministers should have been that partial mobilisation was not possible – Russian military plans were simply not flexible enough to make this a viable option. Certainly there was no time to devise a new plan given the complexities of the troop and rail movements involved in mobilisation – it would take many months to work out the details of such a plan. If the military had told the council that only total mobilisation was an option, with all the risks this involved (almost certain German mobilisation and war), then the ministers might have taken a more cautious approach.

St Petersburg – Evening

The Serbian minister, Miroslav Spalajković, was at his summer villa in Finland when he heard news of the ultimatum. He hurried back to St Petersburg but was unable to see Sazonov until 6 p.m., shortly after the meeting of the council of ministers ended. The two men talked for about an hour and, from a Serbian point of view, the most important outcome was that Spalajković was not advised to accept the ultimatum, though he gained no more than sympathy from Sazonov. The Russian foreign minister condemned the ultimatum and said no sovereign state could accept parts of it. He said Serbia could rely on Russian help but very carefully did not say what that help might be. The Russian account of the meeting says that Sazonov advised 'extreme moderation' in the Serbian reply.

At 7 p.m. Sazonov saw the German ambassador, Poutalès, for the first time that day. According to Pourtalès' telegram to Berlin, Sazonov was 'very much excited and gave vent to boundless reproaches against Austria–Hungary'. Sazonov refused to admit the basic premise of

Austro-Hungarian and German policy that the dispute should be settled between Vienna and Belgrade. He also made it clear that Austria–Hungary could not act as accuser, judge and jury – there would have to be some form of international arbitration. Pourtalès said he did not think Vienna would accept such a solution. Sazonov then stated clearly: 'If Austria–Hungary devours Serbia, we will go to war with her.'[38] However, the German ambassador, somewhat surprisingly, drew the highly misleading conclusion, as he told Berlin, that Russia would only fight if Austria–Hungary annexed Serbian territory and that Sazonov's suggestion of internationalisation of the dispute suggested Russia was unwilling to fight. He was probably telling Berlin what he thought they wanted to hear – in his diary he took a bleaker view, arguing that the Russian council of ministers had considered a breach with Vienna and Berlin and had 'resolved not to hang back from an armed conflict'.[39]

Following this meeting, Sazonov carried out the diplomatic actions agreed at the council of ministers. A telegram was sent to Strandtmann in Belgrade advising Serbia to offer no resistance to an attack. Telegrams were sent to the ambassadors in all the major European capitals about the need to extend the time limit and suggesting Austria–Hungary should agree to put its case to all the powers who would then 'advise' Serbia how to react. At the end of a long and tiring day Sazonov saw Paléologue for a second time. The French ambassador was arguing, optimistically, that Germany could not and would not support Austria–Hungary in view of the likely consequences of doing so. He reassured Sazonov that France would stand by Russia. Sazonov then brought Paléologue up to date with the decisions taken by the council of ministers. When the ambassador returned to the embassy, the telegrams he sent to Paris were deliberately designed to mislead the French government. The first, despatched at 9.12 p.m., did not mention the possibility of partial mobilisation (which was bound to critically affect France) and spoke of the need for solidarity with Russia. The second, sent just after midnight, merely said that there would be a meeting of the council of ministers, presided over by the Tsar, on 25 July. Again it failed to mention partial mobilisation and said that 'M. Sazonov will endeavour to win the day for ideas of moderation' – the exact opposite of the truth.[40]

At the end of the second day of the crisis, the policy-makers in Berlin and Vienna had some reason for optimism. Rome looked as though it might be defecting from the alliance but that was not necessarily a disadvantage. More important, France seemed to be taking a very moderate line and Britain seemed to accept the idea of localisation and had hinted that it would remain neutral if a European conflict did start. What they did not know was that Russia, not linked to Serbia by an alliance, seemed to viewing the issue as a direct threat to its sphere of influence in the Balkans and had decided that it would not repeat the moderate policy it had adopted in recent crises. That undercut the basic assumption on which German policy in particular had been based. (Austria–Hungary always accepted that Russia would probably go to war.) Even more important, Russia was about to take the first military measures to escalate the crisis.

8

SATURDAY 25 JULY

Across Europe the main diplomatic efforts during the morning were focused on obtaining an extension of the time limit in the Austro-Hungarian ultimatum. However, in the time available no concerted intervention was possible (which was what Vienna intended) and anyway Vienna had no intention of bowing to these requests – it had decided on its policy and saw no reason to change its mind at this stage. Desultory efforts also continued to devise a formula for mediation, although Vienna had no intention of accepting this either and Berlin had decided not to support such efforts.

Vienna – Morning

The Russian chargé, Kudashev, carried out the instructions sent the previous evening from St Petersburg and called at the foreign ministry to ask for an extension of the time limit. He saw Macchio who said he would tell Berchtold of the request but there was no possibility of an extension. He also rejected any idea that the other powers could be involved in the dispute. Berchtold sent a telegram to Szápáry in St Petersburg stating that he was to reassure Sazonov that the demand for Austro-Hungarian officials to operate in Serbia was not an infringement of its sovereignty. He explained that the idea was to establish a 'Security Bureau' in Belgrade similar to the Russian bureaux in Paris and Berlin, where Russian officials monitored the activities of the Russian revolutionaries in exile. This was certainly not made clear in the ultimatum (after all, it was intended to be rejected) but there was a significant difference between the two examples. The French and German governments were quite happy to keep the revolutionaries under control, whereas the Belgrade government would be in an impossible position if it had to suppress Serbian nationalists.

Kudashev did not like the message he had received from Macchio (nor the fact that he had been fobbed off with a relatively junior official). He sent a telegram to Berchtold demanding an extension of the time limit. By then Berchtold had already left Vienna by train for Bad

Ischl to be with the Emperor when the Serbian reply was received. He told Macchio that he agreed with his earlier statements. He could tell Kudashev that 'even after the breaking-off of diplomatic relations the unconditional acceptance of our demands could bring about a peaceful solution' (which was no concession at all) though Serbia would then have to pay all of Vienna's costs.[1]

London – Morning

The Russian ambassador, Count Alexander Benckendorff, saw Grey early in the morning to reinforce Sazonov's view expressed the previous day that Britain should back Russia and France in the crisis. He suggested Britain should tell Germany that it might not be neutral if there was a European war. Grey merely replied that he 'had given no indication that we would stand aside'.[2] This was untrue because Grey had, on the previous day, given Lichnowsky a large hint that Britain would be neutral by speaking of a four-power European war.

Grey then saw Lichnowsky and told him he was more optimistic about the situation because of the information from Mensdorff late the previous evening that Austria–Hungary would only mobilise and not invade Serbia. He thought Russia would probably mobilise and suggested that it was only at this point that there should be four-power (Britain, Germany, Italy and France) mediation in the dispute. Putting off diplomatic action until this late in the crisis was a disastrous suggestion. By the time major military measures were underway, it would be much more difficult for the powers involved to pull back and mediation would have little time in which to work and be much more difficult to implement. Grey then repeated what he had said at their meeting the previous day about not wanting to intervene in any purely Austro-Hungarian–Serbian dispute (thereby tacitly supporting German ideas about localisation). Indeed, he said he 'fully recognised the justice of the Austrian demand for satisfaction'. He added: 'nor were European complications a matter of indifference to Great Britain, although she was in no way committed by any sort of binding agreements'. This was a slightly better formulation of the British position than the one he used to Lichnowsky on the previous day but it was hardly likely to change German perceptions of Britain's likely role.[3]

Grey then saw Goschen and told him he should return to his post in Berlin as soon as possible. His last action for the day was to send a telegram to Buchanan in St Petersburg saying: 'I do not consider public opinion here would or ought to sanction our going to war in the Servian quarrel.' He added that he thought Russian mobilisation 'almost inevitable', which was hardly likely to restrain the Russians (though Britain had little influence on this subject). He repeated that he would only launch his idea for four-power mediation after both Vienna and St Petersburg had begun to mobilise. The view in the Foreign Office was that if, as expected, Serbia accepted most of the demands and Austria–Hungary mobilised but did not invade, then the crisis would not be serious and indeed had probably been surmounted already. Shortly after lunch Grey left for his fishing lodge at Itchen Abbas in Hampshire where he normally spent his weekends (he had already postponed his departure from the normal Friday evening).

Stockholm

President Poincaré and his party arrived in the Swedish capital in the morning. The main purpose of the visit was to reassure the Swedes that Russia (which was steadily integrating the nominally independent Finland into Russia) had no intention of attacking Sweden. Immediately on arrival, Poincaré and Viviani were told about the German action in Paris the previous day. They realised that if Germany was insisting that the dispute must be localised, then it was supporting its ally and therefore the chances of successful mediation were much reduced. They decided to continue with the planned visit and the only action they took was to send a telegram to Paris. It suggested working with Russia and Britain, and its only positive idea was to put forward 'at the opportune moment' the precedent of the 1904 Rome conference to combat European anarchists, so that all the powers were involved in an inquiry into Serb nationalist activities.[4]

Meanwhile, at the foreign ministry, the Swedish foreign minister, Wallenberg, saw the German minister, Reichenau. He expressed 'lively approval' of the ultimatum but explained that it was necessary to keep up appearances during the French visit. Nevertheless, if Russia did back Serbia and a Russo-German war started, then the Swedish government 'would not for one moment remain in doubt on whose side they would have to stand'.[5] He confirmed these views in a discussion with the Austro-Hungarian minister. However, Wallenberg was deliberately vague when he saw the Russian minister, Nekludov. He told him: 'Sweden would have regard above all to the defence of her neutrality and of her friendly relations with all her neighbours'.[6]

Berlin – Morning

The British chargé, Rumbold, saw Jagow about supporting a British request to extend the time limit. Jagow told him that he had already asked the German ambassador in Vienna to do this. (This was untrue – he did not do so until after he had seen Rumbold and then only passed on the request and did not support it.) Jagow admitted Serbia could not accept the ultimatum but remained optimistic that the dispute could be localised because Austria–Hungary would give Russia a pledge that it would not annex Serbian territory. He continued that Germany would accept Grey's proposal on mediation (which was not yet an official proposal) if relations between Vienna and St Petersburg became 'threatening'. Jagow lied again in saying Berlin did not know of the ultimatum in advance and added that 'as a diplomatic document [it] left much to be desired'.[7]

Jagow next saw the Russian chargé, Bronevski. He told him Vienna would not give way over the time limit but he would pass on the Russian message (which he did not). Jagow refused to discuss any other matters, saying Russia would have to be satisfied by Austria–Hungary's pledge not to seek territorial acquisitions.

The real German attitude was revealed in the report Szögyény sent to Berchtold. If the Serbian reply was unsatisfactory then Berlin felt:

> our declaration of war and war operations will follow immediately. Here every delay in the beginning of war operations is regarded as signifying the danger that foreign powers might intervene. We are urgently advised to proceed without delay and to place the world before a *fait accompli*.[8]

The German government knew that Austro-Hungarian mobilisation would take over a fortnight to complete and that Vienna, on current plans, did not intend to declare war on Serbia during this period. Because of the slow pace of Austro-Hungarian mobilisation, diplomacy would have had plenty of time to work and put pressure on Vienna to accept a compromise solution. The German suggestion that Vienna should bring forward the declaration of war to just after the breaking-off of diplomatic relations and the start of mobilisation would certainly create a *fait accompli*. The obvious danger in any such action was that it would only serve to escalate the crisis, close off possible lines of retreat and put more pressure on Russia to move further along the road with its own military measures. The German government clearly felt that the strategy agreed with Vienna in early July was working. (It was unaware of developments in St Petersburg.) However, this pressure on Vienna to escalate the crisis was, after the decision to provide Austria–Hungary with a 'blank cheque' early in July, the single most disastrous mistake Berlin made during the crisis. Although Germany knew that its ally wanted a military triumph over Serbia to restore its prestige, the decision to restrict the room for diplomatic intervention was grossly irresponsible. Combined as it was with the Russian decision to begin the early stages of mobilisation, it escalated the crisis to the edge of European war.

Rome

In the morning the British ambassador, Rodd, who had returned from his art-hunting tour of Tuscany, saw di Martino, the secretary-general of the foreign ministry. The latter was gloomy about the situation. He said: 'Austria–Hungary will only be restrained by unconditional acceptance of note by Servia; occupation of Servian territory is contemplated.'[9] San Giuliano made his first visit to Rome during the crisis when he saw the Serbian minister, Mihailjović, who was advised that Serbia should 'yield to the Austrian demands in spite of all their monstrousness. In his opinion Austria would only win a shadow victory thereby; in practice on many points an agreement could be arrived at.'[10]

San Giuliano deliberately did not see the Austro-Hungarian ambassador, Merey, during his short stay in the capital (Merey was at home ill). However, he did ask his secretary, Biancheri, to telephone and ask after the ambassador's health and then state Italy's position. This was that the ultimatum was designed to be unacceptable, Italy had not been consulted and was not, therefore, bound by its alliance obligations and would offer no military support. Any temporary or permanent occupation of territory by Austria–Hungary would require compensation for Italy. Anti-Italian as ever, Merey merely told Vienna that Italy's views should be ignored.

Vienna – Afternoon

The Italian ambassador, the Duke Avarna di Gualtieri, called at the

Ballhausplatz to carry out Rome's instructions sent the previous day, on which Bollati had taken action in Berlin. Avarna could not see Berchtold who was on his way to Bad Ischl and therefore saw Macchio. The ambassador said, according to the Austro-Hungarian note of the talk, that even the temporary occupation of any Serbian territory would mean that Italy would have to be compensated. So far the ambassador had carried out his instructions. He then departed from them even further than Bollati did in Berlin – Avarna was strongly pro-Austrian. He told Macchio that if there was a war between Vienna and Belgrade then Italy 'intends to adopt a friendly attitude consonant with the obligation of the alliance'.[11]

It was no surprise therefore that when Berchtold returned from Bad Ischl he sent a telegram to Merey stating that Avarna's declaration 'has made a most agreeable impression'. He told his ambassador that it had still not been decided whether Serbian territory would be occupied and therefore any discussion of compensation would be 'premature'.[12] Messages were also sent to the embassies in Berlin and London that Italy was supporting the Austro-Hungarian position. Conrad was reassured that the nightmare he had discussed with Berchtold two days earlier – Italian intervention against Austria–Hungary – could be dismissed and that Vienna could concentrate its forces against Serbia and Russia.

The Balkans
In Bucharest the Romanian prime minister, Bratianu, saw the Austro-Hungarian minister, Czernin. Bratianu was worried that if Serbia were defeated then Bulgaria would make gains that would weaken Romania. He suggested an idea that would reappear in many forms later in the crisis – the so-called 'halt in Belgrade'. Under this idea Vienna would do no more than make a military demonstration against Serbia. As Czernin reported, Bratianu wondered whether:

> as the time limit had expired, it would not be possible to make a halt after eventual invasion by our troops and, with the assurance that we purpose no permanent annexation, resume negotiations with Serbia while maintaining provisional occupation.[13]

Romania's ally Greece was being even more cautious. The prime minister, Venizelos, had continued with his journey to Brussels and had now reached Munich. He sent a telegram to Streit, the foreign minister, that he should reserve the Greek position on its alliance with Serbia if Austria–Hungary attacked. Venizelos said that the alliance 'seems to be ruled out by the provocative conduct of Serbia'. However, Greece could not ignore any attack by Bulgaria because of the Greek interests in Macedonia.[14] Streit carried out these instructions when he saw the German minister, Bassewitz. He told him Greece would not intervene in an Austro-Hungarian–Serbian conflict but Bulgaria was different because 'the maintenance of the Treaty of Bucharest was a cardinal question for Greece'.[15]

In Cetinje it seemed that Austria–Hungary was losing the battle to keep Montenegro neutral. The minister, Otto, told Vienna: 'Ministers are agitating for solidarity with Serbia in the event of war.'[16] Nevertheless, the final decision would be made by King Nicholas, and Vienna still felt he was open to persuasion and bribery.

St Petersburg – Morning/Afternoon
The Tsar was at Krasnoe Selo, attending the normal summer review of the army. Numerous diplomats and military attachés were present and they could not fail to notice the long meeting of the council of ministers that lasted most of the morning. The meeting was chaired by the Tsar and Grand Duke Nicholas was also present. The meeting endorsed the decision to move to partial mobilisation against Austria–Hungary if it took action against Serbia. There was still no discussion of the problems involved in this decision. The meeting went further, agreeing that the general staff should implement the measures for the 'period preparatory to war' which had been introduced into Russian military planning by a law of March 1913. These measures, which it was agreed would be discussed by the general staff that evening, were preparatory to general, not partial, mobilisation, against Austria–Hungary. This was a further escalation of the crisis by Russia and one that was bound to directly affect Germany as well as Austria–Hungary.

After the meeting, Sazonov saw Buchanan (the contents of this discussion are covered below) and Paléologue. The latter told Sazonov that France was unreservedly at Russia's side. The French ambassador finally sent word to Paris that the council of ministers had agreed to partial mobilisation against Austria–Hungary and that other preparatory measures were being put in hand. Paléologue also told the Italian ambassador that 'he thought the situation hopeless'.[17]

St Petersburg – Evening

Following the decisions made at the meeting with the Tsar in the morning, the minister of war, General Yanushkevich, chaired a general-staff conference about the preparatory measures to be taken. He said that it was permissible to overstep the 1913 law in order to ensure that the preparations were successful. The meeting made a number of decisions. Troops on manoeuvres would return to barracks. Officers on leave would be recalled and cadets would be promoted to provide enough officers for the units that would form on mobilisation. In addition, all fortresses, fortified cities and frontier posts in Poland and western Russia would be placed on a war footing. Reservists would be recalled to man frontier units. Censorship and security measures were to be tightened, harbours were to be mined and baggage trains and horses for the army were to be made ready. Finally, mobilisation depots would prepare to receive reservists when they were called up. Orders confirming these decisions were issued a few hours later at 1 a.m. and 3.26 a.m. on 26 July.

The Russian government had decided, even before they knew how Serbia would reply to the ultimatum or what Austria–Hungary would then do, to move ahead with military preparations. Moreover, these measures were applicable to general, not just partial, mobilisation. These were the first military moves made by any of the major European powers. Not surprisingly, the preparations were apparent very quickly at Krasnoe Selo. Army manoeuvres were suspended and troops returned to their barracks. A ceremony was held to promote cadets to full officers. Grand Duke Nicholas organised a demonstration in favour of war and at a banquet that evening toasts were drunk to success in war with Austria–Hungary. The German military representative at the army review, General Chelius, guessed what was happening. He immediately sent a telegram to Berlin saying that he believed Russia was starting partial mobilisation against Austria–Hungary.

London – Evening

The telegram from Buchanan recording his talk with Sazonov that afternoon was transmitted quickly and arrived in London at 10.30 p.m. It caused considerable consternation. The first part was relatively innocuous. Sazonov made clear the basis of Russian policy by saying it could not 'allow Austria to crush Serbia and become predominant power in Balkans'. He went on to say that if Serbia appealed for help (which was what St Petersburg had advised it to do) then Russia would stand aside and allow four-power mediation as Grey seemed likely to propose. Sazonov then confirmed that a draft ordering partial mobilisation was being prepared for final approval and that meanwhile preliminary measures were being taken. Buchanan warned him this was dangerous because Germany could not let Russia get a head start. Sazonov went on to say that he thought Berlin was gambling on British neutrality but that, as Buchanan reported, 'if we took our stand with France and Russia there would be no war'. Buchanan deflected this proposal by arguing that Britain could act better as a mediator in Berlin and Vienna as a friend who might join France and Russia rather than as their declared ally. Sazonov then issued a clear threat saying, as Buchanan relayed to London:

> For ourselves position is a most serious one, and we shall have to choose between giving Russia our active support or renouncing her friendship. If we fail her now we cannot hope to maintain that friendly co-operation in Asia that is of such vital importance to us.[18]

This clear piece of blackmail went, as Sazonov knew it would, to the heart of the reasons why Britain had wanted the entente with France and Russia. The protection of India and other imperial interests in Asia and the Persian Gulf meant that Britain could not afford to alienate Russia and Sazonov was pointing out that the price Russia would exact was support in Europe.

Belgrade – Morning

Work on the reply to the ultimatum had continued through the night in the Serbian foreign ministry, but the cabinet now needed to make the crucial decisions about the final text so that work could begin on translating the document into French. As they surveyed the diplomatic scene the picture looked bleak. They had almost no support. Their Balkan allies – Romania and Greece – had carefully avoided committing themselves, but Belgrade assumed that they would not support Serbia against Austria–Hungary. The Montenegrin minister, Mijusković, said his country would go through good and bad times in solidarity with Serbia but advised them to act in accordance with French and Russian advice. France, together with Britain and Italy, was advising Serbia to be as conciliatory as possible.

The most important advice, as in the past, came from Serbia's patron, Russia. The first telegram from Spalajković in St Petersburg recording his talk with Sazonov the previous evening arrived in Belgrade shortly after 4 a.m. and the second took another six hours to arrive. Neither was very encouraging. The condemnation of Austria–Hungary and the general expressions of support for Serbia were to be expected. What was lacking was any clear advice, apart from accepting as much of the ultimatum as possible, and any firm commitments from Russia. Indeed, the main import of the advice seemed to be that Serbia should not offer any resistance to the expected Austro-Hungarian attack, should give up Belgrade and then appeal for international support. It was not until 11.30 a.m. that a third telegram arrived from St Petersburg. It reported that Russia had issued an official communiqué supporting Serbia and mentioned that Russia might begin partial mobilisation. This telegram had little impact on the Serbian reply that had been approved by 11 a.m.

The Serbian cabinet agreed that it would be impolitic to reject the ultimatum outright. Another possibility was to follow the line suggested by Berthelot in Paris and San Giuliano in Rome – acceptance in principle. This would have been the most subtle response. It would have badly wrong-footed Vienna which was expecting rejection. If Serbia had accepted the ultimatum in principle, Vienna would have been forced to engage in a long process of negotiating over the details of its complex demands which would have given Serbia plenty of opportunities to argue and delay while diplomatic pressure was put on Austria–Hungary. It seems that Belgrade never considered this possibility. There were two reasons why it did not. First, it would have been interpreted as humiliating. Second, it would have enraged the extreme nationalists, endangered the survival of the government, which was still weak after the political crisis of late June, and risked revealing the extent of the involvement of parts of the Serbian government in the Sarajevo conspiracy. Pašić was reluctant to make any concessions. As he admitted to the Bulgarian minister two days later: 'If Serbia had been sure of being supported to such an extent by Russia she would never have conceded so much.'[19]

Pašić and the cabinet decided to give the impression that they were accepting as much as possible of the ultimatum while rejecting outright only point six – the participation of Austro-Hungarian officials in the judicial inquiry. In this effort they were remarkably successful – most other European governments thought they had accepted all the other points. In fact, the drafting by Pašić and the foreign ministry was very clever and subtle. Caveats were included on nearly every point which would have enabled Serbia to avoid implementing many of the demands in the event of Austria–Hungary accepting the reply. (The full text of the Serbian reply is in Appendix B.)

The Serbian reply began by claiming they had done nothing since 1909 to alienate Austria–Hungary but that they could not control, and were not responsible for, the activities of private organisations. They said they had expected to be involved in any investigation into the Sarajevo crime but would hand over for trial any Serbian subject whose complicity in the conspiracy was proved. They agreed to publish a declaration in the official journal and issue an army order as suggested by Austria–Hungary. The reply then turned to the nine specific points addressed in the ultimatum. First, it agreed, at the next meeting of parliament, to introduce an amendment to the press law providing punishment for articles inciting hatred towards Austria–Hungary. When the constitution was revised, they would introduce an amend-ment which would allow for the confiscation of publications that broke this new law. However, no timescale was mentioned and there was no commitment that the government would enforce these new rules. Second, it argued that Vienna had produced no proof about the activities of *Narodna Odbrana* (which was correct), but the govern-ment undertook to dissolve it and similar societies. Again, no timescale was mentioned and it would have been easy to form a new society with similar aims. Third, Serbia undertook to remove 'without delay' any propaganda materials in the school system. However, they required Austria–Hungary to provide 'facts and proof' of this propaganda first and they ignored the demand to remove teachers who propagated this material. Fourth, Serbia agreed to remove from military service (though not from the administration as Vienna had also demanded) those whom the judicial inquiry found guilty of acts against the integrity of Austria–Hungary. But this was not what Vienna had demanded – they wanted dismissal for those who engaged in propaganda too and they were all to be dismissed when Austria–Hungary provided 'proofs', not when any Serbian judicial inquiry might find them guilty.

Fifth, the Serbian government claimed it did not understand what Vienna meant by its demand that Austro-Hungarian officials should participate in suppressing subversive movements. They said they would 'admit such collaboration as agrees with the principle of international law, with criminal procedure and with good neighbourly relations'. It was unclear what this meant, but it was effectively a rejection. Sixth,

Serbia said it would open 'an inquiry' against those involved in the conspiracy but they would not accept Austro-Hungarian participation in this process as it would violate both the constitution and criminal procedure. However, in 'concrete cases' communication of the results 'might' be given to Vienna. Seventh, Tankosić had been arrested on 23 July but it had not been possible to locate Ciganović. (The Austro-Hungarian authorities knew how he had been removed from Belgrade with official connivance a month earlier.) Austria–Hungary was asked to provide evidence of their guilt. Eighth, Serbia would reinforce and extend measures to stop smuggling across the border. They would also order an inquiry and 'severely punish' the officials involved in helping the conspirators. Ninth, Serbia agreed to give explanations about remarks made after the assassinations once Austria–Hungary told them what the remarks were and showed that the officials had indeed made the remarks. Finally, Serbia argued that if this reply was not judged to be satisfactory then it was willing to refer the question to either the International Tribunal at The Hague or to the powers that had drawn up the declaration made by Serbia in March 1909.

Although the Serbian reply did involve some concessions and accepted, at least implicitly, the right of Vienna to make such demands, it was very far from the unconditional acceptance that was required. It was clear that point six was rejected and in effect point five as well. Nevertheless, the skilful drafting gave the impression that Serbia was accepting the rest of the ultimatum. In fact, it was not. The only point accepted unconditionally was number eight on the border officials. All the other points were either only partially accepted or had been reworded to avoid the Austro-Hungarian demands and provide let-outs for later Serbian non-compliance. However, had Vienna wanted to seek a diplomatic solution, the Serbian reply could have been a basis for negotiation.

Belgrade – Afternoon

The final text of the reply, which was only subject to minor amendments after 11 a.m., was translated into French under the supervision of Slavko Gruić. By 4 p.m. it was ready for typing on the only machine possessed by the foreign ministry. The typist was nervous and kept making mistakes. Eventually the typewriter broke down and the reply had to be handwritten.

By lunchtime diplomats in Belgrade were aware of the outlines of the reply. At 12.30 Crackenthorpe sent a telegram to London saying that although Serbia would publish the statement as requested by Vienna the other demands were only 'accepted with reserves'.[20] The newly arrived French minister, Boppe, was also able to give Paris an accurate account of the reply. Giesl, at the Austrian legation, knew by 3 p.m., when he saw the minister of commerce, Janković, on a routine matter, that the reply would not be unconditional. He began final preparations to leave Belgrade.

Belgrade – Evening

The two texts of the reply (in Serbian and French as Vienna had demanded) were handed to Pašić by Gruić in an envelope at 5.45 p.m. Nearly all other government officials had left their offices to catch the train for Niš that was due to leave at 6 p.m. Pašić arrived at the Austro-Hungarian legation at 5.55 p.m. (five minutes before the expiry of the deadline) and handed over the reply to Giesl. Speaking in his broken German, he said, 'Part of your demands we have accepted . . . for the rest we place our hopes on your loyalty and chivalry as an Austrian general.' It was a vain hope, as Pašić knew.

After Pašić had left, Giesl read the reply and signed an already typed note. It was taken by messenger to Pašić at the foreign ministry. It told the Serbian government that they had not accepted the Austro-Hungarian demands and that diplomatic relations between the two countries were being broken off. Giesl said that he and his staff would leave Belgrade that evening and that the protection of Austro-Hungarian interests would be placed in the hands of the German legation. At the Austro-Hungarian legation, staff were already burning the code books and the courtyard was crowded with cars packed with luggage. Giesl, his wife and staff drove through the streets of Belgrade where sentries were already posted on every corner. They arrived at the station to find it crowded with other diplomats who were waiting for the delayed train for Niš. Giesl and his party boarded the regular 6.30 p.m. train and ten minutes later crossed the Danube to the frontier station at Semlin. At 6.40 p.m. he sent a short, uncoded telegram to Vienna informing them of the situation. He also spoke by telephone, on the only available line, to Tisza in Budapest. The Austro-Hungarian diplomats then settled down for the overnight journey to Budapest.

Belgrade was now rapidly emptying. Austria–Hungary was expected to invade at any moment and the Serbian government was decamping to Niš, the second largest city in Serbia, though its population was no more than 25,000. The Serbian general staff moved to their war head-quarters at Kragujevać, halfway between Belgrade and Niš. Shortly after 6 p.m. the regent, Crown Prince Alexander, signed the order for general mobilisation. It was the first mobilisation of the crisis. One of the few officials left in the city was Colonel Dragutin Dimitrijvić ('Apis'). He was in his office destroying incriminating papers and waiting for his head of operations in Bosnia–Herzegovina, Rade Malobabić, to cross into Serbia so that they could concert their stories over the conspiracy. Colonel Voja Tankosić was released from custody and was joined at his unit by Milan Ciganović who had mysteriously 'disappeared' and whom the Serbian government had been unable to find.

Bad Ischl – Evening

Berchtold arrived at Bad Ischl by train from Vienna at 5.30 p.m. to see the Emperor. (Franz Josef had spent the afternoon hosting a lunch for the Duke and Duchess of Cumberland and the Duke and Duchess of Brunswick – he was described as being dismal and uncommunicative.) Berchtold sat slumped in a chair for half an hour and then left for his rooms at the Hotel Elizabeth to await the news from Belgrade. While he was waiting, a telegram arrived from Tisza for the Emperor. He was now a convert to immediate and strong action against Serbia. He argued that the expected rejection should be followed by immediate Austro-Hungarian mobilisation. If this was not done, Tisza argued, it 'would gravely injure the reputation of the Monarchy for boldness and initiative'. It would also show weakness and 'result in the most fatal consequences'.[21]

News of the Serbian rejection reached Vienna at 7.45 p.m., when Tisza was able to relay the telephone message from Giesl. (Giesl's *en clair* telegram did not arrive until 9 p.m.) Berchtold was told the news at 8 p.m. and went to see the Emperor; the minister of war, Krobatin, was also present. The three men agreed that Austria–Hungary would continue with the plan agreed in early July. There would be war with Serbia and partial mobilisation of two-fifths of the army would begin on 28 July. They agreed that there would be no deployment along the frontier with Russia in Galicia and a central reserve would be maintained until it was clear how the crisis developed. The instruction to begin implementing the plan reached Conrad in Vienna at 9.23 p.m.

Berchtold then boarded the train back to Vienna where, on news of the Serbian rejection, large crowds had taken to the streets where they were celebrating and singing patriotic songs.

Berlin – Evening

The streets of Berlin were also crowded with people singing patriotic songs and the Austrian national anthem. The chief of the general staff, Moltke, who had returned from his month-long holiday at Carlsbad, held a meeting on the preparations the army should now make. Under pressure from the vice-chancellor, Clemens von Delbrück, the army agreed to limit any preventive measures to be taken against the socialists (Bethmann Hollweg was determined to maintain national unity). The circular issued that evening merely instructed the army to observe the left-wing press but to take no action.

Other action was, however, initiated. Army commanders were recalled to Berlin from leave. Intelligence officers at border posts were also recalled. Instructions were sent to implement the plans to improve intelligence gathering against France and Russia. This involved the so-called *Spannungsreisende* or 'tension travellers'. These were volunteers (some of them army reservists) who would enter France and Russia as businessmen or holidaymakers and make short round trips to gather information about military preparations. As far as the German military were concerned, this was a precautionary move in a period of international tension and not the first stages towards mobilisation which was implemented through very different procedures.

At the end of the third day of the crisis, the first, and easy, part of the Austro-Hungarian/German plan had been successfully concluded – Serbia had, as intended, rejected the ultimatum. However, this only illustrated the inadequacy of the plans made in Vienna and Berlin. The problem they now faced, which they had not clearly thought through, was what to do next. Both capitals knew that it would take a fortnight for Austria–Hungary to be ready to start military operations against Serbia and that Vienna did not intend to declare war until then. Yet this simple fact seems to have been ignored in their planning. Such a long gap would leave plenty of time for the other European powers to exert diplomatic pressure for a settlement – pressure that would be very difficult to resist.

Germany had begun to realise the magnitude of the likely problem the two allies faced when it applied pressure on Vienna to declare war immediately so as to avoid some of the expected diplomatic pressure. However, this was a high-risk strategy that would escalate the crisis and cut off many possible lines of retreat for Vienna. It would therefore further increase the pressure on Russia. The basis of German policy had been that Russia would allow Vienna a free hand to deal with Serbia as it wanted. However, any Austro-Hungarian declaration of war would leave Russia with a stark choice: to allow Austria–Hungary to attack and defeat Serbia, or to begin its own military preparations in an attempt to stop Vienna. What Germany and Austria–Hungary did not know was that Russia had already decided to move down the path of military preparations.

9

SUNDAY 26 JULY

For forty-eight hours after the Serbian rejection of the Austro-Hungarian ultimatum, there was a strange hiatus across Europe. Vienna had broken off relations with Belgrade but had not taken any further action. Although it had decided to begin partial mobilisation this would not start until 28 July. It would not be complete until 12 August. Only then would war be declared. This gave time for mediation to work and on 26 July two proposals emerged that could have resolved the crisis had each side been willing to modify the positions they had taken up. The first was for direct talks between Austria–Hungary and Russia, and the second was a British proposal for a repeat of the conference of ambassadors in London which had resolved the problems caused by the first Balkan War in 1912–13. These two proposals could not operate in parallel – they were incompatible and cut across each other. The danger was that in the confusion neither would be successful.

Vienna

On his return from Bad Ischl the previous evening Berchtold had seen the telegram from Szögyény that had arrived in Vienna at 8 p.m. This conveyed Berlin's opinion that Vienna should declare war on Serbia immediately in order to avoid coming under sustained diplomatic pressure for a settlement. At 12.30 p.m. he held a meeting with Conrad and the German ambassador, Tschirschky. (They were joined later by Macchio and Forgách.) The five men discussed the diplomatic situation. Tschirschky reported that, based on the conversation in Stockholm the previous day, Sweden seemed certain to join the Triple Alliance powers in any war. However, they all agreed that Italy would almost certainly wriggle out of its obligations and Berchtold said he was convinced the Italians would want 'compensation' if Austria–Hungary gained any territory.

After this meeting Berchtold and Conrad held their own discussion about the military and diplomatic options. Berchtold, bowing to

German pressure, said that he now wanted a declaration of war as soon as possible. Conrad said he would not be ready to conduct operations before 12 August. The foreign minister replied: 'the diplomatic situation will not hold as long as that'. The army chief said that he preferred to wait and see how the diplomatic situation developed and that war could always be declared at short notice if the situation demanded. He was faced by the dilemma at the heart of Vienna's war plans. If, on mobilisation, the army were deployed against Serbia then it would leave the frontier in Galicia very vulnerable to a Russian attack. As Conrad put it, 'most important of all, however, was to gain a better understanding of Russia's attitude'. He wanted to wait for about ten days until 4/5 August before making a final decision on how to deploy the army. Berchtold simply said: 'That will not do.'[1]

No final decision was made but preparations were put in hand for a declaration of war. Berchtold seems to have felt that to hesitate now would show weakness and suggest to Berlin that Vienna was an unreliable ally. When he saw Giesl on his return to Vienna that afternoon, he told him: 'the breaking-off of diplomatic relations is not by any means war'.[2] Berchtold explained that he did not think Serbia would resist, particularly given its weak military situation after the Balkan Wars. Serbia would accept the ultimatum unconditionally after Austria–Hungary had made a limited military demonstration, perhaps involving the occupation of the undefended Belgrade. For Berchtold, then, an early declaration of war was simply another way of increasing the pressure on Serbia and showing resolve to Germany – there would be no military operations before 12 August and so the declaration would be little more than a diplomatic gesture. No thought seems to have been given as to how Russia would react. At 4.30 p.m. telegrams were dispatched to the ambassadors in Berlin, Rome, London and Paris saying that war was imminent because Austria–Hungary was faced with 'the necessity of enforcing on Serbia by the sharpest means a fundamental change' in its attitude.[3]

St Petersburg

During the summer months both Sazonov and the German ambassador, Pourtalès, lived at Tsarkoe Selo and on this Sunday morning they travelled together by train to St Petersburg. During the journey they discussed the possible options for mediation in the dispute. Pourtalès objected to a conference, knowing that both Vienna and

Berlin thought this would reduce Austria–Hungary to the same level as Serbia. He therefore suggested direct talks between Russia and Austria–Hungary, even though he appreciated that this would inevitably require some modification of Vienna's position. Sazonov tried to explain that Russia's position did not derive from some vague pan-Slav sympathies but from a realistic assessment of Russia's interests. 'For Russia the balance of power in the Balkans was a vital interest and she could therefore not on any account tolerate the reduction of Serbia to a vassal state of Austria.'[4]

After this discussion Pourtalès decided to take the initiative. He spoke to his colleague Szápáry and told him about his conversation with Sazonov. The Austro-Hungarian ambassador decided that he should see Sazonov that afternoon. At their meeting the foreign minister began by saying that he had been taken by surprise over the contents of the ultimatum when he had seen Szápáry the previous day and had not displayed all the self-command he would have wished. After mutual reassurances the two men agreed to study the ultimatum. Sazonov said that the Austro-Hungarian aims were 'perfectly legitimate', though the method adopted was not the best. He thought many of the points could be made acceptable with only minor amendment. He admitted there were problems with points four, five and six but 'the difficulty regarding the note was one of wording'.[5] Szápáry suggested (though he had no instructions to do this) that Vienna would be willing to discuss contentious points.

Pourtalès then discussed the outcome of the meeting with both men. He reported to Berlin the view in St Petersburg that the ultimatum could be made acceptable. Pourtalès also gave his own personal views to Sazonov about mediation. He thought that if Vienna was willing to modify the form of its demands, as Szápáry had hinted was possible (for example, to allow modification of the Serbian constitution), then direct talks between Austria–Hungary and Russia should take place. Sazonov thought that if they succeeded then St Petersburg would be ready to 'advise' Belgrade to accept the revised document. Pourtalès concluded by telling Berlin: 'I have the impression that Sazonov, perhaps as the result of information from Paris and London, has lost some of his nerve and is now looking for a way out.'[6] His analysis of the reasons was wrong but Sazonov did seem willing to compromise.

Sazonov was now in a mood of considerable optimism. He sent a telegram to the embassy in Vienna suggesting that the government there should authorise Szápáry to start private talks with him for a 'joint revision of some articles' of the ultimatum.[7] (Vienna, of course, had no intention of allowing any such revision.) The Russian foreign minister then saw Paléologue and Buchanan to bring them up to date with events. He told them he would 'use all his influence at Belgrade to induce the Serbian government to go as far as possible in giving satisfaction to Austria'.[8] He also sent a message to Krupensky in Rome to ask the Italian government to tell Vienna that any conflict could not be localised and 'it would be impossible for Russia to refrain from going to the help of Serbia.'[9]

What Sazonov had not revealed to either Pourtalès or Szápáry was the level of Russian military preparations. These were extended further during the day as the Quarter-Master General Danilov, the man in charge of mobilisation plans, arrived back in St Petersburg. All magazines and supply depots were ordered to be fully operational, repairs on the railways were to be completed immediately and all units and depots were to be ready to receive the influx of reservists that would occur when mobilisation was ordered. The German military attaché, Major Eggeling, had already detected signs of Russian activity. A very accurate message was sent to Berlin that he regarded it 'as certain mobilisation ordered in Kiev and Odessa; Warsaw and Moscow doubtful, the rest probably not yet'.[10] The chargé at the United States embassy, Wilson, was only slightly exaggerating when he told Washington: 'Russian government has ordered complete army mobilisation to begin immediately.'[11]

London

During the day Prince Henry of Prussia saw George V. Henry remarked that if Russia did decide on war then it would inevitably mean revolution and the end of the Romanov dynasty. According to the message Henry sent to Berlin (via the German naval attaché at the embassy, who was present at the discussion), George V reassured the Prince that 'England would maintain neutrality in case war should break out between Continental Powers'.[12] This assurance was in line with the response given by Grey to Lichnowsky at the beginning of the crisis and the views expressed privately by Asquith. This message had a major impact in Berlin and convinced the German government that Britain would remain neutral – it was the third time they had heard this view expressed in the last few days. Prince Henry also told Berlin that the fleet, which had been taking part in the annual review at Spithead, was now being dispersed and crews were departing on leave – a clear sign that the British did not expect the military situation to worsen. (It was not until the evening that the dispersal of the fleet was stopped.)

At the Foreign Office, with Grey away in the country, the permanent secretary, Nicolson, was in charge. When he arrived shortly after 10 a.m., he knew that Austria–Hungary had broken off diplomatic relations with Serbia. He quickly read the overnight telegrams and learned that Russian partial mobilisation seemed imminent and that Sazonov had made threats about Britain's position in Asia if it did not cooperate with Russia. He also learned that Berlin had not supported the British request for an extension of the time limit but had merely passed it on to Vienna. He decided that Grey's idea of an ambassadors' conference to take place when relations between Austria–Hungary and Russia became critical would have to be brought forward. He therefore wrote a note to Grey at Itchen Abbas saying 'Germany is playing with us' and enclosing draft telegrams to initiate the proposed conference. He told Grey: 'I am not hopeful' and that the conference was 'a very poor chance – but in any case we shall have done our utmost'.[13] The documents were taken to Grey by messenger and he telephoned his agreement to Nicolson. At 3 p.m. telegrams were sent to the ambassadors in Paris, Vienna, St Petersburg, Berlin and Rome and the minister in Niš, instructing them to ask their respective foreign ministers if they would agree to a conference of ambassadors in London to try 'to find an issue to prevent complications'. While the conference was meeting, all sides were asked to suspend 'active military operations'.[14]

The prime minister, Asquith, was in Berkshire. He spent much of the day playing golf. He was still mainly concerned with the situation in Ireland and its political impact over the coming week. He had to return early to London because the nationalist Irish Volunteers had successfully brought a large consignment of guns ashore at Howth. British troops had tried to disarm some of the volunteers but had then opened fire on a crowd of civilians in Dublin, killing three people and injuring thirty-eight. Before he left for London he wrote a letter to Venetia Stanley, part of which was about the developing European crisis. He thought 'Russia is trying to drag us in'. However, on the ultimatum he thought that 'on many, if not most, of the points Austria has a good & Servia a very bad case'. The problem was that the Austrians were 'the stupidest people in Europe' and they had helped produce 'the most dangerous situation of the last 40 years'.[15] One of

Asquith's Cabinet colleagues, Herbert Samuel (the president of the Local Government Board) was also worried about what might happen in the coming week. He wrote to his mother that by the end of the week Europe might be on the brink of the bloodiest war in its history, adding, 'I hope our country may not be involved. But even of that one cannot be sure. At this stage I think it will not be.'[16] Another minister who, like Grey and Asquith, was out of London was Winston Churchill, the First Lord of the Admiralty. He was taking one of his very rare breaks with his wife and children at Cromer. In his absence, the First Sea Lord, Prince Louis of Battenberg, decided, in the light of the deteriorating European situation, to stop the dispersal of the fleet and maintain its crews at full strength. Churchill confirmed the order when he returned to London late that evening. These were the first British military moves in the crisis.

In the evening, before Grey returned to London, Nicolson, together with Grey's private secretary, Sir William Tyrrell, saw Lichnowsky, the German ambassador. Lichnowsky had been asked by Berlin, which was worried by the first signs of Russian military moves, to ask Grey to use his influence in St Petersburg to try and restrain the Russians. Berlin still hoped to do this on the basis that Austria–Hungary had pledged not to annex Serbian territory and therefore Russia should allow action against Serbia to proceed. The two British diplomats told Lichnowsky about the proposed conference (news of it first reached Berlin through this channel) and then explained their view of the situation. They said it was essential Austria–Hungary did not attack Serbia until the ambassadors' conference met. If, nevertheless, this did happen, Lichnowsky warned Berlin,

> every effort would have been in vain and the world war would be inevitable. The localisation of the conflict as hoped for in Berlin was wholly impossible, and must be dropped from the calculations of practical politics.[17]

Although the Foreign Office officials were taking a slightly stronger line than Grey, Berlin, not surprisingly, chose to believe the statements of Grey, Haldane and the King that Britain would almost certainly remain neutral in a European war.

Berlin

There was little diplomatic activity of any significance in Berlin that

Sunday. In general there was a mood of optimism that German strategy was succeeding. The Kaiser was still on board his yacht *Hohenzollern*, though now on his way back to Germany. Bethmann Hollweg sent him a telegram saying 'St Petersburg is visibly hesitating'.[18] At 6 p.m. the head of the Kaiser's military Cabinet, von Lyncker, who was accompanying the Kaiser, wrote to his wife that all on the yacht were more relaxed and once the Kaiser had assessed the situation on his return to Berlin the next day he would leave for the country. He concluded: 'It looks like beginning to disentangle itself . . . [it] does not look as if a European war were on the point of breaking out.'[19]

Nevertheless, the German general staff was still planning for all eventualities. It prepared a draft of a note to be given to the Belgian government just before Germany intended to violate its neutrality during the first stages of mobilisation. The draft said that Germany had reliable information that France planned to invade Belgium and it was therefore taking counteraction. If Belgium sided with Germany, its integrity and independence would be guaranteed and territorial 'compensations' could be considered. German troops would pay cash for all they needed in Belgium and pay an indemnity for any damage they might cause. If, however, Belgium took a hostile attitude, then no guarantees would be given and the future of the country would be decided by the outcome of the war. Belgium was to respond within twenty-four hours. A note to be sent to the Netherlands was also drafted. It promised German respect for neutrality – violation was no longer part of German military plans following Moltke's amendments to the Schlieffen plan.

Following the telegram from the German military representatives in St Petersburg reporting that Russia seemed to have begun early military moves, the general staff decided to initiate their own preliminary intelligence-gathering measures. Four of the *Spannungsreisende* were ordered to move into Russia. Wilbert E. Stratton, a London businessman who worked for the Pyrene Company (he held a US passport), was sent to St Petersburg. A Herr Beckers went to Moscow and a Herr Ventski travelled to Vilnius, Minsk and Warsaw. Herr Henoumont went to Warsaw and eventually made two trips before the borders were closed later in the week. The German military were not worried about the situation on their western frontier and did not send anybody into France.

Paris

The only important diplomatic event that day in Paris was a call the German ambassador made on the Quai d'Orsay at 5 p.m. He saw Bienvenu-Martin (the temporary foreign minister) and Berthelot (the deputy civil service head). Schoen asked whether the French would be willing to advise Russia to keep out of the conflict now that Vienna had said it would not annex Serbian territory. The French said that Germany should also exercise restraint in Vienna because Serbia had conceded on most points. Schoen's telegram to Berlin records Bienvenu-Martin as saying 'he was most willing to exercise a quietening influence in St Petersburg now that, by the Austrian declaration that no annexation was intended, the conditions for doing so had been created'. In addition, he considered Sazonov's idea that all the powers acting together could pass judgement on Serbia was 'juridicially hardly tenable'.[20] The temporary foreign minister had certainly gone far further towards understanding the Austro-Hungarian position than Poincaré and Viviani would have done. His views about restraining Russia and allowing Vienna a free hand with Serbia did not square with the strong statements of support for Russia that had been given during the state visit and the advice Paléologue was giving in St Petersburg.

Not surprisingly, Schoen was greatly encouraged by his talk at the Quai d'Orsay. After drafting his telegram to Berlin he returned to the foreign ministry where he saw Berthelot (Bienvenu-Martin had already gone home). Schoen said that he would like to make a press statement saying that Germany and France were 'acting in an identical spirit of peaceful co-operation' to find ways of preserving peace. Berthelot refused to agree to such a statement and gave the German ambassador a long lecture saying that Vienna would not be acting as it had without German approval and that Germany was refusing to mediate in Vienna. Schoen responded by arguing that Austria–Hungary only rejected formal mediation and the 'spectre' of a conference where it might be arraigned before what could be seen as a European tribunal. He added that Germany would not refuse to give advice to Vienna in all circumstances. On this sour note the meeting ended.

Berthelot then saw the Russian chargé, Sevastopulo, and told him that the German action earlier in the evening was simply designed to intimidate France into putting pressure on Russia. He then gave his own shrewd assessment of the situation. He thought Austria–Hungary and Germany 'aimed at a brilliant diplomatic victory but not at war at any price, although in the extreme case they would not recoil from it'.[21]

The French took some decisions that Sunday. Messages were sent to *France*, somewhere in the Baltic, advising that the state visits to Denmark and Norway should be abandoned and the presidential party should return to France as soon as possible. Communications were difficult (they were being made via the German radio station at Norddeich near Bremen) and it is unclear whether Poincaré and Viviani received this advice. Meanwhile, Adolphe Messimy, the minister of war, took the first French military measures of the crisis. Officers were recalled from leave and other ranks were recalled from harvest duty. Protection of the railways was instituted, though at this stage only civilians were involved in the task.

Rome

During the morning, San Giuliano had another talk with Flotow at Fiuggi. His main aim was to try to gain German support in tackling Austria–Hungary about 'compensation'. The Italian foreign minister said that Vienna's actions were 'highly questionable' and that the Italian government was worried that if they were successfull against Serbia then the same tactics could be used against them later. He did not believe the assurances about no territorial acquisitions by Austria–Hungary and Italy would therefore make a claim for compensation. Obviously any claim would be strengthened if Germany supported it. Flotow thought such a claim was premature but San Giuliano hinted that if Italy's claims were not recognised it would be obliged 'to step in Austria's way'.[22]

This rather crude attempt at blackmail worked. The diplomats in Berlin were already alarmed that Vienna had treated the Italians badly during the run-up to the crisis by not consulting them (though Germany had agreed with this line). The German military were also convinced that Italian participation was important if a European war did start. Bethmann Hollweg therefore sent a telegram to Tschirschky in Vienna instructing him to tell the Austro-Hungarian government:

> An understanding between Vienna and Rome is necessary. Vienna must not evade this with questionable interpretations of the treaty, but take decisions in keeping with the seriousness of the situation.[23]

This was rather easier for Germany to advocate because it was not its territory that was at stake. The problems the issue of 'compensation' caused in Vienna were explained in a letter Tschirschky dispatched to Jagow following a talk he had with Macchio. The latter pointed out that it was impossible for Vienna to give up the Trentino (which was what Italy wanted) because it was part of the empire and the Emperor and the army would never agree – giving Italy part of the Balkans was a different matter. Indeed, Conrad suggested to Tschirschky that Italy should get Montenegro.

In Rome, that evening, Rodd saw San Giuliano to convey the British proposal for the ambassadors' conference. San Giuliano 'welcomed' the proposal but said he had to consult Berlin and Vienna first.[24] When the Italian foreign minister saw Flotow afterwards he still had to pretend that he was a full supporter of the Triple Alliance (he had to do this to keep German support for 'compensation'). He said it was important not to reject Grey's proposals 'brusquely' because this would 'drive him into the opposite camp, whereas his cooperation is now precious'.[25] However, Rodd had already given London his advice on how Italy's policy was developing. Italy had not been consulted about the Austro-Hungarian action which it would now interpret as 'constructively provoking Russia' and therefore Italy would argue it was not bound by its alliance obligations.[26]

During the course of the evening, the Serbian chargé in Rome, Mihailjović, spoke to officials in the foreign ministry. He gave them the impression that Serbia would now accept the ultimatum unconditionally. However, he was speaking personally and had not received any instructions from Serbia to take this initiative. The Italian foreign ministry misunderstood this and the idea that Serbia would now accept the ultimatum unconditionally formed the basis of Italian policy for much of the rest of the crisis. Meanwhile, across the city the Vatican was continuing with its strong support for Austria–Hungary. It published an official note saying: 'Austria has waited too long in demanding reparation.'

The Rest of Europe

In Bucharest the Austro-Hungarian minister, Czernin, saw King Carol. The King said that Serbia's reply was tantamount to full acceptance and asked whether Vienna contemplated territorial changes for Serbia (which the Romanians feared could only benefit their enemy Bulgaria). The King emphasised that any such changes 'would be unacceptable to Romania' and that the status quo in the Treaty of Bucharest had to be upheld.[27] The message that Vienna sent to Czernin in response simply said that Austro-Hungarian actions would benefit the whole Triple Alliance and they would take no action affecting Romania without consulting them first. But this message contained no guarantees to reassure Bucharest. Romania was told that it was expected to act as a loyal ally if Russia intervened because the defeat of Austria–Hungary and Germany would result 'in the complete abandonment of Romania to Russia and Slav domination'.[28] It was becoming increasingly clear that there were few, if any, common interests between Bucharest and Vienna and their nominal alliance was disintegrating.

Greece was firming up its position that it would support Serbia if Bulgaria intervened but not otherwise. Venizelos was still in Munich when a telegram arrived via Athens from Alexandropulos, the Greek minister in Belgrade. It conveyed a question from Pašić: could Serbia rely on Greek support if it was attacked by Austria–Hungary and also by Bulgaria? Venizelos said his view was that if Austria–Hungary attacked Serbia, Greece would make a decision 'as soon as we were in possession of all the data, taking into account our own capacity to render assistance', i.e. the alliance would not apply. If Bulgaria attacked, the prime minister said he would advise the King 'to send all our forces against Bulgaria'.[29]

In Cetinje, Austria–Hungary made its bid for Montenegrin neutrality. Their representative Otto saw King Nicholas and offered him a bribe of six million kronen to stay neutral in any war between Austria–Hungary and Serbia. The King was non-committal and the diplomatic corps in the town picked up, as usual, different messages about Montenegrin policy. Delaroche-Vernet reported to Paris 'this offer has not been accepted'.[30] The German military attaché reported that the King had told him 'he would do everything to avoid war with Austria'.[31]

In Brussels the secretary of the International Socialist Bureau, Camille Huysmans, summoned a meeting of the various national representatives for Wednesday 29 July. Meanwhile, King Albert of Belgium still planned to leave for his motoring holiday across Europe. He had taken out an International Certificate for Motor Vehicles under the pseudonym he would be using on his travels – Count de Réthy.

MONDAY 27 JULY

Niš

The Serbian government arrived at the new capital in the early hours of Monday morning. The situation was now much clearer than when they had left Belgrade thirty-six hours earlier. Spalajković in St Petersburg reported that Russia was preparing for partial mobilisation against Austria–Hungary and in any war would launch a major offensive in Galicia, which would relieve the pressure on Serbia. The Serbian reply to the ultimatum had, despite all its carefully drafted reservations, been generally welcomed in the European capitals other than Vienna and Berlin. Italy seemed likely to be neutral and this would increase the problems Austria–Hungary faced in any war. Later in the day the Serbian government learned of the British initiative for a conference, which they thought would be advantageous – it would put Austria–Hungary and Serbia in a roughly equal position. The main worry for Pašić was the possible role of Bulgaria and whether it would try to take advantage of an Austro-Hungarian attack to advance into Macedonia in the Serbian rear in an attempt to recover territory lost in the Treaty of Bucharest. Pašić saw the Bulgarian minister and said there would be 'good consequences' if Bulgaria did not cause any complications.[1] It is unlikely that the Bulgarian government took any notice of this vague promise – there was little Serbia could offer its rival and if it did survive an Austro-Hungarian attack it was hardly likely that it would give Bulgaria anything.

The Serbian cabinet met in the morning and agreed that, in view of the improving diplomatic situation and the promise of Russian support, they did not need to take any further action. As Pašić wrote at 6.50 p.m. that evening:

> We have made our last concession – further we will not go, nor will we seek mediation, for that would suggest that we are ready to yield even more. Russia is resolute. Italy neutral.[2]

There was no prospect of Serbia shifting to an unconditional acceptance of the Austro-Hungarian ultimatum – indeed, Pašić felt he had already conceded too much and would not have gone as far as he did had he been surer of Russian support a couple of days earlier. Serbia might not seek mediation but the major powers, especially Russia, could pressurise it into acceptance if they wanted. At this point any significant Serbian impact on the developing crisis came to an end. The Serbian government continued with its military preparations, waited for the expected Austro-Hungarian attack and watched the developing European crisis.

London

News about the decision to keep the fleet concentrated and at full strength was published in the newspapers that morning. The Foreign Office did not know until late evening how the rest of Europe was reacting to its diplomatic initiative for an ambassadors' conference launched the previous afternoon.

On his return to the office, Grey had a clearer picture of the dangers inherent in the situation than he did before the weekend. He decided to see Lichnowsky. He told him he had seen the Serbian reply and thought it agreed with the Austro-Hungarian demands 'to an extent such as he would never have believed possible'. He felt this had to be the result of Russian pressure (which was not correct) but that if Vienna now invaded then such action would prove it had only been seeking an excuse to inflict a military defeat on Serbia. In these circumstances Austria–Hungary would be making a direct challenge to Russia which it would probably be unable to decline. Germany should therefore urge its ally to accept the Serbian reply. Lichnowsky argued Germany would have to support Austria–Hungary against Russia, not on the merits of the dispute but because it could not afford to see its only ally crushed. Grey made a veiled threat that, as he reported to Rumbold in Berlin, 'other issues might be raised that would supersede the dispute between Austria and Servia, and would bring other Powers in, and the war would be the biggest ever known'.[3] Grey was probably more clear-cut in talking to Lichnowsky than he was prepared to acknowledge in his telegram which would be circulated among his colleagues in Whitehall. Lichnowsky reported to Berlin that he was sure Britain:

> would place herself unconditionally by the side of France and Russia in order to show that she is not willing to permit a moral, or perhaps a military, defeat of her group. If it comes to war under these conditions we shall have England against us.[4]

Berlin, believing it had better information about British policy, made only cosmetic changes to its strategy when it received Lichnowsky's telegram.

In the afternoon Grey saw Mensdorff and told him roughly what he had said to Lichnowsky. He added that he thought Austria–Hungary believed it could make war on Serbia without involving Russia. He then used an unfortunate phrase: 'If they could make war on Servia and at the same time satisfy Russia, well and good' but if they could not the consequences would be 'incalculable'.[5] The problem was that Vienna thought it could make war on Serbia and keep Russia out through vague assurances about not annexing Serbian territory. Grey's phraseology was only likely to reinforce such assumptions. After this meeting Grey went to the House of Commons to make a brief statement about the diplomatic situation but there was no debate.

Asquith was mainly involved in a series of meetings about the Irish crisis, which seemed even more intractable after the gun-running and the shootings in Dublin the previous day. In his letter to Venetia Stanley he did not mention the European situation (apart from Grey's statement) but did report the view in some quarters of the government that war might be a way out of the Irish crisis:

> Winston on the other hand is all for this way of escape from Irish troubles and when things looked rather better . . . he exclaimed, moodily, that it looked after all as if we were in for a 'bloody peace'![6]

The cabinet met for an hour in Asquith's room at the House of Commons at 5.30 p.m. Nearly all of the discussion was about Ireland, but at the end Grey raised the possibility of a European war and Britain's position. Grey's assessment of the situation was quite frank, as one member of the Cabinet recorded:

> Both groups are waiting for England's decision. If she kept aloof from France and Russia we should forfeit naturally their confidence for ever, and Germany would almost certainly attack France while Russia was mobilising. If on the other hand we said we were prepared to throw our lot in with the *Entente*, Russia would at once attack Austria. Consequently our influence for peace depended on our apparent indecision. Italy, dishonest as usual, was repudiating her obligations to the Triplice.[7]

There were already signs that opinion in the cabinet was badly divided over whether Britain should support France in a war with Germany. A minority refused to accept intervention on these terms. Others were bellicose from the beginning, as Hobhouse recorded in his diary: 'Churchill was of course for any enterprise which gave him a chance of displaying the Navy as his instrument of destruction.'[8]

The Cabinet endorsed the decision to keep the fleet at full strength and also agreed that the first stage in Britain's war plans should be implemented – warning telegrams were sent to all naval, military and colonial bases ordering them to implement the measures contained in the War Book for the 'precautionary period'. The cabinet also agreed to discuss Britain's obligations to Belgium at their next meeting. Some members were already clear that this was likely to be the crucial issue for Britain. In the evening Lloyd George discussed the situation with the newspaper editor, C. P. Scott. He told him Germany would try to cripple France before dealing with Russia. During this phase the British fleet might have to protect the northern French coast as the French army advanced 'to meet the German invasion across Belgium'.[9] Herbert Samuel was less sure that Britain could keep out of a war than he had been the previous evening. He wrote to his wife: 'I am still inclined to be pessimistic about the outlook.'[10]

Berlin – Morning

When the policy-makers reassembled in Berlin on the Monday morning, they were still optimistic that the strategy they and Austria–Hungary had decided upon some three weeks earlier was working. They still believed that through seizing the diplomatic initiative and dictating the pace of the crisis they could pressurise Russia into allowing Austria–Hungary to secure its extensive aims against Serbia. Even if Russia did decide to intervene militarily they were convinced that Britain would not intervene in a European war, giving Germany and Austria–Hungary a good chance of success.

Remarkably, the German government had still not seen the text of the Serbian reply delivered over thirty-six hours earlier. Their ally had not seen fit to send it to them and in the middle of the morning Tschirschky was asked to obtain a copy. He did not send the text until early the next morning and Germany eventually obtained a copy from the Serbian minister in Berlin on Monday evening. Jagow sent a copy to the Kaiser at Potsdam by special messenger at 9.30 p.m. This delay in obtaining a copy of the reply was to have a fundamental impact on the development of the crisis.

Although the British embassy had still not formally conveyed Grey's suggestion for an ambassadors' conference, the Wilhelmstrasse was aware of the proposal from Lichnowsky's telegram sent the previous day. The German government was still determined to have nothing to do with the idea. Jagow saw Szögyény to warn him that later in the day they would be forwarding the British proposal to Vienna. He told him, as the ambassador reported to Vienna:

> The German Government assures in the most decided way that it does not identify itself with these propositions, that on the contrary it advises to disregard them.[11]

Jagow said that the proposals were only being sent on to satisfy London, because it was vital to ensure that Britain did not side with France and Russia.

During the morning Jagow also saw the French ambassador, Jules Cambon, who called to support the British proposal. Jagow was worried by the early signs of Russian military preparations and said that if Russia did mobilise then Germany would do so 'at once'. He then made a statement that Cambon immediately passed on to Bronevski, the Russia chargé, who in turn told St Petersburg. According to Cambon, Jagow said, 'We shall mobilise either if Russia mobilises on our frontier or if Russian troops invade Austrian territory.' This was to have a significant impact on Russian policy. They interpreted the statement (not unreasonably) as German acceptance of Russian partial mobilisation against Austria–Hungary as long as they did not actually attack in Galicia or mobilise along the German frontier.[12] Bronevski also saw Jagow himself, to follow up Sazonov's proposal made on the previous day for direct talks between Russia and Austria–Hungary. Jagow said, very unenthusiastically, that 'as Szápáry had begun the conversation, he might as well go on with it'. Berlin would not pressurise Vienna to accept the proposal but would 'pass on' their information about the talks, which Jagow argued, rather unconvincingly, would be an indication of German approval.[13]

Late in the morning Bethmann Hollweg sent a telegram to Lichnowsky conveying the official rejection of Grey's proposal:

> We could not take part in such a conference, as we would not be able to summon Austria before a European court of justice in her case with Serbia.

He added that Sazonov's suggestion for direct talks 'appears to me to be feasible'.[14] Although the chancellor did not set out his reasoning in the telegram, it was obvious that Berlin did not want Austria–Hungary and Serbia treated as equals in the dispute and direct talks between

Vienna and St Petersburg would tend to localise the dispute and mean that less pressure was put on Vienna to compromise.

Berlin – Afternoon

The Kaiser arrived back in the capital from his cruise at 1 p.m. He was met at the Wildpark station by Bethmann Hollweg who briefed him on the diplomatic situation. The Kaiser travelled on to Potsdam and called a conference of his advisers for the afternoon. At 3.10 p.m. he saw Bethmann Hollweg and afterwards had a separate meeting with the military chiefs. No specific decisions were taken but the tone of the discussions remained optimistic. The policy initiated at the start of the crisis seemed to be working and no military action was expected for some time. Moltke wrote to his wife: 'The situation continues to be extremely obscure . . . It will be about another fortnight before anything definite can be known or said.'[15] Similarly, General Plessen, the Kaiser's adjutant-general, recorded in his diary:

> The Austrians are not nearly ready! It will be the beginning of August before operations can begin. It is hoped to localize the war! England declares she means to remain neutral. I have the impression that it will all blow over.[16]

Both these assessments were clearly based on the assumption that Austria–Hungary would take sixteen days to mobilise. Even if, as Germany had suggested two days earlier, a declaration of war were made in the next couple of days, in order to restrict the room for diplomatic intervention, this should not change the situation significantly.

In the afternoon the British ambassador, Goschen, finally called at the foreign ministry to put forward Grey's proposal for a conference of ambassadors – something which Germany had already rejected. The British embassy had not acted on the instructions from London for almost twenty-four hours because they were waiting for Goschen to return from London. He travelled overnight by train and boat via Flushing. Because of the short notice, he was only able to secure the last, small, sleeping berth over the wheels which he found 'most uncomfortable'. No doubt the journey did not improve his already gloomy mood as he noted in his diary: 'Rather low in my mind – as Russia can under the circs hardly remain indifferent – and then . . .?'[17] Jagow immediately rejected the British suggestion, describing it as practically a 'court of arbitration'. He said that Germany preferred to take up the suggestion for direct Austro-Hungarian–Russian talks and see how they went. During a discussion about possible military developments, Jagow again said that 'if Russia only mobilised in the south [i.e. against Austria–Hungary] Germany would not mobilise'. However, Jagow did add that the Russian system was so complicated that it might be difficult to judge what was happening and Germany could not allow Russia to gain a head start.[18]

During the day reports from intelligence units along the frontier with Russia began to arrive in Berlin. They indicated that Russian preliminary mobilisation measures were underway. The messages from Königsberg reported that frontier guards along the border with East Prussia had been placed on alert, that troop trains were moving from Kovno towards the border while empty freight trains (to carry the mobilised troops) were moving into Russia away from the border. By the afternoon it was clear that Russian frontier guards all along the border were on a high state of alert, that army units were leaving their summer training grounds for their depots, that rolling stock was being assembled at Vilnius and that martial law had been declared in some areas and fortified towns. At 4 p.m. the general staff intelligence committee concluded that Russia was beginning to implement its 'period preparatory to war'. Nevertheless, there was no pressure to begin similar German preparations and it was expected that the period of tension would last for some weeks. The last of the 'tension travellers' was not due to leave until 4 August. The first report from one of these agents, Ventski, arrived later in the day. He confirmed, through previously agreed phrases in an uncoded commercial telegram, that war preparations had begun in Vilnius.

Berlin – Evening
During the course of the evening, the telegrams from Lichnowsky recording his talk with Grey that morning arrived in Berlin. They provided the first sign that German strategy might not be working. Lichnowsky's assessment that Britain did not think localisation of the dispute between Austria–Hungary and Serbia could be achieved and that Britain would support France and Russia during the dispute, perhaps even to the point of joining them in any European war, did have an impact on Bethmann Hollweg. The information did not produce a radical rethink of German policy but the chancellor did decide that it would be politic not to alienate Britain if at all possible.

He decided Germany should not reject mediation proposals out of hand, if only because of the impression this would create.

Just before midnight he sent a telegram to Tschirschky in Vienna setting out the new approach:

> If we rejected every mediation proposal the whole world would hold us responsible for the conflagration and we would be represented as the ones driving towards war. That would make our own position at home an impossible one where we must appear as the ones being forced into war. We cannot therefore reject the role of mediator . . . I want Count Berchtold's views on the English suggestion and on M. Sazonov's desire to negotiate directly with Vienna.[19]

A couple of hours later a reply was sent to Lichnowsky. It explained that Berlin had rejected the idea that they should put pressure on Austria–Hungary to accept the Serbian reply after Vienna had already rejected it and after Serbia had mobilised. Bethmann Hollweg explained:

> Austria intended – and it is not only her right but her duty – to secure herself against the continuation of the undermining of her own existence through the Greater Serbia propaganda.

After this restatement of the hard-line position taken up by Berlin and Vienna at the start of the crisis, Bethmann Hollweg tried to give some reassurance: 'In the sense desired by Sir Edward Grey we have at once begun mediatory action at Vienna.' He added that they had also asked about the direct talks between Austria–Hungary and Russia.[20] The 'at once' was hardly true – there had been a gap of almost a day – but Germany was no longer rejecting these ideas out of hand as it had at lunchtime. Even so, it had done no more than ask for Vienna's opinions on possible mediation.

Vienna

Policy-makers in Vienna were still trying to decide how to react to the German demand, communicated on Sunday, that Austria–Hungary should declare war on Serbia even though it could not start military operations for over a fortnight. Conrad was still worried that, if Austro-Hungarian forces were deployed against Serbia before they knew what Russia would do, then if Russia did intervene, it would be almost impossible to mount a successful defence against a Russian attack into Galicia. Nevertheless, when Berchtold sent Hoyos to see

Conrad during the morning the latter gave way. He would agree to a declaration of war 'provided diplomatic considerations made it seem necessary'.[21]

Berchtold still wanted to show Berlin that Austria–Hungary was a strong and decisive ally. The diplomatic situation still seemed to be favourable. Szápáry's report of his conversation with Sazonov the previous day suggested that the Russian foreign minister was much calmer and had recognised that Austria–Hungary had legitimate claims to make on Serbia. Szögyény reported from Berlin that Sazonov had told Pourtalès 'Russia would only mobilise if and when Austria–Hungary were to assume a hostile attitude towards Russia'.[22] This was bound to reinforce the view that any conflict with Serbia could be localised. A declaration of war and partial mobilisation directed at Serbia could not be interpreted as directly threatening Russia. The prospect of mediation was still in the air, even if Germany was not supporting it. Berchtold therefore decided to declare war on Serbia. A draft declaration was prepared which the foreign minister forwarded to Franz Josef who was still at Bad Ischl. Berchtold explained it was 'not impossible that the Triple Entente Powers might yet try to achieve a peaceful solution of the conflict unless a clear situation is created by a declaration of war'.[23]

Vienna, rather optimistically, did not expect much to change following the declaration of war on Serbia. No military operations would start for two weeks and a solution might still be found. As the Emperor told Giesl, who was seeing him to report on his actions in Belgrade, 'this still does not mean war . . . we are not at war yet, and if I can, I shall prevent it'.[24] Tschirschky reported to Berlin that the official declaration of war would be made on 28 July, or perhaps the day after, 'in order to cut away the ground from any attempt at intervention'.[25] His report was available in Berlin at 4.37 p.m. and may have played a part in shifting Bethmann Hollweg towards not rejecting all mediation efforts.

During the afternoon, reports arrived in Vienna from the military attaché in St Petersburg. These indicated that Russia was beginning extensive military preparations in the St Petersburg, Moscow, Kiev, Warsaw and Odessa military districts. Although these reports were exaggerated, they caused Conrad considerable alarm. He remained worried about the safety of attacking Serbia if the reserves were needed against Russia. Having committed himself, at least in theory, to the attack on Serbia, he now wanted Germany to resolve Vienna's problems. At a meeting with Berchtold and Tschirschky he suggested a way out of the dilemma. If Russia did, at some point, mobilise against Austria–Hungary, then he wanted, as Tschirschky reported to Berlin, the Germans to say 'this mobilisation constitutes such a threat on the Russian southern and western frontier that corresponding measures would have to be taken'.[26] Conrad may have hoped that this would only be a threat, but it showed a severe misapprehension of his ally's war plans (about which Moltke had briefed him). If Germany mobilised, it inevitably meant war and an attack on France with only minimal forces left against Russia. Such action would be of no help to Austria–Hungary but it would start a European war. Conrad did not know that Jagow had already stated on two occasions that Germany would not mobilise if Russia only mobilised against Austria–Hungary.

St Petersburg

During the morning Sazonov saw Buchanan, who transmitted London's suggestion for the ambassadors' conference. Sazonov was not keen on the idea because he believed he had secured Austro-Hungarian agreement to direct talks on the modification of the ultimatum. Not surprisingly, he preferred to go down this route before reverting to the British proposal if direct talks failed.

Sazonov then saw Pourtalès. The Russian foreign minister was still in an optimistic mood. He said that because Vienna had pledged that it would not annex Serbian territory and had not made any hostile moves, despite breaking off relations, 'the moment had come . . . to seek the means by an exchange of views among the Powers . . . "to build a golden bridge" for Austria'. Sazonov said he was not worried about the exact means used to achieve this and that he had no wish to humiliate Austria–Hungary. He argued, with some justification, that if Serbia had accepted the ultimatum, there would have been a revolution and an even more nationalistic government would have taken power. He 'urgently begged' the German ambassador for cooperation. Pourtalès was in a much less accommodating mood than the previous morning. He did not know whether Vienna would be prepared to modify its demands but thought it was time to put an end to the endless Serbian provocations – 'Europe ought not to try to stay Austria's arm in her present quarrel with Serbia'. Serbia would have to behave like a civilised nation if it wanted equal rights. Sazonov did not expressly reject these arguments. He merely said, 'It must be possible to find some way of giving Serbia a well-merited lesson while respecting her sovereign rights.' This was hardly wholehearted support for Serbia and on this unresolved note the conversation ended.[27]

Sazonov then instructed the minister for war, General Sukhomlinov, to see the German military attaché, Major Eggeling. The latter reported to Berlin that Sukhomlinov gave 'his word of honour that no order for mobilization had been issued as yet' (which was true). He admitted that 'purely preparatory measures' were being taken (which was also true). Sukhomlinov then made a clear statement of the Russian position. If the Austro-Hungarian army crossed the Serbian frontier, then Russia would mobilise in those military districts facing Austria–Hungary – Kiev, Odessa, Moscow and Kazan. But 'in no circumstances on German front: Warsaw, Vilna or St Petersburg'. Eggeling responded by warning that 'even mobilization against Austria alone must be regarded as very dangerous'.[28] During the day Russia decided to extend its preliminary military preparations from European Russia to include the military districts of the Caucasus, Turkestan, Omsk and Irkutsk.

Paris

The messages to the presidential party on *France* finally got through and it was agreed that the state visits to Denmark and Norway would be cancelled. Poincaré and Viviani would return to Paris as quickly as possible, although inevitably the journey would take a couple of days. The president and prime minister discussed the situation as the ship sailed towards the North Sea. Poincaré noted in his diary:

> I passed part of the day explaining to Viviani that weakness towards Germany always resulted in complications and that the only way to remove the danger was to show firm perseverance and impassive *sang froid*. But he is nervous and agitated and doesn't stop pronouncing imprudent words or phrases which reveal a black ignorance in matters of foreign policy.[29]

In Paris there was only desultory activity during the day. Schoen wrote to Berthelot again suggesting France should influence Russia to take a peaceful line. When he visited Abel Ferry, the under-secretary at the foreign ministry, he even made the remarkable suggestion that Germany and France should jointly intervene between Austria–Hungary and Russia. The idea was rejected (and would not have been accepted by Berlin anyway). Schoen was not the only person advising the French to moderate policy in St Petersburg. The British ambassador, Sir Francis Bertie, was doing the same. He reported to London that France should tell its ally 'not to assume the absurd and obsolete attitude of Russia being the protectress of all Slav states, whatever their conduct, for this will lead to war'.[30] London did not act on Bertie's advice – it would have had little impact in St Petersburg and Britain did not want to alienate Russia, given the wider imperial interests at stake.

During the day the French cabinet met and agreed a number of further precautionary military moves. The majority of troops in Algeria and Morocco would be recalled to France. The French military appear to have been worried that if Russia did mobilise only against Austria–Hungary (leaving very few troops to attack Germany), then France might have to face an even stronger German invasion during the first weeks of any war. The cabinet also agreed to institute military protection of the railways.

Rome

During the morning San Giuliano saw Rodd to discuss the British proposal for a conference. The Italian foreign minister thought, correctly, that Germany would not advise its ally to stop any military action even during the meeting of the conference, but perhaps Austria–Hungary would do so on its own accord. He argued that if Serbia now accepted the ultimatum Vienna would be satisfied. He thought Serbia was now ready to do this (a view based on the misleading impression given by Mihailjović the previous evening) and would certainly do so if the conference of ambassadors so 'advised'. This might have been the basis for a solution but San Giuliano made no effort over the next few days in either Berlin or Vienna to develop this approach.

The most active diplomat in Rome that day was the French ambassador, Camille Barrère, who had been in his post since the turn of the century. In the morning he saw the colonial minister, Ferdinando Martini, who told him he did 'not see any possibility of this country marching at the side of Austria'. He then saw the prime minister, Salandra, and gained the impression that Italy 'would like to stay out and maintain an attitude of watchfulness'. In the evening he saw San Giuliano at Fiuggi. The foreign minister expressed 'severe criticism' of the ultimatum but thought Serbia should have accepted it in its entirety so as to place Austria–Hungary 'in an embarrassing position'. San Giuliano denied that Italy had given approval for Vienna's actions and added it had not given any assurance that it would fulfil its alliance obligations.[31]

At the Vatican the Austro-Hungarian minister, Count Pállfy, saw Cardinal Merry del Val, the secretary of state. He reported that 'of gentleness or conciliatoriness there was no trace' in the cardinal's attitude. He thought the note to Serbia was 'sharp' but hoped Vienna would see the affair through to the end and added it was a pity that 'Serbia had not long since been "cut up small"'. Pállfy told Vienna that this was also the view of the Pope, who had for years expressed regret that Austria–Hungary had failed to 'chastize her dangerous neighbour'. The minister concluded that the Pope and the cardinal saw Serbia as 'the rodent ulcer' eating its way into Austria–Hungary which was the Catholic Church's 'stoutest champion in the fight against the Orthodox Church'.[32]

The Low Countries

In Brussels the regular army was put on alert, but no call-up of reservists was instituted. The Belgian government was becoming concerned about its position as the crisis deepened. It was, however, principally worried by France and its policy of all-out attack in war. It thought that French troops might advance into Belgium to meet German troops as far forward as possible and therefore be the first to violate Belgian neutrality. The secretary-general at the foreign ministry, van der Elst, saw the French minister, Klobukowski, to make clear that Belgium would 'employ all resources at the present hour available to it to defend its territory against any violation from wheresoever it may come'.[33]

In The Hague the Dutch foreign minister, Jonkheer Loudon, called the Belgian minister, Baron Fallon, to the foreign ministry. He asked what steps Belgium was taking to defend itself, explaining that the Netherlands was worried that German troops might move through its territory in order to avoid the forts around Liège (which was the basis of the original German plan drawn up by Schlieffen). He argued that the Netherlands and Belgium ought to consider a joint defence and asked to be kept in touch with Belgian planning. Although Fallon reported the talk to Brussels, his telegram was never passed on to the Belgian minister for war and so no action was taken on the suggestion. It was the nearest the two countries came to a coordinated policy and over the next few days they drifted further apart.

Bucharest

When Czernin studied the telegram sent from Vienna the previous day asking him to make vague and nebulous assurances to the Romanian government in return for a pledge of support in any war, he realised this policy would not work. He saw King Carol who merely replied that Austria–Hungary 'could unfortunately scarcely reckon on military support from Romania'. If the pro-German and pro-Austro-Hungarian King was taking this attitude, Czernin realised the situation as far as Vienna was concerned was poor. He told Berchtold:

> Nobody in Romania believes that when we actually have Serbia prostrate we shall content ourselves with acceptance of the 'Note', leaving the now existent Big Serbia intact.

He reported that the Romanian politicians were convinced that Vienna had already 'assigned, perhaps even promised, a large slice of Serbia to the Bulgarians'. He argued that if Romania was to be kept neutral it was 'absolutely necessary to indicate now as soon as possible the territory that is to be assigned to her'.[34]

The Romanian foreign minister, Porumbaro, saw the French minister, Blondel, to respond to a series of questions the minister had raised a couple of days earlier. He stated Romania's position as being one of solidarity with Serbia and Greece to maintain the Treaty of Bucharest if Bulgaria tried to alter it. It would not intervene in any Austro-Hungarian war with Serbia as long as Vienna did not try to modify the Treaty of Bucharest. Meanwhile, the Russians were trying to coax Romania on to their side. On instructions from St Petersburg, the Russian minister, Poklevski, saw the prime minister, Bratianu. He told him Russia could not leave Serbia to its fate, but if Austria–Hungary was successful, then Romania would probably be their next target.

Washington

The European crisis had almost no impact on the United States, which was mainly concerned with the civil war in Mexico, and the government made no attempt at intervention. President Woodrow Wilson spent most of the period of the crisis at the bedside of his wife Ellen (she died on 6 August). His only comment was at a press conference on this Monday. He was asked about the American position and responded that it was the traditional policy of the United States not to take part in political affairs outside of the western hemisphere. The American government played no part in the rest of the crisis – indeed Japan, as we shall see, was more involved than the United States.

By the end of the day, very little had happened to resolve the crisis. The Russians had made their suggestion for direct talks with Austria–Hungary but Vienna had not reacted. The British proposal for a conference of ambassadors had been sidelined in St Petersburg and Rome and effectively rejected in Berlin. However, the first signs were already emerging that the situation might slip rapidly out of control. By the early evening, the German government knew that its ally had responded to their pressure and would declare war on Serbia shortly. This would significantly restrict Russia's room for manoeuvre. It might well push it down the road of military preparation – it had already moved further in this direction than any other country apart from Serbia. France seemed to be encouraging its ally and giving it a free hand to deal with the situation as it saw fit. Russian military preparations were being detected in Berlin, although no counter-measures had yet been taken. The conversion of Berlin, late in the evening, to not opposing the British suggestion for a conference, even if it was not wholeheartedly supporting it, was largely cosmetic and unlikely to have any major impact.

TUESDAY 28 JULY

Vienna

On the previous day a draft declaration of war on Serbia had been prepared, but the most pressing problem on the Tuesday morning was Italy. Overnight a telegram had arrived from Merey, the fervently anti-Italian ambassador in Rome. He warned Berchtold, rightly, not to trust any of the assurances given by Avarna, the Italian ambassador in Vienna. He told the foreign secretary that Avarna was not trusted in Rome and that anyway his friendly remarks were 'primarily, if not exclusively, intended as a preliminary to claims for compensation'.[1] Merey argued that these claims should be denied and that Italy was not strong enough to cause significant trouble. Privately he thought that if Austria–Hungary defeated Serbia it would send a message to Italy about how their claims against the Habsburg empire would be treated.

On his return to Berlin on the previous day, the Kaiser had made it clear that it was 'absolutely essential that Austria should arrive at an understanding with Italy in time for it to be of use'.[2] Tschirschky was instructed to raise the matter immediately with Berchtold. The result was that the German ambassador visited the foreign minister early on the Tuesday morning. He passed on the Kaiser's message and also said: 'the German Government interpreted Article VII in the same way as the Italian' – i.e. any acquisition of territory by Austria–Hungary in the Balkans automatically entitled Italy to compensation. The German ambassador made a 'solemn and emphatic appeal' for Vienna to resolve the problem, telling Berchtold that it would cause Germany military problems if Italy did not join its allies in any war. Under this sort of pressure, Berchtold had little choice but to make a limited concession. Merey was instructed to tell the Italian government that Austria–Hungary did not intend to make any territorial acquisitions (which was untrue), but if a 'purely temporary' occupation was necessary, then it would 'enter upon an exchange of views with Italy on compensation'. Although Vienna had conceded discussions, it had not given way on the principle of compensation nor on the rival inter-pretations of Article VII. The Italians, however, wanted a firm promise of territory before the war started so that they could judge whether it was worthwhile supporting their allies. The core of Austria–Hungary's position was unchanged. In Berlin Szögyény was instructed to tell the German government that 'the question of detaching any portion of the Monarchy could not form the subject of any discussion whatsoever'. Merey was given the same information but told not to reveal it to the Italian government. Berchtold knew that his friend Merey would strongly dislike this policy and tried to reassure him: 'I have decided to meet the Italian standpoint in this matter [!] because the present game is for high stakes, involves considerable difficulties and would be absolutely impracticable without the firm cohesion of the Triplice Powers.'[3]

Once the meeting with Tschirschky was over, the attention of the Vienna government turned to the declaration of war on Serbia. It was signed, just after 11 a.m., by the eighty-four-year-old Emperor Franz Josef at Bad Ischl. He was seated at a small writing table looking out over his favourite hunting terrain. He was in fact signing the death warrant of the Habsburg empire which, within little more than four years, would, under the pressure of all-out war, disintegrate into ruins. The next question for the diplomats in Vienna on 28 July was how to serve the declaration of war now that Austria–Hungary had no diplomatic representative accredited to the Serbian government. They asked their ally to act for them but Germany refused, arguing that the other European powers might think that they had hounded Vienna into declaring war (which was in fact true). The only course open was to send an *en clair* telegram to Niš via Bucharest announcing the declaration of war. It was dispatched shortly after noon.

It was only after the declaration of war had been made that Berchtold saw the Russian ambassador, Shebeko – he had hurriedly returned to Vienna after the outbreak of the crisis. Berchtold had deliberately avoided seeing him the day before so as not to discuss Sazonov's proposal for direct talks between the two countries before Vienna declared war. When Berchtold saw Shebeko in the afternoon, he told him that Austria–Hungary refused to enter into any negotiations on the Serbian reply, which had already been rejected as unsatisfactory. This was not what Sazonov had suggested – Russia was asking for a rewording of the Austro-Hungarian ultimatum so that Serbia could be pressurised into accepting the new draft. Vienna's veto meant that the attempt to start direct talks between Austria–Hungary and Russia had collapsed before it had got off the ground.

After seeing the Russian ambassador, Berchtold attended a meeting with Conrad, Krobatin, Burián, Stürgkh, Forgách and Macchio to discuss the military situation following the declaration of war on Serbia. The meeting agreed to mobilise the navy but was still in a quandary over what military strategy to follow. Berchtold asked whether war with Russia could be carried on if the army was attacking Serbia. As Conrad noted sarcastically, 'this objection certainly seemed belated'.[4] Indeed, if Berchtold was only now appreciating the central problem at the heart of Austro-Hungarian strategy, then it was clear that there had been no integration of diplomatic and military planning in Vienna. That Berchtold could make such a remark reinforces the suggestion that for him the declaration of war was no more than a diplomatic move designed to increase the pressure on Serbia to accept the ultimatum and one which had no military implications. This was a disastrous miscalculation and ignored the impact the declaration of war might have in St Petersburg. Conrad told the meeting that with partial mobilisation due to start the next day he needed to know by 1 August whether there was going to be a war with Russia so that he could decide where to send his reserves.

Faced with this dilemma, Vienna decided to see if Germany could resolve their problem. A telegram was sent to Szögyény in Berlin pointing out that if Austria–Hungary was engaged in operations against Serbia, then even if Russia only mobilised against Austria–Hungary Germany ought to mobilise too, even though this made European war inevitable. The ambassador was to ask Germany to consider issuing 'a friendly reminder' to Russia along these lines by 1 August at the latest.[5] The perceived need to issue such a reminder, which would be seen as a threat by the Russians, only underlined the ill-thought-out and dangerous nature of Vienna's policies.

Niš

It was shortly after 1 p.m. when Pašić received a telegram saying that Austria–Hungary was declaring war. He decided, not surprisingly, that this uncoded telegram, which had come via Bucharest, must be hoax, designed as a trick to make Serbia responsible for any war by initiating attacks on Austria–Hungary. An hour later he saw the German minister, Griesinger, who said that he knew nothing about a declaration of war and therefore could not offer any advice.

Pašić then sent telegrams to his ministers in St Petersburg, London and Paris, telling them about the strange telegram he had received and asking them to find out whether it was true. Only gradually during the afternoon did a series of reports reach Niš from around Europe, confirming that Austria–Hungary had indeed declared war on its neighbour. Just before dusk, the first military action of the European crisis took place as Austro-Hungarian artillery batteries at Semlin began a desultory shelling of Belgrade.

Berlin – Morning

Up until the previous day, Germany had been pushing its ally forward, agreeing that it should take strong measures against Serbia, agreeing that an unacceptable ultimatum should be sent, pressing for an early declaration of war and rejecting mediation efforts by the other powers. Now its policy was to be thrown into chaos by the Kaiser. At 7.30 a.m. he went riding in the park at the Neues Palace with General von Plessen. Afterwards he saw the Serbian reply to the ultimatum, now over forty-eight hours old, which had finally been sent to Potsdam late the previous evening. He, like many others across Europe, was taken in by the clever Serbian drafting and wrote on his copy of the reply:

> A brilliant achievement in a time limit of only forty-eight hours! It is more than one could have expected! A great moral success for Vienna; but with it all reason for war is gone and Giesl ought to have quietly stayed on in Belgrade! After that I should never have ordered mobilization.[6]

This was a volte-face of enormous proportions and showed a severe misunderstanding of Vienna and Berlin's strategy in the previous three weeks – the whole point of the ultimatum was that Serbia had to accept it unconditionally or diplomatic relations would be broken off. Both capitals had agreed a diplomatic success was no longer sufficient and a Serbian military defeat was essential. The Kaiser realised that Germany could not suddenly reverse course and now ask its ally to accept the Serbian reply after it had already been rejected as unsatisfactory. Vienna would have to be given a way out that saved face.

After a discussion with General von Plessen, the Kaiser composed a handwritten note to Jagow which was dispatched by messenger at 10 a.m. The Kaiser stated:

> I am convinced that on the whole the wishes of the Danube Monarchy have been acceded to. The few reservations that Serbia makes in regard to individual points could, according to my opinion, be settled by

negotiation. But it contains the announcement *orbi et urbi* of a capitulation of the most humiliating kind, and a result, all reason for war falls to the ground.

He went on to argue, as a way of finding a palatable exit from the crisis for Vienna, that Serbian concessions had to be turned into deeds. They would try to wriggle out of their concessions because: 'The Serbs are Orientals, therefore liars, tricksters, and masters of evasion.' It would therefore be necessary to use some military force: 'Austria would receive a hostage (Belgrade) as a guarantee' until the Serbians carried out their promises. This would also give the Austro-Hungarian army a sense of achievement and ensure that Vienna's prestige and morale was not damaged. The Kaiser wanted a message sent to Vienna saying: 'Serbia has been forced to retreat in a very humiliating manner . . . as a result, every cause for war had vanished.' On this basis – what became known as the 'halt in Belgrade' – the Kaiser said, 'I am ready to mediate for peace with Austria.'[7] In parallel, the Kaiser sent a similar message to Moltke via Plessen.

This proposal was quite skilful. Austria–Hungary could not draw back now without a severe loss of face (especially after the declaration of war – which was not known in Berlin until 6.30 p.m.). Occupation of Belgrade would bolster its prestige but without all-out war. It was unlikely that Serbia would accept this idea but that was not essential. The key factor was Russia. As became clear later, St Petersburg might accept a limited Austro-Hungarian occupation of Belgrade as long as Germany pressurised Austria–Hungary into negotiating over its demands. Given the state the crisis had now reached, this was probably the only feasible way out.

Berlin – Afternoon

The Kaiser's message probably did not arrive at the Wilhelmstrasse until lunchtime (the Kaiser, unlike the Tsar, did not use the telephone). Although Jagow and Bethmann Hollweg would have needed to discuss the Kaiser's proposal, there was then a long pause before any action was taken – why is unclear. One reason may have been that the chancellor was engaged in discussions with the Socialist leader Albert Südekum. He was trying to persuade him not to oppose government policy as the crisis deepened and the possibility of European war grew. Südekum, on the right wing of the SPD, needed little convincing and gave the chancellor the assurances he wanted.

Even one of the most left-wing Socialists, Rosa Luxembourg, who was on her way to the ISB meeting in Brussels, was equally convinced about her government's policies. She wrote: 'If you ask whether the German government is ready for war there is every reason to reply in the negative.'[8]

When Bethmann Hollweg returned from this meeting shortly after 3pm, he sent a reply to Tschirschky's message of the previous day about Vienna's request for Russia to be threatened with German mobilisation if it mobilised against Austria–Hungary (a request that was being made yet again that afternoon in Vienna). The chancellor informed the ambassador that the rumours of Russian military measures had not been confirmed (even though German intelligence had received such information the previous day) and that neither he nor Moltke would, therefore, take any action to threaten Russia with military counter-measures.

Twenty-five minutes after that telegram was dispatched, a disturbing message was received from Lichnowsky in London. Germany had accepted Vienna's assurances that it had no territorial ambitions in Serbia and that Hoyos had been speaking personally in Berlin on 5 July when he blurted out to Zimmerman the real aims of Austro-Hungarian policy – the dismemberment of Serbia. Lichnowsky reported the conversations he had had with Mensdorff and his staff at the Austro-Hungarian embassy the previous evening. He stated that 'Austria is only out for the overthrow of Serbia'. He added that Mensdorff had also said, 'Vienna absolutely wanted war, because Serbia was to be "flattened out" . . . the intention is to present Bulgaria (and presumably also Albania) with portions of Serbia.' Bethmann Hollweg realised that he had been deceived by Vienna about the real aims of its policy, that Hoyos had been speaking the truth, and that the assurances being given to Russia (and the other powers) about the future of Serbia were false. Serbia was to be partitioned among the other Balkan states and the rump that remained would, after 'frontier rectifications', be turned into a client of Austria–Hungary. He wrote on his copy of the telegram: 'This ambiguity on the part of Austria is intolerable.'[9]

A quarter of an hour later at 4pm, the intelligence section of the general staff issued its daily assessment of the situation. It reported that Russian partial mobilisation against Austria–Hungary was underway in two military districts – Odessa and Kiev. However, the 'period preparatory to war' was being implemented across the whole country, including along the German border. Guards had been established on railway lines and rolling stock for troop transports was being assembled at mobilisation points. No indication of any major action was reported from France, although the decisions made over the previous two days to recall senior officers from leave and to stop some summer training were detected. In Belgium it was reported that some troops had been recalled from leave. Germany decided to take some countermeasures. Units that would be ordered to infiltrate into France to sabotage the railways during mobilisation were put on alert. Troops taking part in training exercises were to be recalled to barracks and military guards were to be placed at key points along the railways. Bethmann Hollweg objected to these measures, but the Kaiser overruled him.

During the course of the afternoon, the Kaiser received a letter Prince Henry had written that morning when he landed at Kiel after his return from Britain. He reported on his talk with George V two days earlier, saying that he had asked for 'a short talk with Georgie'. The King had given him an assurance that the British government 'would leave no stone unturned to localize the war between Austria and Serbia'. This was, the King explained, the reasoning behind the proposal for the ambassadors' conference – 'to try to hold Russia in check' – and he hoped Germany would join these efforts despite its alliance with Austria–Hungary. The Prince added that the King thought Europe was near to a major war and said he was quoting George V 'literally' when he said 'we shall try all we can to keep out of this – and shall remain neutral'. Prince Henry added that he thought the King was sincere and that Britain might be neutral at the start of any war, but in the long run its relationship with France might force it to intervene.[10] This message was bound to reinforce, once again, Berlin's view that Britain might go along with a local war between Austria-Hungary and Serbia (Grey had also indicated the same). More importantly, it might stay neutral in a European war (as Grey had also hinted at the end of the previous week).

Berlin – Evening

It was only in the evening that the Kaiser's proposal for a 'halt in Belgrade' was considered in the light of the diplomatic situation and the evidence from Lichnowsky of Vienna's duplicity about its real aims for the future of Serbia. What followed were several hours of frantic activity. The first action was to try and reassure the other powers that Germany was trying to resolve the dispute. The message sent to

Lichnowsky was not very encouraging. It told him Britain could not 'expect us in our mediatory action to go to the length of trying to coerce Austria–Hungary into indulgence towards Serbia'. But at least it accepted that Berlin was engaged in mediation, something that it had rejected the previous day.[11] Bethmann Hollweg also summoned Goschen to explain that Germany had only rejected the British proposal for a conference because it looked too much like a court sitting in judgement on Austria–Hungary. Instead, he was making every effort to initiate direct talks between Vienna and St Petersburg even though Russia had 'nothing to do' with the dispute between Austria–Hungary and Serbia.[12] Bethmann Hollweg did not know that earlier in the day Vienna had vetoed such talks.

The chancellor then wrote to the Kaiser (the document arrived at Potsdam at 10.15 p.m.) suggesting that he should send a personal message to the Tsar. One of the reasons for the message was to establish Germany's position: 'Such a telegram, should war prove to be inevitable, would throw the clearest light on Russia's responsibility.' (Already the main powers were manoeuvring, not simply to avoid war but to establish their innocence and the culpability of their enemies if war did break out.) The telegram to the Tsar would make it clear that Germany was backing the direct talks between Austria–Hungary and Russia 'for the purpose of explaining unambiguously . . . the object and extent of Austria's procedure against Serbia. The declaration of war that has occurred in the meantime need make no difference.'[13] (The last sentence was optimistic, as events in St Petersburg were to prove.) Bethmann Hollweg followed this up with his own message to Pourtalès in St Petersburg. It told him, 'we are continuing our endeavours to persuade Vienna to have a frank discussion with St Petersburg' to clarify 'the aims and extent' of Austro-Hungarian action. The declaration of war 'does not change this in any way'.[14]

The message to Vienna setting out the Kaiser's proposal (and reflecting Bethmann Hollweg's annoyance over the information from London about Austria–Hungary's real intentions) was sent at 10.15 p.m. Tschirschky was told that Austria–Hungary had consistently reassured its ally that it did not want territorial acquisitions and more Slavs within the empire. However, 'despite repeated interrogations . . . the Austro-Hungarian Government has left us in the dark concerning its intentions'. Berlin now felt that the Serbian reply met Vienna's demands 'in so considerable a measure' that if Austria–Hungary adopted 'a completely uncompromising attitude' then there would be a 'gradual defection from its cause of public opinion throughout all Europe'. Because Austria–Hungary could not begin military operations before 12 August, it would in the meantime be 'placed in the extraordinarily difficult position of being exposed . . . to the mediation and conference proposals' of the other powers. In this situation 'if it continues to maintain its previous aloofness . . . it will incur the odium of having been responsible for a world war . . . even in the eyes of the German people'. It was impossible to fight a war on this basis with domestic support, therefore 'it is imperative that the responsibility for the eventual extension of the war . . . should, under all circumstances, fall on Russia'.

So far the message had done little more than set out very clearly the underlying problems in the strategy that Berlin and Vienna had agreed in early July without thinking through the consequences. Only now did Bethmann Hollweg turn to the Kaiser's proposals. He thought that the latest information from St Petersburg suggested that the Russians did appreciate that Serbia needed to be taught a lesson – Sazonov had used that phrase the previous day. It was therefore vital for Vienna to make clear that it would make no territorial acquisitions and that its military preparations were solely aimed at a temporary occupation of Belgrade and some other territory to ensure Serbia complied with Austro-Hungarian demands; once Serbia complied, the occupying forces would be withdrawn. Tschirschky was instructed to discuss this with Berchtold and ensure that Vienna took the initiative in St Petersburg with such a proposal. In doing so 'you will have to avoid very carefully giving rise to the impression that we wish to hold Austria back' – which was exactly what Berlin was trying to do. Germany still supported the aim of 'cutting the vital cord of the Greater Serbia propaganda, without at the same time bringing on a world war'. If the latter could not be achieved, then this diplomatic initiative would at least improve 'the conditions under which we shall have to wage' any war.[15]

The Kaiser's firm position had been made much less clear-cut in the drafting of the telegram. Much would depend on how Tschirschky interpreted his instructions and how strongly he put the demand to Berchtold for an Austro-Hungarian initiative on the 'halt in Belgrade' to be made to the Russians. Nevertheless, an important threshold had been crossed. Germany was beginning to appreciate the extremely dangerous position in which it was now placed. Two questions remained. Could it persuade its ally to draw back and would any action in St Petersburg be taken in time to avoid a significant worsening of the crisis?

St Petersburg – Morning/Afternoon

The first ambassador to see Sazonov during the morning was Buchanan. He reported to London that the Russian foreign minister was losing the optimism he had shown on Sunday and that he now took 'a pessimistic view of the situation'. Buchanan asked Sazonov whether Russia would accept Vienna's assurances on Serbian independence and integrity. Sazonov replied, 'no engagement that Austria might make on these two points would satisfy Russia'. He then said that Russia would mobilise when Austro-Hungarian troops crossed the Serbian border.[16] (This was the same, clear statement of the Russian position as Sazonov had asked Sukhomlinov to give the German military attaché the previous day.)

Sazonov then saw Szápáry. The ambassador still had no instructions from Vienna about the talks the two men were supposed to hold over the ultimatum and the Serbian reply, even though it was now two days since the idea had first been discussed in St Petersburg. Szápáry reported to Vienna that Sazonov asked to see the full dossier they possessed which proved Serbian complicity in the conspiracy – the Austro-Hungarian government had made no effort to improve its case by giving this information to the Russians. The ambassador repeated to Sazonov the pledge not to annex Serbian territory but reported it 'did not make much impression'. However, the two men had a friendly discussion over the Balkans. Szápáry commented, 'in his disinclination for coming into conflict with us [Sazonov] clutches at straws'. The ambassador noted that in contrast to previous periods of tension the foreign minister did not mention public opinion, Slavdom or the Orthodox Church. Instead, he argued with 'political objectivity' and laid 'particular stress on Russia's interest that Serbia should not be reduced to a state of vassalage'.[17] The talk may have been friendly but it achieved nothing – the differences between the two states over the future of Serbia were fundamental and irreconcilable. The question was whether either would modify their position.

Sazonov's next conversation was certainly not friendly. He saw Pourtalès and accused him of being part of a joint Austro-Hungarian and German plot – 'a well-laid scheme' – to provoke a war. Pourtalès walked out of the meeting. He returned to see officials in the foreign ministry in order to protest over the action of Russian police in putting out of use the radio on board the German steamer *Prince Eitel Friedrich* which was moored in St Petersburg harbour. Afterwards he resumed his talk with Sazonov. It was a sterile exchange. The foreign minister said that the Serbian reply gave Vienna all it could want – if it was not accepted it simply proved Austria–Hungary wanted war. Pourtalès said that he had reports that Russian military preparations were far more advanced than the assurances they had given on the previous day.[18]

St Petersburg – Evening

It was at about 4 p.m. local time that St Petersburg heard of the Austro-Hungarian declaration of war on Serbia. The general staff were already meeting to discuss the military options open to Russia. They were beginning to change the advice given, with so little thought, on 24/25 July that partial mobilisation against Austria–Hungary was a feasible operation. Quarter Master General Danilov had been recalled from an inspection tour of the Caucasus and had arrived back in St Petersburg late on the night of Sunday 26 July. As the expert on mobilisation he knew that improvising plans for partial mobilisation (none existed) would wreck the carefully laid plans for general mobilisation. His views were supported by General Dobrorolski, the head of the mobilisation section (who had given different advice four days earlier) and by General Ronzhin, the head of military transport. The chief of staff, General Yanushkevich, was inclined to stick with the advice he had given the Tsar on 25 July, but in the end decided to go along with the opinions of the experts.

This meeting was still in session when Sazonov saw the French ambassador, Paléologue, shortly after he had heard about the declaration of war on Serbia. The ambassador did not pass on the full message which Poincaré and Viviani had sent from the battleship *France* the previous day. He omitted the part about the two countries working together for a solution. Instead, he told Sazonov of 'the complete readiness of France to fulfil her obligations as an ally in case of necessity'.[19] Such a declaration (which probably coincided with Poincaré's own views expressed during the state visit) could only increase Russian determination to take strong action. In addition, Sazonov had another of his mood swings and was now very bellicose and determined not to be browbeaten by Austria–Hungary. After seeing Paléologue, Sazonov had a brief talk with Yanushkevich who, after the meeting with his mobilisation experts, was now arguing for general mobilisation as the only feasible option. Sazonov still preferred partial mobilisation as a means of putting pressure on Vienna. Their differences were not resolved by the time Sazonov had to leave shortly after 5 p.m. to drive the seventeen and a half miles to Peterhof, where he was due to see the Tsar at 6 p.m. The Tsar's diary merely records: 'At 6 p.m. I received Sazonov who informed me that to-day at noon Austria declared war on Serbia.'[20] It is inconceivable that the two men did not discuss the military options open to Russia, but they seem to have decided to postpone any decisions until the next day. Meanwhile, orders for both partial and general mobilisation would be prepared.

The result of this decision was that the Russian diplomats and military were now working on different lines. On his return from Peterhof, Sazonov sent telegrams to the embassies in Vienna, Paris, London, Rome and Berlin. It explained a change in Russia's diplomatic stance. Following the declaration of war on Serbia, direct talks with Vienna, as proposed on Sunday, were no longer an option. Austria–Hungary would now have to suspend military operations before talks could start, otherwise the talks would simply give them time to annihilate Serbia. (This position was compatible with the Kaiser's 'halt in Belgrade' proposal which was about to be sent to Vienna.) Bronevski in Berlin was told that partial mobilisation would begin in two days (29 July) in the Odessa, Kiev, Moscow and Kazan military districts but that this was not aimed at Germany. However, during the course of the evening Yanushkevich sent a telegram to the commanders of all Russia's military districts. It gave them advanced warning that general mobilisation would be ordered on 30 July and that the formal telegram initiating mobilisation would be sent later. Russian policy was in a state of almost complete confusion. What was clear was that attitudes towards Austria–Hungary were hardening. A military response was becoming almost inevitable following Vienna's declaration of war on Serbia.

Rome

The main development in the Italian capital was a message from Berlin to Flotow telling him 'we support Italian wishes for compensation in so far as we have already pointed out to Vienna the need for an understanding and still do so'.[21] This declaration of German support, which was passed on to San Giuliano, encouraged the Italians to submit a formal note (written in French) to Merey, the Austro-Hungarian ambassador. It stated that for Italy Article VII was a central part of the Triple Alliance and the basis for all its relations with

Austria–Hungary. Therefore negotiations on compensation were now urgent and without agreement Italy would be unable to give diplomatic support to its ally.[22] There was still a huge gulf between the two countries – the most Vienna was prepared to concede under German pressure was that talks on compensation could start after occupation, not in advance as Italy wanted.

In the afternoon San Giuliano saw the British ambassador, Rodd. Neither knew that Germany had rejected the idea of a four-power conference and that Vienna had declared war. The Italian foreign minister was still influenced by the misleading information from the Serbian chargé, Mihailjović, that Serbia might still accept the ultimatum. His idea for mediation was based on indications that Austria–Hungary might be willing to explain exactly what it intended in points five and six of the ultimatum, in particular that these demands did not in fact infringe Serbian sovereignty because they only involved Austria–Hungary in the inquiry and not in the judicial process. San Giuliano accepted that Austria–Hungary could not give this explanation direct to Serbia but could do so to the ambassadors at the conference. On this basis, 'The Powers might then advise Servia to accept unconditionally'.[23] This was a reasonable proposal and, in conjunction with the Kaiser's 'halt in Belgrade' idea, could have been the basis for a settlement if Austria–Hungary and Russia had been willing to compromise. Rodd agreed to see if this idea was acceptable in London.

London

The main diplomatic event in the British capital was final confirmation that Grey's proposal for an ambassadors' conference was dead. Early in the afternoon a telegram arrived from Goschen in Berlin. He had spoken to the French and Italian ambassadors that morning and the three men felt that German objections to the four-power conference were largely about its format. They therefore suggested that Grey should reformulate his proposal and drop the idea of a 'conference' because it sounded too much like a 'tribunal'. Having done this, he should then put the ball back in the German court by asking them to 'suggest lines on which [they] would find it possible to work with us'.[24] This was a shrewd suggestion which would have put Berlin in a very awkward position indeed. However, Grey had already sent a message, which crossed with Goschen's telegram, saying a 'direct exchange of views between Austria and Russia is the most preferable method of all, and as long as there is a prospect of that taking place I would suspend every other suggestion'.[25] The result was that Grey abandoned his conference proposal not knowing that the alternative of direct talks between Russia and Austria–Hungary was already dead in the water. In the evening a telegram arrived from de Bunsen in Vienna, reporting that in his talk with Berchtold the foreign minister made it clear that Vienna 'cannot delay warlike proceedings against Servia and would have to decline any suggestion of negotiations on basis of Servian reply'.[26] When Rodd's telegram reporting his talk with San Giuliano was received, those ideas were therefore also dismissed. All the proposals for mediation in the dispute, which had been launched some forty-eight hours earlier, had failed. Whether, as the pace of military preparations increased, it was possible to devise some other formula remained to be tested.

Asquith spent most of the day discussing the situation in Ulster and dealing with routine business at the War Office (he had, earlier in the year, taken over as secretary of state for war on a temporary basis after a 'mutiny' in army units in Ireland). He did see the King and told him of the blackmail Sazonov was applying over Britain's position in India and the Persian Gulf – 'Russia says to us "If you won't say you are ready to side with us now, your friendship is valueless, and we shall act on that assumption in the future".' At the Foreign Office, Nicolson reflected these fears about Russia in a telegram he sent to Buchanan in St Petersburg:

> Our relations with Russia are now approaching a point where we shall have to make up our minds as to whether we should become really intimate and permanent friends, or else diverge into another path.[27]

News of the Austro-Hungarian declaration of war was available in London during the afternoon (formal confirmation from Crackanthorpe in Niš arrived at 7.45 p.m.). At 5 p.m. a further step in preparations for war was taken when the Admiralty ordered the ships of the First Fleet to proceed, during the night, through the Channel to the North Sea and their war stations. Three ministers, Asquith, Grey and Haldane, were at 10 Downing Street until 1 a.m. discussing the implications of the Austro-Hungarian declaration of war but reached no firm conclusions.

The growing threat that Britain might be involved in a war led to the creation of two organisations. Graham Wallas formed the British Neutrality Committee, which did little beyond collecting a list of names of actual and potential supporters. Norman Angell (a well-known anti-war author) set up the slightly more active Neutrality League. The initial resolution establishing the League spoke of the value of German culture 'racially allied to ourselves' and argued that the main threat to European civilisation came from Russia. It published 500,000 leaflets entitled 'Shall We Fight for a Russian Europe?'

Paris

Poincaré and Viviani were still on the return voyage towards France and in their absence there was little activity in the French capital. The only diplomatic move of any importance came when the German ambassador saw Bienvenu-Martin. The acting foreign minister made it clear that a moderate attitude by Austria–Hungary was the essential starting point for any mediation and that 'the best means of avoiding a general war was by preventing a local one'. The aim of mediation was to 'satisfy Austria by the assurance of guarantees for Serbia's atonement and for her future good behaviour'.[28] However, Bienvenu-Martin made no suggestions as to how such mediation might take place and so the conversation was pointless.

That morning the socialist newspaper *L'Humanité* published a manifesto drawn up the previous evening by the socialist leaders. It showed that they, like their German counterparts, were convinced that their own government was working for peace. French workers were asked 'to gather all efforts for the maintenance of peace. They know that in the present crisis the French Government is most sincerely anxious to avert or to diminish the risks of conflict.' Meanwhile, the ISB meeting to be held in Brussels on 29 July would 'express with the utmost force and unanimity the joint determination of the European proletariat to maintain peace'. The socialist leaders across Europe were, as they had been for years, sincerely convinced of the righteousness not just of the socialists but also of their own countries. They were also powerless and the drafting of long-winded resolutions full of verbiage could achieve nothing.

Brussels

The Belgian government was increasingly concerned about the maintenance of its neutrality. A recall of army reservists was started. The foreign minister, Davignon, saw the British minister, Sir Francis

Villiers, and gave him the same message as the French minister the previous day. Belgium would 'offer resistance to the utmost of their power should the integrity or neutrality of Belgium be assailed from any quarter'.[29] This was not intended as a reassurance but was a warning to Britain not to be the first to violate Belgian neutrality.

The French minister, Klobukowski, and his military attaché, Commandant Génie, remained suspicious about Belgian attitudes. They reported to Paris that the government would not make any declaration of principle about its neutrality and would join whichever side seemed the strongest. They thought the population was badly divided, with the Walloons favouring France and the Flemish supporting Germany. If Germany did attack, they thought the Belgian government would offer only token resistance and then retire to Brussels and Antwerp.

Bucharest

The Austro-Hungarian efforts to bring Romania in as a full member of the Triple Alliance and a supporter of Vienna's actions (which never had much chance of success) were reaching the end of the road. The Emperor Franz Josef sent a message to King Carol asking for no more than 'sincere understanding' of Vienna's actions.[30] However, when the King saw the Austro-Hungarian minister, Czernin, he told him Romania would not carry out the terms of the secret alliance. Berchtold's attempted reassurance that Bulgaria would be neutral and that if it repeated its attack of June 1913 'we should leave Bulgaria to her wretched fate' made no impact.[31]

The prime minister, Bratianu, called on the Russian minister, Poklevski, to respond to the questions raised the previous day. He said he could not state an official Romanian position but 'speaking personally' he could say 'Russia need not expect any hostile move on the part of Romania'. When he conveyed this statement to St Petersburg, Poklevski shrewdly remarked that the Romanian government was worried that if it 'remained neutral [it] would, after the war was over, be exposed to chicanery both from Russia and from Austria'.[32] The problem for Romania was that there were severe problems in allying with either side.

Sofia

King Ferdinand was still away from the capital on a motoring holiday and was not due to return until the end of the month. In his absence the government had already accepted Vienna's advice to remain neutral in the expectation of making major gains when Serbia was defeated. (They were unaware that Vienna had threatened to leave them to their 'wretched fate' if they did attack during the crisis.) Telegrams were sent to all Bulgarian representatives abroad stating Bulgaria would remain neutral.

The Russian minister, Savinsky, called on the prime minister, Radoslavov, to argue that Bulgaria should reverse its position and stand by the Serbs who were fellow Slavs and recreate a Balkan alliance against Austria–Hungary. This appeal had no chance of success and Radoslavov made it clear that Bulgaria would 'take Macedonia with both hands'. If Austria–Hungary attacked Serbia, Bulgaria would send its irregular forces, the *comitaji*, into Macedonia. (This is what Vienna had already secretly suggested.) Savinsky reported the Bulgarian attitude as being 'to look around and then decide according to the course of events which side it would be more profitable for them to join'.[33]

Later in the day the Austro-Hungarian minister, Tarnowski, saw Radoslavov, together with the foreign minister and the minister for war. He told them that following Vienna's declaration of war on Serbia now was the time for the *comitaji* to be sent across the border into Macedonia to start a campaign of terrorism against both Serbian forces and the local population.

Cetinje

Following the Austro-Hungarian declaration of war, King Nicholas sent a message of support to Crown Prince Alexander of Serbia. It told him that the Montenegrin army was 'already at the frontier, prepared to fall in the defence of our independence' (which was very far from allying with Serbia). The message ended: 'Long live our cherished Serbdom.' In the evening mobilisation of the Montenegrin army was announced in the official newspaper – it was justified as a response to the Austro-Hungarian troop concentrations along the border.

King Nicholas was under growing pressure to ally with Serbia but was, as usual, being as devious as possible on the diplomatic front. He decided he should not see the Austro-Hungarian minister, Otto. The foreign minister, Plamenac, did do so and told him that Montenegro was 'still determined to observe strict neutrality "unless we are swept away by public opinion"'. It would help if Vienna could declare 'the war with Serbia was not a war of conquest'. Plamenac then moved on to the purpose of the talk. The King had obviously decided that Vienna's offer of a monetary bribe to stay out of the war was not sufficient. The foreign minister said that although the King had reigned since 1860 and had quadrupled the size of the country it was still not viable, especially as Montenegro had not really benefited from the wars of 1912–13. He thought Vienna should not have stopped Montenegro's southward expansion at the time and now hoped for an Austro-Hungarian 'guarantee of her further independent existence'. Plamenac explained that Montenegro would interpret such a guarantee as 'the assurance of an aggrandizement of Montenegro such as would enable her to continue her existence in complete autonomy and independence' (i.e. no union with Serbia). If Vienna did this, Montenegro would be 'a good, devoted and grateful friend'. Plamenac asked for a reply before the Montenegrin parliament met on 1 August. The Montenegrin attempted blackmail was shameless but in the tradition of its devious diplomacy.

Constantinople

As the crisis deepened the Ottoman government had, like the other Balkan states, to decide how to exploit the situation to its advantage. Russia was its main enemy and Germany seemed the only possible ally. During the day, the Grand Vizier, Said Halim Pasa (who acted as foreign minister and presided over the cabinet) saw the German ambassador, Baron von Wangenheim. Although Said Halim held important posts, he was an Egyptian prince and therefore outside of the ruling group of Turkish officers in the Committee of Union and Progress. This was to cause problems later.

Said Halim proposed an offensive/defensive Ottoman-German alliance directed against Russia. The ambassador immediately passed the proposal to Berlin and at 9.30 p.m. Bethmann Hollweg responded after having consulted the Kaiser. Germany proposed that the Ottomans should take part in any Russo–German war arising from the current crisis but should be neutral in any localised war between Austria–Hungary and Serbia. (Like Bulgaria, it was too dangerous to involve the Ottomans in any purely Balkan war.) The German military mission under General Liman von Sanders would take command of the Ottoman army in any war. Germany would guarantee Ottoman territorial integrity against Russia. The alliance would only last for the current crisis and any immediate consequences which could leave the Ottomans open to a revenge attack by Russia later.

The German government clearly saw the Ottomans as a potentially important ally. In any war, their role in blocking communications between the Mediterranean and the Black Sea would make it very difficult for France (and Britain if it joined in the war) to supply Russia and coordinate strategy.

WEDNESDAY 29 JULY

Vienna

The main question to be resolved in the Austro-Hungarian capital was how the government would react to the German proposal for a 'halt in Belgrade' and an opening of negotiations with Russia. At some point during the day the German ambassador, Tschirschky, did see Berchtold. He reported to Berlin that Berchtold was ready to repeat to the Russians the misleading declaration that Austria–Hungary would make no territorial acquisitions at the expense of Serbia. (Russia had already rejected such a declaration as inadequate.) However, on the military measures suggested by Berlin – the 'halt in Belgrade' – 'he is not in a position to give me an immediate answer'.[1] Tschirschky's dispatch did not arrive in Berlin until 1.30 a.m. the next day (30 July).

Vienna had stalled and refused to respond to its ally's fairly clear request to compromise. The Austro-Hungarian government was still in a highly recalcitrant mood and determined to press ahead with its plans to deal with Serbia. Berchtold probably felt that negotiations, even after the capture of Belgrade, might deprive Vienna of a real triumph and enable Serbia to wriggle out of its intended fate. But these difficulties were inherent in any negotiations and if Vienna really did want a completely free hand to do whatever it wanted to Serbia then that policy was almost certainly not achievable without a European war (as Vienna had recognised on 7 July).

Despite Austro-Hungarian intransigence, the question remains whether Tschirschky did fairly represent the German proposal in his discussion with Berchtold. He had already been reprimanded by the Kaiser for advocating restraint at the beginning of the crisis and was, no doubt, determined to avoid another such rebuke. As de Bunsen reported to London, Tschirschky was 'so identified with extreme anti-Servian and anti-Russian feeling prevalent in Vienna that he is not likely to plead the cause of peace with entire sincerity'.[2] The minutes prepared by Berchtold after his conversation with the ambassador suggest that Tschirschky did indeed misrepresent this vital initiative, emphasising those parts of the message from Berlin with which he agreed.[3]

Meanwhile, military action was underway. An Austro-Hungarian naval flotilla on the Danube began the serious shelling of Belgrade. The diplomatic corps remaining in the city, led by the British vice-consul, hoisted a white flag in a Belgrade park overlooking the Danube and tried to open discussions with the Austro-Hungarian military. Meanwhile, the British embassy in Vienna was negotiating a safe passage for British residents in Belgrade to leave the city by train. During the afternoon there were increasing indications reaching Vienna that Russia might be about to begin partial mobilisation against Austria–Hungary. Army intelligence units in Galicia were picking up the first signs of increasing Russian preparations. Vienna had so far only mobilised about half of its army.

Late that evening, Berchtold drafted a message for Szögyény in Berlin. He was to tell the German government that 'for military reasons our general mobilization must be put in hand at once if the Russian measures for mobilization are not immediately suspended'. No mention was made of the 'halt in Belgrade' proposal, but the ambassador was told that although diplomatic action would continue in St Petersburg and Paris 'we shall naturally not allow ourselves to be dissuaded from our military action against Serbia'.[4] Germany had, in early July, given its ally a free hand in dealing with Serbia and that policy was now being applied with a vengeance.

Rome

Vienna still faced problems in dealing with the Italian claim for compensation. Their ambassador in Rome, Merey, undertook the personally distasteful task of seeing San Giuliano (they could not stand each other) and giving him the statement of Vienna's position – talks between the two countries if and when Austria–Hungary found it necessary to annex or occupy territory. The foreign minister merely took down the key phrases and said he would have to talk to the prime minister. After the meeting Merey sent a petulant message to Vienna saying that although he was the acknowledged expert on Italy:

> I really wonder why we afford ourselves the luxury of an ambassador at Rome . . . and do not rather transfer the representation of our interests in Italy to the German embassy, which is obviously much more competent.[5]

In the afternoon San Giuliano saw Flotow in an attempt to enlist German support for opening immediate talks with Vienna. He did not mention the Austro-Hungarian 'concession' and said that Italy could not support Vienna diplomatically (let alone militarily) without prior agreement to their interpretation of Article VII (which Austria–Hungary had not conceded in its agreement to hold talks at some point). He argued that direct talks would certainly fail if Merey was involved and asked Germany to initiate the talks. But he added, 'time was short'.[6]

San Giuliano and Merey met again in the evening for another frigid discussion. Merey reported to Vienna that the foreign minister explained that Italy was not bound by the terms of the alliance because of Austria–Hungary's failure to consult and its aggressive action against Serbia. Nevertheless, if war did occur Italy would ask itself the question 'whether her interests were better served by taking military action on our side or remaining neutral'. San Giuliano said his preference was for the former option as long as Italy's position in the Balkans was 'safeguarded'.[7] This was totally mendacious, as Merey knew. Italy wanted a clear offer of territory before deciding whether to join its allies or to remain neutral. Its preferred solution was to be bribed to stay neutral – something neither Berlin nor Vienna would countenance under any circumstances.

The first Italian military preparations of the crisis were also put in hand. They were taken by the army without consulting the government and bore no relation to Italy's diplomatic bargaining – they were all based on the assumption that Italy would fight alongside its allies. The decisions affected the Alpine frontier with France – storehouses were reprovisioned, artillery batteries were dispatched to the forts and the four corps in that area recalled all their troops who were on leave. In addition, the corps to be sent through Germany to fight on the Rhine frontier was brought up to full strength.

Paris

President Poincaré and his party docked at Dunkirk shortly after 8 a.m. and were greeted by a large crowd as they landed on the quayside. They travelled by train to Gard du Nord where another large crowd had assembled. Cheering crowds also lined the route to the Elysée Palace. The president was determined to take over control of policy. He wrote in his diary that Viviani would be 'hesitant and pusillanimous' and therefore 'I am determined to take over myself responsibility for Viviani's action'.[8] He was also determined to continue the strong policy he had set in St Petersburg. This had two elements: no restraint on Russian actions, and a determination to place Germany in the wrong so as to cement internal French unity and increase the chances of British intervention by convincing London of French moderation.

At 11.15 a.m. the Russian ambassador, Alexander Izvolsky, called at the Quai d'Orsay to inform them of the telegram St Petersburg had sent the previous evening (saying that partial mobilisation would be instituted shortly). This was hardly the formal consultation required under the Franco-Russian military convention, but Paris raised no objection to this fundamental step that could easily send the crisis spinning rapidly out of control. During the day, Poincaré initiated the first of the daily cabinet meetings which he was to chair for the rest of the crisis. He also held a meeting with Viviani, Messimy, the minister of war and General Joffre, the chief of the General Staff, to discuss the military options. They agreed that it was premature to begin general mobilisation, especially since Germany had taken no military measures at this time. Covering troops would, however, take up their positions from Luxembourg to the Vosges mountains. Poincaré, despite Joffre's strong objections, insisted that they remain at least ten kilometres from the frontier with Germany in order to avoid provoking an incident and to demonstrate French restraint to the British.

Across the city, Madame Caillaux was acquitted at the end of her trial and the newspapers were still giving far more coverage to these sensational events than the developing European crisis. There was also a major demonstration by the League of Patriots, led by the right-wing nationalist, Maurice Barrès. They marched past the statue representing the unliberated city of Strasbourg in the Place de la Concorde to the strains of the *Marseillaise*.

Berling – Morning/Afternoon

In Berlin, as Bethmann Hollweg waited for a reply from Vienna on the 'halt in Belgrade' initiative taken the previous evening, there was an anti-war protest by tens of thousands of demonstrators along the Unter den Linden. The chancellor was not, however, worried by the position of the SPD. Following their discussion the previous day, Albert Südekum had consulted his colleagues among the Socialist leadership and returned that morning to give Bethmann Hollweg the assurances he had asked for. Südekum said that 'because of the wish to serve the cause of peace – no action whatsoever (general strike or partial strike, sabotage or anything similar) was planned or need be feared'.[9] It was clear that the right-wing leadership of the SPD was determined to keep control of the party and marginalise those who still had revolutionary leanings. Later in the day, the party executive sent a confidential letter to the editors of all socialist newspapers asking them to take a moderate line.

After this meeting Bethmann Hollweg read a paper prepared the previous day by Moltke called 'Summary of the Political Situation'. It reflected the growing intelligence available to the German army that Russia was in the early stages of mobilisation. It argued that Austria–Hungary could not safely attack Serbia if Russia had begun partial mobilisation and would have to move to full mobilisation in order to defend Galicia. Moltke argued that the crisis had been structured by the Russians. They had taken the preliminary steps towards full mobilisation while denying they were doing so (which was true). This was, he argued, in order to force Vienna and Berlin into taking the first open steps towards war so as to make their position both with their own people and with wider European opinion much more difficult. Moltke argued that Germany needed to decide whether Russia and France were determined on war. He pointed out, correctly, that 'the military situation is becoming from day to day more unfavourable for us, and can, if our prospective opponents prepare themselves further, unmolested, lead to fateful consequences for us'. He concluded that unless 'a miracle happens . . . at the eleventh hour [there will be] a war which will annihilate for decades to come the civilization of almost the whole of Europe. Germany has no desire to bring about this terrible war'.[10]

During the morning, Bethmann Hollweg saw Moltke and General Erich von Falkenhayn, the Prussian minister for war. Von Falkenhayn argued that the government should proclaim the *Kriegsgefahrzustand* ('state of war danger'), which would enable a number of military measures preparatory to mobilisation to be put into effect. Despite the paper he had just sent Bethmann Hollweg and the increasing signs of Russian preparations, Moltke argued against such a move and the chancellor agreed with him. Any such proclamation would be a major, and very public, escalation of the crisis. Nevertheless, it was agreed that the ambassadors in St Petersburg and Paris should be instructed to tell the Russian and French governments that if they continued to take preparatory military measures then Germany would have to take counteraction. In particular, Pourtalès in St Petersburg was told to say 'further continuation of Russian mobilization measures would force us to mobilize, and in that case a European war could scarcely be prevented'.[11] The message to Paris was more moderate and merely said that Germany might have to declare the *Kriegsgefahrzustand* and this would increase tension. The two messages were sent at 12.50 p.m.

In parallel with this meeting, Szögyény called at the Wilhelmstrasse and saw Jagow. He was carrying out Berchtold's instructions sent the previous evening to try and get Germany to commit itself to general mobilisation as soon as Russia started partial mobilisation against Austria–Hungary. Jagow was in a quandary. This proposal was highly dangerous and would make a European war inevitable and he had previously reassured the Russians that Germany would not mobilise in these circumstances. He tried to play for time by asking Szögyény to produce a memorandum on the subject.

Elsewhere in the foreign ministry, the political director, Wilhelm von Stumm, was considering the draft ultimatum to be sent to Belgium which the general staff had prepared three days earlier. He made a number of amendments. The original asked Belgium to 'take sides' with Germany – Stumm altered this to a request to adopt 'a friendly attitude'. He also made it clear that if Belgium did side with Germany, the promised territorial compensation would be at the expense of France. He then added a piece of waffle about how if Belgium did cooperate, 'the friendly ties which bind the two neighbouring states will grow stronger and more enduring'. Stumm passed the revised draft to Bethmann Hollweg who approved it.

On the previous day Bethmann Hollweg had demonstrated his increasing annoyance about the way Vienna was handling the crisis. This had been brought on by the reluctance of Austria–Hungary to open talks with Italy on compensation and the evidence that it had been less than frank with Berlin over its intentions towards Serbia. Now Bethmann Hollweg wrote to Jagow at the foreign ministry saying they needed to consider sending a new telegram to Vienna on both issues:

> in which we sharply declare that we regard this way of handling the question of compensation with Rome as absolutely unsatisfactory and hold Vienna entirely responsible for any attitude Italy may take in a possible war.

Bethmann Hollweg then put his finger on the fundamental inconsistency at the heart of Austro-Hungarian policy. On the one hand it was saying that it would compensate Italy in the event it made a permanent occupation of territory in the Balkans, yet it was reassuring Russia (and the rest of Europe) that it had no such intentions. The chancellor pointed out that if talks with Italy on compensation did begin, then the Italians would almost certainly tell the Russians what was going on. The chancellor argued that 'we as allies cannot support a policy with a false bottom'. In these circumstances it would be impossible to mediate in St Petersburg and then '[we] will find ourselves hitched to the towline of Vienna'. Bethmann Hollweg said he refused to be put in this position 'even if I risk being accused of turning tail'.[12]

Later in the day, Bethmann Hollweg and Jagow discussed this letter and agreed to send a telegram to Tschirschky in Vienna. It stated: 'I view the behaviour of the Vienna Government and its diverse procedures with the different Governments with growing disapproval.' The telegram then set out what Austria–Hungary had said in different places and what had been learned from Lichnowsky in London. It continued: 'I can only draw the conclusion that its disavowal of Count Hoyos . . . was only meant for the gallery' and that Vienna had plans 'which it thinks had better be concealed from us' because it feared that Berlin would veto them. It argued that Vienna was trying to draw a distinction between taking Serbian territory itself and allowing the other Balkan states to carve up their rival. Although the German analysis of its ally's policy was brutally frank (and correct), Bethmann Hollweg then, as in the telegram about the 'halt in Belgrade', pulled his punches. The information was for Tschirschky's benefit and he was asked to do no more than 'indicate' to Berchtold that 'it would be advisable to take precautions to avert mistrust of his declarations to the Powers on the subject of Serbian integrity'.[13] Germany had indeed found itself hitched to an ally whose policies it was finding increasing difficulty in controlling.

London – Morning

Shortly after arriving at the Foreign Office, Grey saw Lichnowsky to talk about what possibilities might still be open for mediation. Grey said his proposal for an ambassadors' conference had been rejected and that direct talks between Russia and Austria–Hungary seemed likely to fail (as indeed they had). He took up the suggestion made by Goschen in Berlin on the previous day – could Germany now make a proposal that was acceptable to them. Grey thought, based on the false reports from Rome, that Serbia might now accept the ultimatum and asked whether Germany could stop its ally crossing the frontier. He added a very vague threat: 'one could never tell whose house might remain unscorched in the midst of such a conflagration'. Grey continued that there was no desire to humiliate Austria–Hungary but equally Russia could not be humiliated either. Lichnowsky responded with the standard German line agreed at the start of the crisis: 'Serbia did not concern Russia at all' and they had no reason to intervene because Vienna 'had no intention of annexing Serbia'. As Grey astutely pointed out, it was quite possible to turn Serbia into a vassal state without annexation. Then, trying to feel his way towards a proposal that was similar to the Kaiser's 'halt in Belgrade' (of which Grey was unaware), he asked whether it was possible to define Austria–Hungary's military and political objectives so that some reassurance could be given to Russia.[14] Grey emphasised to Goschen in Berlin that he had told Lichnowsky 'mediation was ready to come into operation by any method that Germany thought possible'.[15] The ball was back in the German court.

After this discussion Grey left to attend the cabinet meeting at 10 Downing Street which lasted from 11.30 until 2 p.m. The first item on the agenda was the situation in Ireland and the changes to be made to the Royal Irish Constabulary following the shootings at the weekend. The cabinet then moved on to their first substantive discussion of the European crisis and, in particular, of Belgian neutrality. Grey had prepared a series of papers on 'Belgian Neutrality in 1870', including dispatches, statements in the House of Commons and a copy of the Law Officers opinion given on 6 August 1870 about Britain's obligations under the 1839 treaty.[16] The legal position as stated during the Franco–Prussian War in 1870 was clear: the guarantee of Belgian neutrality could not be conditional on unanimity between the signatories of the 1839 treaty because they were the only powers likely to violate that neutrality. During the cabinet discussion that morning, it became clear that many members, probably a majority, had doubts about this view. They took the position that 'the Powers were really jointly & severally responsible for the fulfilment of the Treaty of 1839'.[17] Whatever legal interpretation was adopted, there was still a series of problems to resolve. Britain was not bound to intervene militarily to restore Belgian neutrality – diplomatic action could be sufficient. This would almost certainly be the case if Belgium did not resist any invasion. It was also clear that Belgium would first have to appeal for support, otherwise Britain might be guilty of violating its neutrality.

Asquith told the cabinet, reflecting the accepted military advice, that 'if the Germans attacked France they would certainly go through Belgium, and would hesitate to attack in any other way'.[18] The problem was that the military thought German troops might only pass through the south-eastern part of the country and not cross the Sambre-Meuse line or attack Liège. In these circumstances Belgium might only offer token resistance and not ask for assistance. Without a Belgian appeal for help and with only a limited violation of neutrality, the British government might decide it was not worth intervening. There was also the possibility that France might be the first to violate Belgian neutrality. However, most of the cabinet accepted that if Germany seemed likely to conquer the whole of Belgium and establish themselves on the Channel coast, then British interests would be directly affected.

During a more general discussion of the situation, Grey described Austria–Hungary's actions as 'brutal recklessness', but it was agreed that Britain should continue its policy of not committing itself. There would be no outright support for France or Russia and neither would there be a declaration of neutrality in all circumstances. As one member described the debate: 'We must do the best for our own interests . . . we discussed the situation from our selfish point of view.' John Morley, a strong non-interventionist, expressed his view, which was shared by most of his colleagues: 'I shall not be a party to any intervention between Austria and Servia. France may be a different thing.'[19] John Burns wrote in his diary: 'It was decided not to decide.'[20] The cabinet then discussed what Grey should tell the French and German ambassadors. It was agreed his statements should be ambiguous. Grey said he would tell Cambon that 'the Austro-Servian quarrel did not concern us . . . Don't count upon our coming in', whereas Lichnowsky would be told 'don't count on our abstention'.[21]

In his report to the King, Asquith tried to sum up the cabinet's conclusions:

> It is doubtful how far a single guaranteeing State is bound under the Treaty of 1839 to maintain Belgian neutrality if the remainder abstain or refuse. The Cabinet consider that the matter if it arises will be one of policy rather than of legal obligation.

He then turned to the question of what France and Germany should be told about Britain's position and summarised it as 'at this stage we were unable to pledge ourselves in advance either under all circumstances to stand aside or in any condition to go in'.[22] In his letter to

Venetia Stanley, Asquith described the cabinet discussion as 'very satisfactory' and continued 'the acute point will arise if & when Germany proposes to invade France by way of Belgium – her shortest route . . . of course we want to keep out of it, but the worst thing we could do would be to announce that in *no circumstances* would we intervene'.[23] Herbert Samuel made the same point in his letter to his wife Beatrice, although he remained pessimistic: 'if both sides do not know what we shall do, both will be less willing to run risks . . . I still think the probabilities are that the fuse which has been fired will quickly bring a catastrophic explosion.'[24]

London – Afternoon
After lunch Asquith told the House of Commons that, following the Austro-Hungarian declaration of war, the situation was grave. There was no debate after his statement, but eleven members of the radical Liberal Foreign Affairs Group met under the chairmanship of Arthur Ponsonby. The outcome was a letter from Ponsonby to Asquith saying that the group did not want to make his situation more difficult by any public action. However, they argued, Russia and France should be told Britain would not intervene and the government's position ought to be that 'Great Britain in no conceivable circumstances should depart from a position of strict neutrality'.[25]

At the Foreign Office Grey saw Mensdorff. The ambassador finally handed over the bulky Austro-Hungarian document on Serbian involvement in the Sarajevo conspiracy. It was in German and it was now too late to have any impact – the Foreign Office did not bother to read it and left it to gather dust in a basement archive. The rest of the meeting was equally unproductive. Grey said Vienna would have support if it accepted the Serbian reply and the other powers would guarantee Serbia stuck to it. Mensdorff responded that it was a purely Austro-Hungarian–Serbian dispute and Russia had to keep out. According to Mensdorff's report to Vienna, Grey replied:

> If the Powers are to advise only Russia to remain passive, that would be tantamount to giving you a free hand, and this Russia will not accept. You would have to give us at least something that we could make use of at St Petersburg . . . Even without territorial gains, we might reduce Serbia to the rank of vassal . . . and thereby eliminate Russia from the Balkans.

Very belatedly, Grey seemed to be grasping the magnitude of the crisis.

Mensdorff observed that Britain wanted to stay out of any war and that 'Russian interests leave England cold' but on the other hand Britain would stand by France.[26]

Grey then carried out the first of the tasks set by the cabinet when he saw Cambon. He told him:

> In the present case the dispute between Austria and Servia was not one in which we felt called to take a stand. Even if the question became one between Austria and Russia we should not feel called upon to take a hand in it . . . If Germany became involved and France became involved, we had not made up our minds what we should do.[27]

Cambon apparently said little in reply except that France could not be neutral in any Russo–German war.

Grey then called Lichnowsky to the Foreign Office for their second meeting of the day. The foreign secretary developed the idea he had raised in the morning. It was, he argued, too late to stop Austro-Hungarian military moves, but even after the occupation of Belgrade 'it might be possible to bring some mediation into existence'. Austria–Hungary might hold Belgrade in order to ensure a settlement and that Serbia paid compensation but would not advance any further while mediation was in progress.[28] According to Lichnowsky's account, Grey then said that Britain wanted Germany's friendship and would be able to:

> stand aside as long as the conflict remained confined to Austria and Russia. But if [Germany] and France should be involved, then the situation would immediately be altered, and the British Government would, under the circumstances, find itself forced to make up its mind quickly. In that event it would not be practicable to stand aside and wait for any length of time.[29]

Grey had finally made the statement that Buchanan in St Petersburg had suggested he might make four days earlier. Grey could have made this statement much earlier in the crisis – it did not commit Britain in any way and merely pointed out to Berlin that there were circumstances in which Britain might not be able to remain neutral. Indeed, instead of making such a statement four days earlier, Grey had dropped hints that Britain might well stay neutral. The impact of Grey's message when it reached Berlin late in the evening was far-reaching. But by then the crisis was beginning to run out of control. If Grey had made his statement four days earlier, it might well have made Germany draw back in time.

Berlin – Evening

Shortly after 4.30 p.m. the Kaiser began a series of meetings with his advisers at Potsdam. The first involved Bethmann Hollweg, Falkenhayn, Moltke and Lyncker. Falkenhayn again argued that the *Kriegsgefahrzustand* should be declared. The chancellor once again responded that this measure was much too close to mobilisation, that diplomacy and overt military measures could not be run in tandem and no response had yet been received from Vienna on the Kaiser's proposal made the previous day for a 'halt in Vienna'. Moltke summed up the latest military intelligence. Russia had completed the protection of its border railways but there was no evidence of mobilisation in the Warsaw military district opposite Germany and there had been no significant recall of reservists. In France there had been no recall of reservists, though trains were being marshalled and the forts at Belfort were now fully armed. Although Germany was significantly behind Russian preparations and slightly behind those of France, Moltke took a moderate line. The Kaiser supported the chancellor and Moltke and it was agreed that only minor military measures would be implemented. The movement of troops from training exercises to their depots would be accelerated, some border posts (mainly in the east) would be reinforced and sentries would be posted on key railway bridges.

At 6.10 p.m. the Kaiser saw Crown Prince Henry and Bethmann Hollweg. During an hour-long discussion the Prince reported on the discussions he had had in London and the assurances about British neutrality he had received from George V. The chancellor suggested that it was time to firm up this general understanding with Britain. At 7.15 p.m. the three men were joined by three admirals – Tirpitz (navy minister), Pohl (naval chief of staff) and Müller (chief of the Kaiser's navy cabinet). Bethmann Hollweg seems to have suggested that if British neutrality were to be obtained it would probably be necessary to offer what the British had wanted for the last few years – an agreement limiting the size of the German navy. The chancellor thought this was a price worth paying. The admirals and the Kaiser did not and the subject was dropped.

Bethmann Hollweg travelled back to Berlin but immediately discovered that the situation had taken a significant turn for the worst. At 5 p.m., while the discussions at Potsdam were still in progress, the Russian ambassador, Serge Sverbeev, who had only just returned to Berlin, called on Jagow. He was finally carrying out Sazonov's instructions, sent the previous evening, to tell Germany that Russia was moving towards partial mobilisation. While the discussion was under-way, a telegram from Pourtalès in St Petersburg arrived giving the same information. Sverbeev argued that Austria–Hungary was also taking military measures in Galicia. Jagow responded that the Russian action meant the end of diplomacy. The ambassador reported that he 'could not conceal . . . [my] amazement', arguing, rightly, that Jagow had earlier promised that Russian partial mobilisation would have no effect on Germany. The discussion ended with mutual recriminations about military preparations.[30]

This was a major new development of which the policy-makers at Potsdam had been unaware. Bethmann Hollweg immediately called a meeting with Jagow, Moltke and Falkenhayn to consider what response to make. Moltke and Bethmann Hollweg again argued against mobilisation or even declaration of the *Kriegsgefahrzustand*. They accepted the Russian assurances that this partial mobilisation, when it happened, would not automatically lead to war and also wanted Russia to take the first and fatal steps in order to improve the German govern-ment's position with both the German public and Britain. Falkenhayn thought the Russians were lying, but said 'our mobilisation, even if two or three days later than that of Russia and Austria, would be more rapid'.[31] However, the meeting did agree that, as a precaution, the draft ultimatum to Belgium should be dispatched in a double-sealed envelope by special messenger to the German minister in Brussels, Klaus von Below-Saleske. He was instructed not to open the package until he received a further message from Berlin.

Bethmann Hollweg then summoned the British ambassador, Goschen, who was dining with Cambon, the French ambassador, and Polo, the Spanish ambassador. He made what Goschen described as a 'strong bid for British neutrality'. (Goschen's telegram to London was drafted in the chancellor's presence and Bethmann Hollweg even made some amendments to it.) The chancellor said that a Russian attack on Austria–Hungary seemed likely in which case there would almost certainly be a European war. He hoped Britain would stay neutral. He knew Britain would not allow France to be crushed but said that 'such a result was not contemplated by Germany'. He then gave an assurance that if Britain stayed neutral 'in the event of a victorious war, Germany aimed at no territorial acquisitions at the expense of France'. (The message sent to Brussels only an hour or so earlier effectively promised Belgium part of France if they allowed the passage of German troops.)

Goschen shrewdly asked about the position of France's colonies and Bethmann Hollweg said he could give no assurances on this point, though he was prepared to give one about Dutch neutrality. This was a maladroit move because Goschen then asked about the position of Belgium. The chancellor responded that he 'could not tell to what operations Germany might be forced by the action of France'. However, if Belgium did not take sides against Germany 'her integrity would be respected after the conclusion of the war'. As Goschen noted, this was virtually an admission that Germany did intend to violate Belgian neutrality. Bethmann Hollweg concluded by saying that he hoped there could be a 'general neutrality' agreement with Britain. Goschen merely responded by saying he thought Britain would wish to keep its freedom to decide its own policy.[32]

Bethmann Hollweg's approach was extremely clumsy and crude. Even if Britain had been sympathetic (as the chancellor thought was the case from earlier indications) this deal gave them nothing. Any offer on the German navy had been removed and Britain was expected to stand aside while Belgian neutrality was almost certainly violated and France stripped of its colonies to Germany's benefit. This approach was, therefore, no more than an attempt by Germany to secure a free hand in Europe. It was only after Goschen had left that Bethmann Hollweg realised the disastrous miscalculation he had made. Lichnowsky's telegram recording his second conversation with Grey in the afternoon (where a clear threat of British intervention was made) was dispatched from London at 6.39 p.m. and reached Berlin relatively quickly at 9.12 p.m. However, it then took time to decode and was not available to the chancellor until after his meeting with the British ambassador.

Berlin – Night

Bethmann Hollweg now realised that the two main German assumptions that had shaped its policy since early July had collapsed almost simultaneously. Russia looked likely to intervene unless Vienna's attack on Serbia could be limited very quickly and in any European war that would almost inevitably follow Russian military action Britain looked unlikely to be neutral. He decided he needed to take rapid diplomatic action on a number of fronts. His actions amounted to a complete reversal of German policy as he scrambled to try and avoid a European war.

There was still no report from Tschirschky in Vienna about the action he should have taken on the Kaiser's 'halt in Belgrade' proposal. (His telegram explaining that Austria–Hungary was stalling on the idea did not arrive in Berlin until 1.30 a.m. and then had to be decoded.) At 10.18 p.m. Bethmann Hollweg sent an uncoded telegram to Vienna asking whether the message of the previous evening (about the 'halt in Belgrade' proposal) had been received. Twelve minutes later he completed a second message saying that a reply was expected 'by return' on the ambassador's discharge of his instructions. (This telegram did not leave Berlin for another two hours because of the pressure of work in the foreign ministry coding room.) The chancellor realised that Grey's proposal to Lichnowsky during their morning talk (that there should be some agreement on limiting Austria–Hungary's military operations and demands) was almost identical to the Kaiser's 'halt in Belgrade'. He therefore sent the full text of Lichnowsky's telegram to Tschirschky telling him to inform Berchtold 'at once'. If, as the Italians were suggesting, Serbia would, under pressure, accept the ultimatum then, Vienna was told, 'we regard such compliance on the part of Serbia as a suitable basis for negotiation', although Austria–Hungary could occupy some territory as a guarantee of compliance.[33]

Just after 11 p.m. Bethmann Hollweg sent a telegram to Pourtalès in St Petersburg. It tried to mollify the Russians by saying that Berlin was working in Vienna for a firm declaration by Austria–Hungary of no territorial acquisitions and only temporary occupation to obtain Serbian guarantees. On this basis Germany hoped Russia would keep negotiating. Next, another telegram was sent to Tschirschky to ask Vienna not to break off bilateral negotiations with Russia (which they had effectively already done). It explained that, although two days earlier Berlin had not supported such talks, now 'in order to prevent a general catastrophe, or at any rate put Russia in the wrong, we must urgently desire that Vienna should begin and pursue conversations'.[34]

After a short break, during which it became clear to Berlin that Vienna had declined talks with St Petersburg, Bethmann Hollweg sent two long telegrams to Tschirschky in Vienna. They set out a new German position. They no longer supported Austro-Hungarian policy and they now expected, in the light of a looming European catastrophe, that their ally would accept immediate mediation and a diplomatic resolution of the dispute. In the first telegram the chancellor explained that following Grey's second talk with Lichnowsky (with its clear threat that Britain might intervene) the situation for Berlin and Vienna was grim. Bethmann Hollweg considered that 'in case Austria refuses all mediation' Germany and Austria–Hungary would be in a difficult position in any war – Britain would be hostile, Italy and Romania neutral. He argued:

> Austria's political prestige, the honour of her arms, as well as her claims against Serbia, could all be amply satisfied by the occupation of Belgrade or of other places. She would be strengthening her status in the Balkans as well as in relation to Russia by the humiliation of Serbia.

Only four days earlier Germany had been urging its ally to declare war and had always accepted that Vienna wanted a military victory over Serbia because a diplomatic triumph would not be sufficient. Now that it was clear where this policy was leading, Vienna was told 'we must urgently and emphatically commend . . . the acceptance of mediation on these honourable conditions'. If this was not done 'the responsibility for the consequences that might otherwise arise would be for Austria and ourselves exceedingly grave'.[35]

Five minutes later the second telegram (and the fifth in this period of frantic activity) was dispatched to Vienna. This explained that, because Vienna seemed to have rejected direct talks with St Petersburg, Berlin had supported Grey's ideas on four-power talks of some sort. Bethmann Hollweg made it clear that Austria–Hungary was not expected 'to submit to a sort of European court of arbitration'. Therefore direct talks with Russia might be preferable:

> We can not expect Austria to deal with Serbia, with whom she is at war. The refusal to hold any exchange of opinions with St Petersburg, however, would be a serious error, as it would be direct provocation of Russia's armed interference.

The chancellor was still angry over the other issue he had raised earlier in the evening: 'on the Italian question, too, Vienna seems to disregard our advice'. The chancellor concluded that Germany would of course fulfil its alliance obligations 'but must decline to be drawn into a world conflagration by Vienna, without having any regard paid to our counsel'. Tschirschky was instructed to speak to Berchtold 'at once' and 'with all impressiveness and great seriousness'.[36]

Two further follow-up messages were then sent. Pourtalès was instructed to tell Sazonov 'we continue to mediate; preliminary condition, however, is suspension for the time being of all hostilities on the part of Russia against Austria'.[37] Lichnowsky was also told to see Grey and thank him for his frank statement about Britain's position and tell him 'we continue to mediate at Vienna and urgently advise acceptance of his proposals'.[38]

There is a clear air of panic about Bethmann Hollweg's actions late in the night of 29 July and in the early hours of the next day. Time was now needed to put pressure on a highly recalcitrant Vienna – perhaps Berlin might even have to make the threat to abandon its ally if it did not change tack. But time was very short and any military measures by Russia could end the attempt to pressurise Vienna into a diplomatic solution. What Bethmann Hollweg did not know was that, even as he was desperately trying to unravel the dangerous situation he had helped to create, Russia was taking action which would end any chance of mediation and a diplomatic solution.

St Petersburg – Morning

There was frantic diplomatic activity in St Petersburg throughout the morning. The various talks centred around three factors. First, attempts to limit any Russian military preparations (which seemed imminent after the discussion the previous evening between Sazonov and the Tsar about partial and general mobilisation). Second, the question of Austro-Hungarian action against Serbia, and third, the possibility of mediation either through direct talks between Vienna and St Petersburg or in some wider forum. The Kaiser's proposal for a 'halt in Belgrade' was not discussed – it had got no further than Tschirschky and Berchtold in Vienna.

At 11 a.m. Pourtalès saw Sazonov. The German ambassador said Berlin was still trying to pressurise Vienna into direct talks with St Petersburg to clarify 'the aims and extent' of Vienna's actions against Serbia (but not the terms of the ultimatum). The foreign minister responded that Austria–Hungary had begun partial mobilisation, which must, at least in part, be directed at Russia, and that therefore Russia would take similar action later in the day. However, he emphasised that this did not mean Russian troops would cross the border. Pourtalès argued that Berlin needed more time to apply pressure on Vienna and pointed out the danger that German mobilisation might follow any Russian military moves. Despite this clear statement of the German position, foreign ministry officials advised Sazonov that Germany was probably only trying to slow up Russian military preparations and that its appeals in Vienna would be ineffective even if they were genuine.[39]

Sazonov then saw Buchanan and told him, correctly, that Germany had promised that it would not mobilise if Russia only undertook partial mobilisation. He reassured the British ambassador that 'it was for this reason that it had been decided not to order the general mobilisation which military authorities had strongly recommended'. He also informed him that because Vienna was rejecting direct talks St Petersburg was now supporting Grey's revised conference proposal that it had rejected only two days earlier.[40] The Russian foreign minister then saw Pourtalès again and told him Russia was now supporting the British proposal, though he emphasised that Austria–Hungary was not expected 'to submit to any kind of European court of arbitration'. The German ambassador warned him again that any form of Russian mobilisation would be 'a grave mistake'.[41]

Szápáry then called on Sazonov to inform him of a new suggestion from Vienna. Austria–Hungary would not discuss the ultimatum or the Serbian reply but was ready to propose 'a far broader basis for the exchange of views'. He re-emphasised that Vienna did not wish to damage Russian interests, did not intend to acquire Serbian territory and did not question Serbian sovereignty. Sazonov replied that he might be satisfied over territory, but the Austro-Hungarian note did infringe Serbian sovereignty. Vienna, he argued, was trying to turn Serbia into a vassal state and change the power balance in the Balkans. He added that Austria–Hungary's 'legitimate demands would be recognised and fully satisfied, but that this would need to be done in a form acceptable to Serbia. It was merely a case of quarrelling over words.' (It was not, of course, a quarrel over words – what was at stake was the future of Serbia and the prestige and power of Austria–Hungary and Russia.) Szápáry tried to argue that Vienna's demands did not concern Russia, to which Sazonov responded 'in this case Russian interests were identical with the Serbian'. The Austro-Hungarian ambassador's proposal for a general exchange of views with Russia might have been productive (though it still seemed to be based on St Petersburg giving Vienna free hand against Serbia), but then a foreign ministry official entered the room. He told Sazonov that Belgrade had been shelled. Sazonov thought this meant that a full-scale Austro-Hungarian invasion of Serbia was underway and told Szápáry that it was now impossible to hold discussions and ended the meeting.[42]

St Petersburg – Afternoon

After the discussion the previous evening with the Tsar, Sazonov assumed that the general staff were preparing the order for partial mobilisation, which had been the agreed Russian response since the meeting of the council of Ministers five days earlier. In fact, Yanushkevich had instructed the general staff to prepare the order for general mobilisation because they had, unilaterally, decided the previous afternoon that this was the only feasible military option. To be valid, the order had first to be signed by the minister of war, the navy minister and the interior minister, and then Sazonov had to gain the Tsar's approval. Yanushkevich instructed General Dobrorolski to gather the necessary signatures. General Sukhomlinov, who had originally been extremely bellicose, was now doubtful but reluctantly signed the order. Dobrorolski then saw the interior minister, Maklakov. He too was very reluctant but, sitting at a table crowded with icons and ritual lamps, crossed himself and signed the order while talking of the inevitable revolution that would follow any war. The navy minister was out of his office. Shortly after 3 p.m., while the first two signatures were being gathered, Yanushkevich saw the German military attaché, Eggeling. He told him there was no change in the situation and that 'there was no mobilisation anywhere', which was still technically correct.[43]

St Petersburg – Evening

At some time around 6 p.m. Pourtalès called on Sazonov for their third discussion of the day. He was carrying out Bethmann Hollweg's instructions sent at 12.50 p.m., following the chancellor's meeting with Moltke and Falkenhayn, to warn Russia about the danger of further military preparations. He told Sazonov that 'further progress of Russian mobilisation measures would compel us to mobilise and that then European war would scarcely be prevented'.[44] Germany had, once again, made its position crystal clear. Sazonov and his officials immediately discussed this development. The foreign minister interpreted the German message as an ultimatum and this reinforced his conviction that Vienna was only being intransigent because of Berlin's support. Although he had previously thought partial mobilisation against Austria–Hungary was a sufficient response, he now began to think a European war was inevitable and Russia had better fight it on the best terms possible by starting general mobilisation immediately.

He seems to have been under the illusion, despite the clear German warnings, that general mobilisation did not mean war, because Russian troops would stay behind the frontier while mobilisation was underway.

Sazonov was suffering from another of his violent mood swings and he did not think through the consequences of what he was now advocating. So far Austria–Hungary had declared war on Serbia, begun partial mobilisation and made a very limited attack on Belgrade. It would be another two weeks before they were ready for any major military operations against Serbia – there was plenty of time in which diplomacy could operate. Sazonov, however, did not know about the Kaiser's 'halt in Belgrade' proposal nor that Germany was about to make a complete volte-face. Partial mobilisation directed at Austria–Hungary would have been a possible response though a very dangerous one. However, just because Russia did not have a plan for partial mobilisation did not mean that it had no alternative but to move immediately to general mobilisation. The preparatory measures put in hand on 25 July already gave Russia a few days lead in mobilisation over its rivals. It could have waited for several days to see how the crisis developed. General mobilisation was not only a disproportionate response to the situation on the evening of 29 July – it was a massive escalation of the crisis that would make a European war almost inevitable. Sazonov might convince himself that it would have no real effect, but he did not consider, despite the clear warnings from Berlin, the impact this decision would have on Germany. The whole of German strategy was based on not allowing Russia a head start in mobilisation and, under Germany's inflexible plans, war began at the very start of mobilisation even though it would be about two weeks before the full army was ready to deploy.

The discussions in the Russian foreign ministry over how to react to Germany's latest message were still continuing when the Tsar rang to tell Sazonov about an optimistic message from the Kaiser. This was a message sent at 1.45 p.m. from Berlin saying that he was exerting all his influence to get Vienna to reach an understanding with Russia. Sazonov told the Tsar of the German threats conveyed by Pourtalès. The Tsar agreed to Sazonov's request that ministers could consider general mobilisation and that in the meantime he would send a message to the Kaiser asking him to explain the discrepancies between the two messages from Berlin. At about 8 p.m. Yanushkevich held a meeting in his office with Sazonov and Sukhomlinov while other senior military figures waited in an outer office. The three men decided 'in view of the small probability of avoiding war with Germany' to recommend immediate general mobilisation.[45] Their decision was endorsed by the Tsar after a short telephone call. General Dobrorolski left to obtain the final signature on the order from the navy minister. This was done by 9 p.m. and he left for the St Petersburg Central Telegraph Office to begin typing the order so that it could be dispatched across the country.

It was just after the Tsar had given approval for general mobilisation that he received another message from the Kaiser. This was a reply to the one the Tsar had sent the previous evening and it asked Russia to show restraint while he tried to mediate in Vienna. The Tsar decided that he could not ignore this appeal and immediately telephoned General Sukhomlinov to countermand the order for general mobilisation. The minister for war tried to dissuade the Tsar by saying that any partial mobilisation would wreck plans for a general mobilisation. He asked the Tsar to speak to the chief of staff, Yanushkevich. He gave the Tsar the same advice as Sukhomlinov but again it was rejected and Nicholas II ordered the cancellation of general mobilisation. Instead, he approved the implementation of the plan agreed on 25 July – partial mobilisation in four military districts together with the Baltic and Black Sea fleets. It had been a busy day for the Tsar as he recorded in his diary: 'During the day we played tennis; the weather was magnificent. But the day was singularly unpeaceful. I was continually being called to the telephone.'[46]

After the discussion with the Tsar, General Yanushkevich called Dobrorolski's office to tell him to hold up the telegrams initiating general mobilisation. He found that Dobrorolski had already left to dispatch them and sent Captain Tugan-Baranovski to run after him and stop the telegrams. He arrived at the telegraph office just in time and general mobilisation was cancelled. Instead, Russia began the first stages of partial mobilisation, although the general staff decided that they would continue with the preparations for general mobilisation, hoping to change the Tsar's mind before chaos ensued.

Sazonov dispatched telegrams to London and Paris informing the ambassadors of Russian partial mobilisation. At 11.45 p.m. he telephoned the French ambassador, Paléologue, to inform him of the decision. The first secretary at the embassy, Chambrun, was sent to the foreign ministry to secure details and the military attaché, General de Laguiche, went for discussions with the general staff. In the chaos that subsequently ensued in communications with Paris over the Russian decision, two points are clear. First, Paléologue took no action to dissuade Sazonov, neither did he demand that France should be consulted before mobilisation began as was required by the military agreement between the two countries. Second, the French embassy was aware that evening that Russia intended to continue its preparations for general mobilisation.

At the end of a very long day Sazonov saw Pourtalès for the fourth time. He informed him of the Russian decision for partial mobilisation, but asked Berlin to take part in four-power talks aimed at persuading Vienna to drop demands detrimental to Serbian sovereignty. The German ambassador was not optimistic, saying that talks were almost impossible 'now that Russia had resolved on the fatal step of mobilization'. Sazonov responded that 'the cancellation of the mobilization order is no longer possible and that the Austrian mobilization was responsible for it'.[47] The European situation was now very grim indeed.

The Low Counties and Denmark

In Brussels the French minister, Klobukowski, reported to Paris that it seemed likely that Brussels would wait to see which was the winning side before joining them. In fact, Belgium was the first country in western Europe to begin mobilisation when a partial mobilisation was ordered during the day. Three classes of reservists were called up to double the number of front-line troops to 100,000 and increase numbers in the forts and frontier defences. Belgian forces were spread out across the country – one division guarded the coast against a potential British invasion, one was along the frontier with Germany, while two were deployed on the longer frontier with France. Two more divisions were retained in Antwerp and Brussels. In neighbouring Luxembourg the prime minister, Eyschen, who had been on holiday at Évian-les-Bains, returned to the country during the evening.

For the first time in the crisis, Denmark had to consider what its position might be. The British minister, Sir Henry Lowther, called on the foreign minister, Scavenius, who told him that Denmark's attitude in any general war 'would be one of strict neutrality'. If Britain were neutral there would be no problem, but if not potential Anglo–German naval operations would mean that 'the geographical position of Denmark would bring her within the danger zone'.[48] (The position of the Kiel canal and German bases made this almost inevitable.) At the same time Jagow in Berlin sent the German minister in Copenhagen,

Brockdorff-Rantzau, a message to reassure the Danish government that Germany had 'no intention to endanger the integrity of the Danish state'. However, he was to explain that there might well be naval operations in Danish waters and that the Danish government therefore needed to decide its attitude towards Germany.[49]

The Balkans

The main diplomatic initiatives during the day came from Austria–Hungary and Russia in an attempt to improve their positions. The Russian ambassador in Bucharest, Poklevski, was instructed to see the prime minister, Bratianu, and build on the recent improvement in relations between the two countries. In particular, he was to let him know 'that we do not rule out the possibility of advantages for Romania if she joins us in a war with Austria'.[50] Similarly, the Austro-Hungarian ambassador in Athens, Szilassy, saw Streit, the foreign minister. He was told Greece would be strictly neutral and only intervene if Bulgaria did so. Szilassy then gave it as his 'personal opinion' that 'Greece might well receive part of Serbia' (probably part of Macedonia). He reported that he found the foreign minister 'very accessible' to the idea.[51] Later, Szilassy was able to reassure Streit that Bulgaria had committed itself to absolute neutrality. Meanwhile, a message arrived from Prime Minister Venizelos who was still in Munich. He sent instructions to be passed on to Alexandropulos, the minister in Niš. These were that Greece would not stand by its alliance with Serbia on the grounds that to do so would require a partial mobilisation of the Greek army and this might only tempt Bulgaria to intervene.

Brussels

The International Socialist Bureau met at the Centre for Workers' Education on the sixth floor of the new wing of the *Maison du Peuple*. Much of the discussion was about the forthcoming Congress of the Second International due to be held in Vienna in September. The Bureau agreed to bring the meeting forward to 9 August and changed the venue to Le Pré-Saint-Gervais, near Paris. They were convinced this left plenty of time for the congress to meet and take action before any European war began. The general mood of the meeting was, however, gloomy. There was no representative from Serbia, but the seriously ill

Victor Adler, accompanied by his son Friedrich, sketched the position in Vienna. He argued that it was impossible to stop the war – the Socialist Party was powerless and incapable of action. His main aim was to try to preserve it as a functioning organisation as war fever grew. The Czech representative, Anton Nemec, supported Adler's assessment. Other delegates, such as Bruce Glasier from Britain, the Russian revolutionary, llya Rubanovich, and the Menshevik, Pavel Axelrod, were convinced that the workers would follow agreed socialist policy. (Maxim Litvinov was supposed to be representing Lenin, who was in exile in Poland, but did not attend.) The Russian representatives forecast revolution if Russia did join the war. When news arrived that Russia was likely to begin partial mobilisation they refused to believe it.

The delegates reflected their differing national positions. Hugo Haase from the SPD in Germany said that the German governing class and industrial leaders did not want war, that Germany had not known of the Austro-Hungarian ultimatum in advance and that only an attack by Russia would bring Germany into the war. On the other hand, Jean Jaurès speaking for the French socialists said:

> We do not have to impose a policy of peace on our government. It is carrying one out . . . the French government is the best ally for peace of this admirable English government which has taken the initiative toward conciliation.

Jaurès argued that the meeting should take no dramatic action – that should be left for the meeting of the congress in ten days' time: 'We need the Congress. Its deliberations and resolutions will give the proletariat confidence.'[52]

In the evening the delegates move to the *Cirque Royal* for a rally in favour of peace. There were speeches from Kier Hardie, llya Rubanovich and Jean Jaurès. Unlike the closed session of the ISB, the speeches reflected great optimism about the prospects for peace and the ability of the European proletariat to bring it about. What the delegates did not know was that Europe was now on the very edge of the precipice and that within twenty-four hours a European war would be inevitable.

THURSDAY 30 JULY

Brussels – Morning
The International Socialist Bureau reconvened for a short meeting early in the morning. It passed a resolution, probably drafted by Jaurès, though it was formally in the name of Haase. It spoke of the growing anxiety of the proletariat about a possible European war and called for more anti-war demonstrations as a matter of urgency. It said that the dispute between Austria–Hungary and Serbia could be solved by arbitration and looked forward to the meeting of the congress in Paris 'which will give powerful expression to the determination of the proletariat of the world to preserve the peace'. There was no call for any common action. That was left to the meeting of the congress on 9 August.

Most of the members left in an optimistic mood. Jaurès told one of the Belgian socialist leaders: 'this is going to be another Agadir, we shall have our ups and downs. But this crisis will be resolved like the others.' Another French socialist, Anton Rosmer, remarked: 'at any rate the threat of a European war is no longer imminent as in the first days. As the situation is developing now the crisis might last days or even weeks.'[1] Jaurès had time to visit the Museum of Art before catching the train to Paris. He slept for most of the journey through northern France and after arriving at Gare de l'Est went immediately to the offices of the socialist newspaper, *L'Humanité*.

Paris – Morning
On the previous evening, after the chaos in St Petersburg over partial and general mobilisation, Sazonov sent a telegram to the ambassador in Paris. It explained that Germany had asked for Russia not to continue with mobilisation and went on 'as we cannot comply with the wishes of Germany, we have no alternative but to hasten on our military preparations and to assume that war is probably inevitable'. The telegram also thanked Paris for Paléologue's declaration of unequivocal support.[2] When the message arrived in Paris in the early

hours of 30 July, the Russian ambassador, Izvolsky, immediately took it to Viviani (the military attaché, Ignatiev, took a copy to Messimy). Although Paris was aware that partial mobilisation might be ordered, the information in the telegram from St Petersburg was unclear. It did not say anything about the decision to continue preparations for general mobilisation, nor that a decision to embark on this fundamental step was imminent. The French had no information from their ambassador in St Petersburg – he had agreed that the Russians should inform Paris via their embassy. He certainly seems to have agreed that the Russians should suppress information about general mobilisation. Paléologue did send his own message just after midnight, but only after changing his codes – the message did not arrive in Paris for almost twenty-four hours (11.15 p.m. on 30 July) and therefore had no influence over the crisis. (The telegram said that Russia was proceeding secretly to the first measures of general mobilisation and the delay on Paléologue's part was probably deliberate.)

At 2 a.m. on 30 July, when Viviani and Messimy had seen the Russian telegram from St Petersburg, they immediately went to the Elysée to wake Poincaré. The three men drafted a telegram to go to Paléologue in St Petersburg. He was to tell the Russian government that it 'should not immediately take any step which may offer Germany a pretext for a total or partial mobilisation of her forces'.[3] The telegram was dispatched at 7 a.m. Paris time, but Paléologue claimed that he did not receive it until 6 p.m. St Petersburg time (4 p.m. Paris time), which was too late to affect the decisions being made in the Russian capital (Paléologue was deliberately misleading in this claim – the telegram arrived in St Petersburg at about 2 p.m. local time, though still too late to have any influence on Russian decisions.) A copy of the French telegram was given to Izvolsky who held further talks with Margerie at the Quai d'Orsay and Ignatiev also had talks with Messimy at the war ministry. The Russians sent their telegram to the foreign ministry in St Petersburg at about 9.30 a.m. This was 11.30 a.m. in the Russian capital, and since the transmission and decoding of telegrams from Paris normally took between three to four hours at a minimum, the telegram from Paris would not have been available in St Petersburg before about 3 p.m. at the earliest, probably later. Again, this was too late to affect the decisions being made in the Russian capital.

Although the French response had no effect on the decisions made by their ally on 30 July, it is important to understand exactly what the French were advising the Russians to do. The French government was unclear as to exactly what the Russians were proposing to do – they knew partial mobilisation could be implemented and that since 25 July their ally had been making a number of moves preparatory to general mobilisation. The French would have been entitled, under the terms of the military convention between the two countries, to demand to be consulted before Russia began general mobilisation because of the impact this would have on Germany and therefore France. It is clear that at no point did the French make such a demand. The French telegram sent to St Petersburg was not a veto on Russian action – it merely advised a cautious approach. The telegram that the Russian embassy sent to St Petersburg was rather more frank about French motives. It said the French would not interfere with Russian preparations, but thought they 'should be of as little overt and provocative a character as possible'. A statement might even be made that they were being slowed down – they could always be speeded up later.[4] Even if either of these messages had arrived in St Petersburg in time to affect the crucial decision-taking, it is unlikely that they would have made a difference.

The real motivations behind French policy became clearer at a cabinet meeting held at 9.30 a.m. The notes made by Abel Ferry (the under-secretary of state for foreign affairs) recorded the decisions made as:

1. For the sake of public opinion, let the Germans put themselves in the wrong.
2. Mobilize but do not concentrate. Do not stop Russian mobilization.[5]

The basis of French policy was to ensure that Germany was seen as responsible for taking the aggressive steps that resulted in war. (The Germans were trying to ensure the same in relation to Russia.) This was believed to be important not just for domestic opinion and internal unity but also to convince Britain that war could not be blamed on France. The second point in Ferry's note makes it clear that the French had no intention of stopping their ally from mobilising, whatever the risks involved – they merely wanted them to do it cautiously so that they could not be blamed for provoking Germany into war. Indeed, if war was inevitable then the French had every reason to ensure that the Russians did mobilise as early and as quickly as possible. The sooner the Russians could put pressure on the Germans in the east the more likely it was that the French would survive the initial German assault.

The last line in Ferry's note refers to the military decisions taken by the cabinet. The chief of the General Staff, Joffre, was pushing hard for precautionary measures to be started. He argued that each day's delay in mobilisation would result in the loss of fifteen to twenty kilometres of French territory. The cabinet was determined that, although they were doing almost nothing to help prevent a war, France should avoid the blame for causing the war. They confirmed the decision made the previous day that troops were to remain ten kilometres from the border. Preparatory measures were put in hand, but they were restricted in scope – no reservists were to be called up, no horses or vehicles were to be requisitioned (though they could be bought on the open market) and no train transports were to be activated. The reasons behind the policy were made clear in a telegram sent to the ambassador in London, Paul Cambon. It explained the cabinet's decisions, particularly to leave part of its territory undefended, and added: 'In doing so we have no other reason than to prove to British public opinion and the British Government that France, like Russia, will not fire the first shot.'[6]

Vienna – Morning

Shortly after dawn, the succession of telegrams which Bethmann Hollweg had sent in the early hours began arriving at the German embassy in Vienna. They made it clear that Germany now expected its ally to compromise and either open direct talks with St Petersburg or accept the British proposal for some form of four-power mediation. Austro-Hungarian military action (there had been none, other than the shelling of Belgrade the previous day) could continue but would be limited to the occupation of Belgrade. This was a fundamental reversal of policy and a desperate attempt to find a solution at the last moment. Exactly what happened in Vienna when these messages were given to the Austro-Hungarian government can be reconstructed, but this has to be done through a fog of misleading information deliberately sent to Berlin by the German ambassador, Tschirschky.

Tschirschky told Berlin he was 'lunching' with Berchtold when the telegrams were brought to him. This is untrue – from the Austro-Hungarian evidence it is clear that the telegrams were available shortly after breakfast and that Tschirschky saw Berchtold in the early morning. As Tschirschky read out the crucial telegrams, Berchtold was 'pale and silent'. The ambassador says he put the new German position: Vienna would get what it wanted and 'a complete refusal of the mediation was out of the question'. Whether he put any pressure on Berchtold, as he was instructed to do by Berlin, remains doubtful. Berchtold then left the meeting to discuss this development with other members of the government. The ambassador remained talking with Forgách, who had taken the notes of the meeting. The latter said 'agreement to the mediation was requisite' but 'the restriction of the military operations now in progress appeared . . . to be scarcely possible'. He also suggested that since Tisza was due in Vienna the next day it would be impossible to take any decisions before he was consulted. Tschirschky's misleading timing of the meeting enabled him to justify not sending a telegram to Berlin describing this discussion until 1.35 a.m. on 31 July.[7]

The German initiative required a fundamental appraisal of Austro-Hungarian policy and Franz Josef was recalled from Bad Ischl for a meeting in the afternoon. Meanwhile, Berchtold seems to have viewed the German initiative as a betrayal of the policy agreed in Berlin on 5 July, which it was. Having backed Vienna, and encouraged it to declare war on Serbia, it was now trying to pull the rug from under Vienna's feet. There were two options open. The first was to accept the German pressure and agree to talks that would inevitably lead to a compromise solution. The second was to escalate the crisis and ensure that Germany was tied to Austria–Hungary irrevocably. Berchtold seems to have felt, as he had since July, that Austria–Hungary's prestige would be badly damaged if it compromised and therefore chose the second option.

After he left Tschirschky, Berchtold discussed the new situation with Conrad. The latter, worried by increasing signs of Russian partial mobilisation and whether it would be safe to attack Serbia in these circumstances, wanted general mobilisation. Berchtold explained the pressure from Germany to commence meaningful negotiations. Hoyos, who was also present, suggested that Conrad should prepare an order for general mobilisation to be discussed that afternoon with the Emperor. Krobatin, the minister for war, then joined the meeting which went on to discuss what Vienna's terms would be if Serbia was prepared to negotiate. They concluded that Serbia would have to accept every word of the ultimatum without qualification. They would also have to refund the entire cost of Austro-Hungarian mobilisation. Serbia would also have to cede its capital, Belgrade, and the Sabac area. Austria–Hungary would construct new fortifications in these areas but Serbia would have to pay for them. These were not terms for a realistic negotiation.

At this point Berchtold must have seen Tschirschky again because the Austro-Hungarian position is reflected in a telegram the ambassador sent to Berlin at 3.20 p.m. This explained that Serbian acceptance of points five and six of the ultimatum would no longer be sufficient for Vienna and pointed out, correctly, that Serbia had also made significant reservations on the other points. Tschirschky said that complete acceptance of the ultimatum by Serbia would have been sufficient but 'now that the state of war has come into force, Austria's conditions would of course be formulated differently'. However, the ambassador very carefully did not spell out these new conditions knowing they would only alienate Berlin still further.[8] Tschirschky did, however, send another telegram to Berlin explaining how Vienna would now enter into negotiations. Once again the telegram was very carefully drafted so as not to reveal the extent to which Vienna was rejecting its ally's demands. He explained that Szápáry in St Petersburg would now 'begin' talks with Sazonov at which he would 'elucidate' the ultimatum and 'receive' any suggestions from Russia while discussing general relations between the two counties. But this was no more than Vienna had offered the previous day and it was not negotiation about the ultimatum and the Serbian reply, which was what Berlin wanted. Tschirschky also said that Berchtold would see the Russian ambassador and tell him that Vienna had no territorial aims in Serbia. He would tell him that 'after the conclusion of peace' there would be 'a purely temporary occupation of territory', and Austria–Hungary would evacuate in stages as Serbia fulfilled the peace terms.[9] This formula bore no relation to the German 'halt in Belgrade' proposal. It would have allowed Austria–Hungary to occupy the whole of Serbia, impose the new terms agreed earlier in the morning, allow the other Balkan states to annex large parts of Serbia and turn the rump state into a vassal of Vienna. This is what Austria–Hungary had wanted all along and what Russia was not prepared to accept. Even under pressure from Berlin (as watered down by Tschirschky) Vienna was still not prepared to amend its extreme aims against Serbia.

What Tschirschky very carefully did not mention in either of these two telegrams to Berlin was that the Emperor was about to be asked to approve general mobilisation.

Vienna – Afternoon/Evening

That the German ambassador saw Berchtold to give him the overnight messages from Berlin long before lunchtime (as he tried to pretend to

Berlin) is clear from two telegrams dispatched from Vienna at lunch-time. At 1.20 p.m. Berchtold sent a message to Szápáry in St Petersburg. He was to see Sazonov 'at once' and report back 'immediately'. He was to explain that he was always ready to 'elucidate' any points in the ultimatum and to say that he would 'very much like . . . to talk over amicably and confidentially' relations between the two countries because there had been misunderstandings in the previous few days. The ambassador was to ask Sazonov what points he would like to discuss and he was instructed to 'enter upon a discussion of matters in general eliminating of course . . . everything running counter to Russian interests'.[10] These proposed general discussions were not what Berlin wanted and were merely designed to give the illusion of negotiation. The most significant omission was any mention of a 'halt in Belgrade' or any willingness by Vienna to stop military action or moderate its stance towards Serbia. Twenty minutes earlier, a telegram was sent to Szögyény in Berlin asking him to request the German government to back these talks in St Petersburg. He was given a statement of Vienna's position: 'In our action against Serbia we plan no territorial gain and have absolutely no intention to destroy the independent existence of the Kingdom.'[11] This statement left quite enough loopholes for all of Austria–Hungary's real aims.

Later in the afternoon Berchtold saw the Russian ambassador, Shebeko. The telegram the ambassador sent to St Petersburg illustrates just how successful the foreign minister was in giving him a totally false impression of Vienna's policy. Shebeko said it had been a 'friendly interview' and added, 'I received the impression that Berchtold would really like to arrive at an understanding with us.'[12] He failed to notice that Berchtold had deliberately omitted to say that negotiations could be opened on either the text of the ultimatum or the Serbian reply (this is what Russia wanted and would have been the point of any nego-tiations, either direct or in a four-power forum). All that was offered were general talks. The ambassador was so optimistic after the talk that he stopped packing his personal belongings (he had expected to be recalled to St Petersburg at any moment) and also told the British and French ambassadors that there were now real grounds for hope.

After this conversation Berchtold left the Foreign Office for the decisive meeting with the Emperor and Conrad. Berchtold gave Franz Josef copies of all the German overnight telegrams together with the misleading information from Rome that Serbia would now accept the ultimatum. The three men discussed the possible Austro-Hungarian terms in any negotiations and agreed with the conclusions reached earlier in the day. Franz Josef said that Serbia would never accept such conditions and Berchtold added that Tisza had always opposed annexation of Serbian territory (he might have added that Vienna had constantly reassured the rest of Europe that it would do no such thing). The discussion then moved on to the military options. Conrad said that he could not now suspend military options (the 'halt in Belgrade' did not require any such suspension at this time). Conrad emphasised the difficulty of just mobilising against Serbia when Russia posed a threat in Galicia. However, this dilemma had been at the heart of Austro-Hungarian strategy since the beginning of the crisis. In order to resolve it, Conrad now argued that it would be 'irresponsible' not to order general mobilisation. The only substantial objection Berchtold made was to the cost if war did not result. The meeting agreed that mobilisation would be ordered the next day once the council of ministers, which was due to meet in the morning, had endorsed the decision. The war against Serbia would continue and mobilisation would be based on this assumption. However, if Russia did intervene, then the main army would be deployed in Galicia. The offer of vague and general talks in St Petersburg was thought to be sufficient to placate Berlin and, meanwhile, the much more dangerous proposal for four-power mediation would be declined – 'a courteous reply will be returned to the English proposal, without accepting it on its merits'.[13]

The Austro-Hungarian government therefore not only rejected the strong pressure from its ally to open negotiations immediately, so as to avoid a European war, but it also decided to escalate the crisis. Why? In most respects the situation on 30 July had not changed from the previous day. Russia seemed to be embarking on partial mobilisation, but Vienna could easily have waited to see what happened – if there were to be serious negotiations it was best to avoid any escalation. What was different was the pressure being applied by Germany. The worry in Vienna was that Germany might be about to back down – it might even decide not to support Austria–Hungary and leave it isolated against Russia. The prospect of negotiations was seen as threatening Austria–Hungary's prestige. General mobilisation, which would be a direct threat to Russia, would help tie Germany to its ally and ensure that they could not backtrack at the last moment.

Tschirschky knew of the agreement between Conrad and Berchtold that they would recommend general mobilisation to the Emperor. His telegram to Berlin at 5.20 p.m. was therefore highly misleading in every respect. It merely stated: 'Instructions emphatically executed. Count Berchtold will reply by return after receiving Emperor Franz Josef's commands.'[14] It omitted the one piece of information Berlin needed to know if it was to stop Vienna. When the Wilhelmstrasse received the telegram at about 8 p.m., Stumm telephoned the ambassador to try to find out what was happening in Vienna. Tschirschky appears to have been rather more frank about Austria–Hungary's determination to reject all compromise, in particular the idea of a four-power conference, but, once again, he did not refer to the imminence of general mobilisation. Even when he sent his telegram at 1.35 a.m. the next morning, reporting on his supposed lunchtime meeting with Berchtold, he merely said that Conrad would be submitting a recommendation for general mobilisation. He did not say what he already knew, which was that Franz Josef had agreed the recommendation. The telegram ended with a massive understatement: 'it was not quite certain whether in the present situation mobilization was still the right course'.[15]

Vienna had rejected the advice of its ally that it should open serious negotiations immediately. It had also decided to escalate the crisis. In practice, the decisions in Vienna were irrelevant and the German pressure, even if it had been accepted, came too late. It was the decisions taken in St Petersburg during 30 July that made a European war inevitable.

St Petersburg – Morning

After the chaos of the previous night, Sazonov had not changed his mind about the necessity for general mobilisation, despite the Tsar's objections. At about 10 a.m. he saw Krivoshein, the minister for agriculture (a hardliner from the very first discussions on 24 July). They talked about the delay in mobilisation and Sazonov asked his colleague to put pressure on the Tsar to change his mind. Shortly after this meeting, Sazonov discussed the situation with Yanushkevich and Sukhomlinov. Yanushkevich was still worried that partial mobilisation, which had been underway for about twelve hours, would wreck the plans for general mobilisation. The three men agreed it was 'imperative to prepare for a serious war without loss of time'. Yanushkevich telephoned the Tsar, but he refused to reverse his decision of the previous night. However, he did agree to see Sazonov at 3 p.m.[16]

Sazonov then met Pourtalès who had asked to see the foreign minister in order to pass on Bethmann Hollweg's message explaining that Berlin was working hard with Vienna for mediation. Sazonov was still not happy with the formula on the fate of Serbia provided by Vienna and so the German ambassador invited him to make his own proposal. He suggested that if Vienna could declare that because the dispute had now taken on a European dimension it was 'ready to eliminate from its ultimatum those points which infringe on Serbia's sovereign rights' then 'Russia agrees to suspend all military preparations'. This was a crucial offer. Although Russia would not accept Vienna's declarations about Serbia's fate, it had offered a way out. Crucially, Russia had not insisted on a suspension of Austro-Hungarian military operations against Serbia as a prerequisite to negotiations. It would not have taken much effort to square this proposal with the German (and British) idea of a 'halt in Belgrade'. As Bethmann Hollweg wrote later that day in Berlin:

> What point of the Austrian ultimatum has Serbia really rejected? To my knowledge only the co-operation of Austrian officials in the judicial proceedings. Austria could forgo this co-operation on the condition that it occupies parts of Serbia with its troops until the completion of negotiations.[17]

Given even a minimum degree of flexibility, a diplomatic solution could have been achieved even at this late hour, given time. The Austro-Hungarian actions that morning in Vienna and Sazonov's own insistence on general mobilisation ensured that time was no longer available.

Sazonov was very far from being frank with the German ambassador. But he was equally mendacious with the British ambassador, Buchanan. The latter reported that Sazonov told him partial mobilisation had been ordered that morning (it was actually the previous evening) and preparations had begun for general mobilisation. The Russian foreign minister read out the text of the formula he had just given Pourtalès and added, 'If Austria rejects this proposal preparations for general mobilisation will proceed and European war will be inevitable.'[18] Yet Sazonov was about to leave to see the Tsar and request the start of general mobilisation before Berlin, let alone Vienna, had any chance to consider his initiative.

St Petersburg – Afternoon

After seeing Pourtalès, Sazonov sent telegrams to the ambassadors in Berlin, Paris, London and Vienna setting out his proposal. He then left for a 'breakfast' at 12.30 in a private room at Donon's restaurant with Krivoshein and Baron Schilling, the senior official in the foreign ministry. All three men favoured immediate general mobilisation because they had convinced themselves war with Germany was inevitable. Sazonov left the restaurant at 2 p.m. for his appointment with the Tsar in Peterhof.

The meeting at the Alexander Palace was also attended by General Tatistchev, the Tsar's personal envoy to the Kaiser. The discussion began at 3.10 p.m. and was dominated by Sazonov's monologue in favour of general mobilisation. The basis of his argument was that, despite the offer he had made to Pourtalès only a few hours earlier, there was no hope of preserving peace. Germany was determined on war, its military preparations were well advanced (both of which were untrue) and therefore Russia must start its preparations as soon as possible. At first the Tsar refused to agree. In these circumstances Sazonov's position was crucial – if he had chosen to disagree with the general-staff view, in order to give diplomacy time to work, then the Tsar would have backed him and mobilisation would not have taken place. Eventually, at about 4 p.m., the Tsar gave way. Sazonov asked for permission to telephone the news to Yanushkevich in St Petersburg (to ensure it was implemented before the Tsar changed his mind again). This was granted and Sazonov rushed to the ground floor of the palace to give Yanushkevich the go-ahead. Three signatures were still required for the order to be valid. They were easily obtained by General Dobrorolski because the council of ministers was meeting at the Mariinski Palace. By 5 p.m. Dobrorolski was once again at the General Telegraph Office issuing the instructions to the military authorities across Russia. The Tsar reacted with insouciance to this fatal decision that would doom both himself and his dynasty: 'After lunch I received Sazonov and Tatistchev. I went for a walk by myself. The weather was hot . . . had a delightful bathe in the sea.'[19]

The Russian decision to order general mobilisation was the one move in the crisis that was bound to produce a European war. The whole of German strategy was based on mobilising faster than the Russians and therefore they could not let them get a head start. Russian general mobilisation made German mobilisation and therefore a European war inevitable. Yet the Russian decision was made with little, if any, thought about the consequences and was wholly disproportionate to the situation they faced on 30 July. The outcome was a massive escalation of the crisis which shifted the threat that Russia posed from Austria–Hungary to Germany.

Sazonov was grossly irresponsible in not thinking through the consequences of Russian general mobilisation. He did not do so primarily because he seems to have been under two major illusions. The first was that general mobilisation could be kept secret. The second was that because the Russian army did not plan to cross the frontier during the mobilisation phase, mobilisation did not mean war and that the other powers, in particular Germany, would allow Russia to complete its military preparations without taking any action. He had been warned consistently by both Pourtalès and Buchanan, among others, that he was wrong and that if Russia mobilised so would Germany. He ignored those warnings.

Once the fatal decision was made, Paléologue again seriously misrepresented the situation to his government in Paris. At 4.31 p.m. he sent a telegram saying:

> This very morning I have recommended to M. Sazonov to avoid all military measures which might furnish Germany with a pretext for general mobilisation.[20]

This telegram uses phrases that are in the telegram sent from Paris at 7 a.m. that morning which Paléologue claimed he did not receive until about an hour and a half later, at 6 p.m. The Paris telegram probably arrived around 2 p.m., but it certainly had not arrived when Paléologue saw Sazonov, together with Buchanan, at about midday. It is therefore almost certain that the ambassador issued no such warning to Sazonov and that the 4.31 p.m. telegram is a deliberate falsification, probably for the public record, to show that France did try to restrain its ally when it was doing nothing of the sort.

When Sazonov returned from Peterhof he saw Paléologue for the second time that day to confirm that general mobilisation was underway and that the order had been issued at 5 p.m. It was only at 9.15 p.m. that the ambassador sent a further telegram to Paris. It stated that Sazonov had come to the conclusion that Germany would not pressurise Austria–Hungary into a settlement, which was a gross misrepresentation of his discussion with Pourtalès earlier in the day. It then stated that Russia also had intelligence that German war preparations were far advanced (if such intelligence existed it was certainly false). Therefore, Russia 'has decided to proceed secretly to the first measures of general mobilisation'.[21] This was a gross misrepresentation of the decision made that afternoon. It either reflects Sazonov's mistaken view or, if Paléologue consulted his military attaché at the embassy, it is a deliberate attempt to mislead Paris.

Berlin – Afternoon/Evening

After the frantic activity during the evening of 29 July and the early hours of 30 July when Bethmann Hollweg tried to pressure Vienna into accepting mediation and a compromise, it is hardly surprising that there were no important developments in Berlin during the morning.

It was at 1 p.m. that the chancellor saw Falkenhayn, Moltke and Tirpitz to discuss the telegram that had arrived from Pourtalès about an hour earlier, confirming that Russia had started partial mobilisation. Also available was the telegram the Tsar had sent to the Kaiser during the night which, in response to the request from the Kaiser to restrain Russian military measures, admitted that Russian military preparations had been underway since 25 July. (The Tsar tried to claim they were purely defensive.) These messages seemed to confirm the military intelligence now available in Berlin. Moltke reported that Russian mobilisation was directed at Austria–Hungary and had not started in the military districts facing Germany. Nevertheless, the Russian 'period preparatory to war' was far advanced and mobilisation could start very quickly. Belgium had stopped military training and was recalling reserves. The forts around Liège were fully operational and the bridges were mined for demolition – this was crucial for German plans that were based on seizing Liège at the very start of mobilisation. The meeting agreed not to take any action but to wait and see how the situation developed.

That afternoon the German government seems to have become convinced that a European war was more likely than not. At 1 p.m. a special edition of the semi-official *Berliner Lokal Anzeiger* was published announcing that German mobilisation had started. All copies of the paper were confiscated by the government and telegrams were dispatched to the major European capitals denying the story. Nevertheless, the incident was bound to heighten the sense of crisis. Szögyény was reflecting this mood when he sent a telegram to Vienna late in the afternoon. He reported that 'a state of nervousness' gripped the German elite and this was not just because a European war seemed near. The ambassador reported worries that Italy would not be an ally and might even be actively hostile. Concessions from Austria–Hungary were therefore required immediately to try and keep Italy friendly. The Kaiser also reacted badly when he saw Lichnowsky's account of his talk with Grey the previous afternoon when the foreign secretary had made a clear threat that Britain might not stay neutral in any European war. He wrote: 'England shows her hand at the moment she thinks we are cornered' and thought the message George V had given Prince Henry about neutrality was 'the grossest deception'. He thought Grey's attitude was a 'threat combined with a bluff' and added that Britain had not issued 'a single, serious, sharp, deterrent word at Paris or St Petersburg' (which was true).[22]

At 5 p.m. Bethmann Hollweg chaired a meeting of the Prussian cabinet at which he reported on the diplomatic situation. Already his thoughts were moving towards allocating the blame for any war, saying, 'the greatest importance must be attached to presenting Russia as the guilty party'. Nevertheless, he argued against the declaration of the *Kreigsgefahrzustand* while diplomatic action, especially the German pressure on Vienna, was still underway. He told the meeting: 'As a political leader I am not abandoning my hope and my attempts to keep the peace as long as my démarche in Vienna has not been rejected.'

Overall, 'there was practically no hope of England', which would side with Russia and France, the position of Italy was unclear and neither Romania nor Bulgaria could be counted on. On all sides the situation seemed grim: 'the situation had got out of hand and the stone had started rolling'. The only bright spot was his discussions with the socialist leaders. He reported that 'nothing much need be feared' from them during the crisis.[23]

At about 8 p.m. Stumm in the Foreign Office talked by telephone to Tschirschky in Vienna. He gained the clear impression that Vienna was going to reject outright German pressure for a compromise. Bethmann Hollweg drafted a telegram that was sent to Vienna at 9 p.m. It stated that Vienna 'declines to give in in any direction since it will scarcely be possible to cast the blame on Russia for the European conflagration now about to break out'. The Kaiser felt he could not reject the Tsar's pleas for mediation, though the situation had deteriorated because Russia had begun partial mobilisation. If Britain did succeed in pushing Paris and St Petersburg towards a compromise 'while Vienna declines everything, Vienna will be giving documentary evidence that it absolutely wants a war' and Russia would be 'free of responsibility'. If this happened, it 'would place us, in the eyes of our own people, in an untenable position'. The chancellor therefore concluded 'we can only urgently advise that Austria accept the Grey proposal [for four-power mediation], which preserves her status for her in every way'. Tschirschky was to see Berchtold, and if necessary Tisza, 'at once' and in the 'most emphatic language' put these points to the Vienna government.[24]

In some respects this telegram was less strongly worded than those sent overnight on 29/30 July, but it was another attempt to pressure Vienna into some form of compromise. Shortly after this telegram was dispatched, disturbing intelligence began to arrive in Berlin. The businessman from London, Mr Wilbert E. Stratton, was in St Petersburg and he sent a commercial telegram to a cover address in Antwerp. It contained coded information that suggested Russian general mobilisation might have started. The information was quickly passed to Berlin. At almost the same time, reports from intelligence units along the East Prussian frontier were received. They said that at two places Russian troops had burned down their own customs sheds, closed public offices in the frontier towns and started removing cash and documents in strong boxes to the interior. These activities were correctly interpreted as the first indications that general mobilisation was underway.

In the light of this new information, Zimmerman began drafting a telegram for Bethmann Hollweg to send to Tschirschky. It ordered him to suspend action on the telegram sent at 9 p.m. because 'military preparations of our neighbours, especially in the east' were underway and Germany now urgently needed to know Vienna's decisions, 'especially those of a military nature'.[25] Before this message could be sent, the Kaiser received a telegram from George V saying that Britain was acting in Paris and St Petersburg to seek a suspension of military activities if Vienna agreed to limit its military actions in Serbia (a sort of 'halt in Belgrade'). Bethmann Hollweg decided not to send Zimmerman's draft but instructed Tschirschky that the 9 p.m. telegram was not to be acted on. He was, however, to give Berchtold the British message and ask for his immediate reaction. But this was far short of exercising pressure in favour of acceptance.

The impact that Russian general mobilisation had on Berlin can clearly be seen in the very rapid change of course away from negotiation shortly after 9 p.m. when the first intelligence indications arrived.

London

There was little diplomatic activity in London during the day and there was no cabinet meeting. Most newspapers were now taking a line strongly opposed to Austria–Hungary and Germany. In particular, *The Times* was in favour of British intervention in any European war. But some, especially the liberal papers, remained anti-Serbian. The *Manchester Guardian* declared, 'we care as little for Belgrade as Belgrade for Manchester', and the *Daily News* argued, 'we must not have our western civilization drowned in a sea of blood in order to wash out a Serbian conspiracy'. The parliamentary Labour Party adopted a resolution that although a European war might not be avoided, Britain should remain neutral in all circumstances. The Liberal Foreign Affairs Group under Ponsonby met again, this time with twenty-two MPs present. They agreed a letter to be sent to Asquith saying that if Britain did intervene in a war then they would withdraw their support from the government. However, they immediately undermined the threat in the letter when they acknowledged that Britain had treaty obligations that it would have to uphold.

Asquith told Venetia Stanley that the situation was 'very black'.[26] Herbert Samuel wrote to his wife with a shrewd analysis of the situation. He thought that Germany and Russia seemed reluctant to go to war but:

> the headstrong recklessness of Austria is too much for them. Austria, which is really embarking on war in order to prevent the break-up of her own dominions, is utterly selfish and cares nothing at all whom else she involves.

He thought there was a 'faint hope' of a settlement 'but it is an exceedingly faint one'. He also thought that the Cabinet would hold together during the crisis though there was still a possibility it might split.[27] The main political development of the day came when the Conservative leader, Bonar Law, and the leader of the Ulster Unionists, Edward Carson, called on the prime minister. They suggested putting off legislation on Ulster in view of the international situation. Asquith discussed the suggestion with Lloyd George and Grey and then gratefully accepted the proposal as at least a short-term way out of the Ulster impasse.

At the Foreign Office the main development was the formal British response to Bethmann Hollweg's bid for British neutrality made late the previous evening. At 3.30 p.m. Grey told Goschen: 'You must inform the German Chancellor that his proposal that we should bind ourselves to neutrality on such terms cannot for a moment be entertained.' Britain could not afford to see France end its position as a great power and the bargain Bethmann Hollweg suggested was a 'disgrace'. Neither was Britain prepared to bargain away 'whatever obligation or interest we have as regards the neutrality of Belgium'.[28] This telegram crossed with one from Goschen recording a talk with Jagow during the course of the morning. It asked Britain to do something to restrain St Petersburg while Germany tried to put pressure on Vienna for a 'halt in Belgrade'. At the end it noted that Jagow had mentioned that Lichnowsky's telegram containing Grey's threat that Britain would not remain neutral had only arrived in Berlin late the previous evening. If it had arrived earlier, Bethmann Hollweg 'would, of course, not have spoke to me in way he had done'.[29]

Lichnowsky also saw Grey to see if Britain would restrain Russia and at 7.35 p.m. a telegram was sent to Buchanan in St Petersburg. It said that Berlin was trying to persuade Vienna to agree that after taking Belgrade and some frontier areas it would stop military activities, while the major powers arranged that 'Serbia should give satisfaction sufficient to pacify Austria'. He therefore hoped that Russia would agree to discussions and 'suspend military preparations'. The ambassador in Paris was asked to support this action with the French government. At the end of the message to Buchanan, Grey said, 'it is a slender chance of preserving peace, but the only one I can suggest'.[30] A similar message was sent from George V to Berlin and it was this that caused the slight hesitation in the German capital late that evening.

The message to St Petersburg took a long time to arrive – the British government no longer trusted the security of the telegraph network across Germany and sent the message via Aden. Even if Grey's message had arrived quickly, it would have been too late. Russia had already taken the fatal step of general mobilisation. Had the initiative been made earlier and had Vienna showed the slightest willingness to accept the Kaiser's 'halt in Belgrade' proposal made two days earlier, then a compromise along these lines might well have been possible. After 30 July there was no realistic chance of a diplomatic settlement. European governments were manoeuvring (as both Paris and Berlin had already demonstrated) to blame their opponents for the outbreak of a European war that was now only a matter of hours away.

14

FRIDAY 31 JULY

St Petersburg

Sazonov's illusion that general mobilisation could be kept secret was shattered early in the morning as the notices announcing the call-up, printed on red paper, were posted on every street in the Russian capital. Pourtalès immediately saw the foreign minister. Sazonov tried to explain that the measures were entirely precautionary and that Russia would not make any irrevocable moves. The ambassador replied that Russia seemed to be bent on war. He returned to his embassy and at 10.20 a.m. sent an urgent message to Berlin reporting that Russia had begun general mobilisation.

The French ambassador knew of the Russian decision the previous evening. At 6.30 a.m. Paléologue knew that the mobilisation notices were being pasted up across the city. He then took until 10.43 a.m. to send a telegram to Paris (although he timed it at 8.30 a.m.). It was marked *extrême urgence* but was sent, because Paléologue, like the British Foreign Office, did not trust the security of messages sent across Germany, via Scandinavia. The result was that the message did not arrive in Paris until 8.30 p.m. and it then took another thirty minutes to decode. It stated: 'An order has been issued for the general mobilization of the Russian army.'[1] The result of Paléologue's actions was that for the whole day Paris was in ignorance of this fundamental step taken by its ally (again without any consultation). It was another example of the ambassador failing to keep Paris informed of developments. He did not even need to send a coded telegram via a circuitous route – the information was public knowledge in St Petersburg and could have been sent to Paris via an *en clair* telegram.

As soon as he heard the news, the Austro-Hungarian ambassador, Szápáry, sent a message to Vienna saying that there was no longer any point in holding discussions with Sazonov about the general relations between the two countries. It was later, after he received a report from Vienna on Berchtold's talk with the Russian ambassador the previous afternoon, that he decided to go and see Sazonov. The ambassador explained that his instructions predated Russian mobilisation but the foreign minister tried to reassure him by repeating his own illusions when he said the Russian army would not move and therefore 'mobilization had no significance'. Szápáry explained that Vienna welcomed talks and that there was no real difference between 'modification' and 'elucidation' of the ultimatum (which was not what Vienna thought). Sazonov's mood swung once again and he was now optimistic about a solution. The simple fact was the two men had not discussed the most important issue – Russian mobilisation.[2]

Sazonov clearly did misinterpret this conversation because he sent a message to the Russian ambassadors in the major capitals saying Vienna had agreed to 'a discussion on the content of the ultimatum presented to Serbia'. Sazonov now wanted talks in London, although Szápáry had already told him Vienna would not be enthusiastic about this venue. Austria–Hungary was to stop military operations 'on Serbian territory' (it had not yet invaded) – Sazonov said this was an 'important', though not essential, precondition. Russia was not offering to rescind mobilisation, merely to maintain a 'waiting attitude'.[3] The two men were deluding themselves and this diplomatic initiative was rapidly overtaken by military developments.

Later in the day Pourtalès asked to see the Tsar. He pointed out that the Russian general mobilisation was contrary to the assurances given that the military preparations were only for partial mobilisation. He told the Tsar that mobilisation would have a terrible impact in Berlin and would also end any chance of mediation. He reported that the Tsar seemed unaware of the consequences and said that it was now impossible to rescind the order – however, Russian troops would not make any hostile moves. The Tsar merely recorded in his diary: 'It has been a grey day, in keeping with my mood'.[4]

Perhaps the most accurate description of the situation in St Petersburg was given by Pašić to the Serbian chief of staff, General Putnik. This was based upon reports from the Serbian minister, Spanlajković:

> Russia is now talking and drawing out the negotiations in order to gain time for the mobilization and concentration of her army. When that is complete she will declare war on Austria.[5]

That was just what Berlin and Vienna were not prepared to allow Russia to do.

Vienna

The Austro-Hungarian government was unaware that Russia had begun general mobilisation until the afternoon, although it knew that Germany suspected that some measures had been taken the previous evening. The first meeting of the day was at 8 a.m. between Berchtold, Conrad, Krobatin, Tisza, Stürgkh and Burián. They discussed the messages from Moltke on the previous day urging mobilisation against Russia. It was agreed Conrad should send a reply which had been drafted the previous afternoon. It said that Franz Josef had agreed 'to carry through the war against Serbia' but that the rest of army would be mobilised later in the day and would concentrate in Galicia.[6] It is probable that, although this message reflected the decisions made by the Emperor the previous afternoon, the information was not sent to Berlin immediately in case Germany tried to stop Austro-Hungarian general mobilisation while mediation efforts were still in progress.

After this meeting those present assembled for a formal council of ministers at which they were joined by Bilinski and Rear-Admiral von Kailer, the deputy chief of the navy. Hoyos once again took the minutes.[7] The discussion illustrates the continuing intransigence of the Austro-Hungarian government in the face of pressure to compromise. It confirms that Austria–Hungary had always wanted a military solution of the 'Serbian problem' even if this made a European war inevitable. Berchtold began by reporting on the diplomatic action of the previous day and the decisions the Emperor had made, although he did not make clear the full extent of the pressure Berlin had placed on Vienna. He explained that a reply to Berlin was being drafted which would be based on three fundamental principles. First, operations against Serbia must continue. Second, there could be no negotiations on the British proposals for a limitation on military action against Serbia until Russian partial mobilisation was stopped. (The Russians had been more flexible on the previous day and did not ask for similar Austro-Hungarian restraint.) Third, the Austro-Hungarian ultimatum to Serbia could not be subject to any negotiation. These conditions were no more than a reformulation of the existing Austro-Hungarian position. They meant that Vienna had not changed its position from the beginning of the crisis – it was to be given a free hand to deal with Serbia in whatever way it thought fit. Berchtold was worried about four-power mediation because Britain, France and Italy would all back Russia, leaving Germany as Austria–Hungary's sole supporter. Moreover, if the talks took place in London, Lichnowsky was 'a very doubtful support' and 'anything might sooner be expected from Prince Lichnowsky than that he would warmly represent our interests'. Berchtold therefore concluded:

> If this whole action ended in nothing else than a gain in prestige, it would . . . have been undertaken altogether in vain. A mere occupation of Belgrade would be no good to us; even if Russia would allow it.

If there was a 'halt in Belgrade', Russia would pose as the saviour of Serbia and the Serbian army would remain intact. Two to three years later 'we could expect a renewed attack of Serbia under far more unfavourable conditions'.

Bilinski spoke next and said that partial mobilisation by Austria–Hungary and Russia had altered the situation. Therefore, 'proposals which might have been acceptable at an earlier date, are no longer acceptable now'. Tisza strongly supported Berchtold and argued that it was far too dangerous to get involved in any British-sponsored mediation, suggesting that there should be no negotiations until Russia stopped partial mobilisation, although Austro-Hungarian military operations would continue.

The meeting then went on to consider the position of Italy. Berchtold explained the background and that Germany was supporting Italian claims that Article VII of the Triple Alliance referred to any territorial gains by Vienna anywhere in the Balkans, not just at the expense of the Ottomans as Austria–Hungary were trying to maintain. Neither could Vienna guarantee that in no circumstances would it annex Serbian territory. Berchtold admitted the essential duplicity at the core of Vienna's policy – they were reassuring the other powers that they had no intention of making territorial acquisitions, yet with Italy they had to consider what would happen if 'we should be forced against our will to undertake a non-temporary occupation'. The council agreed to 'promise Italy a compensation in the eventuality of a lasting occupation of Serbian territories on our part'. Italy would receive Valona if it 'actually fulfilled its duties as an ally', otherwise it would get nothing. In return, Austria–Hungary would take a 'decisive influence' in northern Albania. This was a concession by Vienna. At the very beginning of the crisis in early July, Berchtold had told Tschirschky that if Vienna did move against Serbia then Italy would demand Valona 'and to that we could not agree'.[8]

The discussion at the council took no account of the developing European crisis. It was clear that Romania would not join the war and there was very little likelihood that Italy would do so. Vienna was also aware of what Grey had said to Lichnowsky about the possibility that Britain would not remain neutral. Yet there was no discussion of how Austria–Hungary and Germany could fight a European war on this basis with any chance of ultimate success. But if there were a European war then any solution of the Serbian problem would depend on a successful outcome. The Austro-Hungarian government was sticking to the plan and the objectives it had set at the beginning of the crisis regardless of the wider consequences and without any assessment of the likelihood of success.

Later in the day Berchtold finally sent a telegram to Szögyény in Berlin giving the formal response to the German pressure for mediation (it did not arrive at the embassy in Berlin until 3.45 a.m. on 1 August). Vienna would be 'willing to enter more closely' into the British proposals but military action would, 'for the time being', have to take its course. Britain was to prevail on Russia to stop its mobilisation against Austria–Hungary. If it did, Vienna would end its 'defensive military counter-measures in Galicia'.[9] Vienna had taken thirty-six hours to give even this limited reply, which did not accept the Kaiser's 'halt in Belgrade' proposal, let alone the Russian conditions, and which was still based on giving Austria–Hungary a 'free hand'. Earlier, at 1 p.m., Franz Josef sent a message to the Kaiser, which stated that at the moment Vienna received the British mediation proposals they had heard of Russian partial mobilisation and he had, therefore, ordered full mobilisation. The army operations against Serbia 'can suffer no interruption' and any 'fresh rescue of Serbia by Russian intervention' would have the 'most serious consequences' for Austria–Hungary and therefore Vienna 'cannot possibly permit such intervention'.[10] This telegram accurately reflects the continuing intransigence of the Austro-Hungarian government.

The Emperor's telegram was dispatched only after Austro-Hungarian general mobilisation had been ordered at 12.23 p.m. – some twenty hours after Russia issued a similar order. The first day of mobilisation was set as 4 August which, because conscripts were allowed a day to put their personal affairs in order, meant that it would be 5 August before the process began. Conrad had decided, despite Moltke's pressure to deploy against Russia, to continue with the mobilisation plans already underway for a full deployment against Serbia. (He had told the council of ministers on 7 July that it would be possible to alter deployment plans up until the fifth day of mobilisation

– i.e. 1 August.) Indeed, even at 8 p.m. that evening, orders were sent to the 2nd army command in Budapest specifically stating that the deployment to the Balkans would continue, even though by then Vienna knew of Russian general mobilisation and therefore of the threat this would pose to both Galicia and Germany.

It is likely that Conrad decided to continue with the deployment against Serbia because he still hoped to crush Austria–Hungary's real enemy. Also, he was receiving advice from the railway division of the General Staff that a change in mobilisation plans would be catastrophic. These plans were based on all trains moving at the same speed – that of the slowest train on the worst line – normally a maximum of eighteen kilometres an hour. All trains also stopped for six hours a day for the troops to be fed, even though there were field kitchens on the trains. Feeding had to take place in stations and therefore the troops often received two meals in the middle of the night and then nothing for hours. By the late afternoon of 31 July, 132 troop trains had already left for the Serbian frontier. Conrad decided that it would be bad for morale for the trains to reverse direction and return the troops to their depots so that they could then deploy to Galicia.

Berlin

Austria–Hungary had already ordered general mobilisation before it knew of the similar Russian decision. It was therefore in Berlin that Russian general mobilisation had its greatest impact. At about 7.30 a.m. the General Staff intelligence section received a coded telegram from Captain Erich Otto Volkmann, the head of the army intelligence unit at Allenstein. He reported that in several places along the border red mobilisation notices had been posted up in Russian villages. Moltke was immediately informed and he telephoned the chief of staff at Allenstein, Colonel Emil Hell. Moltke said that he wanted firm evidence before taking any action and asked Hell to get hold of one of the Russian notices. The intelligence unit decided to use one of their local agents, Pinkus Urwicz, a tradesman in Kolno. The border was still open because war had not been declared and he crossed into Russia and took a copy of one of the notices. He returned to Allenstein where, shortly before noon, Captain Volkmann was able to telephone the exact text of the order through to Berlin.

From early morning, therefore, the indications from the east were that Russia had begun to mobilise. When Goschen called on Bethmann

Hollweg shortly before 10 a.m. to convey the British rejection of his bid for neutrality, the chancellor showed little interest in the reply (he knew he had made a tactical mistake in ever suggesting it). Bethmann Hollweg explained that Russian general mobilisation seemed to be underway and that Germany would probably have to take some serious steps later in the day. After seeing the ambassador, the chancellor held a meeting with Moltke and Falkenhayn about the military situation. Shortly after 11.40 the telegram which Pourtalès had sent from St Petersburg at 10.20 (8.20 Berlin time) was brought into the meeting – it arrived just before the confirmation of mobilisation sent from Allenstein. The three men agreed that the *Kriegsgefahrzustand* should be proclaimed and an ultimatum sent to St Petersburg demanding a halt to mobilisation. The Kaiser's authority was needed for these moves and, for what seems to have been the only time in the crisis, the telephone was used to alert Wilhelm II at Potsdam. He decided to travel to Berlin immediately. Up until this point, the Kaiser had remained optimistic about the crisis and thought it would be resolved by diplomatic means, possibly his own 'halt in Belgrade' proposal.

The Kaiser arrived in the capital at lunchtime and after a brief meeting agreed to the proposed measures. The *Kriegsgefahrzustand* was declared with immediate effect. It involved a series of measures. Martial law was proclaimed, press censorship of military news was imposed, full military protection of the railways was started, soldiers on leave were recalled, all troops returned to their bases, censorship of overseas mail began, private road traffic in frontier areas was banned, covering troops moved to the frontiers, and military and naval protection of the North Sea islands was instituted. In German plans this phase was regarded as leading inevitably to general mobilisation within a matter of hours, which was why both Moltke and Bethmann Hollweg had been reluctant to agree to it earlier. At 1.45 p.m. a telegram was sent to Tschirschky informing him of the decision and saying that mobilisation would follow within forty-eight hours at most. The message ended 'we expect from Austria immediate active participation in the war against Russia'.[11]

Between 3.10 and 3.30 p.m. messages were sent to the ambassadors in all the major European capitals explaining the proclamation of the *Kriegsgefahrzustand* and the ultimatum to Russia. Pourtalès was to tell the Russian government that German mobilisation would follow if 'Russia does not suspend every war measure against Austria-Hungary and ourselves within twelve hours'.[12] There was almost no chance that such a demand would be accepted, but it was useful in trying to place the blame on Russia and it filled in the time before Germany could start mobilisation. There was a major omission from the German message: it did not make clear that for them, unlike Russia, mobilisation did mean war. The telegram sent to Schoen in Paris described the action being taken in St Petersburg. He was instructed to 'ask the French Government if it intends to remain neutral in a Russo–German war'. If France did, 'as is not to be presumed', opt for neutrality, then Schoen was to say 'we shall have to demand the turning over of the fortresses of Toul and Verdun as a pledge of neutrality'. The French were given until 4 p.m. on 1 August to return an answer, although Berlin did not expect acceptance of such a far-fetched proposal.[13] The telegram to Rome said, 'we definitely count on Italy's fulfilment of the engagements into which she has entered'.[14]

The most pressing problem Berlin faced was to coordinate military strategy with its ally now that it expected to be at war with Russia within approximately twelve hours. The problem was that Vienna was still intent on sending its troops south to Serbia, while German plans required as much help as possible from Austria–Hungary in the east as the bulk of its forces invaded France. At 4.05 p.m. the Kaiser sent a message to Franz Josef informing him that preparatory mobilisation measures were underway and that these would become definitive within twenty-four hours at most. He stated: 'I am prepared, in fulfilment of my alliance obligations, to go to war against Russia and France immediately.' The real point of the message came next: 'In this struggle it is of the greatest importance that Austria directs her chief force against Russia and does not split it up by a simultaneous offensive against Serbia.' The German army would be tied up in France and 'in this gigantic struggle . . . Serbia plays a quite subordinate role, which demands only the most absolutely necessary defensive measures'. Franz Josef was also told that it was necessary to bring Italy into the war with 'the greatest possible deference to her wishes'.[15]

This message came as a bombshell to Vienna. The whole object of its policy – the humiliation and carve-up of Serbia – was now to be subordinated to German plans which came into effect in any wider European war. Shortly after 6 p.m. a message from Moltke was telephoned to Vienna asking Conrad whether he intended to leave Germany in the lurch during a war with Russia and France. Conrad's reply, which reached Berlin at about 10.30 p.m., repeated Vienna's intention to move against Serbia and asked for further information about German mobilisation and what Vienna was expected to do. Conrad then sent another message to Berlin via the German military attaché in Vienna, Kageneck, saying that Germany was creating very grave problems for Austria–Hungary because its mobilisation against Serbia was already far advanced and difficult to reverse. The two allies were not able to reach any agreement on their military strategy that night.

Despite the difficulties with Vienna, the policy-makers in Berlin, especially the military, were in a buoyant mood during the afternoon of 31 July. By declaring general mobilisation, the Russians had started down the road to war and resolved Germany's problems – Russia could be portrayed as the aggressor and Germany could claim to be acting defensively. The Bavarian military representative in Berlin, General von Wenninger, visited the Prussian war ministry early in the afternoon and described the scene: 'Everywhere beaming faces, people shaking hands in the corridors, congratulating one another on having cleared the ditch.'[16] In the foreign ministry a junior official, Rosenberg, began drafting a declaration of war on France.

Paris

As already seen, the French government had no knowledge of the Russian decision to start general mobilisation until late in the evening of 31 July, even though that decision had been taken by the Tsar more than twenty-four hours earlier. The French cabinet met for three hours in the morning, but only discussed financial measures to cope with the growing panic across Europe.

The cabinet agreed to meet again at 4 p.m. Thirty minutes before the meeting, Joffre sent Messimy a note threatening resignation if mobilisation was not ordered that evening. He argued that the general staff had strong intelligence that they were at least thirty hours behind Germany in mobilisation (possibly forty-eight hours) because Berlin had called up tens of thousands of reservists secretly by individual notification rather than by public notice. Such an operation was technically impossible, as Joffre well knew, and Germany was in fact behind both France and Russia in its military measures at this time. The cabinet meeting lasted until 6.30 p.m. and shortly after 5 p.m. it accepted some of Joffre's demands, in particular allowing movement of covering troops along the frontier. Mobilisation was not agreed, although it was decided to stop German citizens of military age from leaving France. Messimy discovered after the meeting that the government had no power to do this.

It was only while the cabinet meeting was in progress that the first indication of the rapidly deteriorating situation became apparent. A telegram from Cambon in Berlin arrived saying that Germany had declared the *Kriegsgefahrzustand* in response to Russian general mobilisation and would be making demands in St Petersburg. Just after the meeting ended, Schoen saw Viviani and delivered the message from Berlin asking whether France would remain neutral. He did not raise the question of the Toul and Verdun fortresses because he knew it would be rejected. (The French later decoded the German instructions from Berlin and found out about the demand.) The request was irrelevant because France would never have opted for neutrality. Following Cambon's telegram from Berlin, Poincaré and Viviani discussed what they would do if Germany did make a demand for neutrality. They agreed they would say nothing until the deadline and then would merely state that France would look after its own interests.

After this meeting Margerie, who had been present at the talk with Schoen, drafted a telegram for Viviani to send to Paléologue. It provided an update on the situation in Paris and how France would respond to the German request on neutrality. It then asked the ambassador to report 'as a matter of urgency' on Russian mobilisation. This telegram raises a number of problems. Paris made no attempt to find out about Russian general mobilisation even after getting the report from Cambon in Berlin, which was supported by numerous press agency reports. It only acted after Schoen saw Viviani. Even then the telegram feigns complete ignorance of general mobilisation and does not make any attempt to dissuade the Russians or suggest any action that might avoid war, apart from a vague statement about Paris being sure Russia 'would avoid anything which might open up the crisis'.[17] The first part of the telegram was sent at 9 p.m., probably just before Paléologue's message was decoded after its twelve-hour journey around Europe. The second part of the telegram to St Petersburg was sent, unaltered, at 9.30 p.m. even though Paris was fully aware of Russian general mobilisation. The actions of the French government confirm the suspicion that it was mainly interested in ensuring it could portray itself in public as not simply acquiescing in Russian mobilisation (which is what it had done the previous day). France did not want to restrain its ally (any attempt to do so might fracture the alliance and leave France dangerously isolated). Its main preoccupation was to demonstrate to Britain, and its own public opinion, that it was the innocent party and that Germany had taken every aggressive action. Later in the evening the Russian ambassador, Izvolsky, saw Messimy and reported to St Petersburg the French government's 'firm resolve to fight'. He also noted that the French General Staff hoped that 'all our efforts will be directed against Germany and that Austria will be regarded as a negligible quantity'.[18] France was treating its ally in the same way as Germany treated Austria–Hungary – the actual cause of the conflict was now to be subordinated to the needs of a general European war.

The French cabinet met again at 9 p.m., once Russian general mobilisation had been confirmed by Paléologue's telegram. It was agreed that it was now too late to issue mobilisation orders that day. The Cabinet therefore agreed to wait until 4 p.m. the next day (1 August) before declaring mobilisation – this was the last time at which action could be taken if 2 August (now the earliest practicable date) was to be the first day of mobilisation. The Cabinet felt that by waiting (which involved no delay in mobilisation) they would probably be able to appear as responding to German action rather than initiating military measures.

It was while the cabinet was in session that, at about 9.50 p.m., news was brought in that Jean Jaurès had been assassinated. Jaurès had always generated great hatred on the right of French politics. On 17 July Maurice de Waleffe, writing in *Paris-Midi*, said that on the eve of any war a general should order some men 'to put Citizen Jaurès up against a wall and pump the lead he needs into his brain at point-blank range'. A week later Charles Maurras wrote in the journal of his movement Action Française: 'we have no wish to incite anyone to political assassination but M. Jean Jaurès may well shake in his shoes!'

After his return from the ISB meeting in Brussels on 30 July, Jaurès was stalked by a fanatical right-winger, Raoul Villain. Although Villain had plenty of opportunities, he did not strike that day. On 31 July Jaurès spent the morning at home talking to his old friend Lucien Lévy-Bruhl. He spent the afternoon at the Palais Bourbon talking to various ministers and Socialist Party colleagues. He had seen Viviani on his return from Brussels the previous day but now the foreign minister was too busy to see him – he spoke to his deputy Abel Ferry instead. At 8 p.m. Jaurès went to the offices of the socialist newspaper *L'Humanité* to oversee the production of the paper for the next day. An hour later, before writing the leading article he, together with a few colleagues, adjourned to the nearby Café du Croissant for a light dinner. They sat near the window for their meal and were just getting up to leave at about 9.40 p.m. when Villain fired the two fatal shots. Jaurès fell to the ground. Pierre Renaudel smashed Villain over the head with a bottle, knocking him unconscious. By the time a doctor arrived Jaurès was dead. (Villain was acquitted at his trial in March 1919 and eventually died fighting in the Spanish Civil War as a member of Franco's forces.)

The news of Jaurès' assassination caused great concern in the cabinet and real fears that it would increase civil unrest and perhaps even interfere with mobilisation. Ministers agreed to keep two cavalry regiments in Paris rather than send them to the eastern frontier. A government manifesto was posted up across the country appealing for calm and associating itself with the mourning for Jaurès. President Poincaré respected Jaurès, despite their acute political differences. He wrote in his diary that evening: 'if war breaks out, he would have been amongst those who would have known how to do their duty . . . *Quel crime abominable et sot.*'[19]

London

The British government could do no more than watch the key decisions being taken in the other European capitals. Its main worry was the rapidly deepening financial crisis. Asquith saw the governor of the Bank of England and gave approval for the doubling of bank rate to 8 per cent and the suspension of gold payments (this had last been done between 1797 and 1821). The Stock Exchange was also closed for the first time in its history. Despite the escalating diplomatic and financial crisis, ministers still intended to leave for their usual weekend breaks. Lloyd George was due to travel to Dieppe and Asquith confirmed plans to travel to Chester as an excuse to spend the weekend at Penrhos on Anglesey where his lover Venetia Stanley was staying.

In the morning Grey saw Lichnowsky to discuss possible mediation plans. The two men did not know of Russian general mobilisation that made these ideas redundant. The main interest of the talks is therefore in the positions taken by each man. Grey still spoke of arbitration. He said that if Germany could get Vienna to agree a 'reasonable proposal' (the 'halt in Belgrade' would fall into this category) then Britain would advocate it in Paris and St Petersburg and say 'if Russia and France would not accept it His Majesty's Government would have nothing more to do with the consequences'.[20] Although Grey said he added a rider that 'if France became involved we should be drawn in', it is not surprising that Lichnowsky reported: 'to-day for the first time I have the impression that . . . in a possible war, England might adopt a waiting attitude'. Grey continually emphasised that Britain 'was bound by no treaties' and that if Berlin and Vienna showed flexibility and Russia put itself in the wrong, 'he could sponsor the idea of not immediately taking the part of France'.[21]

Grey then attended the Cabinet meeting at 11 a.m. It was a desultory discussion at which little was decided. Grey told his colleagues about the German approach for British neutrality, but it made little impact. As Herbert Samuel told his wife, 'nothing untoward happened at the Cabinet today'.[22] Churchill was bellicose for intervention, but most of the others were more cautious. However, Lewis Harcourt, the colonial secretary, went too far in the pencilled note he sent Jack Pease, the president of the board of education, saying 'it is now clear that *this* Cabinet will not join the war'.[23] Harcourt also wrote, clearly reflecting Grey's line, 'if Russ[ia] unreasonable we wash our hands'.[24] Pease himself described the general view in his diary: 'British opinion would not now enable us to support France – a violation of Belgium might alter public opinion, but we could say nothing to commit ourselves.'[25] The one action that the cabinet did agree was that Grey should approach both Germany and France to enquire about their attitude to Belgian neutrality (this was no more than Britain had done in 1870). The necessary telegrams were sent at 5.30 p.m.

After lunch Grey saw the French ambassador, Paul Cambon. He told him about the German approach for neutrality and then, according to Cambon, said that following the cabinet meeting Britain was 'unable to guarantee to us their intervention'. In the light of the financial crisis, the cabinet felt 'British neutrality might be the only way of averting the complete collapse of European credit'. Cambon argued, wrongly, that Britain had given a pledge to support France and then 'requested Sir E. Grey to submit the matter once more to the cabinet and to insist on pledges being given to us without delay'. Grey refused, although Nicolson, the permanent secretary, told the ambassador the cabinet would meet the next day and Grey would renew the discussion. In practice Cambon knew Grey supported France and, as he told Paris, he was 'a partisan of immediate intervention'.[26]

News of Russian general mobilisation reached London at about 4.30 p.m., either via Schubert, the secretary of the German embassy, who explained what action Germany was taking, or via the news agencies. This was just before Buchanan's telegram from St Petersburg giving official confirmation arrived at 5.20 p.m. This caused the hardliners in the British government – Nicolson and Crowe in the Foreign Office and General Sir Henry Wilson at the War Office – to argue for immediate British mobilisation and intervention on the side of France. They tried to concert their activities but Asquith refused to see them.

During the day the British section of the Second International issued a manifesto against joining a European war. It was signed by Kier Hardie and the secretary of the section, Arthur Henderson. The Liberal Foreign Affairs Group met twice but, ineffective as usual, decided to do nothing until after the weekend. Early in the evening, Grey left the Foreign Office to dine at his club in St James's with his parliamentary private secretary, Arthur Murray. After dinner the two men played billiards. Meanwhile, Asquith described it as 'a most disappointing day', not because of Russian mobilisation, but because he had had to postpone his trip to Chester and Anglesey to see Venetia Stanley.[27]

It was late in the evening when a formal message from the German embassy arrived at the Foreign Office explaining the ultimatum sent to Russia and the action taken in Paris to enquire about French neutrality. Grey's private secretary, Sir William Tyrrell, immediately took the message to 10 Downing Street where he, together with Asquith and his private secretary, Maurice Bonham-Carter, drafted a message for George V to send to the Tsar appealing to him to stop mobilisation. When the draft was ready, Asquith and Tyrrell managed to find a taxi and went to Buckingham Palace where they got the King out of bed. George V agreed the draft message after reading it in his dressing gown and it was sent to St Petersburg shortly before 2 a.m.

Rome

The Italian Cabinet was also unaware of Russian general mobilisation when it met at 10 a.m. and agreed that Italy would remain neutral in any European war, although no announcement was to be made at this stage. Immediately after the meeting, however, San Giuliano saw the French ambassador, Barrère, and, under terms of 'the most complete secrecy', told him Italy regarded the Austro-Hungarian attack on Serbia as 'an act of aggression' and that this absolved Italy 'from action in favour of Austria'. He went on to tell Barrère that the agreement the ambassador had negotiated in 1902, while compatible with the Triple

Alliance (which was very doubtful), enabled Italy 'without failing in the loyalty she owes to her allies, to abstain from participation in any conflict'. He emphasised that he needed 'restraint' from Russia and France for Italy to remain neutral (if they became the aggressors, the terms of the Triple Alliance would drag Italy into the conflict).[28]

It was not until late in the afternoon that Flotow received the telegram from Berlin telling him of the German response to Russian mobilisation and saying that Italy was expected to fulfil its alliance obligations. The German ambassador saw San Giuliano at 8 p.m. and received a frosty response. Immediately after this meeting the Italian foreign minister saw Salandra, the prime minister. Their meeting lasted until about midnight when a statement was issued to the press saying that Italy would be neutral.

Western Europe

In Brussels the first person to hear of the German declaration of the *Kriegsgefahrzustand* was the French minister, Klobukowski. He called on the foreign minister, Davignon, and gave him an assurance (though he had no authority to do so) that France would not be the first to violate Belgian neutrality. Davignon said that the Belgian government had every reason to believe that Germany would not do so either. The secretary-general of the foreign ministry, Baron van der Elst, was sent to the German legation where he saw the minister, Below-Saleske. The minister told him he was sure that there had been no change in the previous pledges Germany had given not to violate Belgian neutrality. (Below-Saleske was unaware of the Schlieffen plan.)

When Britain sent the messages to Berlin and Paris asking them about their attitude to Belgian neutrality, a copy was sent to the British minister in Brussels, Sir Francis Villiers. He was asked to obtain an assurance from the Belgian government that they 'will to the utmost of [their] power maintain neutrality'. Davignon gave Villiers that assurance but added that Belgium's relations with all its neighbours were 'excellent' and 'there was no reason to suspect their intentions'. If there was 'any violation', Belgium was 'in a position to defend the neutrality of their country'.[29]

Following the British message, King Albert presided over a meeting of the council of ministers at 7 p.m. Although some members were hesitant, the council agreed to declare general mobilisation as from 1 August. The aim was to provide a strong defence against either France or Germany. In The Hague the government began the call-up of all army and navy reservists and the units along the German frontier were strengthened. Similarly, in Berne the Swiss federal council ordered mobilisation as from 1 August as soon as it was aware of the German *Kriegsgefahrzustand*.

During the afternoon the prime minister of Luxembourg, Eyschen, sent telegrams to the ministers in Paris and Berlin asking them to obtain assurances of respect for Luxembourg neutrality. He also called personally at the French and German legations to ask for similar declarations. Neither France nor Germany replied. The French had already decided in 1912 that Luxembourg was effectively a German vassal and that they would take no action if Germany did invade. Later in the day, Eyschen sent a protest to Berlin about the cutting-off of food supplies (Luxembourg was a member of the German customs union).

The Balkans

Both sides were still trying to obtain Romanian support. The Kaiser sent a message to King Carol reminding him of his family loyalty. He congratulated him that he had 'created a civilized state on Europe's eastern march and thereby erected a dam against the Slav tide'. The Kaiser went on: 'I am confident that as King and Hohenzoller you will remain loyal to your friends and fulfil your engagements under the alliance to the utmost.'[30]

Although the King would, personally, have been willing to do so, there was no likelihood that Romania would join Germany and Austria–Hungary. Indeed, it was being tempted to do the opposite. Sazonov sent a message to the Russian ambassador, Poklevski, that he should tell the Romanian government that Austria–Hungary planned to attack them. He was to suggest that if Romania sided with Russia 'we would declare our willingness to promise our support for the acquisition by Romania of Transylvania'. When Poklevski put this offer to the prime minister, Bratianu, the latter shrewdly asked whether Britain and France would support this policy.[31]

Russia was also trying to barter other territory in the Balkans – this time from the country for whom it was going to war, Serbia. Sazonov sent a message to Strandtmann, the acting minister in Niš, that he should consult the Serbian government as to whether Russia should put out feelers to Bulgaria 'in order to ensure not only its effective neutrality but even its military support by consenting to territorial compensation in the event of Serbia's receiving an equivalent else-where'.[32] In plain language what this meant was that Bulgaria would regain territory in Macedonia that Serbia had taken under the Treaty of Bucharest in 1913 in return for Serbia gaining Bosnia–Herzegovina at the expense of Austria–Hungary.

Meanwhile, both Berlin and Vienna were trying to put pressure on Greece. The Kaiser tried to get King Constantine to join Germany and Austria through appeals to monarchical solidarity and the memory of his assassinated father and with threats about attacks from Italy, Bulgaria and Turkey if Greece did not support Germany. Vienna preferred bribery. Berchtold instructed the minister in Athens, Szilassy, to see the foreign secretary and speak 'personally' about 'the possible assignment to Greece of a bit of Serbia'.[33] Greece had already had the nerve to ask Serbia, which was under attack from Austria–Hungary, to move some of its troops to the Bulgarian border to deter an attack on Greece.

In Cetinje the Montenegrin government had not accepted Vienna's bribe to stay out of the war and Austria–Hungary had not reacted to its proposal to remain neutral in return for territorial gains. It is doubtful whether King Nicholas and the government ever trusted Vienna to keep its word (it had not done so in the past) and realised that if Austria–Hungary did dismember Serbia, then Montenegro would be badly isolated and might be the next to suffer similar treatment. During the morning, the foreign minister, Plamenac, told the Austro-Hungarian minister, Otto, that Montenegro could only stay neutral as long as Russia did so. Indeed, since Russia was the mainstay of Montenegrin finances, the government in Cetinje had little choice in the matter. This confirms the suspicion that Montenegro's bid for Austro-Hungarian support two days earlier was based on the possibility of a limited war only involving Serbia in which Montenegro would be able to stay neutral. News of Russian general mobilisation reached Cetinje about lunchtime and strongly increased the pressure for war with Austria–Hungary.

Constantinople

For the previous few days Berlin had been stalling on the proposed alliance with the Ottoman empire. The main reason was that it did not want an extension of the alliance beyond the current crisis, as far ahead as 1918, as Constantinople wanted. At 3 p.m. Wangenheim sent a message to Berlin saying 'if we mean to conclude with Turkey it is high time'.[34] When the message arrived, Berlin knew it was facing a European war and, after consulting the Kaiser, Bethmann Hollweg responded at 6.15 p.m. Wangenheim was instructed to tell the Grand Vizier 'without delay' that Germany was now ready for an immediate agreement and that it accepted the Ottoman demand for the alliance to last until 1918. The only condition was that 'it must, however, first be ascertained whether in the present war Turkey can and will undertake some action worthy of mention against Russia'.[35]

15

Saturday 1 August

St Petersburg – Morning

Pourtalès did not receive the instructions sent from Berlin during the afternoon of 31 July until shortly before midnight. It was therefore in the early hours of 1 August that he called on Sazonov to deliver the German ultimatum requiring Russia to cease all military preparations within twelve hours. The foreign minister spoke of 'the technical impossibility of suspending the war measures' and attempted to argue that Germany had 'overestimated the significance of a Russian mobilization'. The ambassador asked for a guarantee that Russia 'intended to keep the peace, even in the event that an agreement with Austria was not reached'. Sazonov refused to give such an assurance and Pourtalès responded that in the circumstances 'nobody can blame us for our unwillingness to allow Russia a longer start in mobilization'. Sazonov offered the Tsar's assurance on his 'word of honour' that the Russian army would not move, though it would obviously continue to mobilise.[1] Such an assurance was worthless to Germany. Their strategy was based on two points: they could not allow Russia to get a head start in mobilisation and for them (though not the other European powers) mobilisation was the equivalent of war. Certainly, Sazonov never grasped this latter fact. Even if Germany had plans to mobilise without war, it is very doubtful whether the European powers could have faced each other for weeks with fully mobilised armies without going to war. In practice, mobilisation led automatically to war for all of them.

This meeting in the early hours of 1 August ended with no agreement between the two men. In theory, Russia was required to provide an answer to the ultimatum by noon, but Sazonov made no effort to do so and the Russian government never considered stopping mobilisation now that it was underway. Pourtalès reported his conversation to Berlin, but similarly made no effort to see Sazonov again before the noon deadline. The only other action Pourtalès took was at 7 a.m. that morning. He wrote to Count Fredericks, the minister at the court of the Tsar, whom he had met the previous afternoon when he saw the Tsar, to give his personal warning about the situation and how close the two countries were to war.

Shortly after breakfast, Szápáry called on Sazonov to convey a message from Vienna (sent the previous afternoon) that it was 'ready to negotiate with Russia on a broad basis, but especially inclined to discuss the text of our note as far as interpretation was concerned'. (This was once again Vienna's distinction between 'elucidation'/ 'interpretation' on the one hand and 'modification' on the other.) Szápáry added that he did not know how Vienna had reacted to Russian general mobilisation. Sazonov said the Russian army would not move while talks continued and that the message from Vienna was a 'proof of goodwill'. He once again suggested talks in London. Szápáry told Vienna there was a basis for negotiation if they still wanted to do so after Russia had mobilised.[2] This discussion had taken place far too late but it illustrates what could have happened had Russia not mobilised precipitately when it had no overriding need to do so.

Vienna

Almost exactly the same conversation as took place in St Petersburg occurred when Shebeko called on Berchtold that morning. The ambassador suggested talks in London and argued that Russian military measures 'bore no hostile character'. Russia was merely insisting that Austria–Hungary 'did not solve the conflict with Serbia without consulting Russia' (which was exactly what Vienna had intended to do from the beginning of July). Berchtold tried to broaden the discussion saying Russia should not 'always and entirely make the fate of the Balkan States the touchstone of her attitude towards us'. The ambassador responded that Russia had 'many obligations . . . as an orthodox and Slav state'.[3] The talk in Vienna was even less productive than in St Petersburg.

The most important question that Vienna still had to resolve was its military strategy. All planning so far had been on the basis of a war against Serbia, with Germany providing assistance to help protect Galicia if Russia was hostile. Conrad complained to Moltke that 'only on 31 July came suddenly the definite declaration on the part of Germany that she herself now intended to carry through the major war against France and Russia'. This required Austria–Hungary to change direction, put off the attack against Serbia and move the bulk of its forces into Galicia to divert Russian forces while Germany attacked France. Vienna had little choice but to abandon the purpose for which the whole crisis had been instigated – the attack on Serbia. Conrad reassured his German colleague that Austria–Hungary would now 'employ the main weight of our strength in the north' despite the problems involved in moving troops from the Serbian frontier now that mobilisation was fully underway.[4] In practice, Conrad decided that it would be too difficult to alter the mobilisation plans. The reserves mobilised the previous day when general mobilization was declared would move to Galicia. However, the troops already moving towards the Serbian frontier would complete their journey and then wait for about ten days until the main mobilization was completed. Then they would get back on their trains and move to Galicia where they would join the main army by 18 August. On one of the trains moving slowly south towards the Serbian border was a twenty-two-year-old Croat-Slovene industrial apprentice, Josep Broz, who had been conscripted for his two years' military service in 1913. Thirty years later he would be better known as Tito, the partisan leader who went on to be the ruler of Yugoslavia for more than thirty years.

Vienna still had to resolve the dispute with Italy over compensation, following the decision of the council of ministers the previous day to make a compromise offer. On the evening of 31 July there were talks involving the German ambassador, Tschirschky, and on the Saturday morning Berchtold saw the Italian ambassador, Avarna. He told him Austria–Hungary adopted 'the Italian interpretation of Article VII of the Triplice treaty on condition that Italy in the present conflict completely fulfils her obligations under the alliance'.[5] Although Avarna accepted the offer, Rome had no intention of doing so because it required Italian entry into the war. They also knew that Vienna would not give them what they wanted – the Trentino – particularly if they were victorious in a European war.

Paris – Morning
The newspapers were dominated by the murder of Jaurès. In *Temps*, where Tardieu had written in March 1913 that Jaurès acted 'against the national interest as an advocate for the foreigner' and was 'a sinister agent of negation and disruption', the assassinated socialist was now acclaimed as 'a great force'. The paper also spoke of 'the fine dignity of his life'. *La Guerre Sociale* was more predictable with its triple

headline: 'National Defence above all', 'They have assassinated Jaurès', 'We will not assassinate France'. *Matin* was enthusiastic about the forthcoming war, saying 'never has war offered itself under aspects more favourable to us'. It argued that with Austria–Hungary fully committed in the Balkans, Germany would have to face Russia and France alone and therefore war 'will bring us the reparations which are our due'.

At 8 a.m. General Joffre saw the war minister, Messimy. He told him that intelligence suggested that five classes of German reservists had been recalled for the next day and the purchase of horses had started on 30 July. He said that by 4 August Germany would be 'entirely mobilised . . . even without the order for mobilisation having been issued'.[6] These assertions were nonsense – Germany had still not begun mobilisation and it was as incapable of carrying out the secret operation Joffre outlined as any other European state. Nevertheless, Joffre once again threatened to resign unless mobilisation was ordered by 4 p.m. at the latest. The French cabinet met at 9 a.m. with Joffre present. The important diplomatic news was from Barrère in Rome, confirming Italy would be neutral. Joffre therefore decided that the covering troops intended to move to the south-eastern frontier should remain at their depots and be ready to entrain for the north-east to face the German attack. The cabinet agreed that the mobilisation notices should be posted at 4 p.m. that afternoon, with the first day of mobilisation to be 2 August. Meanwhile, all troops would remain outside of the ten-kilometre zone from the frontier to avoid any incidents. The members of the cabinet were generally agreed on moving to mobilisation even though Germany had not yet done so (its intentions were clear, however). The main doubter was Senator Couyba, the minister of work and social affairs, and Viviani also had reservations.

Viviani was called out of the Cabinet meeting to see the German ambassador, Schoen, at the Quai d'Orsay. The ambassador repeatedly asked whether France would stay neutral and Viviani would say no more than that France would look after its own interests. The report on the talk that Viviani sent to his ambassadors afterwards was grossly misleading and designed for later publication. It said Russia had accepted the British proposal for a halt in military preparations (which was completely untrue) and that Vienna was ready for talks (at best only partially true). It argued that it was only Germany that was driving the crisis on. It neglected to mention the Russian decision to start general mobilisation, tacit French approval of that action and the decision, just taken by the French cabinet, to begin mobilization.

Shortly before 1 p.m., after the cabinet had dispersed, a telegram arrived from Paléologue in St Petersburg. It was another of his misleading messages. It stated Pourtalès had told Sazonov that Germany would begin mobilization later that day. In fact, he had set out the twelve-hour deadline and Paris knew this to be the case because Schoen had given them the correct information the previous evening. The telegram seems to have been a rather clumsy attempt to ensure Paris did not intervene in St Petersburg and suggest moderation before the German deadline expired – the French government had no intention of doing so anyway. As the ministers awaited developments, Poincaré remained optimistic. Although his appeal to George V for British intervention had been brushed aside, he remained confident that if France ensured that it appeared to be defensive and made Germany the aggressor, then Britain would eventually join France and Russia. He noted in his diary: 'I do not despair; the Foreign Office is very well disposed towards us; Asquith also; the English are slow to decide, methodical, reflective, but they know where they are going.'[7]

London – Morning
Poincaré might have been less sanguine had he known of the doubts and divisions within the British government. In the early morning telegrams from Paris and Berlin arrived giving the responses to the British enquiry, made the previous afternoon, about attitudes to Belgian neutrality. The French government gave the necessary assurance, but the report from Goschen of his discussion with Jagow was worrying. The German foreign minister refused to give a reply, saying that if he did so it 'could not fail, in the event of war, to have the undesirable effect of disclosing to a certain extent part of their plan of campaign'.[8] Although the German government could argue that if they gave an assurance on Belgian neutrality this might enable the French (if they believed the assurance) to deduce that the weight of the German attack would fall elsewhere, the reply was, correctly, regarded by the Foreign Office as highly suspicious.

At 10.30 a.m. Asquith, Grey and Haldane met at 10 Downing Street for a talk before the cabinet meeting. Exactly what was said is unknown but the outcome was of fundamental importance. There seems to have been a general feeling, reflecting the mood of the cabinet on the previous day, that France was too closely tied to Russia and that it was Russia that was provoking a European war by mobilising. Britain had stood by France in the Moroccan disputes of 1906 and 1911 because Morocco formed part of the Anglo-French colonial agreements. Was this the case now? Did Britain have to support France just because its ally had intervened in the dispute between Austria–Hungary and Serbia – a dispute in which Britain had no direct interest? Grey had, at the previous day's cabinet meeting, hinted that Britain might make a proposal, and if Russia and France rejected it, then Britain would wash its hands of the consequences.

It was as a result of this discussion that Grey took action which was to have a profound effect in Berlin later in the day. According to Lichnowsky, Grey telephoned to make an extraordinary proposal. The foreign secretary asked whether, if France remained neutral in any Russo–German war, Germany would pledge not to attack France. The ambassador immediately gave such an assurance. His telegram, dispatched to Berlin at 11.14 a.m., added that Grey would make use of this assurance at the cabinet meeting and that Grey had also told him he hoped that afternoon to give the ambassador 'some facts which may prove useful for the avoidance of the great catastrophe'.[9] At lunchtime Grey took even more extraordinary action. He sent his private secretary, Tyrrell, to see Lichnowsky at the German embassy. It was, as Lichnowsky reported to Berlin at 2.10 p.m., advance warning that 'Sir E. Grey will this afternoon make proposals to me regarding English neutrality, even for the eventuality of our being at war with both Russia and France'.[10] The idea in the morning proposal that France would stay out of a Russo–German war and allow its ally to be defeated was simply wishful thinking. Lichnowsky was obviously happy to give the assurance Grey wanted because if it had ever been implemented it would have transformed Germany's strategic situation and greatly increased the likelihood of success in the war. The lunchtime proposal for British neutrality – which the British had rejected when Bethmann Hollweg suggested it – is very difficult to understand.

While the German ambassador was telegraphing this unexpected development to Berlin, the British cabinet met for two and a half hours from 11 a.m. The discussion was general but heated, and little was decided. Grey discussed the replies from France and Germany on Belgian neutrality, but most members thought there was little real difference between the two statements. The strongest advocate of immediate intervention was Churchill. Asquith described him as 'very bellicose' and added 'it is no exaggeration to say that Winston occupied at least half of the time'. The rest of the cabinet, apart from Grey and Asquith, did not believe that Britain ought to intervene simply to support France and that public opinion would not support such action. Grey said if British policy was to be non-intervention in any circumstances, which was not what the overwhelming majority of the cabinet believed, then he would resign. Asquith described Lloyd George as being 'all for peace' but added he was for 'keeping the position still open'.[11] During the meeting, Lloyd George sent a note across the table to Churchill saying 'if patience prevails and you do not press us too hard we might come together'.[12] Lloyd George's view was correct – if the cabinet was forced to decide simply on the issue of supporting France, it would almost certainly split. However, events, in particular any German invasion of Belgium, would change that position very quickly. Only John Morley was utterly opposed to intervention in any circumstances and even argued that the guarantee to Belgium was joint and not individual. John Burns, another strong opponent of intervention, wrote in his diary: 'no decision as in all our minds there rested the belief and hope for agreement'.[13] Asquith thought Morley would resign whatever decision was made and told Venetia Stanley: 'we came, every now & again, near to the parting of the ways' but that at the end of the meeting 'we parted in a fairly amicable mood'.[14] Herbert Samuel was not optimistic as he reported to his wife: 'we may be brought in under certain eventualities . . . I am less hopeful than yesterday of our being able to keep out of it'.[15]

The cabinet did make a number of decisions on military matters. Churchill's request for full mobilisation of the Royal Navy was rejected. It was also agreed that the British Expeditionary Force would not be sent to the Continent if Britain did join any European war. The cabinet's decision was probably no more than a way of keeping the doubters in line by reassuring them Britain was not committed to a Continental war. Asquith, who was still acting as secretary of state for war, ordered that army training was not to be stopped (the return of troops to barracks would be a preliminary to dispatch of the expeditionary force). He also stated that the government had never promised France that the expeditionary force would be sent (which was correct). Two days earlier General Sir John French had been called to the War Office and told that he would command any expeditionary force sent to the Continent.

Berlin – Afternoon

Little happened during the morning in Berlin as the government waited for replies from Paris and St Petersburg to the ultimatums sent the previous afternoon. The only information they had from Pourtalès was the report on his meeting with Sazonov in the early hours of the morning. It implied that the Russian response, if there was to be one, would be negative. Shortly before 1 p.m., a telegram was sent to St Petersburg containing two texts (in French) of the declaration of war to be used depending on whether the Russian reply was unsatisfactory or simply not given. The declaration was to be handed over at 5 p.m. Berlin time, 7 p.m. St Petersburg time.

Berlin continued to wait for news throughout the afternoon. Finally, shortly after 4 p.m., the Kaiser telephoned Bethmann Hollweg and said that he was ready to sign the mobilisation order. The chancellor, together with Falkenhayn, Moltke and Tirpitz departed to see the Kaiser at Berlin Schloss. There they were joined by the Kaiser's military advisers, Lyncker and Plessen. At 5 p.m. the Kaiser, seated at a table made from the timbers of HMS *Victory*, signed the mobilisation order. Germany was still unaware whether Russia had accepted the ultimatum or not, although seven hours had elapsed since the expiry of the deadline.

Just as the order was signed, Jagow rushed into the room saying that an important message had arrived from London at 4.25 p.m. and was being decoded – the text would arrive shortly. Despite Tirpitz's objections, Moltke and Falkenhayn left to issue the orders for mobilisation. Ten minutes later the text of the telegram was brought into the meeting. It was the message Lichnowsky had sent at 11.14 a.m. saying that he had given Grey the pledge that if Germany did not attack France in any Russo–German war, then Britain would secure French neutrality and, by implication, its own too. It was, he added, following the words given to him by Tyrrell, vital that German troops did not violate French territory at this stage. Moltke and Falkenhayn were immediately recalled and returned to find all those at the Schloss in a high state of excitement. The British seemed to be offering not only their own neutrality but also that of France so that Germany and Austria–Hungary could concentrate on fighting Russia. German diplomacy seemed to have achieved its objective – British neutrality and a limited war in the Balkans. In many ways it was even better than a localised Austro-Hungarian–Serbian war because France would be neutral and therefore Russia could be defeated.

A jubilant Kaiser announced that Germany would simply deploy all its forces in the east. Moltke intervened to say this was not possible – the Kaiser must know that Germany had made no plans for war with Russia alone and it was impossible to improvise such a mobilisation plan at short notice. He also said, quite reasonably, that he did not believe the British could get France to agree to the idea and even if they did it would be far too dangerous to send all German forces to the east if France remained fully mobilised in the west. Bethmann Hollweg argued for stopping the deployment against France and after a number of violent arguments threatened to resign. Tirpitz intervened to say that he supported the Kaiser and the chancellor – it was simply impossible to reject the British proposal. Falkenhayn then asked for permission to withdraw in order to discuss the matter separately with Moltke. When the two men returned to the room, Falkenhayn announced that Moltke had reluctantly agreed to a compromise. The British proposal would be accepted, but mobilisation along the French frontier would continue. However, the possibility of redeploying forces to the east would be studied.

Jagow, Bethmann Hollweg, Falkenhayn and Moltke then adjourned to a separate room to draft a reply to Lichnowsky in London. It said:

> Germany is prepared to accede to the English proposal if England guarantees with her entire armed strength the unconditional neutrality of France in the Russo–German conflict, a neutrality which must last until the final settlement of the conflict. It must rest with Germany to decide when this settlement is attained.

The telegram went on to state that German mobilisation had been decreed and that it was impossible to stop the concentration of the army in the west at this late stage. However, German forces would not cross the French frontier before 7 p.m. on 3 August – British acceptance was required by that time.[16] Under Moltke's pressure, the German reply had conceded very little. While the telegram was being drafted, Tirpitz suggested that the Kaiser should send a personal message to George V supporting the proposal. This was written by Tirpitz and Admiral Müller and sent to London at 7.02 p.m. The telegram to Lichnowsky followed thirteen minutes later. Jagow later sent a telegram to Schoen telling him of the offer and asking him to 'please keep the French quiet for the time being'.[17]

After the telegrams to London had been sent, Bethmann Hollweg remembered that elements of the 16th Division at Trier were due to seize the Luxembourg railways (which were under German management and control) as soon as mobilisation started, in order to forestall similar action by the French. He argued this action would not only be a violation of neutrality but would also be seen as a clear threat by the French. The Kaiser agreed and instructed his aide-de-camp to send a message to the 16th Division ordering it not to move. Moltke refused to sign the order and the Kaiser told him to leave the meeting. The order was telephoned through to Trier. Tirpitz argued the declaration of war on Russia should be stopped, especially since no operations could take place for several days. The Kaiser disagreed and no action was taken.

After the meeting the Kaiser sat with his family in the small garden of the Schloss. When Szögyény arrived with a message from Franz Josef, he found the Kaiser in a state of euphoria. The Kaiser was full of praise for Bethmann Hollweg's brilliant diplomacy that had pulled off a spectacular coup. Germany and Austria–Hungary would now be fighting Serbia and Russia in the most favourable possible circumstances.

Paris – Afternoon

After the cabinet meeting in the morning, the mobilisation order was signed by Poincaré, Viviani, Messimy and Augagneur (the navy minister), but held by Messimy until it was required. At 3.30 p.m. Joffre sent General Ebener to Messimy's office to collect the order. At 3.45 p.m. he took it to the Paris Central Telegraph Office where, ten minutes later, the telegrams announcing general mobilisation were dispatched across France. Notices headed MOBILISATION GENERALE were posted up outside the main Paris post offices shortly after 4 p.m. They were accompanied by a two-page government proclamation, drafted by Viviani, approved by Poincaré and signed by all government ministers. It was defensive in tone and tried to justify the government's action. It argued 'mobilisation is not war', though it is doubtful whether many believed the assurance, and said that it was 'the best means of assuring peace with honour'. The proclamation concluded:

> In this hour, there are no parties. There is *la France éternelle*, peaceful and resolute France. There is the *patrie* of right and justice, completely united in calm, vigilance and dignity.

France mobilised an hour before Germany.

France – Afternoon

At about 5 p.m. the church bells across France began tolling and the mobilisation notices were posted up outside the numerous *mairies*. France is the only country in Europe where there is a record of how the general population reacted to the news of mobilisation and imminent war. The minister of public education, Albert Sarraut, ordered teachers across the country to record what happened in France during August 1914. Numerous records have been preserved – in Charente, for example, they cover 316 out of the 424 communes. The most common reaction was one of surprise and astonishment – despite the diplomatic crisis, few people seem to have expected war as the outcome. The teacher at La Magdelaine recorded:

> Even though the news on the last few days of July was alarming, the pacifist-minded rural population did not believe that war would break out. The order to mobilize was therefore greeted with a real feeling of stupefaction.[18]

In nearly 60 per cent of communes for which records survive, the reaction to mobilisation was generally negative. About a fifth were described as 'calm'; in only a quarter were there signs of patriotic fervour. The most frequent words used in the reports were 'consternation', 'tears', 'sadness', 'resignation' and 'agitation'. In Benest the teacher recorded:

> This sad news was made known to the public to the accompaniment of pealing bells and the beating of drums. In less than an hour, all the inhabitants of the commune had gathered before the town hall. What consternation![19]

In Champniers commune the report noted that 'an immense sadness can be seen on the faces'.[20] There were no signs of resistance – the power of the state was simply too great. As Péricat, one of the leaders of the militant CGT trade union recalled: 'Though I believed neither in frontiers nor in nations, I lacked the force of character not to serve. I admit it; I was afraid.'[21]

The greatest of the English war poets, Wilfrid Owen, who was to die just days before the armistice in 1918, was then a twenty-one-year-old student living in France and teaching English. His postcards home to his mother Susan during the last week of July betray absolutely no sense of crisis. On 31 July he left Bordeaux to spend August at the Léger villa at Bagnères-de-Bigorre in the Pyrennes, where he was to teach English to Mme Léger and her eleven-year-old daughter Nénette. His long letter home to his mother, written on 1 August, gave a lengthy description of the Villa Lorenzo and the Léger family, and concluded:

> The news of war made a great stir in Bagnères. Women were weeping all about; work was suspended. Nearly all the men have departed . . . Our food is already much dearer . . . Nobody is very gay.[22]

London – Afternoon

The financial panic in London worsened during the day. For four hours a group of ministers – Lloyd George, Haldane, Harcourt, McKenna, Simon, Runciman and Samuel – met, both on their own and with representatives from the City, to try and deal with the crisis. Bank rate was raised again, this time to 10 per cent and payment of bills of exchange that fell due was postponed until the end of August.

While these meetings were underway, Grey saw Lichnowsky. He told him that the German attitude towards Belgian neutrality was a matter of 'very great regret'. The ambassador then asked Grey a direct question: would Britain stay neutral if Germany respected Belgian neutrality? The foreign secretary responded that it 'would not be possible for him' to make such a declaration. What he did not say was that a large proportion of the cabinet would have agreed with the proposition.[23] The two men did discuss the idea of French neutrality – Grey admitted that he had not kept his promise to use Lichnowsky's pledge (that Germany would not attack France if it remained neutral) during the cabinet discussion. But the idea that France could afford to stand aside while Germany defeated its ally and then moved all its forces back to the west was absurd. As the Kaiser wrote on his copy of Lichnowsky's report of Grey's idea: 'The fellow is mad or an idiot!' The ambassador concluded: 'they want to keep out of the war if at all possible', although the German response on Belgian neutrality had created 'a bad impression'.[24]

Grey then saw the French ambassador, Cambon. According to Grey's record of his conversation he said, 'I have definitely refused all *ouvertures* to give Germany any promise of neutrality and shall not entertain any such suggestion unless it were on conditions that seemed real advantages for France.' This was, to say the least, a highly ambiguous way of describing the offer Grey had made to Germany that morning. (It is hard to see how French and British neutrality in a German war with Russia could have 'real advantages for France'.) He went on to report that the cabinet had agreed 'we could not propose to Parliament at this moment to send an expeditionary force to the continent'. Grey also claims that he told Cambon that the current situation was very different to the Agadir crisis in 1911, because that involved Morocco which was part of the spheres of influence agreement in the Anglo-French entente. Now, however:

> Germany would agree not to attack France if France remained neutral in the event of war between Russia and Germany. If France could not take advantage of this position, it was because she was bound by an alliance to which we were not parties . . . This did not mean that under no circumstances would we assist France, but it did mean that France must take her own decision at this moment without reckoning on an assistance that we were not now in a position to promise.

This part of the discussion probably reflects the talk between Haldane, Grey and Asquith before the cabinet meeting and the proposal put to Lichnowsky. If Germany offered France neutrality and they did not accept because of their treaty with Russia, then Britain might argue it was absolved from any obligation it might have to France. Such a position would probably have been endorsed by a majority of the cabinet. In their view any British intervention in a European war should not be determined by France but by any violation of Belgian neutrality if Germany did attack France. (Such a position was also far more acceptable to Parliament and the country.) There was always an important distinction between support for France and for Belgian neutrality. The majority of the cabinet did not want to go to war just to support France (and Russia) against Germany (and Austria–Hungary). Grey claimed that he also told Cambon 'as to the question of our obligation to help France, I pointed out that we had no obligation'.[25]

Copies of these telegrams were circulated among a number of Grey's colleagues in Whitehall and there must be a strong suspicion that the wording was designed to reassure them that the foreign secretary was following the lines of their discussion at that morning's meeting. Cambon's record of the meeting provides a very different version of their talk. It says Grey told him that the expeditionary force might not operate on the French left flank (as the plans devised in 1905–6 and updated regularly since required) but that it might go elsewhere. The operation Grey had in mind was a direct intervention in Belgium, which had been considered by the cabinet in 1911, and which might appeal to public opinion as being a more obvious defence of Belgian neutrality. He then told Cambon that he would make two proposals to the cabinet, which was probably going to meet on Sunday. They were that he should declare in the House of Commons that Britain would not permit any violation of Belgian neutrality and that it would not permit the German fleet to enter the Channel and attack the northern coast of France. The ambassador concluded his report by saying, 'Sir Edward Grey insisted that, for the moment, he could do no more.'[26]

The question of British protection of the northern French coast was probably first raised in a discussion between Cambon and Grey's permanent secretary, Nicolson. In 1912 Britain and France had agreed that the French fleet would be concentrated in the Mediterranean, while the British fleet was in the North Sea deployed against Germany. The supporters of British intervention alongside France (Grey, Asquith and Churchill) deliberately misrepresented the nature of the 1912 agreement which was very carefully drafted to make it clear that each country was making their deployments on their own and not as part of an overall agreement. It specifically stated that they did not create an engagement to cooperate in any war. Nevertheless, whatever the wording, the agreement did create a political and moral commitment to follow through the implications of these deployment decisions – that Britain would protect the northern French coast.

St Petersburg – Evening

The German ambassador had taken no action to discover whether Russia would reply to the ultimatum he had delivered in the early hours of the morning and neither had Sazonov made any attempt to reply. However, when Pourtalès received the telegram sent from Berlin just before 1 p.m. containing the declaration of war, he immediately asked to see the Russian foreign minister. Sazonov was at a meeting of the council of ministers on Elagin Island which began at 2 p.m. and did not finish until about 6 p.m.

Pourtalès finally saw Sazonov at 7 p.m. and immediately asked him whether he was able to give a favourable response to his earlier message about the suspension of Russian military measures. The foreign minister refused to do so, but said that Russia wanted to continue negotiations. The ambassador repeated his question twice more, each time emphasising that serious consequences would flow from a Russian rejection. After two further refusals, Pourtalès handed over the declaration of war as drafted in Berlin. Neither man noticed that it contained both versions of the text – one to be used if Russia rejected the ultimatum and the other for use if it refused to respond. Pourtalès was leaning on one of the windows in Sazonov's office in tears as the Russian foreign minister merely glanced at the document. The two men embraced and Pourtalès asked for his passports – it was agreed he and his staff would leave St Petersburg the next day.

Pourtalès returned to the embassy and sent a telegram at 8 p.m. announcing that Germany was now at war with Russia. It never reached Berlin. At the same time Sazonov telephoned Buchanan to give him the news. Paléologue, as usual, was slow in reacting. He did not send a telegram to Paris until 1.19 a.m. the next morning (it did not arrive until the afternoon of 2 August). As before, the French government found out what had happened through the Russian ambassador in Paris. Later in the evening, Sazonov sent a message to Shebeko, the ambassador in Vienna, saying that he was to remain at his post. Although Russia had begun its military preparations to try to deter Austria–Hungary, it was now at war with Germany. Meanwhile, there was to be no breach of relations with Germany's ally. Russian troops were ordered to withdraw two kilometres from the frontier to avoid any clashes with Austro-Hungarian forces.

Paris – Evening

Shortly after 10 p.m., Poincaré summoned the minister of war, Messimy, to the Elysée Palace. The president had heard that French cavalry had penetrated into the ten-kilometre zone next to the frontier. At 10.30 p.m. an order was issued threatening a court martial if there was any repetition of the incident. At 11 p.m. the Russian ambassador, Izvolsky, received news from St Petersburg of the German declaration of war. He immediately went to see Poincaré to ask how France would respond. Poincaré was keen to avoid any debate about the Russian alliance in the national assembly and he did not want to declare war on Germany both for domestic reasons and in order to demonstrate to Britain that France was pacific. He reassured the ambassador that there was no question of France not fulfilling its alliance obligations, but, as he noted in his diary:

> It would be better that we were not obliged to declare it [war] ourselves and that it be declared on us. That was necessary for both military and domestic political reasons: a defensive war would raise the whole country.[27]

As Poincaré was talking to the ambassador the first regular army units were marching through the streets of Paris to the Gare de l'Est and Gare du Nord where they entrained for the journey to the frontier.

London – Evening

The British section of the Second International issued 'An Appeal to the British Working Class', arguing that Britain should not cooperate with 'Russian despotism' and calling for action for peace. What that action was to be remained unspecified. At 8 p.m. news arrived from Paris that mobilisation was underway but that French troops would still remain ten kilometres from the border. Grey also saw the Japanese ambassador to discuss the implications of the situation for Britain's ally. He told him that 'if we do intervene, it would be on the side of France and Russia and I therefore do not see we were likely to have to apply to Japan under the alliance'.[28] Japan, however, had its own interests in the Far East, in particular the possibility of gaining German possessions in the area if it did enter the war.

After Grey left the Foreign Office, he again went to his club to dine and play billiards with Murray, his parliamentary private secretary. It was in the middle of the evening when Grey was summoned to Buckingham Palace. The Kaiser's telegram (sent shortly after 7 p.m.) had arrived and Grey was required to explain why Germany thought Britain and France were going to be neutral in a Russo–German war. Grey simply denied that any such exchange had taken place with Lichnowsky and drafted a misleading reply for the King to send to the Kaiser. Grey then saw Asquith and the two men agreed the cabinet should meet the following morning for a major discussion about British policy. For Asquith, it had been a dreadful day, but not because of the international situation. He wrote to Venetia Stanley: 'I have never had a more bitter disappointment' – he had to cancel the trip to see her in Anglesey.[29]

Berlin – Evening

The Kaiser had retired to bed when George V's reply to his telegram arrived, at about 11 p.m. The message simply said that there must have been a misunderstanding and only referred to Grey's afternoon conversation with Lichnowsky and ignored the important exchanges during the morning. Moltke was immediately summoned to the Schloss. The

Kaiser, who had simply thrown an overcoat over his bedclothes, handed over the telegram from London and told Moltke that he could now do whatever he wanted and that all hope of peace had gone. Moltke immediately sent a telegram to Trier to order a resumption of the invasion of Luxembourg.

Rome

During the morning, San Giuliano saw Flotow to discuss the Austro-Hungarian offer of compensation if Italy entered the war. The Italian foreign minister rejected the offer from Vienna – Valona 'he would not have at any price', he only wanted to ensure that Austria–Hungary did not get part of Albania. San Giuliano argued that if Italy stayed neutral this could benefit its erstwhile allies because it might help persuade Britain to be neutral too. Flotow was not impressed by this weak argument.[30]

The outcome of this meeting was that Flotow and Merey decided to see San Giuliano together that afternoon to make one last appeal for Italy to join its allies. According to Flotow, they 'sharply insisted' on Italy fulfilling its alliance obligations. Merey no doubt took pleasure in reminding the foreign minister that Vienna's offer of 'compensation' was only valid if Italy took part in the war. San Giuliano kept insisting that it was too risky to join Germany and Austria–Hungary because the long Italian coastline would then be subject to British attack.[31] After the meeting Merey told Berchtold that if Italy did not join the war it should be regarded as having left the Triple Alliance. Both Berlin and Vienna rejected this advice as too risky – it might encourage Italy to join France and Britain.

At 10 p.m. the Italian cabinet met. It considered the pressure from Germany and Austria–Hungary but endorsed the decision, which had been announced twenty-four hours earlier, that Italy would be neutral.

Brussels

During the morning, Camille Huysmans issued what proved to be the last circular the International Socialist Bureau sent out. It merely informed the affiliated parties that because of the deteriorating international situation the congress to be held in Paris was cancelled. It was no more than a confirmation of the powerlessness of the Second International that had been apparent for years.

Across the city, the French minister, Klobukowski, called on the foreign minister, Davignon. He gave him, as instructed by Paris, an official declaration that France would respect Belgian neutrality. However, it did include the rider that if another power violated this neutrality, then France reserved the right to modify its attitude. Shortly afterwards, the Belgian minister in Berlin, Beyens, reported that Germany had been unable to answer the British question about Belgian neutrality. This naturally increased suspicions about what Germany was planning. Davignon issued instructions to the Belgian representatives in the main European capitals that they were now to deliver the message they had been sent on 24 July and enquire how the parties to the 1839 treaty regarded their commitments. He also sent his private secretary, Bassompierre, to see the German minister, Below-Saleske, to tell him the French guarantee was being released to the press. The German minister merely said that he had no instructions on the matter.

The lack of any guarantee from Germany worried King Albert and he summoned the head of the foreign ministry, van der Elst, and together the two men drafted a message to be sent to the Kaiser. It reminded him of the Belgian attitude in 1870–1 (strict neutrality) and asked for the previous German promises about respect for that neutrality to be repeated. The message was translated into German by the Queen and sent to Berlin.

Luxembourg

Late in the evening, the prime minister, Eyschen, sent a telegram to Berlin to protest that at around 7 p.m. German troops had occupied the railway station at Ulflingen and begun tearing up the tracks. The troops involved were an infantry company of the 69th Regiment commanded by Lieutenant Feldmann. They were carrying out the first stages of the German mobilisation plan and had crossed the border before the Kaiser's order to stop the invasion had reached Trier. When that order arrived, another group of soldiers crossed the border in motor cars to recall the troops, who were back in Germany by about 7.30 p.m. Eyschen's telegram demanded an assurance of German respect for Luxembourg neutrality.

On the other side of the Duchy, French troops had begun tearing up the railway tracks on their side of the border at Mont St Martin Longwy.

The Balkans

In Bucharest, Germany decided to add its weight to Austria–Hungary's attempts to ensure Romania joined its nominal allies. This was now even more imperative following the outbreak of war with Russia. The German chargé, Waldburg, saw King Carol and told him that if Germany won the war 'as a reward for the fulfilment of its engagements and for active participation in the war . . . Romania should receive Bessarabia'.[32] The King merely responded that Romania, like Italy, would be neutral because both countries regarded Austria–Hungary as engaging in a war of aggression. Waldburg also saw the prime minister, Bratianu, who was sceptical about whether Romania could afford to alienate its powerful neighbour Russia by taking its territory. He told the German minister:

> Bessarabia . . . would only be of value to Romania if Russia were made to cede territory to Austria and Germany and be so weakened that this province would actually remain permanently with Romania.[33]

Germany had more luck in Constantinople where final agreement was reached on the terms of the alliance between the two countries – Germany effectively accepted the Ottoman terms.

In Cetinje, Austria–Hungary was making yet another effort to secure Montenegrin support. The message from Vienna for their minister, Otto, told him that they viewed Montenegrin neutrality as being of 'great importance'. He was to give the misleading reassurance that Austria–Hungary was not engaging in a war of conquest against Serbia and that there would be 'no permanent seizure' of Serbian territory. In response to the message from King Nicholas that he would like to be bribed with money and territory to stay out of the war, Vienna said there would be 'ample financial aid' if Montenegro remained neutral. Vienna effectively rejected the bid for territory in Albania, but instead offered territory in the Sanjak at the expense of Serbia.[34]

It was unlikely that such an offer would ever have been accepted. However, it arrived after the Montenegrin parliament, the Skupština, met and voted in favour of war with Austria–Hungary. Late that evening the King addressed the members of the Skupština who had gathered in the courtyard of his palace. Their vote was not binding on the government, but the King thanked them for their patriotism and asked them to remain calm. He gave no indication as to what he would decide to do.

*

By the end of 1 August, all four major continental powers had begun mobilisation. Germany and Russia were at war, as were Austria–Hungary and Serbia. Because of the alliance obligations, it was inevitable that Germany and France would be at war within a matter of hours. Remarkably, the two powers whose actions had done most to bring about the European war, Austria–Hungary and Russia, were still not at war and had not even broken off diplomatic relations. The focus of attention now began to switch to Britain, the last of the major European powers to decide its policy.

16

SUNDAY 2 AUGUST

Berlin – Morning

At 2.30 a.m. Chancellor Bethmann Hollweg summoned Jagow, Zimmerman and three senior foreign office officials, together with Moltke, Falkenhayn and Tirpitz. Berlin still did not know whether it was at war with Russia or not. The message Pourtalès sent from St Petersburg the previous evening at 8 p.m. (6 p.m. Berlin time), announcing that he had given Sazonov the declaration of war, never reached Berlin – the Russians cut all communications with Germany on the evening of 1 August.

The chancellor raised the question of the need for a declaration of war on France – under the German mobilisation plans, the attack on Belgium would begin in about twenty-four hours and war with France was needed as a justification. Tirpitz still opposed war and argued that the army should change its plans to concentrate on Russia. Moltke and Falkenhayn said that as far as they were concerned war with France had already started and a formal declaration was not needed. Bethmann Hollweg pointed out, correctly, that under Article 1 of the 1907 Hague Convention on the Outbreak of Hostilities, a formal declaration was legally required. A long argument ensued. Moltke insisted that it was now too late to change the only mobilisation plan that Germany had and it was also too late to avoid an invasion of Belgium. He argued that the ultimatum to Belgium should be delivered as late as possible and that Germany should not declare war on France, in the hope they would attack first.

The first problem was resolved when, shortly after 4 a.m., the general staff learned that Russian troops had crossed the border and attempted to destroy the railway at Johannisburg. At 4.30 a.m. a public statement was issued that Germany was now at war with Russia. Two hours later messages were sent to the ambassadors in Rome and Vienna. Flotow was to tell the Italian government that Russia had attacked Germany and that war with France would follow and therefore 'we expect from Italy fulfilment of her obligations as an ally'.[1] Tschirschky was given the same information and told 'we expect of Austria fulfilment of her allied obligations and immediate vigorous intervention against Russia'.[2] This message was backed up by one from Moltke to Conrad. The main thrust of Austro-Hungarian military efforts should be directed against their 'mortal enemy', Russia. This should involve 'all available forces' because 'Serbia can be kept in check with limited forces'.[3]

There was still concern in Berlin over what to do about France and Belgium. At 9 a.m. Jagow sent a message to Schoen in Paris enclosing the declaration of war that had been completed in the foreign ministry the previous evening. Ten minutes later Bethmann Hollweg sent a telegram cancelling that instruction. At 10 a.m. the chancellor, Moltke, Tirpitz and Plessen met the Kaiser at the Berlin Schloss. Moltke repeated the argument he had made in the early hours of the morning – Germany was already at war with France. Tirpitz now made a volte-face and agreed that no declaration was needed. Bethmann Hollweg restated the legal position and pointed out that the ultimatum to Belgium, which was already in the legation safe in Brussels, did not make sense unless Germany was at war with France. His arguments won the day but infuriated the military. Moltke and Tirpitz made a blistering attack on the foreign ministry and demanded that Jagow be sacked. The Kaiser refused.

Vienna

Early in the morning, Tschirschky called on Berchtold to carry out the instructions sent from Berlin. Berchtold resisted the German pressure to declare war on Russia. He argued Austria–Hungary was in the middle of deploying its forces against Serbia and, although the main group of reservists would go to Galicia, war could not be declared until the units moved from the Serbian frontier to Galicia in the middle of August. Conrad supported these arguments and advised that there should be no declaration of war on Russia while mobilisation and redeployment were underway.

It was only after further pressure was applied on Vienna through Szögyény that Berchtold submitted a draft declaration of war on Russia to Franz Josef that evening. However, even after approval, it was not to be presented in St Petersburg before 5 August at the earliest and probably considerably later. Tschirschky reported the decision to Berlin by telephone and then followed up with a telegram trying to justify the decision: 'Vienna would like to avoid incurring the odium of aggression through a spontaneous declaration of war.'[4]

Rome

Flotow went to see San Giuliano to carry out his instructions. He reported to Berlin that the Italian government had decided that Austria–Hungary had launched a war of aggression, it had not been consulted about the ultimatum and (a new excuse) it had not had time to make any military preparations. Therefore 'she would for the time being have to remain neutral, reserving decisions to be taken later in favour of her allies' (few can have believed the last part). Flotow correctly deduced that fear of Britain lay behind the Italian decision and advised 'practically nothing will be achieved here unless English participation in the war can be prevented'.[5]

A brutally honest appraisal of Italy's position was sent, later in the day, from Rome to Avarna in Vienna and Bollati in Berlin, both of whom thought Italy should fight alongside its allies. San Giuliano argued that Italy could only join an Austro-Hungarian war of aggression if the Italian people 'can be shown benefits commensurate with the danger and sacrifices'. In any such war, Italy faced heavy maritime attack, probable loss of its fleet to the superior French and British navies, problems in maintaining control of its North African colonies and a long-term loss of influence in the Mediterranean. The commensurate benefits would, it was implied, therefore have to be very high. However, if Germany and Austria–Hungary managed a 'bare victory' (which San Giuliano thought was the best they might achieve), they 'would not be in a position to give us adequate compensation'. And even if they did unexpectedly achieve the complete defeat of France and Russia, 'there would be neither the interest nor the will to give us compensation proportionate to our sacrifices'. Berlin and Vienna had refused to define exactly what Italy might get, but it was obvious Austria–Hungary would never give up 'the Italian provinces of Austria'.[6] This was an admission of the total failure of Italian policy – it was in the wrong alliance system. If it did not want to fight France and Britain and wanted to be rewarded with parts of Austria, it could never achieve these aims inside the Triple Alliance. The July crisis had made that crystal clear. The logic of the Italian position dictated that it should join Britain and France and hope that if they were successful Italy would get what it wanted.

Luxembourg

Shortly after dawn, German troops crossed the frontier and occupied Luxembourg. In the middle of the morning both Eyschen and Grand

Duchess Marie Adelheid sent protests to Berlin. At 2.10 p.m. Jagow replied to Eyschen, telling him the occupation was necessary because Berlin had information that French troops were advancing on the Grand Duchy (which was untrue). Jagow offered no more than that Germany would pay compensation for any damage and made no commitment on the future of Luxembourg. The French minister, Mollard, was still in the capital sending messages to Paris. The Germany army commander, General Fuchs, asked for advice on what should be done. While Fuchs was waiting for instructions, Paris sent Mollard the French declaration of respect for Luxembourg neutrality – this was not done until Paris knew that Germany had occupied the territory. The declaration belatedly stated that France would respect the 1867 treaty guaranteeing Luxembourg neutrality but added the proviso that the German violation meant that France would now 'let herself be guided in regard to this by the consideration of her defence and her own interests'.[7]

London – Morning

The French ambassador asked to see Grey as soon as he heard of the invasion of Luxembourg. He brought with him the text of the 1867 treaty (Britain, France and Prussia were among its signatories). Grey said that he took the same view as his predecessor had done in 1867 – it was a collective guarantee and therefore not the same as that given to Belgium in 1839. Grey argued that an individual power was not obliged to act on its own. The simple fact was that Britain had no interest in the preservation of Luxembourg neutrality and would not take any action. Later, Grey brushed aside the Luxembourg government, saying that their protests to Berlin and 'the serious matters to which they allude will engage the earnest attention of His Majesty's Government'.[8]

Grey also had to consider the telegram which Bertie, the perplexed ambassador in Paris, had sent him about his proposal the previous day for French neutrality (and, by implication, British too) in a Russo–German war. Bertie asked what he was to do and pointed out that this scheme would simply allow Germany to defeat Russia before turning on France. Since the question revolved around France's treaty with Russia, 'Am I to enquire precisely what are the obligations of the French under the Franco-Russian alliance?'[9] At 10.50 a.m. Grey sent the ambassador a message to forget about the subject.

With full-scale European war a matter of hours away, the only major power that still had to decide its policy was Britain. Although a German attack on Belgium might be close, no action had yet been taken. The British government therefore faced a dilemma. Some members of the cabinet wanted to support France in a war with Germany regardless of whether Belgian neutrality was violated. A large group would not accept this argument (which appeared to be the logical outcome of the ententes signed with France and Russia for imperial reasons). Without a violation of Belgian neutrality, it was far from clear that the cabinet would be able to remain united. The debates in the cabinet that morning were the most dramatic of the crisis.

Shortly before the cabinet met, Haldane set out his views in a letter to his sister:

> The ideas that on the one hand we can wholly disinterest ourselves and on the other that we ought to rush in are both wrong. And the real course, that of being ready to intervene if at a decisive moment we are called on, is difficult to formulate in clear terms. Yet I think this is what we must attempt.[10]

Haldane held this view throughout the crisis, but he would find it almost impossible to articulate it at the cabinet meeting. A group of ministers also met at Lloyd George's office at 11 Downing Street at 10.15 a.m. Those who discussed the situation with the chancellor of the exchequer were Pease, Harcourt, Beauchamp, Simon and Runciman. None of these men was determined on neutrality in any circumstances but neither were they supporters of Grey's position – they had real doubts about what course to take. Pease summed up their conclusions: 'all agreed we were not prepared to go into war now, but that in certain events we might reconsider position, such as the invasion wholesale of Belgium'. This left open what 'wholesale' meant and some of those present also had doubts about the commitment to Belgium: 'Harcourt not prepared to rely on treaty of 1839 as now binding. Simon arguing too that 80 years had created wholly different circumstances.'[11]

The cabinet met at 10 Downing Street for three hours from 11 a.m. Grey opened the proceedings by saying the time had come for 'plain speaking'. He was due to see Cambon at 2.30 p.m. and needed to tell him what Britain would do to help France in the war. He argued that France was 'relying on the entente' and said: 'I believe war will come & it is due to France they shall have our support.'[12] This was a terrible mistake. The idea that France was 'due' British support because of the secret agreements made over the previous eight years was exactly what most of the cabinet would not accept. As Herbert Samuel noted: 'cabinet almost resulted in a political crisis to be super-imposed on the international and financial crises. Grey expressed a view which was unacceptable to most of us.'[13] Harcourt passed a note across the table to Lloyd George asking him to 'speak for us' because 'Grey wishes to go to war without violation of Belgium'.[14] The majority view around the cabinet table was expressed by Samuel:

> We were not entitled to carry England to the war for the sake of our goodwill for France, or for the sake of maintaining the strength of France and Russia against that of Germany and Austria. This opinion is shared by the majority of the cabinet with various degrees of emphasis on the several parts of it.[15]

Grey made it clear that if the cabinet decided for neutrality he would resign. (The overwhelming majority of the cabinet had always rejected the idea of neutrality in all circumstances.) If Grey went, it seemed likely that Asquith, Crewe and Churchill would go with him. At about midday a letter to Asquith from the Conservative leader, Bonar Law, was brought in and the prime minister read it to his colleagues. It argued:

> It would be fatal to the honour and security of the United Kingdom to hesitate in supporting France and Russia at the present juncture; and we offer our unhesitating support to the Government in any measures they may consider necessary for that object.

Although the letter opened the possibility of a pro-war coalition being formed from the small minority in the cabinet who supported war alongside France in any circumstances and the opposition, in practice the letter had little impact on the discussion.

That discussion now turned towards possible compromises. The situation of Belgium was still uncertain and the cabinet was unsure whether a minor violation of neutrality by Germany and only token resistance by Belgium would activate the British guarantee. However, there was a tacit understanding that a full-scale German invasion of Belgium would result in British intervention and that the overwhelming majority of the Cabinet would support such a policy. Certainly, Lloyd George expected this to happen and consequently wanted to put off any final decisions for as long as possible while waiting on events. The meeting therefore concentrated on the proposal to guarantee the northern and Atlantic French coasts from German attack. At first glance this might have seemed a pro-French move, but that was not how the cabinet viewed the proposal. Britain could not allow the German fleet to operate in the Channel without impairing its own security and it was unlikely that Germany, with its much smaller fleet, would challenge a British decision to keep the German fleet out of the area. A guarantee would provide security for the French but without necessarily involving Britain in the war at all. When the cabinet discussed the details, some members, including McKenna (a former First Lord of the Admiralty), Pease and Samuel, tried to persuade Grey that French warships should be excluded from the Channel too. He refused saying, correctly, that the cabinet had to recognise that such a declaration was bound to favour France. The cabinet did, however, agree that Germany would be allowed to send destroyers and cruisers into the North Sea in order to protect its merchant ships. The overwhelming majority of the cabinet was prepared to give a declaration to France that the Royal Navy would protect the French coast. They did so because it helped square the circle in the cabinet – it gave some help to France but it was in Britain's own interest not to allow the German fleet unhindered access to the Channel.

John Morley was one of the main opponents of intervention who, in tears, told his fellow ministers, 'if you persevere in intervention I cannot return to this room'. But as one of his colleagues cruelly noted, 'As he had said the same thing about once a month for 3 years, no one took this very seriously.'[16] Eventually, Morley agreed to stay for the moment because he found the argument over the Channel acceptable, though Samuel thought his views were 'sadly inconsequent and inconsistent.'[17] The only member of the cabinet who did threaten to resign (apart from the tearful Morley) was John Burns. He felt the decision, even to defend the French coast, was one step too far along the road of increasing commitment to France which Grey and Asquith had been treading since 1906. He thought it symbolised 'an alliance with France with whom no such understanding had hitherto existed'.[18]

Asquith had spent much of the meeting writing a letter to Venetia Stanley. From it, he read out to his colleagues the conclusions of the meeting:

1. We have no obligation of any kind either to France or Russia to give them military or naval help.
2. The despatch of the Expeditionary Force to help France at this moment is out of the question & wd. serve no object.

3. We mustn't forget the ties created by our long-standing & intimate friendship with France.
4. It is against British interests that France shd. be wiped out as a Great Power.
5. We cannot allow Germany to use the Channel as a hostile base.
6. We have obligations to Belgium to prevent her being utilised & absorbed by Germany.[19]

The cabinet agreed to reconvene at 6.30 p.m.

Paris

There was a generally calm atmosphere during the first full day of French mobilisation. In the morning the Socialist Party issued a statement declaring its intention to defend France in the event of war. The government carried out only a handful of arrests on the Carnet B list of suspected subversives. There were anti-German demonstrations across Paris and both German and Austrian shops were looted – there were also major attacks on the German food company Maggi. Poincaré instructed Malvy, minister of the interior, to tell Hennion, the prefect of police in the capital, to maintain order at all costs – if necessary the instigators of the riots were to be charged before a military court.

The cabinet met at 2 p.m. They agreed to a few measures designed to emphasise national unity. The decree closing certain religious establishments was suspended and an amnesty granted to those who had broken the press laws. However, the cabinet did not allow Prince Roland Bonaparte to serve in the government – he was banned from doing so under an 1886 law excluding claimants to the throne. (The Prince donated his house in Paris to be used as a hospital.) The military reported that two German officers had been shot on French soil after they had been caught requisitioning supplies. A formal protest was sent to Berlin and the cabinet agreed that French troops could now enter the ten-kilometre zone along the frontier – they were authorised to expel German troops on French territory but were not allowed to cross the border themselves.

The cabinet agreed a proclamation of a state of emergency – the national assembly now had to meet within forty-eight hours, by which time it was hoped Germany would have attacked France. Poincaré began to compose his message to be delivered at that meeting. His first draft contained the passage: 'at last we could release the cry, until now smothered in our breasts: "Vive L'Alsace Lorraine".' Other ministers persuaded him that any such declaration would be bad for foreign opinion (especially in ·Britain) and make the war appear as one of revenge and aggression. The President agreed to delete the passage.[20]

Across France, reservists and mobilised men were beginning to depart for their various mobilisation depots. There were still few signs of enthusiasm. The reports from around the country suggested that most people felt that they had no choice but to submit – it was their duty and obligation, which it was impossible to avoid. The most frequent expression in the reports were 'we can't avoid it' and 'it has to be done.'[21] To most observers the enthusiasm that was displayed seemed artificial. One teacher in Aubeterre reported: 'the songs of those who were blustering and boasting rang false to me and it seemed that they had drunk in order to screw up their courage and hide their fear'. A teacher from Mansle thought the same and added: 'the affectedness of this clamorous gaiety is easy to grasp'.[22] Cabinet ministers were probably right to advise Poincaré to drop references to Alsace and Lorraine. The reports on popular sentiment in France showed that 'revenge' was mentioned in only 6 per cent of cases and Alsace and Lorraine even less frequently. By far the most frequent response was that of duty and the need to defend France against an aggressive Germany.

Berlin – Afternoon

As German mobilisation began, a message was sent at 2.05 p.m. to the minister in Brussels, Below-Saleske, saying that he was to open the envelope he had received from Berlin on 29 July. He was to present the ultimatum at 7 p.m. local time. Just over three hours later, Lichnowsky in London was informed of the action that would be taken in Brussels. He was to explain to the British government that the actions were 'self-defence against French menace' and say that the integrity of Belgium would be restored in the peace settlement. However, he was not to take any action until the following morning – after the ultimatum had been presented and the Belgian reply received.

Although Germany intended to violate Belgian neutrality, it had great hopes that the Swiss would not be neutral and would soon declare themselves as allies. During the afternoon Moltke wrote to Jagow to tell him that Switzerland had begun mobilisation. He also informed him that 'a treaty of alliance with Switzerland has been prepared by me, one copy of which is in my hands and the other in the hands of the Chief of Swiss General Staff'. This treaty would 'put all Swiss armed forces under the control of the German High Command'. Moltke emphasised that the existence of the treaty had to kept absolutely secret until the political negotiations with Switzerland were concluded, because the Swiss government had not approved the military talks, let alone the draft alliance.[23] (Moltke's minute was judged to be too sensitive to include in the official German collection of papers published after the war.)

In Munich there was a huge patriotic demonstration in the front of the Feldherrnhalle on Odeonplatz. The crowd was singing '*Die Wacht am Rhein*' and '*Deutschland über alles*'. A photograph of the scene taken by Heinrich Hoffman shows that in the middle of the crowd there was an ecstatic twenty-five-year-old purveyor of indifferent water-colours – Adolf Hitler. Hitler had left Vienna to escape Austro-Hungarian conscription and had been living in Munich since March 1913. On the outbreak of war he immediately volunteered for the Bavarian army. Hitler should have been returned to Austria–Hungary, but due to a bureaucratic mix-up he was allowed to enlist in the Bavarian army on 16 August and he served with distinction on the western front until the end of the war, being gassed on more than one occasion. Hoffman later became Hitler's court photographer. The future Nazis who were to join Hitler were scattered across Germany. Hermann Goering was serving with 112 Baden Regiment ('Prince Wilhelm') in the garrison at Mühlhausen. Heinrich Himmler was a thirteen-year-old schoolboy on holiday with his father, a professor of classics, at Tittmoning near the Austrian border. He was noting down the main events of the crisis in his diary. Joseph Goebbels was a partially crippled seventeen-year-old schoolboy at Rheydt near Düsseldorf.

Back in Berlin, the Czech writer Franz Kafka was largely ignoring the crisis. After breaking with his fiancée, he went bathing on the Baltic coast and on his return to the capital noted in his diary: 'Germany had declared war on Russia, – swimming in the afternoon.'[24] In the German capital there were reports that the French had bombed the outskirts of Nuremberg, although these were rapidly revealed to be false. Military action was, however, underway elsewhere. The German navy had the cruiser *Goeben* in the Mediterranean. During the day it asked to take on coal in the Italian port of Messina. The Italians refused permission and the ship was only able to refuel with 2,000 tons of coal from a German merchant ship. It was ordered to sail towards the North

African coast to be ready to attack French ports in the area and stop army transports on their way to France. Almost immediately, the French ordered units of their fleet to sail from Toulon to protect the transports.

London – Afternoon/Evening

When the cabinet meeting ended at about 2 p.m. Asquith went upstairs at 10 Downing Street to have lunch. He was joined by Birrell and Pease from the cabinet, his private secretary Bonham-Carter, his wife Margot and other members of the family. There was an air of forced cheerfulness over the meal as the group discussed various word derivations and the soundness of Dryden's English. After the lunch Asquith asked Pease to track down Burns and try to dissuade him from resignation. Pease did not find him until after 4 p.m., but was unable to change his colleague's mind – Burns was convinced Grey was dragging the cabinet into war. Asquith drove to London Zoo where he spent an hour in the bird sanctuary.

The rest of the cabinet broke up into various groups that lunched together. Half a dozen members were at Lord Beauchamp's house in Belgrave Square. Apart from the host, those present included Lloyd George, Harcourt, Simon, and Samuel. They were all worried and tried to steer a middle course between neutrality and automatic intervention. A similar group of McKenna, Runciman and Masterman were lunching at McKenna's house in Smith Square. Later in the afternoon, when Samuel called at the house, he found McKenna lying exhausted in bed.

Absent from these lunches was Grey. He was seeing Cambon at the Foreign Office. He gave him the assurance agreed by the cabinet:

> if the German fleet comes into the Channel or through the North Sea to undertake hostile operations against the French coasts or shipping, the British fleet will give all the protection in its power.

In addition, Grey explained that Britain would not be sending an expeditionary force to the Continent if it was involved in the war. In his telegram to Bertie in Paris, Grey explained the thinking behind the decision. How the war might develop was unknown and 'it was impossible to send our military force out of the country'. Indeed, the sending of two or four divisions to the Continent 'would entail the maximum of risk . . . and produce the minimum of effect'.[25]

During the discussion, Cambon asked whether the First Lord of the Admiralty, Churchill, was correct when he told the French naval attaché that information about the declaration on the protection of the French coast had been given to the German embassy as well. Grey reassured him that this information was 'quite wrong' and 'nothing has been said to any foreign representative except yourself, or will be said until a public statement is made'.[26] That statement was a lie – the information had been given to Lichnowsky by Grey himself earlier in the morning. At 12.19 p.m. the military attaché at the German embassy sent a message to the German general staff and navy staff. He explained Grey had told Lichnowsky that the German navy should refrain from incidents that might challenge the Royal Navy, in particular there should be no attacks on the northern coast of France. Attacks on Russian forces would not cause any problems. The attaché added: 'for the time being the English will not approach German waters and expect reciprocity from us'.[27] Tirpitz immediately endorsed this proposal. Clearly, the British were hoping that by alerting Germany their 'guarantee' of the northern French coast would never have to come into operation.

During the afternoon there were a number of anti-war meetings across the country. The largest was that organised by the British section of the Second International in Trafalgar Square. There were a dozen speeches all condemning any alliance with despotic and reactionary Russia and arguing that Britain had no interests in the Austro-Hungarian quarrel with Serbia. The attendance at the meeting was poor and it was generally regarded as a flop.

Half an hour before the cabinet was due to reconvene, a number of ministers from the broad central group who were waiting on events met to agree tactics. Among those attending were Lloyd George, Samuel, Crewe and Birrell. When the cabinet did meet at 6.30 p.m. it was a much easier meeting than in the morning. Pease described it as 'a friendly cabinet . . . no discordant note struck'.[28] The meeting discussed the speech Grey was to make in the House of Commons the next after-noon, but refused to agree an exact formula which would trigger British intervention over Belgium. It was generally agreed that only a substantial violation would cause Britain to act. If Belgium reacted like Luxembourg and made a token protest or did not resist the transit of German troops through the south-east of the country, then Britain could not intervene – it was impossible to be 'more Belgian than the Belgians'. However, most members of the cabinet expected that a major German invasion was likely within the next couple of days and that Belgium would resist. In this case Britain would join the war but in circumstances that did not rely on the various arrangements made with France or any obligations that might flow from them. Only Burns and Morley indicated that they could not accept this position.

After the cabinet meeting, some ministers – Lloyd George, Simon, Masterman and the Liberal chief whip Illingworth – dined with Lord Riddell, the chairman of the Newspaper Proprietors Association. Also present was Ramsay MacDonald, the leader of the Labour Party. Riddell noted in his diary that Lloyd George was 'in favour of intervention in certain circumstances'.[29] Although Lloyd George had kept open his communications with the more sceptical members of the cabinet, just in case it was possible to avoid war or a cabinet split, his position had always been that Belgian neutrality would eventually bring about British intervention. MacDonald noted more cynically:

> Discussed war. Masterman jingo, George ruffled, Simon broken. George harped on exposed French coasts and Belgium but I gathered that excuses were being searched for.[30]

It was during this meeting that Simon decided he was going to resign. He drafted a letter and showed it to Lloyd George, who merely returned it without comment. If war was inevitable, then the chancellor of the exchequer was not about to join his colleagues and give up power.

Many other politicians were also deciding where they stood that evening. One junior minister, Charles Trevelyan, decided he should resign. He would not support Belgium if Germany invaded just to attack France. However, if they tried to seize Antwerp and the coast, then he might reconsider – British interests would be directly involved at this stage. Many Liberal backbenchers could not believe that their government would decide to intervene. Richard Holt wrote in his diary:

> What England will do seems uncertain tho' it is almost impossible to believe that a Liberal Government can be guilty of the crime of dragging us into this conflict in which we are in no way interested.[31]

Not all Conservatives agreed with the views of the party leadership that Britain had to intervene simply to support France. Lord Selbourne wrote to Edith Lyttleton, the wife of one of his colleagues:

Any sympathies I have are with Austria, and for us to be involved in this Armageddon seems as indefensible as intolerable . . . If Belgium or Holland summoned us, then my conscience would be clear because that would be a *casus foederis*.[32]

That evening there were large crowds in front of Buckingham Palace until 1 a.m., cheering and singing. Asquith wrote to Venetia Stanley: 'war or anything that seems likely to lead to war is always popular with the London mob . . . How one loathes such levity.'[33] At the Admiralty Churchill issued instructions to begin naval cooperation with France. The French navy would be able to use British bases, common codes were instituted and intelligence information about the position of German ships in the Mediterranean and Pacific was exchanged.

The 'Neutral' Capitals

In Berne the Swiss government knew nothing of the agreement made between their army chief and Moltke. Indeed, the German foreign ministry knew that such a deal was very unlikely ever to be brought into operation. During the afternoon, the Swiss made a formal complaint to the German minister, Romberg, that German troops had used a Swiss road. Zimmerman sent an immediate and profuse apology and assurance that no such incident would happen again.

The German government seemed more likely to secure Sweden as an ally than Switzerland. Moltke thought they could be bribed into the war if Germany 'unhesitatingly granted all her wishes for the recovery of Finland' and the deployment of Swedish troops along the border would be a major threat to Russia.[34] Secret talks between the two countries may have been underway in Berlin. The British were also picking up signs that Sweden might ally with Germany. The British minister in Stockholm, Esme Howard, saw the foreign minister, Wallenberg. He asked for a categorical assurance of Swedish neutrality. Wallenberg replied, 'Sweden was determined to maintain neutrality as long as possible.' Howard naturally asked in what circumstances they would not be neutral. Wallenberg responded, 'if Great Britain joined Russia, Sweden would be forced to take the other side', but refused to state why this was the case.[35]

In neighbouring Norway, which had been independent of Sweden for less than ten years, the British minister, Findlay, ascertained that the government had taken measures for the defence of its neutrality, but they feared a German ultimatum which it might not be able to resist. In

Copenhagen the government told Berlin that it was starting the call-up of 30,000 men to the armed forces, but reassured the German government that this action was purely defensive. In Madrid, where the Spanish government took no part in the crisis, the foreign minister reassured the French ambassador that it was safe for French troops to be withdrawn from the Pyrenean frontier.

Although Japan was allied with Britain, the German government hoped they could tempt it to repeat its attack on Russia that had been so successful in 1904–5. In Berlin Moltke argued 'we can promise Japan everything she desires of us in this respect'.[36] In Tokyo the German ambassador, Count Rex, called at the foreign ministry to carry out the instructions sent by Berlin that day to tell Japan that Germany would soon be at war with Russia and that they should 'draw the necessary consequences'.[37] When Rex made this point to the Japanese foreign minister, Kato, his reply was blunt. Japan's relations with Russia were 'very friendly' and no deterioration was expected. Japan wanted to be neutral (which was untrue) but he explained 'the final decision of Japan depends on England'. Japan 'must intervene' if Britain claimed help and it would happen automatically if Germany attacked British territory in the Far East.[38]

In the Balkans the position of the various powers was becoming clearer. Romania would be neutral. Although Germany demanded 'the immediate mobilization of the Romanian army and its entry into war against Russia', there was no chance of this happening.[39] The German minister in Bucharest, Baron von Waldthausen, who had only just returned to his post, made the remarkable suggestion to Bratianu that 'Romania might in the first place declare that she would not attack Bulgaria if Bulgaria attacked Serbia'.[40] This betrayed a complete lack of understanding of the Romanian position from the beginning of the crisis – they would not allow Bulgaria to use the crisis to overthrow the settlement in the 1913 Treaty of Bucharest. After Bratianu heard of the German declaration of war, he immediately went to see the Russian minister, Poklevski, to ask whether a Romanian declaration of neutrality would be regarded as a friendly gesture by Russia. The minister reassured him that it would.

In neighbouring Bulgaria the government gave the German and Austro-Hungarian ministers the text of a treaty of alliance. If Bulgaria were attacked, the two powers would give unconditional support. If Romania allied with Russia, 'Bulgaria would have a free hand to reassert her claims to the Dobruja' (which had been lost in the 1913 settlement).[41] Bethmann Hollweg accepted these terms that evening. He did, however, suggest separate Bulgarian treaties with Germany and Austria–Hungary so that Italy did not, as a formal member of the Triple Alliance, have to be involved.

Meanwhile, the Greek government was betraying its alliance with Serbia. Venizelos, who was back in Athens after the Ottomans had suspended negotiations on an alliance now that they were joining the German side, sent instructions to Alexandropulos in Niš. He was to try to convince Pašić 'without entering into an examination of the obligations resulting from the alliance with Serbia' that Greek benevolent neutrality would really be much better for Serbia. If Greece intervened in the war, it would 'greatly harm her' and might even lead to the loss of Salonika, the only port which could supply Serbia. It was better to maintain the Greek army intact 'to keep Bulgaria in order'.[42] The flaw in the Greek argument was that all of these factors were obvious when Greece signed the alliance in 1913. Nevertheless, Serbia did not ask Greece to carry out its alliance obligations. King Constantine also rejected the Kaiser's appeal for Greece to intervene. Venizelos had convinced the King that because Britain and France controlled the Mediterranean Greece had to side with them. The prime minister told the French chargé in Athens: 'Greece would in no case be found in a camp opposed to that of the Triple Entente.' On participation in the war, Greece would 'wait to receive the advice of those three Powers'.[43]

Brussels

During the morning the British minister, Villiers, called on the foreign minister, Davignon, to tell him that Germany had failed to give any assurance about Belgian neutrality. Davignon said Belgium had 'no reason to suspect Germany of an intention to violate neutrality' and that it had not considered making an appeal to the guarantor powers. If a violation did take place, the Belgian government had not considered outside intervention and 'would rely upon their own armed force as sufficient to resist aggression, from whatever quarter it might come'.[44] After this meeting, Davignon sent a message to the Belgian ministers in Paris, London and St Petersburg saying that he was not worried by the lack of a German assurance since one had been given only a year earlier and 'the neutrality of Belgium is established by treaty which Germany intends to respect'.[45]

The Belgian government, despite the invasion of neighbouring

Luxembourg, thought that the lack of German action during the day was a hopeful sign. Klobukowski, the French minister, was suspicious about the situation. He told Paris that the lack of any German assurance combined with 'this tranquillity on the part of Belgium' gave rise to the strong suspicion of 'some sort of connivance between the two countries'.[46] Later in the day he sent another message to Paris saying he was sure King Albert had obtained 'certain assurances of a tranquillizing nature' from the Kaiser and that Germany had approved Belgian mobilisation which was directed primarily against France.[47] His assessment was shown to be wrong within the next few hours.

When the German minister, Below-Saleske, received the telegram sent from Berlin at 2.05 p.m. he opened the double-envelope package he had received by special messenger four days earlier. Inside he found the ultimatum that was to be given to the Belgian government at 7 p.m. He was shocked by its contents – he knew nothing of the Schlieffen plan and had only that morning given an interview to *Le Soir* (which was published the next day) expressly stating that German troops would not enter Belgium. The ultimatum, which was in German, was typed into a formal document at the legation. At 6.30 p.m. Below-Saleske telephoned the Belgian foreign minister, Davignon, to ask for an immediate interview at 7 p.m. At that meeting the German minister handed over the ultimatum and asked for a reply within twelve hours. Because of the difficult phraseology in the document, it took the foreign ministry staff nearly an hour to translate the ultimatum into French.

The Belgian *chef du cabinet* (the title prime minister was only introduced after the war), Charles de Broqueville, was alerted as soon as the ultimatum was delivered. At 8.10 p.m., after he had read it, he left to see King Albert and also summoned the cabinet. The King and de Broqueville immediately decided there was no option other than to reject the ultimatum. The council of ministers met at 9 p.m. and endorsed this decision, although it is difficult to know the exact nature of the discussion because no minutes were kept. At 10 p.m. there was a further meeting of ministers together with a number of senior officials and politicians outside of the government who constituted the Conseil de la Couronne.

This meeting lasted almost two hours and discussed the options open to Belgium. The King said that they needed to be clear what would be involved in a war – almost certainly the occupation of most, if not all, of the country. The army chief of staff, General Selliers, said that the army would not be able to offer effective resistance – mobilisation could be completed, Liège and Namur might hold out for a month at best and Antwerp might be defended if the field army could protect the fortifications. His deputy, General Ryckel, who was a favourite of King Albert, rejected the Selliers plan and, unrealistically, argued for defending the line of the Meuse and launching attacks into Germany towards Aachen and Cologne. De Broqueville said that even if Belgium complied with the ultimatum and remained technically neutral, it would, if Germany won the war, be turned into a client state or even annexed. The meeting endorsed the decision to reject the ultimatum. It was also agreed that no appeal would be made to the protecting powers for more than diplomatic support until a violation of neutrality actually took place. A small group of officials and ministers began the task of drafting the reply to be delivered early on the morning of 3 August.

17

Monday 3 August

Brussels
Shortly after midnight, three members of the Conseil de la Couronne began drafting the Belgian reply to the German ultimatum. The group comprised: Carton de Wiart, the minister for justice; Paul Hymans, minister of state; and Professor van den Heuvel of Louvain University (a professor of international law), who had been summoned shortly after the ultimatum was translated. The three men began work at a corner of the table around which the conseil were seated but, finding that too noisy, they adjourned to the foreign ministry where they were joined by its political director, Baron Gaiffier, who had begun drafting a reply while the conseil was meeting. At 1.30 a.m., while drafting was still in progress, the German minister, Below-Saleske, saw the secretary-general of the foreign ministry, van der Elst. He told him the German government had information that French troops had crossed the German frontier and begun bombing operations (the information was untrue). Van der Elst merely said that this had nothing to do with Belgium. At 3.05 a.m. Below-Saleske sent a telegram to Berlin saying that he expected a negative reply from the Belgian government.

By the time that telegram was sent to Berlin, the conseil had met and agreed the Belgian reply. The essence of the response was:

> The Belgian government, if they were to accept the proposals submitted to them, would sacrifice the honour of the nation and betray at the same time their duties towards Europe . . . The Belgian government are firmly determined to repel, by all the means in their power, every encroachment on their rights.

The conseil also agreed that no appeal was to be made to the guarantor powers. Although the reply was ready shortly before 3 a.m., it was not given to Below-Saleske until the last minute before the expiry of the ultimatum at 7 a.m. The moment it was received, the military attaché at the embassy left, as instructed by Moltke, and drove to the Union Hotel in Aachen. Here he told General von Emmich, who was in command of the operation to seize the fortifications at Liège, of the

Belgian response. That operation could now get underway. Below-Saleske did not send the formal telegram informing Berlin of the rejection until 10.55 a.m. and the text of the Belgian reply did not follow until after midday.

The Belgian government had not consulted the guarantor powers before replying and neither did it intend to publish the ultimatum and their response. However, Baron Gaiffier, who had delivered the reply to Below-Saleske, met the French minister, Klobukowski, on his return from the German legation and told him about the overnight events – the two were old friends, having served together in Cairo a few years earlier. Klobukowski immediately gave the details to the Havas press agency and it was quickly published in special editions of the Brussels newspapers. Klobukowski sent a telegram with the news to Paris at 8.20 a.m. The British minister knew of the ultimatum about an hour later and immediately sent the information to London – he did not have the text of the documents until late in the afternoon.

The Belgian cabinet met for two hours at 10 a.m. It again confirmed the decision not to ask for military assistance from the guarantor powers. At noon Klobukowski was told: 'in the present circumstances we do not appeal to the guarantee of the Powers'.[1] A message was also sent from King Albert to George V, but this only asked for 'the diplomatic intervention of Your Majesty's Government to safeguard the integrity of Belgium'.[2] Belgian troops along the frontier with France were under orders to fire on any French troops attempting to cross the border. As the day progressed and no action was taken by Germany, even after the delivery of an ultimatum with such a short timescale, suspicions grew in Brussels about German motivations. The Belgian government suspected that the ultimatum could have been designed to provoke France into an invasion.

Similar doubts were also present among the diplomats in Brussels, especially by the evening when Germany had still taken no action. Just before 7 p.m. Klobukowski sent a message to Paris saying that the German ultimatum was 'a manoeuvre to induce us to be the first to intervene in Belgium, thus causing an initial conflict between the Belgian army and our own'.[3] A few minutes later, Villiers sent a telegram to London informing them that Belgium would not ask for military help 'so long as Belgian soil is not violated by formidable bodies of German troops'.[4] Again this wording left open the possibility that Belgium might not react to a minor violation of its neutrality.

The 'Neutral' Capitals

The German minister at The Hague, Müller, had, like Below-Saleske in Brussels, been sent a message on 2 August instructing him to open the sealed envelope received a few days earlier. He was given a copy of the ultimatum to Belgium but he was instructed to reassure the Dutch government that their neutrality would not be violated. He was, however, told not to deliver this message until the morning of 3 August. Müller therefore saw the Dutch foreign minister, Jonkheer Loudon, at 9 a.m. to tell him that Germany expected benevolent neutrality from the Netherlands and if this was forthcoming 'the neutrality of the Netherlands will be fully respected by Germany'.[5] Loudon made no response at that meeting.

Shortly afterwards, the Belgian minister, Fallon, called on Loudon to say that the Brussels government wanted their commander at Liège, General Leman, to begin talks with the Dutch governor of Maastricht about joint defence of the region. Belgium had not responded to similar Dutch proposals made on a number of occasions since 27 July and now, knowing of the German offer, Loudon avoided responding to the Belgian request. In the afternoon, after consulting his colleagues, Loudon saw Müller and told him 'the Netherlands would on principle strictly maintain neutrality towards all quarters'.[6] The Dutch government did not inform either the French or the British governments of these exchanges.

During the day, the German minister in Berne, Romberg, called at the foreign ministry to give the formal German assurance of strict respect for Swiss neutrality. He was followed by the French minister, Beau, who gave a similar assurance. In Stockholm, however, the British were increasingly worried by signs that Sweden was about to ally with Germany. The British minister, Howard, saw the foreign minister for the second time in two days. Wallenberg slightly modified the position he had taken the previous day. If Britain did not go to war, then Sweden would remain neutral. However, if Britain was at war, 'extreme circumstances' might arise which would force Sweden to decide its position and 'it was impossible for Sweden to fight on the same side as Russia'.[7] Even though this was not a firm commitment to join Germany, it still left plenty of scope for such a decision. The language used by Wallenberg only strengthened the suspicions that Sweden was negotiating with Germany. During the day, the German ambassador in Constantinople told the Grand Vizier that Sweden would fight on the German side and in Vienna Berchtold gave Conrad the same information – indeed, he went further and said Sweden would invade Finland.

Another small European state, Portugal, was much more favourable to Britain, having a treaty of alliance that stretched back several centuries. The government in Lisbon instructed its minister in London, Teixera Gomes, to enquire what attitude Britain wanted Portugal to adopt. During the day, Eyre Crowe wrote to the Portuguese minister to tell him Britain 'would earnestly beg the Portuguese Government to defer for the present issuing any declaration of neutrality'.[8]

The Balkans

The Ottoman government had signed the treaty of alliance with Germany and it came into force now that Germany was at war with Russia. However, the Ottomans began to backtrack. The Grand Vizier told the German ambassador that he should not expect an immediate declaration of war. The government was divided over policy and wanted to move slowly to see how the international situation developed. At this stage the government in Constantinople only started mobilisation and declared a state of armed neutrality. Most members wanted to postpone a final decision until two warships under construction in Britain – *Sultan Osman* and *Resadiye* – were delivered and an alliance with Bulgaria concluded.

During the day the Grand Vizier saw the Bulgarian ambassador, Toshev, and told him about the alliance concluded with Germany. However, Toshev had no instructions from Sofia (the government had deliberately not given him any while they decided what to do) and so the discussion got nowhere. Later, news was received from Britain that the government had seized the two Ottoman warships for use by the Royal Navy. Not surprisingly, this infuriated the hardline elements in the Ottoman government. One of them, Enver Pasha, the minister of war, saw the German ambassador, Wangenheim, and, without the agreement of his colleagues, invited the German government to send warships to Constantinople – it would be a clear breach of neutrality if they did dock in an Ottoman port. On receiving this news, Berlin immediately instructed Rear-Admiral Souchon, the commander of the Mediterranean squadron, to sail to Constantinople with his two main ships – *Goeben* and *Breslau*.

In Bucharest the German government was still trying to entice King Carol into carrying out his alliance obligations. Bethmann Hollweg sent a message saying that talks over an alliance with Bulgaria were going well (which was untrue) and asking 'if formal undertaking by Bulgaria to give up Dobruja so long as Romania remains with Triplice would satisfy . . . and Romania would then move with us against Russia'.[9] This was a poor offer – it merely confirmed Romania in possession of a territory it already controlled in return for going to war. A better offer was on the table from Russia. They had consulted France and Poincaré had agreed 'that in order to exercise pressure on Romania . . . Transylvania must be offered to her'.[10]

The Romanian crown council met during the afternoon at King Carol's summer palace at Sinaia. The meeting was attended by the Crown Prince, government ministers and nearly all other senior politicians, including every living ex-prime minister. The main theme of the meeting was how to avoid joining Austria–Hungary in any war. The King was asked to read out the secret treaty with the Triple Alliance, which he did (in French). It was clear that it only applied if Austria–Hungary was attacked without provocation on its part. The general feeling of the meeting was that since Italy also regarded the war as stemming from Austro-Hungarian aggression, then Romania could not join a war in which Italy was neutral. Bratianu, the prime minister, had asked to speak last. He said the government favoured neutrality, had not been consulted by Austria–Hungary and needed to consider the position of the Romanian population in Transylvania. He argued for waiting to see how the war developed. A messenger entered the room and gave Bratianu a telegram. It confirmed that Italy would remain neutral. King Carol threatened to abdicate, but after a vote in which only one member supported the King's position (Carp, who had been prime minister in 1911–12), he too accepted that Romania would remain neutral. To placate the King, it was decided not to use the actual term 'neutrality'.

Bratianu then saw the German and Austro-Hungarian ministers – Waldburg and Czernin. He told them that the treaty did not come into effect because Romania had not been consulted about the ultimatum. He then made a crucial concession that he hoped would keep both Germany and Austria–Hungary friendly if they did win the war. Romania would accept a revision of the Treaty of Bucharest to allow Bulgaria to intervene against Serbia and take part of Macedonia. This would, Bratianu argued, enable Austria–Hungary to move more troops to face Russia than Romania could have deployed if it had joined the war. This was a reversal of Romanian policy throughout the crisis and for the previous year – it was now willing to allow Bulgaria to stab Serbia in the back as long as Berlin and Vienna interpreted this as a friendly gesture.

In Niš the Serbian government was worried that its patron Russia was trying to tempt Bulgaria into the war with the promise of Serbian territory, even though Serbia would be compensated with Bosnia–Herzegovina. However, given Serbia's dependence on Russia, it had little choice but to go along with the proposal. Pašić saw the Russian chargé Strandtmann to respond to the Russian suggestion. He was worried that 'the Bulgarians would regard Serbian proposals as a sign of weakness and ask too much'. He wanted the Russians to take the initiative in Sofia and appeal to 'Slav solidarity' and get the Bulgarians to state what they wanted to join the war against Austria–Hungary. If this was acceptable then there could be direct negotiations between Serbia and Bulgaria, but they would have to be under Russian supervision.[11]

In neighbouring Montenegro the situation was slipping into farce. The government in Vienna decided to cut off telegraph links with the Montenegrin capital, Cetinje. Unfortunately they forgot that this was the only way their minister, Otto, had of communicating with them. However, the Austro-Hungarian legation had one of the few cars in Cetinje and the military attaché was able to use it to drive to the coastal town of Kotov where it was still possible to send telegrams to Vienna over a commercial link. These journeys along the dusty mountain road were short-lived because the Montenegrin government responded by impounding the car. Then, despite the fact war had not been declared, the Montenegrins stopped the mail service to the legation and in a final gesture cut off its electricity supply. All Austro-Hungarian subjects of military age who were left in Cetinje were arrested.

Rome

The Italian government was still under pressure from Berlin and Vienna to carry out its alliance obligations despite its declaration of neutrality. Relations between the three governments were disintegrating badly. At 9 a.m. the King saw Lieutenant Colonel von Kleist, a personal emissary of the Kaiser, who presented a message asking for immediate mobilisation. The King made clear where his personal sympathies lay, saying, as Kleist reported, 'he personally was wholeheartedly with us', but Austria–Hungary had alienated Italian public opinion.[12] The King also sent a message to the Kaiser saying that the Triple Alliance did not require Italy to go to war in the current circumstances. He then, rather unwisely, signed the message: 'Your Brother and Ally'. An enraged Kaiser wrote on his copy of the letter: 'Insolence. Scoundrel.'[13]

The German ambassador, Flotow, saw San Giuliano. The ambassador argued that the Triple Alliance was applicable because France had attacked Germany (which it had not). The Italian foreign minister responded that the war had begun because of Austro-Hungarian aggression. Flotow reported to Berlin:

> My argument with him about it reached such a degree of acrimoniousness that its resumption seems to me inadvisable. He reproaches us with having concocted the whole game with Austria in order to face Italy with a *fait accompli.*

San Giuliano ended the talk by saying: 'we should see what would become of Austria in this conflict. She was a corpse that could never be brought to life again. She would now be entirely destroyed.'[14] Flotow recommended that an open breach with Italy should be avoided, telling Berlin: 'it must also be borne in mind that from hints dropped by Marquis San Giuliano it cannot entirely be ruled out that Italy might turn against Austria'.[15]

In this atmosphere it is hardly surprising that the talk between San Giuliano and the Austrian ambassador, Merey, was even more undiplomatic. San Giuliano explained that if Italy did join its allies, 'the enormous sacrifices and dangers were out of all proportion to the gains'. The Italian foreign minister then mused about the possible gains: 'not only was Nice French, but it had been ceded by Italy herself. Tunis was a fine colony, but Italy already had too many of them.' Albania could only be of interest to a state of mixed nationalities such as Austria–Hungary. Then, for the first time in the crisis, San Giuliano stated openly what it was that Italy wanted. 'It would be a different matter . . . if the Trentino were in question. That would be the only conceivable compensation.' Merey reacted predictably. He told Vienna that he cut short the conversation and told San Giuliano that he had often in the past spoken 'undiplomatically sharply', but that he would now atone for that fault 'by not answering his inadmissible suggestions with abuse.'[16]

In Berlin the Italian ambassador, Bollati, refused to go to the foreign ministry to present the formal note from the government in Rome declaring its neutrality. He pretended he was 'extremely indisposed'.

Vienna

When the Italian ambassador, Avarna, called on Berchtold to convey a similar note on neutrality, the Austro-Hungarian foreign minister said that it reflected 'no very friendly attitude' by Italy and was a breach of the Triple Alliance. Avarna made it quite clear that he, like Bollati, did not agree with his government. Berchtold thought it was 'very unwise' of Italy to stand aside 'at such a turning-point of history'. If Italy did stick with its allies, then 'an opportunity offered itself for her to realize far-reaching aspirations such as Tunis, Savoy etc.'. This was exactly what San Giuliano was rejecting in Rome. All the pressure and bribery by Berlin and Vienna failed – Italy remained neutral.

In Vienna the mood among the diplomats was confused and uncertain as the wider European war unfolded. Neither the French nor British ambassadors knew what to do. The former, Dumaine, did see Macchio in the foreign ministry and said 'as the situation did not oblige one to leave Vienna immediately, I might stay on unless relations were to be entirely broken off'.[17] The Russian ambassador, Shebeko, reported to St Petersburg that he was, as instructed, remaining in touch with officials in the foreign ministry. The two countries were still not at war and the ambassador thought (wrongly) that 'Austria would not be unwilling to negotiate with us for a possible way out of the dangerous situation created by her ultimatum to Serbia'. He described the mood in Vienna as one of 'deep depression'.[18]

One Russian exile who was worried about what would happen to him if the two countries were at war was Leon Trotsky, the Menshevik who had been the leader of the St Petersburg Soviet during the attempted revolution in 1905. He had just returned from a visit to the ISB in Brussels with his fellow revolutionaries Martov and Plekhanov where they had held unsuccessful talks about healing the Menshevik–Bolshevik split. Trotsky went to see the Austrian socialist leader, Friedlich Adler, at the offices of the *Arbeiterzeitung* newspaper during the morning of 3 August. At 3 p.m. Adler took Trotsky to see the chief of the Vienna political police to ask him what he proposed to do with the Russian exiles in the city. The police chief obligingly told the two men he was drawing up a list of the revolutionaries who would shortly be interned. He advised Trotsky to leave as soon as possible. Within a couple of hours Trotsky and his family had packed their belongings and at 6.10 p.m. they left the *Westbanhof* on the train for Zurich, where Trotsky was to continue his exile. (Of the other future Soviet leaders, Lenin was in exile at Poronin in Galicia and Stalin, who was eventually to have Trotsky murdered, was a little-known revolutionary in the second year of his four-year internal exile at Kureyka near the Arctic Circle in central Siberia.)

London – Morning

Early in the morning, Grey saw the Japanese ambassador. With war against Germany now more likely, he changed the line he had taken earlier and looked for Japanese assistance. He said, 'if the fighting should extend to the Far East, and an assault on Hong Kong and Wehaiwei were to occur, H. M. government would rely on the support of the Japanese government' in accordance with the 1902 alliance.[19] Next, Grey saw Cambon. He did not disclose what he was going to say to the House of Commons in the afternoon, but he confirmed the pledge to defend the northern French coast. Indeed, he went slightly further by adding: 'the British fleet would intervene in order to give French shipping its complete protection, in such a way that from that moment Great Britain and Germany would be in a state of war'. Britain would also, for its own strategic reasons, stop the German fleet moving from the North Sea into the Atlantic.[20] Finally, he saw Lichnowsky. The German ambassador conveyed an assurance from Berlin that 'a threat to the French north coast on our part will not take place as long as England remains neutral'.[21] He also gave Grey an assurance about Belgian 'integrity' being maintained after the war.

It was only after these three meetings, and shortly before 11 a.m., that the Foreign Office knew of the German ultimatum and its rejection by Belgium. Grey took this information to the cabinet, which met from 11.15 until 2 p.m. Before the meeting, Asquith had received resignation letters from Burns, Morley and Simon, and at the meeting Beauchamp offered his resignation too. Grey said that 'he felt some responsibility for the resignations and felt it acutely'.[22] Pease, who was a Quaker and president of the Peace Society, announced that he would stay. Lloyd George said that for him the probable attack on Belgium made all the difference and appealed to the four men to stay or at least to wait until after Grey's speech in the afternoon. They agreed to do so. Nevertheless, feelings ran high during the meeting. Samuel wrote to his wife: 'the cabinet was very moving. Most of us could hardly speak at all for emotion.' However, in most quarters there was little sympathy for those who intended to resign. Samuel said that 'those four men have no right to abandon us at this crisis – it is a failure of courage'.[23] Charles

Hobhouse was particularly incensed by one of his colleagues: 'in Simon's case almost despicable because he pretended to a special and personal abhorrence of killing in any shape'.[24] In terms of policy there was little for the cabinet to decide. It had been tacitly accepted, although not clearly articulated, at the two meetings on the previous day that a German attack on Belgium would result in British intervention. Now that the situation was becoming clearer the cabinet was much more united. The minority who were prepared to enter the war to help France (Churchill, Grey, Asquith and probably Crewe) were joined by the overwhelming majority who accepted intervention was necessary but who wanted a more acceptable reason than the entente and the secret agreements with France. This left a small minority opposed to intervention whatever the reason and that minority would get smaller still by the next morning.

One problem that had to be resolved in Whitehall was the position of secretary of state for war which Asquith had held for the past few months. If Britain were to be at war, it would be impossible for the prime minister to do both jobs. The obvious successor, who had undertaken much of the routine work at the ministry in the past few days and been secretary of state for war at the beginning of the Liberal government, was Haldane. However, he was seen as being too pro-German to be acceptable. Asquith decided, reluctantly, that the only choice was Lord Kitchener, the commander of British forces during the Boer War, who was now the ruler of Egypt. He had been on leave in England but was now returning to Egypt. In the middle of the morning he left his home at Broome near Canterbury to catch the Dover ferry. About noon a message from Asquith arrived recalling him. Staff were sent after Kitchener but did not reach him until he was already on board the 12.55 p.m. boat. It was only because the sailing was delayed, awaiting the arrival of the boat train from London, that Kitchener was located and told to travel immediately to London. One departure that did take place was that of Shackleton's expedition to Antarctica, which left despite the imminence of war. On the other hand, one of the highlights of the social season, the Cowes Regatta, was cancelled.

London – Afternoon/Evening

After the cabinet meeting, Samuel had a quick lunch with Lloyd George at 11 Downing Street. The two men then drove to the House of

Commons through cheering crowds waving Union Jacks. Samuel described the scene for his wife:

> 'This is not my crowd' he said. 'I never wanted to be cheered by a war crowd.' It was a moving sight and I could not help thinking and saying that they all know little what was meant, and that there will be a different spirit three months from now.[25]

Grey gave the only major statement on the crisis to a packed Commons chamber at 3 p.m. It was a muted occasion and Grey's speech was far from clear. He very carefully never mentioned Russia – he knew that subject was far too unpopular with his own back-benchers. Neither did he discuss who was responsible for the European war. Instead, he concentrated on 'British interests, British honour and British obligations'. He explained that the entente was a grouping, not an alliance, and although Britain had supported France over Morocco in 1905–6 and again in 1911, that was because it was the subject of a direct agreement between the two countries. However, the military and naval agreements made with France in 1906 and 1912 were not binding. In addition, this conflict was different because it arose from France's alliance with Russia. Nevertheless, Grey thought Britain did have obligations to France and argued that Britain could not stand aside and see Belgium occupied and France defeated.

In many ways it was a strange speech and quite personal in tone. It was not as strong as it might have been – for example, Grey did not mention the clumsy German bid for British neutrality. It was also difficult to interpret – Lichnowsky, who was sitting in the gallery, was optimistic that Britain might stay out of the war; Charles Trevelyan, a junior minister was, on the other hand, appalled:

> I was prepared for bad news, but in no way for the bare-faced appeal to passion. He gave not a single argument why we should support France. But he showed he had all along been leading her to expect our support.[26]

Asquith also made a strange comment when he told Pease privately: 'the anti-German note in Grey's speech was the only adverse criticism possible'.[27] After Grey finished, the Conservative leader, Bonar Law, and the Irish Nationalist leader, Redmond, promised support. The leader of the Labour Party, Ramsay MacDonald, with the agreement of his party, argued for neutrality. It seemed the best way of staking out a position different from that of the Liberals once it was clear that Lloyd George would not lead an anti-war group. When the House of Commons met again in the evening, there was little support for Grey –

fifteen Liberal MPs spoke, and only four supported the foreign secretary and two of those endorsements were equivocal. It was at this point that Arthur Balfour, a former leader of the Conservatives, insisted that the debate should be stopped.

The cabinet assembled again for a short meeting at 6 p.m. It agreed that a message on Belgium should be sent to Berlin the next day. However, the text was not approved by the meeting. Despite the fact that the cabinet knew of the German ultimatum and its rejection, no warning was sent to Berlin that evening explaining what would happen if they did invade Belgium (no German troops crossed the frontier for another twelve hours). After the meeting, Asquith wrote separately to two of the dissidents, Simon and Beauchamp. He almost certainly offered them promotion in the near future if they did not resign. By the next morning they had withdrawn their resignations. During the evening, Asquith and Pease played bridge with various members of the Asquith family. For the prime minister, the impending European war brought relief from the domestic crisis: 'The one great spot in this hateful war was the settlement of Irish civil strife . . . God moves in a mysterious way his wonders to perform.'[28]

Berlin

It was lunchtime before the German government received confirmation that Belgium had rejected their ultimatum. During the afternoon there were a number of discussions about how to proceed. It was finally agreed there would be no declaration of war because there was still the hope that Belgium might offer no more than token resistance to the German invasion. Moltke drafted a message that was sent to Below-Saleske in Brussels at 10.35 p.m., for delivery early the next morning.

With German mobilisation well underway, it was also necessary to declare war on France, not just to provide an excuse to invade Belgium, but also because German plans would soon involve attacks on French forces. The original declaration of war was scrapped, even though it had been agreed by the Kaiser. It had dealt with the diplomatic disputes since 23 July and the failure of France to declare its position following the outbreak of war between Germany and Russia. During the morning, Jagow in the foreign ministry produced a new draft. It set out a long list of frontier infringements by France and also included allegations about French bombing of railways near Karlsruhe and Nuremberg. (The latter were false and known to be false by the

German General Staff.) The note concluded that France had created a state of war. The message was sent to Schoen in Paris at 1.05 p.m. and it instructed him to deliver the note to the French government at 6 p.m. and ask for his passports.

Paris

During the morning, Poincaré carried out a reshuffle of the government. The main change was the replacement of Viviani as minister for foreign affairs by Gaston Doumergue. The president had never trusted Viviani's judgement but he remained as prime minister. Across the city, there were queues of young couples in front of the *mairies* of the working-class 6th and 5th arrondissements waiting to get married before the men went to their mobilisation depots. Military police were already stationed at the main road junctions and on the bridges across the Seine. Marcel Proust, who was working on *À l'ombre des jeunes filles en fleurs*, the second part of his great novel *À la recherche du temps perdue*, drove through the city to Gare de l'Est with his brother, a medical officer, who was travelling to his wartime post at Verdun.

Across France, the mood was sombre. The men marched out of the villages without any singing and the women lining the road were in tears. The troop trains from the Norman towns of Rouen, Le Havre and Evreux departed in silence. In St Etienne a group of anarchists fled into the woods in the Monts du Forez to avoid the call-up. They were captured within a week. In Brittany some of the peasants in the remote areas of Finistère and Morbihan did not respond to the mobilisation notices because they did not understand French.

When the 1.05 p.m. telegram from Berlin arrived at the embassy in Paris, the text was so garbled that much of it could not be deciphered. The declaration of war therefore had to be redrafted once more. The only parts that could be understood were the false allegations about French bombing raids and so they were included as the main justification for war. Schoen then spoke to the American ambassador to arrange for the United States embassy to look after German interests in France. All of this took time and Schoen was therefore late when he left at 6.15 p.m. to drive to the Quai d'Orsay. Outside the embassy two men forced their way into his car and started shouting abuse. The ambassador called three of the gendarmes protecting the embassy and they ejected the men. Schoen was extremely flustered when he eventually arrived at the French foreign ministry – the US embassy had already alerted the ministry to the reason for the German ambassador's call. He began by protesting about the incident at the embassy for which Viviani apologised profusely. Schoen then read out the formal declaration of war he had drafted at the embassy. Viviani protested strongly about the false allegations before Schoen asked for his passports. Viviani accompanied Schoen to the courtyard where the ambassador bowed deeply, got into his car and left. Germany was now formally at war with both Russia and France.

Probably the most relieved man in Paris was President Poincaré. His strategy of trying to place the responsibility for the war on Germany, so that public opinion in France would rally behind the government and the British would be impressed by French restraint, was finally successful. Now the alliance with Russia would not be the focus of debate and Italy would also be neutral. A war to recapture Alsace-Lorraine could be fought on the best possible terms. He wrote in his diary:

> Never before had a declaration of war been welcomed with such satisfaction . . . It was indispensable that Germany, who was entirely responsible for the aggression, should be led into publicly confessing her intentions.[29]

18

Tuesday 4 August

Tokyo

The earliest action of the day occurred in Tokyo. The Japanese cabinet met for five hours from 9.30 a.m. to discuss the situation created by the European war. The government wanted to join the war in order to gain German possessions in China and the Pacific. However, unless Germany attacked British possessions in these areas, the 1902 alliance would not be activated. After a long discussion it was agreed to issue a public statement that Japan hoped to be strictly neutral but that it was ready to take all necessary steps in accordance with the British alliance. The British ambassador, Sir William Greene, was called to see the foreign minister, Kato, to be given more details about the Japanese position. He was told that if British territory was attacked then Japan would respond immediately 'if called upon'. This latter phrase caused considerable confusion. The British government thought it meant that the Japanese would wait for a British request and the Japanese government was told that Britain hoped to avoid dragging Japan into the war. What the Japanese meant by this phrase was that any attack on British possessions in the Far East would automatically bring Japan into the war and only if there was an attack on British ships on the high seas would they consult London first. The Japanese also told the British that part of their fleet was being mobilised. There was little the Japanese government could do until an incident occurred. Kato told the Russian ambassador, Malevski, 'Japan will not declare her neutrality but will wait to see what attitude Great Britain will adopt in the present crisis.'[1]

Brussels

At 6 a.m. the German minister, Below-Saleske, gave the Belgian foreign minister, Davignon, the note sent from Berlin the previous evening. It stated that the German government 'will find itself, to its deep regret, compelled to take – if necessary by force of arms – the measures of security indicated as indispensable in view of French threats'.[2] Two hours later, the first German cavalry units crossed the border at Gemmenich. They were followed shortly afterwards by infantry units whose objective was to secure the bridges over the Meuse near Liège. Their task was to control the routes to the forts in the area. These bridges, which had been mined some days earlier, were destroyed. When German forces tried to cross the river they came under heavy attack from Belgian troops. Nevertheless, by nightfall, German units had crossed the Meuse at Visé, north of Liège. There had already been a number of incidents between Belgian irregular units and German forces – the village of Battice was burned to the ground as a reprisal.

The news of the German invasion had not reached Brussels when, early in the morning, the King addressed parliament where he spoke of his hope that an invasion would not take place. By the time the cabinet met at 11 a.m., news of the German attack had reached the capital. Ministers drafted a note to be sent to Britain, France and Russia. It stated that Belgium would resist the German invasion and it asked the three powers 'to co-operate in the defence of her territory' through 'concerted and joint action' to ensure the future independence and integrity of Belgium. There was still considerable distrust of France and Britain and what action they might take. King Albert insisted that a final sentence should be added to the note, stating 'Belgium is happy to declare that she will assume the defence of her fortified places'. It was not until late in the evening that the British and French ministers were told of the Belgian appeal and the information did not reach London and Paris until the early hours of 5 August.[3] The action which the Belgian government did take immediately was to send Below-Saleske a note saying relations between the two countries were broken off and enclosing his passports.

The 'Neutral' Capitals
In neighbouring Luxembourg no formal protest over the German occupation was sent to Berlin and the Luxembourg minister in the German capital was not withdrawn. The German General Staff did not reply to General Fuchs's question of 2 August about how the French minister in the capital was to be treated. Fuchs therefore decided, on his own authority, to order him to leave. Under duress, the prime minister, Eyschen, backed up the German order and at 2.15 p.m. Mollard left in his own car and drove to the French border. Before he left, Eyschen took the opportunity to protest over the French attitude towards

Luxembourg neutrality – the fact that Germany had violated it did not give them the right to do so.

In The Hague the permanent head of the Dutch foreign ministry saw the British minister, H. G. Chilton. He only told Chilton that Germany had not presented an ultimatum but that if it did so the reply would be the same as that given by Belgium. He did not reveal the assurance given by Germany nor the Dutch declaration of neutrality given to the German minister.

In Berne the Swiss government issued a formal declaration of neutrality. The military remained strongly pro-German – not only had the chief of staff signed a secret alliance, but Germany had been supplied with military intelligence on a regular basis since 1910. Many of the German-speaking population supported Germany. Karl Scheurer, the head of the military department of Canton Berne, wrote in his diary: 'on general cultural grounds as well as political I believe that a German victory is desirable'.[4]

In Madrid King Alphonso XIII saw the French ambassador, Leon Geoffray. He apologised for the fact that Spain was too weak to enter the war, but all Spanish sympathies were with France and they would do what they could to help. The King added, 'France was defending the independence of the Latin nations and hence of Spain.'[5] In neighbouring Portugal the prime minister saw the British ambassador, Sir Launcelot Carnegie, and told him that Portugal wished 'to act in complete co-operation with Great Britain in whatever course the latter may adopt'.[6] Grey's message to Lisbon said that for the moment Britain 'would be satisfied if the Portuguese government refrained from proclaiming neutrality'. However, it gave a reassurance that if Germany attacked any Portuguese possession, including its colonies, then Britain would be bound by the long-standing alliance between the two countries.[7] This declaration was slightly ironic because Britain had, a few years earlier, reached an agreement with Germany on how to divide up the Portuguese colonies between themselves.

In Copenhagen the Danish government issued a formal declaration of neutrality, as did the Swedish government in Stockholm. The Swedish minister in London saw Grey and told him neutrality was the 'settled desire' of his government. However, he once again stated that if Sweden was forced into the war 'it would be impossible for her to take the side of Russia'. Grey said he would seek a declaration from France and Russia on Swedish independence and integrity if it stayed neutral.[8]

The situation in Constantinople was growing more confused by the day. The government was badly divided and many ministers did not know of the alliance with Germany. Others were worried by Bulgaria – were they just waiting for the Ottomans to be embroiled in war with Britain, France and Russia before attacking? The German government was getting more anxious about the failure to implement the recently signed alliance as the fighting on the eastern front with Russia intensified. Jagow told Wangenheim: 'Turkish declaration of war against Russia today if possible appears of the greatest importance.'[9] There was no prospect of any such declaration. What the German ambassador did not know was that the Ottoman cabinet met during the day and agreed a set of demands Germany was unlikely to be able to meet. The Ottomans would not join the war until Bulgaria did so and Romanian neutrality was assured. Germany was also to pledge itself to end all the extra-territorial privileges granted to the European powers. Germany was not to conclude peace until all occupied Ottoman territory was evacuated and the government in Constantinople was to share in any war indemnity. Hopes for a rapid intervention of the Ottomans against Russia had faded.

In Washington the American government took its only concrete action of the entire crisis. President Wilson sent a message to all the main European heads of state stating he was willing to work for peace if required. They all told him his offer was too late. The Kaiser did not bother to reply until 14 August and the Tsar took even longer to send his rejection of the offer – it was finally dispatched on 26 August. It was just before midnight that a young German, Joachim von Ribbentrop, the twenty-one-year-old son of a former major in the German army crossed the border from Canada into the United States on the evening train from Montreal to New York. He left hurriedly to avoid being interned and after reaching New York took a boat to Germany where he volunteered for the cavalry. Later, he was foreign minister under Adolf Hitler.

Berlin – Morning
Early in the morning a note was sent to Below-Saleske in Brussels, instructing him to tell the Belgian government that at any time Germany was willing to negotiate an acceptable modus vivendi for its troops operating in Belgium. However, the essential part of any such agreement would be a Belgian assurance not to destroy railways and

bridges and for 'the opening of Liège to the passage of German troops'.[10] The note was never delivered because Belgium had broken off relations by the time it arrived in Brussels. At 10.20 a.m. a telegram was sent to Lichnowsky asking him to 'dispel any mistrust' in the British government by repeating the 'formal assurance that, even in the case of armed conflict with Belgium, Germany will, under no pretence whatever, annex Belgian territory'. The note even said German sincerity was demonstrated by its pledge to uphold Dutch neutrality.[11] The German government can have had no realistic expectation that this action would have any effect or that 'mistrust' in London could be dispelled by mere words. This was confirmed when the message to London crossed with one from their ambassador saying that Belgian neutrality was central to British concerns and Britain would intervene unless Germany evacuated Belgian territory 'in the very shortest possible time'.[12]

Bethmann Hollweg was still angry over the failure of Austria–Hungary to declare war on Russia. This failure was compounded by the arguments between the two countries over Italy and the way Vienna had misled Berlin over its intentions towards Serbia. At 11.40 a.m. he sent a strong message to Tschirschky:

> We are compelled by Austria's action to go to war and may expect that Austria will not try to gloss over this fact but will publicly proclaim that threat of intervention (mobilization against Austria) [by Russia] in Serbian conflict forces Austria to war.[13]

Although this was a fair statement of the position, it did neglect the fact that Germany had approved the Austro-Hungarian action and at one stage pushed its ally forward. The Austro-Hungarian ambassador, Szögyény, told the foreign ministry later in the day that the declaration of war would be sent to the embassy in St Petersburg the next morning. It was not served on Russia for another thirty-six hours after that.

War with France was underway and early in the morning Admiral Souchon on the *Goeben* was ordered to sail to Constantinople where, at the invitation of Enver Pasha, it was hoped the Ottoman government could be pushed into joining the war. Before turning around, the *Goeben* and *Breslau* continued on their original mission to North Africa. When they were off the French ports of Philippeville and Bône, they ran up the Russian flag before bombarding the towns to interrupt the movement of troops to southern France. Then they turned to the east. Shortly after 9.30 a.m., they encountered two British warships,

Indomitable and *Indefatigable*, which had been trailing them for some hours. With the two countries not at war, the ships sailed past each other at a distance of about five miles. The German ships put on full speed (twenty-four knots) and, followed by the British ships, sailed towards Constantinople. In the evening the British ships lost contact with the German vessels in fog off the coast of Sicily and were unable to stop their mission.

The staff of the French embassy in Berlin were locked in a dispute with German officials over how they were to leave the country following the declaration of war. Jules Cambon wanted to depart by the direct route through either the Netherlands or Belgium. The Germans refused, presumably because the French might gain useful military intelligence. Instead, the French were offered a route through Vienna, but that suggestion was then withdrawn. Eventually, it was agreed that they would travel via Denmark. They left on a special, locked train. When it arrived near the Kiel Canal, German troops boarded the train and drew down the blinds. Cambon had to pay 3,611 marks and 75 pfennigs in gold for the journey – a sum the German government later reimbursed via the Spanish embassy in Paris.

London – Morning
The British government was unaware of the German invasion of Belgium when, at 9.30 a.m. a telegram was sent to Goschen in Berlin. It referred to the German ultimatum and its rejection by Belgium over twenty-four hours earlier, and instructed the ambassador to tell the German government that Britain was:

> bound to protest against this violation of a treaty to which Germany is a party in common with themselves, and must request an assurance that the demand made upon Belgium will not be proceeded with, and that her neutrality will be respected by Germany. You should ask for an immediate reply.[14]

This telegram, which contained no direct threat that Britain might go to war over the issue, could have been sent the previous evening when it might have had an effect on Germany policy. By now it was too late. Just over an hour later telegrams were sent to the British representatives in Brussels, The Hague and Christiania (Oslo), but, significantly, not Stockholm. They were to explain that, if these countries were pressured by Germany to depart from neutrality, Britain expected that 'they will resist by any means in their power'. Britain would support such resistance and would join France and Russia in immediately offering 'an alliance for the purpose of resisting use of force against them' and providing a guarantee for the future.[15] Within less than two hours, the Foreign Office realised that it had made a major mistake in the wording of these telegrams, At 12.30 emergency telegrams were sent withdrawing the word 'alliance' and substituting 'common action'. At 2 p.m. the offer was withdrawn.

The cabinet met briefly during the morning for a routine discussion. There appears to have been no discussion of the action to be taken in Berlin later in the day. Simon and Beauchamp had withdrawn their resignations and were present at the meeting. John Burns and John Morley were not present having stuck to their resignations. But they were lightweight political figures and their departures were hardly noticed.

At 11.20 a.m. a message arrived from Brussels saying that Germany was likely to invade. Confirmation of the invasion came via the Belgian legation an hour or so later – a telegram from the British minister in Brussels giving the same information did not arrive in London until 4.20 p.m. Even though the British government knew of the invasion shortly before lunch, it did not know how Belgium would respond – no appeal for assistance, other than diplomatic, had so far been made by the Belgian government. Nevertheless, Asquith and Grey drafted a further telegram to Berlin that was dispatched at 2 p.m. It instructed Goschen to repeat the request for German assurances about Belgian neutrality (which were redundant after the invasion) and for a reply to the telegram sent at 9.30 a.m. These were to be received in London by midnight. If this was not done, 'you are instructed to ask for your passports and to say that His Majesty's Government feel bound to take all steps in their power to uphold the neutrality of Belgium'.[16] In many respects it was a strange ultimatum – it did not actually state that Britain would declare war, although that was the obvious implication.

After the telegram was sent, Grey saw Cambon. The French ambassador immediately asked whether, as previously planned, the bulk of the British army would be sent to fight on the French left flank to meet the German sweep through Belgium. Grey replied, 'No, we shall blockade all the German harbours. We have not contemplated the despatch of a military force to the continent.' He added that the army was needed for home defence and that public opinion was opposed to sending it to France.[17] While Asquith was making a statement in the House of Commons about the message sent to Berlin, Grey saw the

Austro-Hungarian ambassador, Mensdorff. Although the Foreign Office had begun drafting a declaration of war on Austria–Hungary, Mensdorff reported that Grey said there was 'no cause for quarrelling with us so long as we do not go to war with France' (nothing was said about Russia). The British ambassador, de Bunsen, was not being recalled. Grey's private secretary, Tyrrell, then gave the ambassador the militarily sensitive information that the French fleet in the Mediterranean would not sail into the Adriatic.[18] Grey confirmed the situation when he told de Bunsen in Vienna that Britain would neither break relations nor take any initiative. He told Rodd in Rome: 'I do not suppose we shall declare war upon Austria unless some direct provocation is given, or she declares war on us.'[19]

The speed of events across Europe caught up with the British Neutrality Committee which held its first meeting during the day – its last was the next day. In total it spent £20 on its 'campaign'. Few people noticed that at Southampton one of the regular ocean liners from South Africa docked. It had left Durban on 18 July, before the crisis broke. On board was an Indian lawyer – Mahatma Gandhi – accompanied by his wife Kasturbai, their children and one of his supporters, Hermann Kallenbach. Gandhi, who was dressed in a European suit for the occasion, had, in June, ended his eight-year-long satyagraha campaign for Indian civil rights in South Africa, after wringing some concessions out of the prime minister, Jan Smuts. Gandhi was on his way back to India where he was to become the charismatic leader of the campaign against British rule.

Paris

The funeral of Jean Jaurès was held during the morning. Among those present were Viviani and the speakers of the two chambers of the French parliament. While the funeral service was underway, the German ambassador, Schoen, left Paris – with less difficulty than Cambon in Berlin. General Joffre, who had continued to move more French forces to the left flank to try and counter the expected German attack through Belgium, set up his war headquarters. They were in a school at Vitry-le-François on the Marne. From this point, he was easily able to reach his five army headquarters in his car driven at 70 mph by an ex-racing driver, Georges Bouillot.

At 3 p.m. the national assembly met to hear an address by President Poincaré. He had no constitutional right to address parliament and so his speech was read in the Senate by the minister of justice and in the Chamber of Deputies by Viviani. Poincaré had accepted the advice of the Cabinet and dropped any references to Alsace and Lorraine. Instead, he stressed the defensive nature of French policy since 1871 and during the crisis of the previous thirteen days. He claimed that France represented liberty, justice and reason. He called for a *union sacrée*. Poincaré's real thinking during the crisis was well set out in a diary entry written in January 1915:

> I have always believed, of course, that the French did not want to declare war for Serbia. I even believed that France would not rise up together to keep the promises of the alliance with Russia and that, if we had been led into declaring war, the country would be cruelly divided. But I had never had doubts about France in the event in which she were attacked, even if it was over Serbia.[20]

Poincaré had therefore achieved the outcome he wanted: a German declaration of war on France. However, his essentially passive policy leaves open the question of how far France really tried to avoid the war or restrain its ally Russia and how far it simply wanted to fight Germany on the best possible terms.

Berlin – Afternoon/Evening

At the same time as Poincaré's speech was being read out in the French parliament, Bethmann Hollweg was addressing the Reichstag. (The hot, dry conditions, which had dominated the European weather during the crisis so far, had ended and it was pouring with rain in the German capital.) Bethmann Hollweg's speech was, like Poincaré's in Paris, full of omissions and distortions. The chancellor admitted that the invasions of Luxembourg and Belgium were breaches of international law but argued 'necessity knows no law'. He added that Britain had been told Germany would not attack the northern French coast and that the territorial integrity and independence of Belgium would be respected at the end of the war. In response to the speech, the SPD leader, Haase, pledged Socialist support for the war. The previous day the party had secretly voted by seventy-eight to fourteen to support the granting of war credits. Now he said:

> The victory of Russian despotism, sullied with the blood of the best of its own people, would jeopardize much, if not everything, for our people and their future freedom. It is our duty to repel this danger and to safeguard

the culture and independence of our country . . . we shall not abandon our native land in its hour of need.

While Bethmann Hollweg was making this speech, the 9.30 a.m. telegram from London arrived at the British embassy. Goschen composed a formal aide-mémoire and went to see Jagow, who was at the Reichstag for the chancellor's address. Jagow said that he was unable to give the requested assurance on Belgium. He explained that German troops had crossed the frontier that morning and that Belgium had acted, 'quite naturally', in response.[21] The second telegram from London, containing the ultimatum, arrived in Berlin at about 6 p.m. Goschen wrote another aide-mémoire and went to see Jagow at the foreign ministry at about 7 p.m. Jagow explained that there had been no change in the German position. Goschen therefore asked to see the chancellor.

The talk between Goschen and Bethmann Hollweg began shortly after 7 p.m. and was conducted in English. The ambassador presented his aide-mémoire and, after it was clear Germany would not accept the British terms, asked for his passports. Goschen described what followed as 'a harangue which lasted for about twenty minutes'. Bethmann Hollweg said it was 'intolerable' that when Germany was trying to save itself Britain 'should fall upon them just for sake of the neutrality of Belgium' and that therefore Britain was 'entirely responsible' for what now happened. Goschen responded that Britain was 'bound in honour' to preserve a neutrality which it had guaranteed. The chancellor added, 'But at what price!'[22] The accounts of the talk by both men are in agreement until this point. Goschen's account then adds that Bethmann Hollweg used the notorious phrase that Britain was going to war for 'a scrap of paper'. The ambassador's account was not written that evening but was composed in the Foreign Office with the intention that it should be made public. It was written on 18 August but published with the false date of 6 August. There must be a strong suspicion that Bethmann Hollweg did not use the phrase, though he may have used something like it, and that it was an invention designed to bolster British wartime propaganda. What is not in dispute is that Goschen was in tears at the end of the meeting and had to wait in an anteroom to compose himself before he was seen by Bethmann Hollweg's staff.

The German government was unclear what the British ultimatum meant. Theodore Wolff, the editor of the *Berliner Tageblatt*, was at the foreign ministry shortly after Goschen saw Jagow and he was given permission by Stumm to print the story. Later in the evening, a special edition reached the streets of Berlin, saying Britain had declared war on Germany. The foreign ministry was less sure that this was the case and at 9.30 p.m. Zimmerman was sent to the British embassy to see Goschen. He asked the ambassador whether the request for his passports was merely the breaking-off of diplomatic relations or whether it meant war. Goschen was unclear about London's instructions too and replied that it implied war would be declared. After the news of the 'declaration of war' (which had not taken place) reached the Berlin streets, a crowd gathered in front of the British embassy and began throwing stones, breaking some of the windows. Goschen and his staff retreated to the first floor. The ambassador then telephoned the foreign ministry and they arranged for a detachment of mounted police to clear the street. Late that night Jagow called at the embassy to offer the formal apologies of the German government.

London – Evening

The British government was in the dark about what was happening in Berlin. The only information from Goschen was about his talk with Jagow at the Reichstag in the afternoon. A draft declaration of war on Germany was prepared which authorised a state of war as from 11 p.m. This was the wrong time – the ultimatum was due to expire at midnight London time. A small group of ministers – Asquith, Grey and Lloyd George – gathered in the cabinet room at 10 Downing Street – they were in a sombre mood.

At about 9.40 p.m. a news agency report was brought in saying that Germany had already declared war. A new declaration of war by Britain was hastily drafted and taken in a sealed envelope to the German embassy by a Foreign Office official, Lancelot Oliphant. About an hour later it was realised that the news agency report was false. Harold Nicolson, the son of the Foreign Office permanent secretary, was sent off to the German embassy to recover the earlier note and substitute the correct declaration. He saw the ambassador, Lichnowsky, who asked him to give his best wishes to his father. London was still officially unaware of how Germany would react to the ultimatum – although the outcome was now pretty clear – when the order was given to begin operations against Germany. Although

Austria–Hungary, which had instigated the crisis, was still only at war with Serbia, a European war, involving all the major powers, was now underway.

PART FOUR

Epilogue

19

AFTERMATH

By the morning of Wednesday 5 August the major European powers were at war, but there was still very little fighting. The German attack on the forts at Liège began in the morning and on the East Prussian frontier there was sporadic fighting with Russian units. Elsewhere, all the major powers were still embroiled in the complexities of mobilisation schedules as the conscripted men arrived at the depots, changed into uniforms, collected their weapons and joined the trains which were beginning to move towards the frontiers on their predetermined timings. The only major change in the situation was that on 6 August the British cabinet reversed the basis on which it had been working for the previous two weeks and decided that the British Expeditionary Force would, after all, be sent to France to fight along-side the French. Another set of mobilisation schedules ground into action.

Across Europe, the loose ends of the crisis were being tidied up. In Berlin the British ambassador called at the foreign ministry on the morning of 5 August to formally request the return of his passports. The Kaiser sent his aide-de-camp to call at the embassy to apologise for the demonstration of the previous evening. The Kaiser also sent his regrets for what had happened between the two allies of Waterloo and formally renounced his honorary titles of British Field Marshal and Admiral. On 6 August Goschen left Berlin, travelling by side streets, to catch a train (the Belgian minister, Baron Beyens, was a fellow traveller) which reached the Dutch border the next day. Goschen then crossed from the Hook of Holland to Harwich and by special train to Liverpool Street. The previous day the German ambassador, Lichnowsky, had travelled in the opposite direction. There was a special military guard of honour at Harwich pier to mark his departure.

On 5 August Austria–Hungary broke off diplomatic relations with Russia and the next day formally declared war. This immediately raised the question of France's relations with Austria–Hungary. They were broken off on 6 August, but there was then a pause while each side waited for the other to act first. Eventually, on 12 August, both Britain and France declared war. France cited as a reason the presence of Austro-Hungarian troops fighting alongside the German army in Alsace-Lorraine. This was untrue. In London Grey wrote a personal letter to Mensdorff:

> I cannot express the sorrow which I feel in having to make to you personally the announcement contained in my official letter . . . I should like to see you to say good-bye, and to shake hands, and to assure you how much my personal friendship remains unaltered.[1]

In the Balkans both sides were still manoeuvring for position. At 5.30 p.m. on 5 August the Austro-Hungarian minister in Cetinje was given a formal note by the Montenegrin government expelling him from the country and declaring war. The legation staff left Montenegro the next day. On the same day Russia formally offered Romania an alliance and the promise of Transylvania at the end of the war. Germany also accepted the Bulgarian terms for an alliance and instructed their ambassador in Sofia, Michahelles, to conclude an alliance immediately. That did not happen for more than a year. On 6 August a Bulgarian–Ottoman alliance was concluded but neither told the German government. Meanwhile, after a series of fiascos, the German ships *Goeben* and *Breslau* evaded the Royal Navy and arrived in Constantinople on the afternoon of 10 August. They were allowed to dock on the authority of Enver Pasha. It was a clear breach of the declared Ottoman neutrality but it was uncertain what the implications of this action would be. The Ottoman government remained bitterly divided over what course to adopt and it was not until late October, when the German ships left to bombard Russian ports in the Black Sea, that the situation was resolved. By early November, the Ottoman empire was at war with Britain, France and Russia.

Japan entered the war long before the Ottomans. The government was determined to seize the opportunity without waiting for British territory in the Far East to be attacked. Britain was soon trying to restrain its erstwhile ally – they were worried that Japan would capture German territory in the Pacific such as Samoa and Nauru that had already been promised to New Zealand and Australia. The Japanese decision to join the war was effectively taken by the cabinet on 7 August, but they waited until 15 August before giving Germany an unacceptable ultimatum. They were to withdraw all their warships from Chinese and Japanese waters and hand over, without compensation, the entire leased territory of Kiaochow in China. A reply was required within eight days. The German government did not accept the terms and Japan declared war on 23 August.

Meanwhile, in Europe, the disintegration of the socialist movement continued as it adjusted to the realities of a major war. On 6 August the British head of the Second International, Kier Hardie, wrote an editorial in *Labour Leader* saying 'the great outstanding fact' demonstrated by the crisis was 'the impotence of the moral and Labour forces of Europe'. On the same day Ramsay MacDonald resigned as leader of the Labour Party. On the previous day he had opposed the party's decision to support the Liberal government in Parliament and the vote in favour of war credits. The pacifist and anti-war movement was in similar disarray. On 6 August L. T. Hobhouse wrote to one of the ministers who had resigned from the Cabinet, John Burns. He argued:

> We cannot continue criticism of the policy which has led to this war as we did in the case of South Africa, for our safety is at stake. We can none of us now think of anything but this one object.[2]

Later in the month the German Peace Association took an even stronger line:

> We German pacifists have always recognized the right and obligation of national self-defence. Each pacifist must fulfil his common responsibilities to the Fatherland just like any other German.[3]

As the war spread across Europe during August, it was easy to forget the reason why it had started – the conflict between Austria–Hungary and Serbia. Even though Vienna had, largely at the behest of Berlin, sent the majority of its forces into Galicia to face Russia, it did launch an attack on its real enemy, Serbia. The attack, which began on 23 August, was easily repulsed. The ramshackle Serbian army even launched a counter-attack into Bosnia–Herzegovina. When Austria–Hungary had more forces available it launched another offensive and captured Belgrade on 6 November. In less than a month a Serbian counter-attack recaptured their capital and routed the Austro-Hungarian forces.

Meanwhile, the Austro-Hungarian inquiry into the assassinations, under the chief investigating judge in Sarajevo, Leo Pfeffer, was completed during September. Both Princip and Čabrinović had expected martyrdom on 28 June rather than capture and interrogation. They had not agreed what they would say and they soon exposed the whole conspiracy. The only significant participant to escape was

Mehmedbašić who fled to Montenegro before reaching Serbia. The conspirators were formally indicted on 28 September and their trial lasted from 12 October until 23 October. All except Princip seemed genuinely shocked at the consequences of their conspiracy for the whole of Europe.

The conspirators were sentenced on 28 October. Under Austro-Hungarian law nobody under the age of twenty could be sentenced to death – the authorities in Vienna thought the conspirators had been deliberately chosen with this in mind. Princip, who was just under twenty at the time of the assassinations, Čabrinović and Grabež, who were still nineteen, were all sentenced to twenty years hard labour. Those who had helped them generally got lighter sentences – Čubrilović and Popović received sentences of sixteen and thirteen years respectively. The twenty-four-year-old Danilo Ilić, who had organised the conspiracy in Sarajevo, was sentenced to death. He was hung on 3 February 1915.

Overall, thirteen people were sentenced to jail terms. Only five came out alive. Of the chief conspirators, Čabrinović and Grabež died of TB in 1916. Princip, the man who had fired the fatal shots, was held in jail at Theresienstadt in Bohemia. His mental and physical health deteriorated steadily. He had to have an arm amputated and on 28 April 1918 he too died of TB. Of the other direct participants in Sarajevo, Čubrilović and Popović were freed when the Austro-Hungarian empire collapsed in October 1918. The bodies of the conspirators were taken back to Yugoslavia in 1920. After the war, Mehmedbašić, the only one to avoid standing trial, returned to Sarajevo (now, like the rest of Bosnia–Herzegovina, part of Yugoslavia) where he worked as a gardener. On 2 February 1930 a marble plaque was unveiled on the house in front of which Princip had stood to fire the fatal shots. Its inscription read: 'On this historic spot on 28 June 1914 on *Vidovdan* Gavrilo Princip proclaimed freedom.' A religious ceremony was conducted by the Orthodox Archbishop of Sarajevo. It was attended by relatives of the other dead conspirators – Čabruiović and Grabež. The secretary of Narodna Odbrana Milan Bozić, led the crowd in singing hymns to the 'hero' and 'martyr' Princip.

The organisers of the conspiracy in Belgrade were also dead before the end of the war. Major Vojin Tankosić was killed in October 1915 in the severe fighting which led to the expulsion of the Serbian government and army from the country. The government took up residence in Salonika and it was here, on 15 December 1916, that

Colonel Dragutin Dimitrijvić ('Apis') was arrested together with other senior members of *Ujedinjenje ili Smrt*. Dimitrijvić was charged with plotting to kill Crown Prince Alexander and the prime minister, Pašić. Whether there was a genuine conspiracy to mount such a coup is unclear, but Alexander and Pašić were suspicious about the continuing activities of *Ujedinjenje ili Smrt*.

During his trial in April 1917, 'Apis' confessed that he had organised the Sarajevo conspiracy so as to weaken the military and the anti-Serbian elements in Vienna. This was a catastrophic misjudgement, if it was true – his more likely motivation was to weaken the Serbian government and strengthen the hardline nationalists in *Ujedinjenje ili Smrt*. Apis said he only approved the conspiracy after the Russian military attaché, Artamonov, promised that Russia would support Serbia and after he had also provided the money to fund the operation. The balance of probability is that his confessions are true – they are certainly consistent with the other evidence available about the conspiracy. 'Apis' was sentenced to death for the conspiracy against Alexander and Pašić. Both Britain and Russia intervened to try and stop the sentence being carried out but he was executed by firing squad on 26 June 1917.

The surviving conspirators kept their extreme Serbian nationalist ideals to the end of their lives. Čubrilović, who had stood near the Čumurja bridge on 28 June but lost his nerve and failed to take any action, gave a lecture in Belgrade in 1937. In it, he outlined a programme for the expulsion of the majority Albanian population in the Kosovo province, the historic heartland of Serbia. He argued that 'the only method and the only means is the brutal force of an organised governmental power, and we have always been above them in this'.[4] His lecture was not published until 1988. Just over ten years later, a Serbian nationalist government did use its power to try and expel the Albanians from Kosovo.

20

CONSEQUENCES

The European war brought about by the assassinations at Sarajevo and the diplomatic crisis of July 1914 did not turn out to be the short war that most military planners expected. The defects inherent in the German plans were painfully apparent within a month of the outbreak of fighting. The mobilization plan worked well and the bulk of the German army was able to march through Belgium into northern France. Then, as could have been foreseen, it ran out of steam as it tried to march faster than the French could relocate their forces using the railway network. The turn to the east of Paris exposed, as predicted, the German right flank. In early September the German attack was first halted and then turned back in a series of battles along the Marne. The limited German forces in East Prussia scored a stunning success against an incompetently led Russian attack, but there was no prospect of following this up to score a decisive victory as Russian mobilisation poured forces into Poland. Within little more than a month, German strategy was in ruins and their prospect of a quick and stunning victory had passed.

In the west, the armies tried to manoeuvre round each other, Brussels and Antwerp fell to the German army and the Belgian government was left holding on to a tiny piece of the country. By the late autumn, the armies had reached the sea and a long line of trenches and fortifications stretched from the Channel to the Swiss frontier. As the stalemate continued, the network of trenches and defences became ever more complicated. The power of the defence relying on trenches, fortifications, barbed wire and machine guns proved almost impossible to overcome. Various offensive weapons were devised – poison gas and tanks – but they could not achieve a breakthrough. Neither could massive artillery bombardments. The attacks that were launched rapidly faltered in the face of defensive power and the inability to control offensive operations – telephone lines were easily destroyed and man-portable radios were not available. The attacks that did take place became battles of attrition and some, such as the German attack at Verdun in 1916, were launched for exactly this purpose. Along the eastern front, trench systems did not develop on an extensive scale, and open and relatively fast-moving warfare remained the norm. The front line ebbed and flowed, but decisive results were not obtained because of the large distances involved.

At sea there were no decisive battles – the full British and German fleets met only once at Jutland and the result was a draw slightly favouring the Germans. The British established a blockade in an attempt to starve Germany into submission. Germany responded with U-boat warfare in the Atlantic designed to do the same to Britain. As the war dragged on it developed into a test of economic and social strength. Peacetime economies were mobilised as a war of production developed and social mobilisation became ever more important as more men were drafted into the armed forces and women took their place in the factory and elsewhere. The development of warfare on this scale meant that as the casualties and costs rose, war aims widened too. The sacrifices on each side meant that only total victory became acceptable.

The war expanded to include nearly the whole of Europe. Italy joined the Allies in early 1915 after receiving promises of the territory it wanted to gain from Austria–Hungary. Its military performance was so bad that it was more of a liability than an asset. Six months later Bulgaria finally joined Germany and Austria–Hungary. It was a joint offensive that finally conquered Serbia in October 1915 and drove the Serbian army, government and much of the population out of the country. In 1916 Romania joined the Allies, attacked Austria–Hungary and was defeated. In that year Portugal joined the war too, though fighting with German forces in Africa had been underway since late 1914. The most fundamental development, with profound implications for future international relations, was the entry of the United States into the war in April 1917. It was the consequence of the German decision to launch unrestricted submarine warfare in the North Atlantic in an attempt to starve Britain into submission.

The entry of the United States saved the Allies who were, by early 1917, on the brink of defeat. Russia collapsed into revolution in February. After numerous inconclusive offensives, the French army mutinied and refused to do more than stay on the defensive. Britain, which had been financing the war effort of its allies and buying munitions on a vast scale in the United States, was only weeks away from bankruptcy as its gold and dollar reserves were exhausted. Although it took the United States more than a year to mobilise, train and equip its armed forces, its financial and economic strength kept

Britain and France in the war. Germany launched one last, great offensive in the spring of 1918 that brought Britain and France to the edge of defeat. During the summer and autumn, German forces were slowly pushed eastwards but were still on Belgian and French soil when they sued for peace.

When the armistice came into effect on 11 November 1918, Europe had been ruined by the largest war ever fought. The European nations mobilised over sixty million men into their armed forces. Of these, eight and a half million were killed and over twenty-one million wounded. The greatest proportion of casualties were in France and Russia, where three-quarters of those mobilised were either killed, wounded, taken prisoner or missing – almost sixteen million men. In Germany almost two-thirds of those mobilised were casualties. Large areas, particularly in northern France and Belgium, were devastated by four years of intensive fighting. France lost about half of its national wealth. The civilian casualties were difficult to count. Some were killed in the combat areas or in reprisals, a few more from the limited bombing raids by airships and aircraft. Far more were weakened by starvation, especially in Germany as the British blockade took effect. At the end of the war millions were killed as a wave of influenza affected already weakened populations.

By November 1918 much of the old European order and those who had begun the war had been swept away. The Russian state was the least able to withstand the pressures of total war. As many of the governing elite had prophesised in July 1914, revolution was the almost inevitable outcome. The Tsar abdicated in February 1917 and he and his family were later shot by Bolshevik revolutionaries. The government set up after the revolution proved unstable and, with peasants demanding land and soldiers peace, the Bolsheviks seized power in October. That government negotiated a separate peace with Germany early in 1918 and Russia disintegrated into a civil war that lasted for more than three years. The Emperor Franz Josef died in 1916 and within little more than two years the Austro-Hungarian empire disintegrated, as allied armies advanced through the Balkans from their base at Salonika. The empire, which had been one of the strongest European powers for more than four centuries, collapsed and was replaced by the petty states that continued to quarrel over the complex national and ethnic map of Eastern Europe and the Balkans. Serbia survived and came to dominate the new Yugoslavia which incorporated nearly all the areas of 'Greater Serbia' that the extreme

Serb nationalists demanded. The great rival of the Habsburg empire since the fourteenth century – the Ottoman empire – was defeated and also collapsed in the autumn of 1918. As the German armies slowly retreated eastwards in the autumn of 1918, the ruling elite that dominated decision – taking in July 1914 tried to avoid taking the responsibility for negotiating peace. The German state created in 1871 disintegrated in early November with a mutiny among the fleet at Kiel and revolution in Berlin. The Kaiser fled into exile in the Netherlands. The Socialist Party took over the government, a republic was declared and they were left with the unenviable task and the opprobrium of negotiating the armistice.

By the end of the war, the three great empires which had dominated European politics only four years earlier and which had plunged Europe into war so recklessly – Russia, Austria–Hungary and Germany – were all consigned to the dustbin of history. In his speech at the Cirque Royale in Brussels on 29 July 1914, just forty-eight hours before he was murdered, the French socialist leader, Jean Jaurès, forecast with uncanny accuracy what would happen if Europe did go to war:

> When typhus finishes the work begun by bullets, disillusioned men will turn on their rulers whether German, French, Russian or Italian, and demand their explanation for all those corpses.

Appendices

Appendix One

The Austro-Hungarian Ultimatum to
Serbia, 23 July 1914

On 31 March 1909 the Royal Serbian Minister at the court of Vienna by order of his Government made the following declaration before the Imp. and Royal Government:

'Serbia acknowledges that none of its rights have been touched by the situation created in Bosnia and Herzegovina and that it will therefore accommodate itself to the decisions which the powers will resolve with regard to the Article XXV of the Treaty of Berlin. Serbia, in following the advice of the Great Powers, pledges itself to give up the attitude of protest and resistance which it adopted since last October with regard to the annexation and it pledges itself furthermore to change the course of its present policy towards Austria–Hungary and to live on terms of friendly and neighbourly relations.'

The history of latter years and especially the grievous events of 28 June have given proofs of a subversive movement in Serbia, whose ultimate aim it is to separate certain portions from the territory of Austria–Hungary. This movement, which has developed under the eyes of the Serbian Government, has resulted in acts of terrorism outside the frontiers of the kingdom, in a series of attempts at murder and in murders.

Far from keeping the formal promises given in the declaration of 31 March 1909, the Royal Serbian Government has done nothing to suppress this movement. It tolerated the criminal doings of the diverse societies and associations directed against the Monarchy, the outrageous language of the press, the glorification of the instigators of the plots; it allowed officers and officials to take part in subversive plans, tolerated a most unhealthy propaganda in public instruction and gave permission for manifestations, which caused the Serbian population to hate the Monarchy and despise its institutions.

The toleration, of which the Serbian Government was guilty, lasted until the very moment when the events of 28 June showed all the world the horrible consequences of such toleration.

The depositions and confessions of the criminal perpetrators of the plot of 28 June prove, that the murder of Sarajevo was prepared in Belgrade, that the murderers had received the weapons and bombs, with which they were armed, from officers and officials, belonging to the Narodna Odbrana and that the conveyance of criminals and weapons to Bosnia had been prepared and carried through by Serbian frontier organs.

The above-quoted results of the judicial inquiry do not permit the Imp. and Royal Government to keep up its attitude of patient observation, maintained for years in the face of criminal dealings, which emanate from Belgrade and thence spread to the territory of the Monarchy. These results make it the duty of the Imp. and Royal Government to put an end to such doings, which are constantly threatening the peace of the Monarchy.

To attain this end, the Imp. and Royal Government finds itself obliged to demand from the Serbian Government an official assurance that it condemns the propaganda directed against Austria–Hungary and in their entirety the dealings whose ultimate aim it is to separate parts of the territory belonging to the Monarchy and that it pledges itself to suppress with all the means in its power this criminal and terrorist propaganda.

With a view to giving these assurances a solemn character, the Royal Serbian Government will publish the following declaration on the first page of its official press organ of 26 July:

The Royal Serbian Government condemns the propaganda directed against Austria–Hungary, that is the entirety of the ambitions, whose ultimate aim it is to separate parts of the territory belonging to the Austrian–Hungarian Monarchy and regrets sincerely the horrible consequences of these criminal ambitions.

The Royal Serbian Government regrets that Serbian officers and officials have taken part in the propaganda above-mentioned and thereby imperilled the friendly and neighbourly relations, which the Royal Government had solemnly promised to cultivate in its declaration of 31 March 1909.

The Royal Government, which condemns and rejects every thought and every attempt to interfere on behalf of the inhabitants of any part of Austria–Hungary, considers it a duty to warn officers, officials and indeed all the inhabitants of the kingdom, that it will in future use great severity against such persons, as will be found guilty of similar acts, which the Government will make every effort to suppress.

This declaration will at the same time be communicated to the Royal army by an order of His Majesty the King, and will besides be published in the official organ of the army.

The Royal Serbian Government will moreover pledge itself to the following:

1. to suppress every publication likely to inspire hatred and contempt against the Monarchy or whose general tendencies are directed against the integrity of the latter;

2. to begin immediately dissolving the society called Narodna Odbrana; to seize all its means of propaganda and to act in the same way against all the societies and associations in Serbia, which are busy with propaganda against Austria–Hungary; the Royal Government will take the necessary measures to prevent these societies continuing their efforts under another name or in another form;

3. to eliminate without delay from public instruction everything that serves or might serve the propaganda against Austria–Hungary, both where teachers or books are concerned;

4. to remove from military service and from the administration all officers and officials who are guilty of having taken part in the propaganda against Austria–Hungary, whose names and the proofs of whose guilt the Imp. and Royal Government will communicate to the Royal Government;

5. to consent that Imp. and Royal Officials assist in Serbia in suppressing the subversive movement directed against the territorial integrity of the Monarchy;

6. to have a judicial inquiry instituted against all those who took part in the plot of 28 June, if they are to be found on Serbian territory; the Imp. and Royal Government will delegate organs who will take an active part in these inquiries;

7. to arrest without delay Major Voija Tankosić and a certain Milan Ciganović, a Serbian government official, both compromised by the results of the inquiry;

8. to take effective measures so as to prevent the Serbian authorities from taking part in the smuggling of weapons and explosives across the frontier; to dismiss from service and severely punish those organs of the frontier service at Schabatz and Loznica, who helped the perpetrators of the crime of Sarajevo to reach Bosnia in safety;

9. to give the Imp. and Royal Government an explanation of the unjustified remarks of high Serbian functionaries in Serbia as well as in foreign countries, who, notwithstanding their official positions, did not

hesitate to speak in hostile terms of Austria–Hungary in interviews given just after the event of 28 June;

10. to inform the Imp. and Royal Government without delay that the measures summarized in the above points have been carried out. The Imp. and Royal Government expects the answer of the Royal Government to reach it not later than Saturday, 25 inst., at six in the afternoon.

ÖUA 10395

Appendix Two

The Serbian Government Reply to Austria–Hungary, 25 July 1914

The Royal Serbian Government have received the communication of the Imperial and Royal Government of 23rd inst., and are convinced that their reply will remove any misunderstanding which may threaten to impair the good neighbourly relations between the Austro-Hungarian Monarchy and the Kingdom of Serbia.

Conscious of the fact that the protests which were made both from the tribune of the national Skupština and in the declarations and actions of the responsible representatives of the State – protests which were cut short by the declarations made by the Serbian Government on 31 March 1909 – have not been renewed on any occasion as regards the great neighbouring Monarchy, and that no attempt has been made since that time either by the successive Royal Governments or by their organs, to change the political and legal state of affairs created in Bosnia and Herzegovina, the Royal Government draw attention to the fact that in this connection the Imperial and Royal Government have made no representations except one concerning a school book, and on that occasion the Imperial and Royal Government received an entirely satisfactory explanation. Serbia has several times given proofs of her pacific and moderate policy during the Balkan crisis, and it is thanks to Serbia and to the sacrifice that she has made in the exclusive interest of European peace that that peace has been preserved. The Royal Government cannot be held responsible for manifestations of a private character, such as articles in the press and the peaceable work of societies – manifestations which take place in nearly all countries in the ordinary course of events, and which, as a general rule, escape official control. The Royal Government are all the less responsible, in view of the fact that at the time of the solution of a series of questions which arose between Serbia and Austria–Hungary they gave proof of a great readiness to oblige, and thus succeeded in settling the majority of these questions to the advantage of the two neighbouring countries.

For these reasons the Royal Government have been pained and

surprised at the statements, according to which members of the Kingdom of Serbia are supposed to have participated in the preparations for the crime committed at Sarajevo; the Royal Government expected to be invited to collaborate in an investigation of all that concerns this crime, and they were ready, in order to prove the entire correctness of their attitude, to take measures against any persons concerning whom representations were made to them. Falling in, therefore, with the desire of the Imperial and Royal Government, they are prepared to hand over for trial any Serbian subject, without regard to his situation or rank, of whose complicity in the crime of Sarajevo proofs are forthcoming, and more especially they undertake to cause to be published on the first page of the *Journal officiel*, on the date of 26 July, the following declaration:

'The Royal Government of Serbia condemn all propaganda which may be directed against Austria–Hungary, that is to say, all such tendencies as aim at ultimately detaching from the Austro-Hungarian Monarchy territories which form part thereof, and they sincerely deplore the baneful consequences of these criminal movements. The Royal Government regret that, according to the communication from the Imperial and Royal Government, certain Serbian officers and officials should have taken part in the above-mentioned propaganda, and thus compromised the good neighbourly relations to which the Royal Serbian Government was solemnly engaged by the declaration of 31 March 1909, which declaration disapproves and repudiates all idea or attempt at interference with the destiny of the inhabitants of any part whatsoever of Austria–Hungary, and they consider it their duty formally to warn officers, officials and the entire population of the kingdom that henceforth they will take the most rigorous steps against all such persons as are guilty of such acts, to prevent and to repress which they will use their utmost endeavour.'

This declaration will be brought to the knowledge of the Royal Army in an order of the day, in the name of His Majesty the King, by his Royal Highness the Crown Prince Alexander, and will be published in the next official army bulletin.

The Royal Government further undertake:

1. To introduce at the first regular convocation of the Skupština, a provision into the press law providing for the most severe punishment for incitement to hatred or contempt of the Austro-Hungarian Monarchy, and for taking action against any publication the general tendency of which is directed against the territorial integrity of

Austria–Hungary. The Government engage at the approaching revision of the Constitution to cause an amendment to be introduced into Article XXII of the Constitution of such a nature that such publication may be confiscated, a proceeding at present impossible under the categorical terms of Article XXII of the Constitution.

2. The Government possess no proof, nor does the note of the Imperial and Royal Government furnish them with any, that the Narodna Odbrana and other similar societies have committed up to the present any criminal act of this nature through the proceedings of any of their members. Nevertheless, the Royal Government will accept the demand of the Imperial and Royal Government and will dissolve the Narodna Odbrana Society and every other society which may be directing its efforts against Austria–Hungary.

3. The Royal Serbian Government undertakes to remove without delay from their public educational establishments in Serbia all that serves or could serve to foment propaganda against Austria–Hungary, whenever the Imperial and Royal Government furnish them with facts and proofs of this propaganda.

4. The Royal Government also agree to remove from military service all such persons as the judicial inquiry may have proved to be guilty of acts directed against the integrity of the territory of the Austro-Hungarian Monarchy, and they expect the Imperial and Royal Government to communicate to them at a later date the names and acts of these offices and officials for the purpose of the proceedings which are to be taken against them.

5. The Royal Government must confess that they do not clearly grasp the meaning or the scope of the demand made by the Imperial and Royal Government that Serbia shall undertake to accept the collaboration of the organs of the Imperial and Royal Government upon their territory, but they declare that they will admit such collaboration as agrees with the principle of international law, with criminal procedure, and with good neighbourly relations.

6. It goes without saying that the Royal Government consider it their duty to open an inquiry against all such persons as are, or eventually may be implicated in the plot of 28 June, and who happen to be within the territory of the kingdom. As regards the participation in this inquiry of Austro-Hungarian agents or authorities appointed for this purpose by the Imperial and Royal Government, the Royal Government cannot accept such an arrangement, as it would be a violation of the Constitution and of the law of criminal procedure;

nevertheless, in concrete cases communications as to the results of the investigation in question might be given to the Austro-Hungarian agents.

7. The Royal Government proceeded, on the very evening of the delivery of the Note, to arrest Commandant Voija Tankosić. As regards Milan Ciganović, who is a subject of the Austro-Hungarian Monarchy and who up to 28 June was employed (on probation) by the directorate of railways, it has not yet been possible to arrest him.

The Austro-Hungarian Government are requested to be so good as to supply as soon as possible, in the customary form, the presumptive evidence of guilt, as well as the eventual proofs of guilt which have been collected up to the present, at the inquiry at Sarajevo for the purposes of the later inquiry.

8. The Serbian Government will reinforce and extend the measures which have been taken for preventing the illicit traffic of arms and explosives across the frontier. It goes without saying that they will immediately order an inquiry and will severely punish the frontier officials on the Schabatz–Loznica line who have failed in their duty and allowed the authors of the crime of Sarajevo to pass.

9. The Royal Government will gladly give explanations of the remarks made by their officials whether in Serbia or abroad, in interviews after the crime which according to the statement of the Imperial and Royal Government were hostile towards the Monarchy, as soon as the Imperial and Royal Government have communicated to them the passages in question in these remarks, and as soon as they have shown that the remarks were actually made by the said officials, although the Royal Government will itself take steps to collect evidence and proofs.

10. The Royal Government will inform the Imperial and Royal Government of the execution of the measures comprised under the above heads, in so far as this has not already been done by the present note, as soon as each measure has been ordered and carried out.

If the Imperial and Royal Government are not satisfied with this reply, the Serbian Government, considering that it is not to the common interest to precipitate the solution of this question, are ready, as always, to accept a pacific understanding, either by referring this question to the decision of the International Tribunal of The Hague, or to the Great Powers which took part in the drawing up of the declaration made by the Serbian Government on 31 March 1909.

ÖUA 10648 – French version, ÖUA 10860 – German version

APPENDIX THREE

INDIVIDUALS INVOLVED IN THE

THIRTEEN DAYS

Austria–Hungary

Ambrozy, Count Ludwig   First Counsellor, Rome embassy
Berchtold, Count Leopold   Minister for Foreign Affairs
Bienerth, Baron Military   Attaché, Berlin
Bilinski, Leon Common   Finance Minister
Burián, Baron István von   Hungarian representative in Vienna
Conrad von Hötzendorf, Franz   Chief of the General Staff
Czernin von und zu Chudenitz, Count Ottakar   Minister, Bucharest
Forgách, von Ghymes und Gacs, Count Janos   Chief of Section,
Ministry of Foreign
Affairs
Gellinek, Otto   Military Attaché, Belgrade
Giesl von Gieslingen, Baron   Minister, Belgrade
Hoyos, Count Alexander   Chef du Cabinet of Foreign Minister
Krobatin, Alexander von   Minister for War
Macchio, Karl, Freiherr von   Senior official, Ministry of Foreign
Affairs
Mensdorff, Pouilly-Dietrichstein Count Albert   Ambassador, London
Merey, von Kapos-Mere, Kajetan   Ambassador, Rome
Montenuovo, Prince Alfred   Chief Controller, Imperial Household
Musulin, von Gomirje Baron Alexander   Head of Chancery,
Ministry of Foreign Affairs
Otto, E   Minister, Cetinje
Pallavicini, Margrave Janos   Ambassador, Constantinople
Pállfy, Count   Minister, Holy See
Pfeffer, Leo   Investigating judge, Sarajevo
Potiorek, Oskar, von, General   Governor, Bosnia–Herzegovina
Stürgkh, Count Karl   Prime Minister of Austria
Szápáry, Graf, Friedrich   Ambassador, St Petersburg
Szécsen, von Temerin, Count Miklos   Ambassador, Paris

Szilassy, von Szilas und Pilas, J   Minister, Athens
Szögyény-Marich, Count   Ambassador, Berlin
Tarnowski von Tarnow, Count   Minister, Sofia
Tisza, Count István   Prime Minister of Hungary
Wiesner, Friedrich von   Legal Counsellor, Ministry of Foreign
                    Affairs

Belgium
Bassompierre, Albert de   Secretary to Minister of Foreign Affairs
Beyens, Baron Napoleon   Minister, Berlin
Broqueville, Charles de   Chef du Cabinet (Prime Minister)
Carton de Wiart, H.   Minister for Justice
Davignon, J.   Minister for Foreign Affairs
Elst, van der, Baron L.   Secretary-General, Ministry of Foreign
                    Affairs
Fallon, A.   Minister, The Hague
Gaffier, Baron D'Hestroy   Political Director, Ministry of Foreign
                    Affairs

Bulgaria
Radev, S.   Minister, Bucharest
Radoslavov, V.   Prime Minister
Toshev, M.   Minister, Constantinople

France
Barrère, Camille   Ambassador, Rome
Beau, Jean   Minister, Berne
Berthelot, Philippe   Director, Ministry of Foreign Affairs
Bienvenu-Martin, J. B.   Minister of Justice, Acting Minister of
                    Foreign Affairs
Blondel, Jean   Minister, Bucharest
Bompard, Maurice   Ambassador, Constantinople
Boppe, Jules   Minister, Belgrade (from July 1914)
Cambon, Jules   Ambassador, Berlin
Cambon, Paul   Ambassador, London
Delaroche-Vernet, P. H.   Minister, Cetinje
Descos, Léon   Minister, Belgrade (until July 1914)

Doumergue, Gaston   Minister for Foreign Affairs (from August 1914)
Dumaine, Alfred   Ambassador, Vienna
Ferry, Abel   Under-Secretary, Ministry of Foreign Affairs
Geoffray, Léon   Ambassador, Madrid
Jaurès, Jean   Socialist deputy
Joffre, General Joseph   Chief of the General Staff
Klobukowski, A. W.   Minister, Brussels
Margerie, Bruno   Political Director, Ministry of Foreign Affairs
Messimy, Adolfe   Minister for War
Mollard, Armand   Minister, Luxembourg
Paléologue, Maurice   Ambassador, St Petersburg
Poincaré, Raymond   President
Viviani, René   Prime Minister, Minister for Foreign Affairs (until
        August 1914)

Germany
Bassewitz, Count K. von   Chargé, Athens
Below-Saleske, Klaus von   Minister, Brussels
Bethmann Hollweg, Theobald von   Imperial Chancellor
Capelle, Vice-Admiral   Acting Navy Minister
Chelius, General Oskar von   Kaiser's representative at Russian Court
Falkenhayn, General Erich von   Minister for War
Flotow, Hans von   Ambassador, Rome
Jagow, Gottlieb von   Minister for Foreign Affairs
Lerchenfeld, Count   Bavarian Minister, Berlin
Leuckart, Freiherr von   Saxon military representative, Berlin
Lichnowsky, Prince von   Ambassador, London
Lyncker, General Baron   Head, Kaiser's Military Cabinet
Michahelles, Gustav   Minister, Sofia
Moltke, General Helmuth von   Chief of the General Staff
Müller, F. von   Minister, The Hague
Plessen, General Hans von   Adjutant-General to Kaiser
Pohl, Admiral   Naval Chief of Staff
Pourtalès, Count Friedrich   Ambassador, St Petersburg
Rex, Count von   Ambassador, Tokyo
Romberg, Freiherr von   Minister, Berne
Schoen, Freiherr Wilhelm   Ambassador, Paris
Stumm, Wilhelm von   Political Director, Ministry of Foreign Affairs
Tirpitz, Grossadmiral Alfred von   Navy Minister

Tschirschky und Bögendorff, Heinrich von Ambassador, Vienna
Waldburg zu Wolfegg und Waldsee Graf, von Chargé, Bucharest
Waldthausen, Baron Julius Minister, Bucharest
Wangenheim, Baron H. von Ambassador, Constantinople
Zimmerman, Alfred Under-Secretary, Ministry of Foreign Affairs

Italy

Avarna di Gualtieri, Duca Giuseppe Ambassador, Vienna
Biancheri, Chiaporri Secretary to Ministry of Foreign Affairs
Bollati, Riccardo Ambassador, Berlin
Carlotti di Riparbella, Marquis Ambassador, St Petersburg
Faschiotti, Baron Carlo Minister, Bucharest
Garroni, Marquis Ambassador, Constantinople
Imperiali di Francavilla, Marquis Guglielmo Ambassador, London
Martino, Giacomo di Secretary-General, Ministry of Foreign Affairs
Salandra, Antonio Prime Minister
San Giuliano, Marchese Antonio di Minister for Foreign Affairs
Tittoni, Tommaso Ambassador, Paris

Montenegro

Plamenac Foreign Minister
Vukotic Prime Minister

Romania

Bratianu, Joan Prime Minister
Porumbaro, N. Foreign Minister

Russia

Artamonov, General Victor Military Attaché, Belgrade
Benckendorff, Count Alexander Ambassador, London
Bronevski, A. Chargé, Berlin
Dobrorolski, General Sergei Chief of Mobilisation Section
Fredericks, Baron Vladimir Minister at Russian Court
Giers, A. Minister, Cetinje
Hartwig, Nicholas Minister, Belgrade
Ignatiev, Lieutenant Colonel Military Attaché, Paris

Izvolsky, Alexander   Ambassador, Paris
Krivoshein, A. V.   Minister for Agriculture
Krupensky, A.   Ambassador, Rome
Kudashev, N.   Counsellor at embassy, Vienna
Potapov, General N.   Military Attaché, Cetinje
Savinsky, A.   Minister, Sofia
Sazonov, Serge   Minister for Foreign Affairs
Schilling, Baron von   Head of Chancery, Ministry of Foreign Affairs
Sevastopulo   Counsellor at embassy, Paris
Shebeko, N.   Ambassador, Vienna
Strandtmann, B.   Counsellor at legation, Belgrade
Sukhomlinov, General   Minister for War
Sverbeev, Serge   Ambassador, Berlin
Yanushkevich, General   Chief of the General Staff

Serbia

Bogicević, Miloš   Chargé, Berlin
Čabrinović, Nedeljko   Sarajevo conspirator
Ciganović, Milan   Serbian railway official, Sarajevo conspirator
Čubrilović, Vaso   Sarajevo conspirator
Dimitrijvić, Colonel Dragutin ('Apis')   Head of Serbian army
                                         intelligence
Grabež, Trifko   Sarajevo conspirator
Gruić, Slavko   Secretary-General, Ministry of Foreign Affairs
Ilić, Danilo   Sarajevo conspirator
Jovanović, Jovan   Minister, Vienna
Jovanović, Ljuba   Minister of Public Instruction
Mehmedbašić, Mohammed   Sarajevo conspirator
Mihailjović, Ljuba   Chargé, Rome
Pacu, L.   Minister of Finance
Pašić, Nicholas   Prime Minister
Popović, Major Rade   Serbian frontier official, Sarajevo conspirator
Princip, Gavrilo   Sarajevo conspirator, assassin of Archduke Franz
                  Ferdinand and Sophie
Protić, S.   Minister of the Interior
Putnik, General Radomir   Chief of Staff, Serbian army
Sajinović, Dr   Chief, political section, Ministry of Foreign Affairs
Spalajković, Miroslav   Minister, St Petersburg
Tankosić, Major Voija   Sarajevo conspirator

United Kingdom

Asquith, Henry   Prime Minister
Barclay, Sir George   Minister, Bucharest
Beauchamp, William, Earl of   Lord President of the Council
Bertie, Viscount, Sir, F.   Ambassador, Paris
Bonham-Carter, Sir Maurice   Private Secretary to Prime Minister
Buchanan, Sir George   Ambassador, St Petersburg
Bunsen, Sir Maurice de   Ambassador, Vienna
Carnegie, Sir Launcelot   Ambassador, Lisbon
Chilton, H. G.   Chargé, The Hague
Churchill, Winston   First Lord of the Admiralty
Crackanthorpe, D.   Chargé, Belgrade
Crewe, Lord   Secretary of State for India
Des Graz, C. L.   Minister, Belgrade
Goschen, Sir William   Ambassador, Berlin
Greene, Sir William   Ambassador, Tokyo
Grey, Sir Edward   Secretary of State for Foreign Affairs
Haldane, Viscount Richard   Lord Chancellor
Howard, Esmé   Minister, Stockholm
Kitchener, Horatio, Earl   Agent and Consul-General, Egypt
Lloyd George, David   Chancellor of the Exchequer
Lowther, Sir Henry   Minister, Copenhagen
MacDonald, Ramsay   Chairman, Parliamentary Labour Party
McKenna, Reginald   Home Secretary
Masterman, Charles   Chancellor, Duchy of Lancaster
Morley, Viscount John   Lord Privy Seal
Nicolson, Sir Arthur   Permanent Secretary, Foreign Office
Pease, J. A.   President, Board of Education
Rodd, Sir J. Rennell   Ambassador, Rome
Rumbold, Sir Horace   Chargé, Berlin
Runciman, Walter   President, Board of Trade
Samuel, Herbert   President, Local Government Board
Simon, Sir John   Attorney-General
Tyrrell, Sir William   Private Secretary to Sir Edward Grey
Villiers, Sir Francis   Minister, Brussels

Notes

Abbreviations

ÖUA	Austro-Hungarian Documents
BD	British Documents
DD	German Documents (Kautsky collection)
DDI	Italian Documents
DF	French Documents
DSP	Serbian Documents
Geiss	July 1914: Selected Documents

2 The Conspiracy

1. Hehn, *The Origins of Modern Pan-Serbism*, pp. 159–63
2. MacKenzie, *Apis*, pp. ix–x
3. FO 3711472, Serbia, Annual Report, 1911

3 The Reaction

1. DF. 3. x. 464/474
2. Redlich Diary, 29.6.14
3. De Bunsen Diary, 28.6.14
4. Haupt, *Socialism and the Great War*, p. 184
5. Albertini, *The Origins of the War of 1914*, Vol. 2, p. 217
6. BD. xi. 36. 7.7.14
7. BD. xi. 49. 9.7.14
8. NEFF Box 1. Letter to Franz Josef

4 Europe in 1914

1. CAB/1/32/3. 1.1.14
2. FO 371/2076. 21.7.14
3. BD. vi. 575. 15.4.12
4. BD. x. ii. 540. 27.4.14
5. FO 800/373 21.4.14

6. BD. viii. 311
7. Helmrich, 'Belgian Concern over Neutrality and British Intentions', p. 422
8. B-M Archiv. W10/50279. No. 94. 18.5.14
9. Röhl, *1914: Delusion or Design*, pp. 31–2
10. Cd 7748. Q40788
11. FO 371/1991 24.6.14
12. BD. ix. ii. 467. 31.1.13

5 The Twenty-Four Days
1. FO 800/372 19.1.14
2. FO 800/374 5.5.14
3. Conrad Memoirs. Geiss, p. 64
4. Geiss, pp. 64–5
5. ÖUA. viii. 9978. 1.7.14
6. ÖUA. viii. 9966. 1.7.14
7. ÖUA. viii 9984. 4.7.14
8. Ibid.
9. Conrad Memoirs, Vol. 4, p. 36
10. Geiss, pp. 67–8
11. Ibid., pp. 64–5
12. Albertini, op. cit., Vol. 2, pp. 485–6
13. ÖUA. viii. 10058. 5.7.14, 7.35 p.m.
14. Falkenhayn to Moltke. Geiss, pp. 77–8
15. Plessen Diary, 5.7.14. Geiss, p. 71
16. Betrab to Moltke, 6.7.14. Albertini, Vol. 2, p. 142
17. ÖUA. viii. 10076. 6.7.14
18. ÖUA. viii. 10118. 7.7.14
19. Rauchensteiner, 'Der Tod des Doppeladlers'. p. 75
20. ÖUA. viii. 10116. 8.7.14
21. ÖUA. viii. 10145. 8.7.14
22. Geiss, pp. 106–8
23. Ibid., p. 107
24. Ibid., p. 109
25. ÖUA. viii. 10215. 12.7.14
26. DD. i. 40. 14.7.14
27. ÖUA. viii. 10252/3. 13.7.14
28. Geiss, pp. 114–15
29. Ibid., p. 113
30. Ibid., p. 131

31. Ibid., pp. 151–4
32. BD. xi. 76. 21.7.14
33. FO 371/1899 5.7.14
34. De Bunsen MSS. Box 15. 7.7.14
35. Geiss, pp. 104–5
36. Goschen Diary, p. 40
37. FO 371/2076 8.6.14
38. Ibid., 21.7.14
39. BD. xi. 50. 16.7.14
40. BD. xi. 56. 17.7.14
41. F. Maurice, 'Haldane 1856–1915', pp. 349–52
42. Geiss, pp. 158–9
43. BD. xi. 60. 18.7.14
44. DD. i. 42. 14.7.14 & DD. i. 51. 15.7.14
45. ÖUA. viii. 10550. 23.7.14
46. DDI. 101. 7.7.14
47. DSP. 449. 16.7.14
48. DSP. 462. 18.7.14
49. Geiss, pp. 127–30
50. DD. i. 100. 21.7.14
51. DD. i. 72. 18.7.14
52. Stone, 'Hungary and the crisis of July 1914', p.169
53. ÖUA. viii. 10459. 21.7.14

6 **Thursday 23 July**
 1. ÖUA. viii. 10554. 23.7.14
 2. DD. i. 136. 23.7.14
 3. ÖUA. viii. 10592. 23.7.14
 4. Hansard, Col. 727. 23.7.14
 5. Goschen Diary, 23.7.14, p. 290
 6. Cecil, 'Albert Ballin', p. 207
 7. Albertini, Vol. 2, p. 346
 8. DSP. 498. 24.7.14
 9. R. Clark, 'Freud: The Man and his Cause', p. 364
10. Haupt, op. cit., p. 187
11. Jarausch, 'The Illusion of Limited War', p. 62

7   **Friday 24 July**

1.   Albertini, Vol. 2, p. 349
2.   DSP. 505. 24.7.14
3.   DSP. 511. 24.7.14
4.   DDI. 473. 24.7.14
5.   Geiss, pp. 173–4
6.   Ibid., p. 192
7.   ÖUA. viii. 10685. 24.7.14
8.   ÖUA. viii. 10571. 24.7.14
9.   Geiss, pp. 194–5
10. BD. xi. 103. 24.7.14
11. Albertini, Vol. 2, p. 590
12. Geiss, p. 179
13. ÖUA. viii. 10608. 24.7.14
14. BD. xi. 102. 24.7.14
15. Geiss, pp. 175–6
16. BD. xi. 101. 24.7.14
17. Ibid.
18. CAB 41/35/20. 25.7.14
19. Asquith to Venetia Stanely, 24.7.14, pp. 122–3
20. BD. xi. 99. 24.7.14
21. DD. i. 157. 24.7.14
22. DDI. 4. xii. 314-15. 24.7.14
23. DD. i. 156/168/ 24.7.14/25.7.14
24. DD. i. 244. 25.7.14
25. Albertini, Vol. 2, p. 319
26. DD. i. 150. 24.7.14
27. Albertini, Vol. 3, p. 360
28. AEB. Correspondence politique. Légations. Allemagne. 24.7.14
29. ÖUA. viii. 10846. 24.7.14
30. Albertini, Vol. 3, p. 629
31. ÖUA. viii. 10598. 24.7.14
32. DF. 3. xi. 17 & 24. 24.7.14
33. ÖUA. viii. 10595. 24.7.14
34. Geiss, p. 189
35. Ibid., pp. 174–8
36. BD. xi. 101. 24.7.14
37. Lieven, *Russia and the Origins of the First World War*, pp. 141–4
38. Geiss, pp. 185–6

39. Albertini, Vol. 2, p. 301
40. DF. 3. xi. 34. 25.7.14

8   **Saturday 25 July**
 1. Geiss, p. 200
 2. BD. xi. 132. 25.7.14
 3. Geiss, pp. 205–6
 4. DF. 3. xi. 54. 25.7.14
 5. Albertini, Vol. 3, pp. 664–5
 6. Ibid.
 7. BD. xi. 122. 25.7.14
 8. ÖUA. viii. 10656. 25.7.14
 9. BD. xi. 113. 25.7.14
10. Albertini, Vol. 3, pp. 266–7
11. ÖUA. viii. 10680. 25.7.14
12. ÖUA. viii. 10746. 25.7.14
13. ÖUA. viii. 10662. 25.7.14
14. Albertini, Vol. 3, p. 629
15. DD. i. 189. 25.7.14
16. ÖUA. viii. 10667. 25.7.14
17. Albertini, Vol. 2, p. 308
18. BD. xi. 125. 25.7.14
19. Albertini, Vol. 2, p. 372
20. BD. xi. 114. 25.7.14
21. ÖUA. viii. 10708. 5.7.14

9   **Sunday 26 July**
 1. DD. i. 213. 26.7.14
 2. Albertini, Vol. 2, p. 375
 3. ÖUA. viii. 10714. 26.7.14
 4. DD. i. 217. 26.7.14
 5. ÖUA. viii. 10835. 26.7.14 (wrongly dated to 27.7.14)
 6. Geiss, pp. 230–1
 7. Albertini, Vol. 2, p. 406
 8. BD. xi. 198. 26.7.14
 9. Albertini, Vol. 2, p. 311
10. DD. i. 216. 26.7.14
11. FRUS 1914. Supplement. p. 15. 26.7.14

12. DD. i. 207. 26.7.14
13. BD. xi. 144. 26.7.14
14. BD. xi. 140. 26.7.14
15. Asquith to Venetia Stanley, 26.7.14, pp. 125–6
16. Wasserstein, *Herbert Samuel*, p. 160
17. DD. i. 236. 26.7.14
18. DD. i. 221. 26.7.14
19. Albertini, Vol. 2, p. 437
20. Geiss, p. 229
21. Albertini, Vol. 2, p. 397
22. DD. i. 211. 26.7.14
23. DD. i. 202. 26.7.14
24. BD. xi. 154. 26.7.14
25. DD. i. 225. 26.7.14
26. BD. xi. 148. 26.7.14
27. ÖUA. viii. 10795. 26.7.14
28. Albertini, Vol. 3, p. 630
29. Ibid.
30. DF. 3. xi. 105
31. DD. ii. 284

10 **Monday 27 July**

1. Albertini, Vol. 3, p. 588
2. DSP. 588. 27.7.14
3. BD. xi. 176. 27.7.14
4. DD. i. 258/265. 27.7.14
5. BD. xi. 188. 27. 7. 14
6. Asquith to Venetia Stanley, 28.7.14, p. 129
7. Hobhouse Diary, p. 177
8. Ibid., p. 178
9. Scott MSS. Add. MS. 50901 ff144
10. Wasserstein, p. 160
11. ÖUA. viii. 10793. 27.7.14
12. Geiss, p. 245; Albertini, Vol. 2, p. 530
13. Geiss, p. 244
14. Ibid., pp. 237–8
15. Albertini, Vol. 2, p. 437
16. Ibid., p. 438
17. Goschen Diary, 26.7.14, p. 291

18. BD. xi. 185. 27.7.14
19. DD. i. 277. 27.7.14
20. DD. i. 278. 28.7.14
21. Albertini, Vol. 2, p. 456
22. ÖUA. viii. 10788. 27.7.14
23. ÖUA. viii. 10855. 27.7.14
24. Albertini, Vol. 2, pp. 375–6
25. DD. i. 257. 27.7.14
26. DD. i. 281. 27.7.14
27. Geiss, pp. 241–2
28. DD. i. 242. 27.7.14
29. Papiers Poincaré. xxxvi. Notes Journalières. 10627. 27.7.14
30. BD. xi. 192. 27.7.14
31. DF. 3. xi. 144, 153 & 159. 27.7.14
32. ÖUA. viii. 10993. 29.7.14
33. DF. 3. xi. 178. 27.7.14
34. ÖUA. viii. 10798 & 10876. 27.7.14

11 **Tuesday 28 July**
1. ÖUA. viii. 10912. 28.7.14
2. DD. i. 244, note 2 by Kaiser. 27.7.14
3. ÖUA. viii. 10909. 28.7.14
4. Albertini, Vol. 2, pp. 483–4
5. ÖUA. viii. 10863. 28.7.14
6. DD. i. 271. 28.7.14
7. DD. ii. 293. 28.7.14
8. Haupt, p. 206
9. DD. ii. 301. 28.7.14
10. DD. ii. 374. 28.7.14
11. DD. ii. 314. 28.7.14
12. BD. xi. 249. 28.7.14
13. Geiss, pp. 258–9
14. DD. ii. 315. 28.7.14
15. Geiss, pp. 259–60
16. BD. xi. 247. 28.7.14
17. ÖUA. viii. 10999. 28.7.14
18. DD. ii. 338. 28.7.14
19. Albertini, Vol. 2, p. 537
20. Ibid., p. 569

21. DD. ii. 321. 28.7.14
22. ÖUA. viii. 10988. 28.7.14
23. BD. xi. 231. 28.7.14
24. BD. xi. 223. 28.7.14
25. BD. xi. 218. 28.7.14
26. BD. xi. 227. 28.7.14
27. BD. x. ii. Appendix 1. 28.7.14
28. Geiss, pp. 257–8
29. BD. xi. 243. 28.7.14
30. ÖUA. viii. 10873. 28.7.14
31. ÖUA. viii. 10874. 28.7.14
32. Albertini, Vol. 3, p. 569
33. Ibid., p. 589

12 Wednesday 29 July
1. DD. ii. 388. 29.7.14
2. BD. xi. 307. 30.7.14
3. ÖUA. viii. 10939. 29.7.14
4. ÖUA. viii. 10937. 30.7.14 (1 a.m.)
5. ÖUA. viii. 10991. 29.7.14
6. DD. ii. 363. 29.7.14
7. ÖUA. viii. 11090. 29.7.14
8. Notes Journalières, BN nafr 1602. 29.7.14
9. Haupt, p. 212
10. Geiss, pp. 282–4
11. Ibid., p. 285
12. DD. ii. 340. 29.7.14
13. DD. ii. 361. 29.7.14
14. DD. ii. 357. 29.7.14
15. BD. xi. 263. 29.7.14
16. CAB 37/120/95. BD. viii. 311
17. Pease Diary, pp. 43–5
18. Ibid.
19. Ibid.
20. Burns Diary, 29.7.14. Add. MSS 46336
21. Pease Diary, op. cit.
22. CAB 41/35. 29.7.14
23. Asquith to Venetia Stanley, pp. 132–3
24. Wasserstein, p. 160

25. Morris, *Radicalism Against War*, p. 409
26. ÖUA. viii. 10973. 29.7.14
27. BD. xi. 283. 29.7.14
28. BD. xi. 285. 29.7.14
29. DD. ii. 368. 29.7.14
30. Albertini, Vol. 2, p. 499
31. Ibid., p. 502
32. BD. xi. 293. 30.7.14 (1.20 a.m.)
33. DD. ii. 384. 29.7.14
34. DD. ii. 385. 30.7.14 (12.30 a.m.)
35. DD. ii. 395. 30.7.14 (2.55 a.m.)
36. DD. ii. 396. 30.7.14 (3 a.m.)
37. DD. ii. 392. 30.7.14 (2.55 a.m.)
38. DD. ii. 393. 30.7.14 (2.55 a.m.)
39. Geiss, p. 281
40. BD. xi. 276. 29.7.14
41. DD. ii. 365. 29.7.14
42. ÖUA. viii. 11003/11094. 29.7.14
43. DD. ii. 370. 29.7.14
44. DD. ii. 342. 29.7.14
45. Geiss, pp. 296–9
46. Albertini, Vol. 2, p. 569
47. DD. ii. 401/412. 30.7.14 (4.30 a.m. & 9.30 a.m.)
48. BD. xi. 646. 29.7.14
49. DD. ii. 371. 29.7.14
50. Albertini, Vol. 3, p. 569
51. ÖUA. viii. 11017
52. Haupt, pp. 250–65

13 Thursday 30 July

1. Haupt, pp. 204–5
2. Geiss, pp. 295–6
3. Ibid., pp. 312–13
4. Albertini, Vol. 2, p. 606
5. MAE. Papiers d'agent, Abel Ferry. 30.7.14
6. DF. 3. xi. 316. 30.7.14
7. Geiss, pp. 308–9
8. DD. ii. 432. 30.7.14 (3.20 p.m.)
9. DD. ii. 393. 30.7.14 (2.31 p.m.)

10. ÖUA. viii. 11092. 30.7.14
11. ÖUA. viii. 11020. 30.7.14
12. Albertini, Vol. 2, p. 622
13. Ibid., pp. 670–1
14. DD. ii. 434. 30.7.14
15. Geiss, pp. 308–9
16. Ibid., pp. 309–12
17. DD. ii. 421. 30.7.14
18. BD. xi. 302 30.7.14 (1.30 p.m.)
19. Albertini, Vol. 2, p. 569
20. DF. 3. xi. 328. 30.7.14
21. DF. 3. xi. 359. 30.7.14
22. DD. ii. 368. 30.7.14
23. DD. ii. 456. 30.7.14
24. DD. ii. 441. 30.7.14 (9 p.m.)
25. DD. ii. 451. 30.7.14
26. Asquith to Venetia Stanley, 30.7.14, p. 136
27. Samuel MSS A/157. 30.7.14
28. BD. xi. 303. 30.7.14
29. BD. xi. 305. 30.7.14
30. BD. xi. 309. 30.7.14

14 **Friday 31 July**
1. DF. 3. xi. 432. 31.7.14
2. ÖUA. DA III. 97. 1.8.14 (10.45 a.m.)
3. Albertini, Vol. 2, p. 683
4. Ibid., p. 569
5. Albertini, Vol. 3, p. 59
6. ÖUA. viii. 11119. 31.7.14
7. ÖUA. viii. 11203. 31.7.14
8. ÖUA. viii. 10006, 2.7.14
9. ÖUA. viii. 11155. 31.7.14
10. ÖUA. viii. 11118. 31.7.14 (1 p.m.)
11. DD. ii. 479. 31.7.14 (1.45 p.m.)
12. DD. ii. 490. 31.7.14 (3.30 p.m.)
13. DD. ii. 491. 31.7.14 (3.30 p.m.)
14. DD. ii. 492. 31.7.14 (3.30 p.m.)
15. DD. ii. 503. 31.7.14 (4.05 p.m.)
16. B. Schulte, 'Neue Dokumente zu Kreigsasbruch und Kriegsverlauf

1914', *Militärgeschichtliche Mitteilungen*, Vol. 25, 1979, p. 140
17. DF. 3. xi. 438. 31.7.14 (9 p.m./9.30 p.m.)
18. Albertini, Vol. 3, p. 83
19. Poincaré. Notes Journalières, BN nafr 16027. 31.7.14
20. BD. xi. 340. 31.7.14
21. DD. ii. 484/498. 31.7.14
22. Samuel MSS A/157. 31.7.14
23. Pease Diary, 31.7.14, p. 45
24. Harcourt MSS 522. 31.7.14
25. DF. 3. xi. 445. 31.7.14
26. BD. xi. 369. 31.7.14
27. Asquith to Venetia Stanley, 31.7.14, p. 139
28. DF. 3. xi. 411. 31.7.14
29. BD. xi. 395. 31.7.14
30. DD. ii. 472. 31.7.14
31. Albertini, Vol. 3, p. 569
32. Ibid., p. 567
33. ÖUA. viii. 11115. 31.7.14
34. DD. ii. 517. 31.7.14
35. DD. ii. 508. 31.7.14

15   Saturday 1 August

1. Geiss, p. 326
2. Ibid., pp. 340–2
3. Ibid., pp. 342–3
4. Albertini, Vol. 3, pp. 49–50
5. Ibid., pp. 293–4
6. Ibid., pp. 99–100
7. Notes Journalières, BN nafr 16027. 1.8.14
8. BD. xi. 383. 1.8.14 (3.30 a.m.)
9. DD. iii. 562. 1.8.14 (11.14 a.m.)
10. DD. ii. 570. 1.8.14 (2.10 p.m.)
11. Asquith to Venetia Stanley, 1.8.14, p. 140
12. Lloyd George MSS C/14. 1.8.14
13. Burns Diary, 1.8.14. Add. MSS 46336
14. Asquith, op. cit.
15. Wasserstein, p. 161
16. DD. iii. 578. 1.8.14 (7.15 p.m.)
17. DD. iii. 587. 1.8.14 (8.45 p.m.)

18. Becker, 'That's the Death Knell of our Boys', p. 20
19. Ibid., p. 21
20. Ibid., p. 23
21. Goldberg, *The Life of Jean Jaurès*, p. 564
22. Owen & Bell, *Wilfred Owen: Collected Letters*, Letter 278, pp. 270–2
23. BD. xi. 448. 1.8.14
24. DD. iii. 596. 1.8.14
25. BD. xi. 419, 426 & 447. 1.8.14
26. DF. 3. xi. 532. 1.8.14
27. Notes Journalières, BN nafr 16027. 1–2. 8. 14
28. BD. xi. 462. 1.8.14
29. Asquith to Venetia Stanley, 1.8.14, p. 139
30. DD. iii. 566. 1.8.14
31. DD. iii. 614. 1.8.14
32. DD. iii. 506. 1.8.14
33. DD. iii. 582. 1.8.14
34. ÖUA. viii. 11143. 31.7.14

16 **Sunday 2 August**
1. DD. iii. 628. 2.8.14
2. DD. iii. 627. 2.8.14
3. Albertini, Vol. 3, p. 50
4. DD. iv. 772. 2.8.14
5. DD. iii. 675. 2.8.14
6. DDI. 5. i. 2–3. 2.8.14
7. DF. 3. xi. 591. 2.8.14
8. BD. xi. 466. 2.8.14
9. BD. xi. 453. 2.8.14
10. Haldane MSS 6012. 2.8.14
11. Pease Diary, 2.8.14, p. 46
12. Ibid., pp. 46–7
13. Wasserstein, p. 162
14. Lloyd George Papers C/14. 2.8.14
15. Wasserstein, op. cit.
16. Hobhouse Diary, pp. 179–80
17. Wasserstein, op. cit.
18. Burns Diary, 2.8.14. Add. MSS 46336
19. Asquith to Venetia Stanley, 2.8.14, p. 146

20. Poincaré, Notes Journalières, op. cit., 4.8.14
21. Becker, op. cit., p. 28
22. Ibid., p. 29
23. Geiss, p. 350
24. M. Brod, 'The Diaries of Franz Kafka', 2.8.14
25. BD. xi. 487. 2.8.14
26. DF. 3. xi. 626. 2.8.14
27. DD. iii. 669. 2.8.14 (12.19 p.m.)
28. Pease Diary, op. cit.
29. Lord Riddell, 'War Diary', p. 8
30. Ramsey MacDonald Papers, 'Memorandum on Outbreak of War', p. 8
31. Morris, p. 404
32. Chandos Papers, I 5/19
33. Asquith to Venetia Stanley, 3.8.14, p. 148
34. DD. iii. 667. 2.8.14
35. BD. xi. 511. 2.8.14
36. DD. iii. 662. 2.8.14
37. DD. iii. 545. 1.8.14
38. DD. iii. 785. 2.8.14
39. DD. iii. 646. 2.8.14
40. DD. iii. 667. 2.8.14
41. DD. iii. 673. 2.8.14
42. Albertini, Vol. 3, p. 633
43. DF. 3. xi. 577. 2.8.14
44. BD. xi. 476. 2.8.14
45. Belgian Grey Book, No. 38
46. DF. 3. xi. 586. 2.8.14
47. DF. 3. xi. 630. 2.8.14

17 **Monday 3 August**

1. DF. 3. xi. 664/676. 3.8.14
2. Belgian Grey Book, No. 25
3. DF. 3. xi. 687. 3.8.14
4. BD. xi. 562. 3.8.14
5. DD. ii. 426 & DD. iii. 671/674
6. DD. iv. 797. 3.8.14
7. BD. xi. 570. 3.8.14
8. BD. xi. 594. 3.8.14

9. DD. iii. 729. 3.8.14
10. Albertini, Vol. 3, p. 570
11. Ibid., p. 598
12. DD. iv. 771. 3.8.14
13. DD. iv. 745. 3.8.14
14. Ibid.
15. DD. iv. 748. 3.8.14
16. Albertini, Vol. 3, p. 334
17. DF. 3. xi. 747. 3.8.14
18. Albertini, Vol. 3, p. 533
19. BD. xi. 571. 3.8.14
20. Geiss, p. 356
21. DD. iii. 714/715. 3.8.14
22. Pease Diary, 3.8.14, p. 147
23. Wasserstein, p. 164
24. Hobhouse Diary, p. 180
25. Wasserstein, p. 164
26. Morris, p. 417
27. Pease Diary, p. 49
28. Ibid.
29. Notes Journalières, BN nafr 16027. 3.8.14

18 **Tuesday 4 August**
1. Albertini, Vol. 3, p. 694
2. Belgian Grey Book, No. 27
3. BD. xi. 654. 4.8.14
4. J. Steinberg, 'Why Switzerland?' p. 54
5. DF. 3. xi. 746. 4.8.14
6. BD. xi. 601. 4.8.14
7. BD. xi. 610. 4.8.14
8. BD. xi. 642. 4.8.14
9. DD. iv. 836. 4.8.14
10. DD. iv. 804/805. 4.8.14
11. Geiss, p. 358
12. Geiss, p. 359
13. DD. iv. 814. 4.8.14
14. BD. xi. 573. 4.8.14
15. BD. xi. 580. 4.8.14
16. BD. xi. 594. 4.8.14

17. DF. 3. xi. 754. 4.8.14
18. Albertini, Vol. 3, p. 535
19. BD. xi. 591. 4.8.14
20. Notes Journalières, BN nafr 16029. 8.1.15
21. BD. xi. 666. 4.8.14
22. BD. xi. 671. 4.8.14

19 Aftermath

1. BD. xi. 673
2. K. Robbins, 'The Abolition of War', p. 39
3. R. Chickering, 'Imperial Germany and a World Without War', p. 322
4. Anzulovic, *Heavenly Serbia*, p. 93

BIBLIOGRAPHY

Primary Sources

Official Documents

ÖUA Bittner, L. and Übersberger, H. (eds), Österreich-Ungarns Aussenpolitik von der bosnichen Krise 1908 bis Zum Kriegsausbruch 1914. Diplomatische Aktenstücke des Osterreich-ungarischen Ministeriums des Ausseren, Vienna 1930 (9 vols)

BD Gooch, G. P. and Temperley, H. (eds) British Documents on the Origins of the War 1898–1914, London 1926–1938 (11 vols)

DD Montgelas, M. and Schüking, W. (eds), Outbreak of the World War: German Documents Collected by Karl Kautsky, New York 1924 (4 vols)

DDF Ministère des Affaires Etrangères, Documents diplomatiques français 2me & 3me series, Paris 1930–1953

DDI I documenti diplomatici italiani 4th & 5th series, Rome 1954–1964

DSP Dedijer, V. and Antic, Z. (eds), Dokumenti o spolnoj politici Kraljevine Srbije, Belgrade 1980

Other Documents

Geiss Geiss, I. (ed.), July 1914: The Outbreak of the First World War: Selected Documents, London 1967

Brock, M. and E., H. H. Asquith: Letters to Venetia Stanley (Oxford, 1982)

David, E., Inside Asquith's Cabinet: From the Diaries of Charles Hobhouse, (London, 1977)

Howard, C., 'The Vienna Diary of Berta de Bunsen, 28 June–17 August 1914', *Bulletin of the Institute of Historical Research*, Vol. 51, 1978, pp. 209–55

Howard, C., The Diary of Edward Goschen 1900–1914 (London, 1980)

Wilson, K., 'The Cabinet Diary of J. A. Pease 24 July–5 August 1914', *Proceedings of the Leeds Philosophical and Literary Society*, Vol. XIX, Part III, 1983, pp. 39–51

Books

Albertini, L., *The Origins of the War of 1914*, 3 vols. (London 1952–7).

Anzulovic, B., *Heavenly Serbia: From Myth to Genocide* (London, 1999).

Becker, J., *The Great War and the French People* (Leamington Spa, 1985).

Berghahn, V., *Germany and the Approach of War in 1914* (2nd edn London, 1993).

Bosworth, R., *Italy and the Approach of the First World War* (London, 1983).

Bridge, F., *From Sadowa to Sarajevo: The Foreign Policy of Austria–Hungary 1866–1914* (London, 1972)

Calleo, D., *The German Problem Reconsidered: Germany and the World Order 1870 to the Present* (Cambridge, 1978).

Cassels, L., *The Archduke and the Assassin: Sarajevo 28 June 1914* (London, 1984).

Cecil, L., *Albert Ballin: Business and Politics in Imperial Germany 1888–1918* (Princeton, 1967).

Crampton, R., *The Hollow Détente: Anglo-German Relations in the Balkans 1911–1914* (London, 1977).

Dedijer, V., *The Road to Sarajevo* (London, 1967).

Donia, R. and Fine, J., *Bosnia and Hercegovina: A Tradition Betrayed* (London, 1994).

Evans, R. and Pogge von Strandmann H., *The Coming of the First World War* (Oxford, 1988).

Farrar, L., *The Short-War Illusion: German Policy, Strategy and Domestic Affairs August–December 1914* (Oxford, 1973).

Fay, S., *The Origins of the World War*, 2 vols (New York, 1928).

Fischer, F., *Germany's Aims in the First World War* (London, 1967).

Fischer, F., *War of Illusions* (London, 1975).

Geiss, I., *German Foreign Policy 1871–1914* (London, 1976).

Goldberg, H., *The Life of Jean Jaurès* (Madison, 1962).

Gooch, J., *Plans of War: The General Staff and British Military Strategy 1900–1917* (Oxford, 1974).

Hall, R., *The Balkan Wars 1912–1913: Prelude to the First World War* (London, 2000).

Haupt, G., *Socialism and the Great War* (Oxford, 1972).

Hazlehurst, C., *Politicians at War, July 1914 to May 1915: A Prologue to the Triumph of Lloyd George* (London, 1971).

Hinsley, H., *British Foreign Policy under Sir Edward Grey* (Cambridge, 1977).

Jarausch, K., *The Enigmatic Chancellor: Bethmann Hollweg and the Hubris of Imperial Germany* (New Haven, 1973).

Joll, J., *The Origins of the First World War* (London, 1984).

Judah, T., *The Serbs: History, Myth and the Destruction of Yugoslavia* (London, 1997).

Keiger, J., *France and the Origins of the First World War* (London, 1983).

Keiger, J., *Raymond Poincaré* (Cambridge, 1997).

Kennedy, P., *The War Plans of the Great Powers 1880–1914* (London, 1979).

Kennedy, P., *The Rise of Anglo-German Antagonism 1860–1914* (London, 1980).

Kiraly B., and Djordjevic, D., *East Central European Society and the Balkan Wars* (Boulder, 1987).

Koch, H., *The Origins of the First World War: Great Power Rivalry and German War Aims* (London, 1984).

Lafore, L., *The Long Fuse* (London, 1966).

Langdon, J., *July 1914: The Long Debate 1918–1990* (Oxford, 1991).

Lieven, D., *Russia and the Origins of the First World War* (London, 1983).

MacKenzie, D., *Apis: The Congenial Conspirator. The Life of Colonel Dragutin T. Dimitrijević* (Boulder, 1989).

Maurer, J., *The Outbreak of the First World War: Strategic Planning, Crisis Decision Making and Deterrence Failure* (Westport, 1995).

Malcolm, N., *Bosnia: A Short History* (London, 1994).

May, E., *Knowing One's Enemies: Intelligence Assessment Before the Two World Wars* (Princeton, 1984).

Midlarsky, M., *The Onset of World War* (Boston, 1988).

Miller, S. et al, *Military Strategy and the Origins of the First World War* (Princeton, 1991).

Millett, A and Murray, W., *Miliary Effectiveness, Vol. 1: The First World War* (Boston, 1988).

Mommsen, W., *Imperial Germany 1867–1918: Politics, Culture and Society in an Authoritarian State* (London, 1995).

Morris, A., *Radicalism Against War 1906–1914* (London, 1972).

Nish, I., *Alliance in Decline* (London, 1975).

Offer, A., *The First World War: An Agrarian Interpretation* (Oxford, 1989).

Petrovich, M., *A History of Modern Serbia 1804–1918, Vol. 2* (New York, 1976).

Porch, D., *The March to the Marne: The French Army 1871–1914* (Cambridge, 1981).

Remak, J., *The Origins of World War 1* (New York, 1967).

Ritter, G., *The Schlieffen Plan: Critique of a Myth* (London, 1958).

Röhl, J., *1914: Delusion or Design?* (London, 1973).

Röhl, J., *The Kaiser and His Court: Wilhelm II and the Government of Germany* (Cambridge, 1994).

Rossos, A., *Russia and the Balkans 1909–1914* (Stanford, 1971).

Schmidt, B., *The Coming of the War, 1914,* 2 vols (New York, 1930).

Snyder, J., *The Ideology of the Offensive: Military Decision Marking and the Disasters of 1914* (Ithaca, 1984).

Steiner, Z., *The Foreign Office and Foreign Policy 1898–1914* (Cambridge, 1969).

Steiner, Z., *Britain and the Origins of the First World War* (London, 1977).

Stone, N., *The Eastern Front 1914–1917* (London, 1975).

Taylor, A., *War by Timetable: How the First World War Began* (London, 1969).

Treadway, J., *The Falcon and the Eagle: Montenegro and Austria–Hungary 1908–1914* (West Lafayette, 1983).

Tuchman, B., *August 1914* (London, 1962).

Turner, L., *Origins of the First World War* (London 1970).

Wasserstein, B., *Herbert Samuel: A Politicial Life* (Oxford, 1992).

Williamson, S., and Pastor, P., *Essays on World War I: Origins and Prisoners of War* (New York, 1983).

Williamson, S., *Austria–Hungary and the Origins of the First World War* (London, 1991).

Wilson, K., *The Policy of the Entente: Essays on the Determinants of British Foreign Policy 1904–1914* (Cambridge, 1985).

Wilson, K., *Empire and Continent: Studies in British Foreign Policy from the 1880s to the First World War* (London, 1987).

Wilson, K., *Decisions for War, 1914* (London, 1995).

Wohl, R., *The Generation of 1914* (London, 1980).

Articles

Abbreviations

AHR   *American Historical Review*

CEH   *Central European History*

HJ   *Historical Journal*

IHR   *International History Review*

JCH   *Journal of Contemporary History*

JIH   *Journal of Interdisciplinary History*

JMH   *Journal of Modern History*

P & P   *Past and Present*

Andrew, C., 'German World Policy and the Reshaping of the Dual Alliance', *JCH*, Vol. 1, No. 3, 1966, pp. 135–51.

Becker, J., 'That's the Death Knell of Our Boys', in P. Fridenson, *The French Home Front 1914–18* (Oxford, 1992), pp. 6–21.

Bestuzhev, I., 'Russian Foreign Policy February–June 1914', *JCH*, Vol. 1, No. 3, 1966, pp. 93–112.

Bridge, F., 'The British Declaration of War on Austria–Hungary in 1914', *Slavonic and East European Review*, Vol. 47, 1969, pp. 401–22.

Chickering, R., 'Patriotic Societies and German Foreign Policy 1890–1914', *IHR*, Vol. 1, 1979, pp. 470–89.

Collins, D., 'The Franco-Russian Alliance and Russian Railways 1891–1914', *HJ*, Vol. XVI, 1973, pp. 777–88.

Corrigan, H., 'German–Turkish Relations and the Outbreak of War in 1914: A Re-assessment', *P & P*, No. 36, 1967, pp. 144–52.

Crampton, R., 'The Decline of the Concert of Europe in the Balkans 1913–14', *Slavonic and East European Review*, Vol. 52, 1974, pp. 393–419.

Crampton, R., 'The Balkans as a Factor in German Foreign Policy 1912–14', *Slavonic and East European Review*, Vol. 55, 1977, pp. 370–90.

Ekstein, M., 'Some Notes on Sir Edward Grey's Policy in July 1914', *HJ*, Vol. 15, 1972, pp. 321–4.

Ekstein, M., 'Sir Edward Grey and Imperial Germany in 1914', *JCH*, Vol. 6, No. 3, 1971, pp. 121–31.

Epstein, K., 'Gerhard Ritter and the First World War', *JCH*, Vol. 1, No. 3, 1966, pp. 193–210.

Evera van, M., 'Why Co-operation Failed in 1914', *World Politics*, Vol. 38, 1985, pp. 80–117.

Farrar, L., 'The Limits of Choice: July 1914 Reconsidered', *Journal of Conflict Resolution*, Vol. 16, 1972, pp. 1–18.

French, D., 'The Edwardian Crisis and the Origins of the First World War', *IHR*, Vol. 4, 1982, pp. 207–21.

Geiss, I., 'The Outbreak of the First World War and German War Aims', *JCH*, Vol. 1, No. 3, 1966, pp. 75–91.

Gilbert, B., 'Pacifist to Interventionist: David Lloyd George in 1911 and 1914: Was Belgium an Issue?', *HJ*, Vol. 28, 1985, pp. 863–85.

Gordon, M., 'Domestic Conflict and the Origins of the First World War: The British and German Cases', *JMH*, Vol. 46, 1974, pp. 191–226.

Groh, D., 'The "Unpatriotic Socialists" and the State', *JCH*, Vol. 1, No. 4, 1966, pp. 151–77.

Hatton, P., 'Britain and Germany in 1914: The July Crisis and War Aims', *P & P*, No. 36, 1967, pp. 138–43.

Hatton, P., 'Harcourt and Self: The Search for an Anglo-German Understanding Through Africa 1912–14', *European Studies Review*, Vol. 1, 1971, pp. 130–42.

Hayne, M., 'The Quai d'Orsay and Influences on the Formulation of French Foreign Policy 1898–1914', *French History*, Vol. 2, 1988, pp. 427–51.

Hehn, P., 'The Origins of Modern Pan-Serbism: The 1844 Nacertanije of Ilija Garašanin: An Analysis and Translation', *East European Quarterly*, Vol. 9, 1975, pp. 153–71.

Helmreich, J., 'Belgian Concern over Neutrality and British Intentions', *JMH*, Vol. 43, 1971, pp. 416–27.

Herwig, H., 'Disjointed Allies: Coalition Warfare in Berlin and Vienna, 1914', *Journal of Military History*, Vol. 54, 1990, pp. 265–80.

Holsti, O., 'The 1914 Case', *American Political Science Review*, Vol. 59, 1965, pp. 365–78.

Howard, C., 'MacDonald, Henderson and the Outbreak of War, 1914', *HJ*, Vol. 20, 1977, pp. 871–91.

Jarausch, K., 'The Illusion of Limited War: Chancellor Bethmann Hollweg's Calculated Risk, July 1914', *CEH*, Vol. 2, 1969, pp. 48–76.

Jelavich, B., 'Romania in the First World War: The Pre-War Crisis 1912–14', *IHR*, Vol. XIV, 1992, pp. 441–51.

Joll, J., 'The 1914 Debate Continues', *P & P*, No. 36, 1967, pp. 100–13.

Kaiser, D., 'Germany and the Origins of the First World War', *JMH*, Vol. 55, 1983, pp. 442–74.

Kann, R., 'Dynastic Relations and European Power Politics 1848–1918', *JMH*, Vol. 45, 1973, pp. 387–410.

Kennedy, P., 'The First World War and the International Power System', *International Security*, Vol. 9, 1984, pp. 7–40.

Kitch, J., 'The Promise of the New Revisionism', *P & P*, No. 36, 1967, pp. 153–65.

Lammers, D., 'Arno Mayer and the British Decision for War: 1914', *Journal of British Studies*, Vol. 12, 1973, pp. 137–65.

Langhorne, R., 'The Naval Question in Anglo-German Relations 1912–14', *HJ*, Vol. 14, 1971, pp. 354–72.

Leslie, J., 'The Antecedents of Austria–Hungary's War Aims: Policies and Policy-Makers in Vienna and Budapest before and during 1914', *Wiener Beitrage zur Geschichte der Neuzeit*, Vol. 20, 1985, pp. 307–94.

Lieven, D., 'Pro-Germans and Russian Foreign Policy 1890–1914', *IHR*, Vol. 2, 1980, pp. 34–54.

Maehl, W., 'The Triumph of Nationalism in the German Socialist Party on the Eve of the First World War', *JMH*, Vol. 24, 1952, pp. 15–41.

Mayer, A., 'Domestic Causes of the First World War', in L. Krieger and H. Holborn, *The Responsibility of Power* (London, 1968), pp. 286–300.

Mommsen, W., 'The Debate on German War Aims', *JCH*, Vol. 1, No. 3, 1966, pp. 47–72.

Mommsen, W., 'Domestic Factors in German Foreign Policy Before 1914', *CEH*, Vol. 6, 1973, pp. 11–43.

Neilson, K., ' "My Beloved Russians": Sir A. Nicolson and Russia 1906–16', *IHR*, Vol. 9, 1987, pp. 521–54.

North, R., 'Perception and Action in the 1914 Crisis', *Journal of International Affairs*, Vol. 21, 1967, pp. 103–22.

Prete, R., 'French Strategic Planning and the Deployment of the BEF in France in 1914', *Canadian Journal of History*, Vol. XXIV, 1989, pp. 42–62.

Prete, R., 'The Preparation of the French Army Prior to World War I: An Historiographical Reappraisal', *Canadian Journal of History*, Vol. XXVI, 1991, pp. 241–66.

Remak, J., 'The Healthy Invalid: How Doomed the Habsburg Empire?', *JMH*, Vol. 41, 1969, pp. 127–43.

Remak, J., '1914 – The Third Balkan War: Origins Reconsidered', *JMH*, Vol. 43, 1971, pp. 353–66.

Renzi, W., 'Italy's Neutrality and Entrance into the Great War: A Re-Examination', *AHR*, Vol. 73, 1967–8, pp. 1414–32.

Rogger, H., 'Russia in 1914', *JCH*, Vol. 1, No. 4, 1966, pp. 95–119.

Röhl, J., 'Admiral von Muller and the Approach of War 1911–14', *HJ*, Vol. 12, 1969, pp. 651–73.

Schroeder, P., 'World War I as Galloping Gertie: A Reply to Joachim Remak', *JMH*, Vol. 44, 1972, pp. 319–45.

Stengers, J., 'The Safety of Ciphers and the Outbreak of the First World War', in C. Andrew and J. Noakes, *Intelligence and International Relations* (Exeter, 1987), pp. 29–48.

Stern, F., 'Bethmann Hollweg and the War: The Limits of Responsibility', in L. Krieger and H. Holborn, *The Responsibility of Power* (London, 1968), pp. 252–85.

Stone, N., 'Hungary and the Crisis of July 1914', *JCH*, Vol. 1, No. 3, 1966, pp. 152–70.

Stone, N., 'Moltke and Conrad: Relations between the Austro-Hungarian and German General Staffs 1909–14', *HJ*, Vol. IX, No. 2, 1966.

Sweet, D., 'The Baltic in British Diplomacy before the First World War', *HJ*, Vol. 13, 1970, pp. 455–7.

Torrey, G., 'Rumania and the Belligerents 1914–16', *JCH*, Vol. 1, No. 3, 1966, pp. 171–91.

Trumpener, U., 'War Premeditated? German Intelligence Operations in July 1914', *CEH*, Vol. 9, 1976, pp. 58–85.

Turner, L., 'The Significance of the Schlieffen Plan', *Australian Journal of Politics and History*, Vol. XIII, No. 1, 1967.

Turner, L., 'The Russian Mobilization in 1914', *JCH*, Vol. 3, No. 3, 1968.

Valiani, L., 'Italian–Austro-Hungarian Negotiations 1914–15', *JCH*, Vol. 1, No. 3, 1966, pp. 113–36.

Vigezzi, B., 'Italian Socialism and the First World War: Mussolini, Lazzari and Turati', *Journal of Italian History*, Vol. 2, 1979, pp. 232–57.

Valone, S., ' "There must be some misunderstanding". Sir Edward Grey's Diplomacy of August 1, 1914', *Journal of British Studies*, Vol. 27 1988, pp. 405–24.

Watt, D., 'The British Reactions to the Assassination at Sarajevo', *European Studies Review*, Vol. 1, 1971, pp. 233–47.

Wolfe, B., 'War Comes to Russia-in-exile', *Russian Review*, Vol. 20, 1961, pp. 294–311.

Wolfe, B., 'War Comes to Russia', *Russian Review*, Vol. 22, 1963, pp. 123–38.

Williamson, S., 'Influence, Power and the Policy Process: The Case of Franz Ferdinand 1906–14', *HJ*, Vol. 17, 1974, pp. 417–34.

Williamson, S., 'The British Cabinet's Decision for War, 2 August 1914', *British Journal of International Studies*, Vol. 1, 1975, pp. 148–59.

Wilson, K., 'Understanding the "Misunderstanding" of 1 August 1914', *HJ*, Vol. 37, 1994, pp. 885–9.

Wilson, T., 'Britain's "Moral Commitment" to France in August 1914', *JMH*, Vol. 48, 1976, pp. 644–65.

Zinnes, D., 'A Comparison of Hostile Behaviour in Decision-Takers in Simulate and Historical Data', *World Politics*, Vol. 18, 1965, pp. 474–502.

Index